WILEY CIAexcel EXAM REVIEW

FOCUS NOTES 2018

WILEY CIAexcel EXAM REVIEW

FOCUS NOTES 2018

PART 3

Internal Audit Knowledge Elements

S. RAO VALLABHANENI

WILEY

Cover image: John Wiley & Sons, Inc.
Cover design: John Wiley & Sons, Inc.

Published by John Wiley & Sons, Inc., Hoboken, New Jersey.
Published simultaneously in Canada.

For general information on our other products and services or for technical support, please contact our Customer Care Department within the United States at (800) 762-2974, outside the United States at (317) 572-3993 or fax (317) 572-4002.

Wiley publishes in a variety of print and electronic formats and by print-on-demand. Some material included with standard print versions of this book may not be included in e-books or in print-on-demand. If this book refers to media such as a CD or DVD that is not included in the version you purchased, you may download this material at http://booksupport.wiley.com. For more information about Wiley products, visit www.wiley.com.

Library of Congress Cataloging-in-Publication Data:

ISBN 978-1-119-48303-8 (Paperback); ISBN 978-1-119-48305-2 (ebk); ISBN 978-1-119-48306-9 (ebk);
ISBN 978-1-119-48299-4 (Part 1); ISBN 978-1-119-48295-6 (Part 2)

Printed in the United States of America

Contents

Preface xiii

CIA Exam Study Preparation Resources xv

CIA Exam-Taking Tips and Techniques xix

CIA Exam Content Specifications xxi

Domain 1   Governance and Business Ethics (5–15%) 1
    Corporate/Organizational Governance Principles *1*
    Roles and Responsibilities of the Audit Committee 17
    Business Ethics 18
    Corporate Social Responsibility 29

Domain 2   Risk Management (10–20%) 34
    Corporate Risk Management 34
    Enterprise Risk Management 37

Domain 3   Organizational Structures, Business Processes, and Risks (15–25%) 40
    Risk/Control Implications of Different Organizational Structures 40
    Types of Organizational Structures 41
    Schemes in Various Business Cycles 51
    Business Process Analysis 65

Business Process Reengineering and Business Process Improvement 67
Benchmarking 68
Production Process Flows 69
Design of Performance Measurement Systems 70
Performance 71
Productivity 72
Components of Productivity Measurement 73
Criteria for Productivity Improvement 73
Balanced Scorecard System 76
Inventory Management Techniques and Concepts 78
Electronic Data Systems 104
Business Development Life Cycles 112
International Organization for Standardization Framework 115
Outsourcing Business Processes...123

Domain 4 **COMMUNICATION (5–10%)**..**132**
Communication Skills 132
Stakeholder Relationships 140

Contents   **vi**

Domain 5 **Management and Leadership Principles (10–20%)**..................................**150**

Strategic Management 150
Strategic Planning Process 153
Global Analytical Techniques 155
Porter's Competitive Strategies 159
Industry Environments 163
Evolution of Global Markets 166
Strategic Decisions...167
Portfolio Techniques of Competitive Analysis.........................169
Forecasting 172
Quality Management 176
Decision Analysis..195
Decision Making..204
Organizational Behavior 215
Group Dynamics..221
Human Resource Management..226
Risk/Control Implications of Different Leadership Styles..........233
Management Skills 235

Contents vii

Team Building		242
Negotiation and Conflict Management		251
Project Management and Change Management		263
Change Management Techniques		271

Domain 6   **INFORMATION TECHNOLOGY AND BUSINESS CONTINUITY (15–25%)**   **275**

Security	275
System Security	282
Firewalls	293
Routers	304
Sensors	307
Hardware and Software Guards	308
Demilitarized Zones	311
Information Protection	313
Identification and Authentication	333
Encryption	347
Application Development	366

System Infrastructure 412
Database Systems 427
Cloud Computing Systems 435
Functional Areas of Information Technology Operations 444
Enterprise-Wide Resource Planning System, Customer-Relationship
Management System, and Software Licensing and Piracy Management............ 453
Data and Network Communications and Connections......................... 463
Business Continuity 531

Domain 7   **Financial Management (13–23%)** **559**
Financial Accounting and Finance: Basic Concepts of
Financial Accounting 559
Intermediate Concepts of Financial Accounting................................. 565
Advanced Concepts of Financial Accounting....................................... 571
Financial Statement Analysis 584
Types of Debt and Equity.. 590
Financial Instruments 596
Cash Management 599

Contents

Valuation Models 613
Capital Budgeting.. 621
Cost of Capital Evaluation... 629
Taxation Schemes.. 638
Mergers, Acquisitions, and Divestitures 640
Managerial Accounting: General Concepts.. 647
Costing Systems 648
Cost Concepts 656
Relevant Costs... 668
Cost-Volume-Profit Analysis 669
Transfer Pricing 676
Responsibility Accounting 679
Operating Budgets 681

Domain 8   **Global Business Environment (0–10%)... 687**
Economic/Financial Environments... 687
Cultural/Political Environments.. 703
Legal and Economic Concepts 713
Impact of Government Legislation and Regulation on Business 718

Contents   **x**

Appendix **Sarbanes-Oxley Act of 2002**... **735**

Title II—Auditor Independence... 736

Title III—Corporate Responsibility 737

Title IV—Enhanced Financial Disclosures 739

About the Author.. 741

Index... 743

Contents

Preface

The Wiley CIAexcel Exam Review Focus Notes 2018 are developed for each of the three parts of the Certified Internal Auditor (CIA) exam sponsored by the Institute of Internal Auditors (IIA). The purpose of the Focus Notes is to digest and assimilate the vast amounts of knowledge, skills, and abilities tested on the CIA exam in a clear, concise, easy-to-read, and easy-to-use format anywhere and anytime to achieve success in the exam.

Each of the Focus Notes book topics is organized in the same way as the Wiley CIAexcel Exam Review book topics, that is, one Focus Notes book for each of the three-part review books. This clear linkage makes the exam study time more efficient and long-lasting, and provides the ability to recall important concepts, tools, and techniques, and the IIA *Standards* tested on the CIA exams. The Focus Notes can be used with any other study materials that you have determined works best for you to prepare for the CIA Exam. The Focus Notes provide a quick and easy refresher to the material that you are studying.

The Wiley Focus Notes are similar to index cards and flash cards in terms of purpose. The Focus Notes complement and supplement, not substitute for, the Wiley Review books, where the former provides a summarized theory and the latter provides a detailed theory.

For those students who are exclusively studying with Wiley's preparation resources, we sincerely recommend the CIA Exam candidate study the Focus Notes and Glossary section for each part a few weeks prior to taking the actual exam for maximum retention and recall of the subject matter, assuming that the candidate has previously studied the Wiley CIAexcel Exam Review books.

The Focus Notes books will be especially useful to auditors who are traveling on an audit assignment, as well as others who are not traveling, due to their small and compact size, giving portability. The simplified summaries included in this material will help you learn the essential knowledge as well as help you retain them for years to come. The Focus Notes book can also be used as a desk reference on a post-exam basis, similar to a dictionary.

CIA Exam Study Preparation Resources

We recommend the following study plan and three review products for each Part of the CIA Exam to succeed in the exam:

- Read each part's review book (Theory)

- Practice the web-based online test bank software (Practice)

- Reinforce the theoretical concepts by studying the Focus Notes (Theory)

A series of **review books** have been prepared for the candidate to utilize for all three parts of the new CIA exam. Each part's review book includes a comprehensive coverage of the subject matter (theory) followed by some sample practice multiple-choice (M/C) questions with answers and explanations (practice). The sample practice M/C questions included in the review book are taken from Wiley's web-based online test software to show you the flavor of questions. Each part's review book contains a glossary section, which is a good source for answering M/C questions on the CIA Exam.

The **web-based online test bank software** is a robust review product that simulates the format of the actual CIA Exam in terms of look and feel, thus providing intense practice and greater confidence to the CIA Exam candidates. The thousands of sample practice questions (5,275 plus) included in the online test bank can provide greater confidence and solid assurance to CIA exam candidates in that they are preparing well for all the required topics tested in the exam. All practice questions include explanations for the correct answer and are organized by domain topics within each part. Visit www.wileycia.com.

The following is a part summary showing the number of sample practice questions included in the online test bank and the number of questions tested in the actual CIA Exam.

Part Summary	Wiley Sample Practice Questions	CIA Exam Actual Test Questions
Part 1	750+	125
Part 2	725+	100
Part 3	3,800+	100
Total Questions in Three Parts	5,275+	325

Focus Notes provide a quick review and reinforcement of the important theoretical concepts, which are presented in a summary manner taken from the details of the review books. The Focus Notes can be studied just before the exam, during travel time, or any other time available to the student.

When combined, these three review products provide a great value to CIA Exam students and we are positive that they will recognize the value when they see it, feel it, and experience it.

We suggest a sequential study approach in four steps for each part of the exam, as follows:

Step 1. Read the glossary section at the end of each part's review book for a better understanding of key technical terms

Step 2. Study the theory from the each part's review book

Step 3. Practice the multiple-choice questions from the online test bank for each part

Step 4. Read the Focus Notes for each part for a quick review and reinforcement of the important theoretical concepts

In addition, the CIA Exam candidates should read **Practice Guides** from the IIA because these guides provide detailed guidance for conducting internal audit activities. They include detailed processes and procedures, such as tools and techniques, audit work programs, and step-by-step audit approaches, as well as examples of audit deliverables. These Practice Guides are not included in the Wiley Review Books due to their voluminous size and the fact that they are available from www.theiia.org.

CIA Exam-Taking Tips and Techniques

The types of questions a candidate can expect to see in the CIA Exam are objective and scenario-based multiple-choice (M/C) questions. Answering the M/C questions requires a good amount of practice and effort. The following tips and techniques will be helpful in answering the CIA Exam questions:

- Stay with your first impression of the correct choice.

- Know the subject area or topic. Don't read too much into the question.

- Remember that questions are independent of specific country, products, practices, vendors, hardware, software, or industry.

- Read the last sentence of the question first followed by all choices and then the body (stem) of the question.

- Read the question twice or read the underlined or circled keywords twice, and watch for tip-off words, such as **not, except, all, every, always, never, least, or most**, which denote absolute conditions.

- Do not project the question into your organizational environment, practices, policies, procedures, standards, and guidelines. The examination is focusing on the IIA's Professional Standards and Publications and on the CIA's exam syllabus (i.e., content specifications).

- Try to eliminate wrong choices as quickly as possible. When you get down to two semifinal choices, take a big-picture approach. For example, if choice A and D are the semifinalists, and choice D could be a part of choice A, then select choice A; or if choice D could be a more complete answer, then select choice D.

- Don't spend too much time on one question. If you are not sure of an answer, move on, and go back to it if time permits. The last resort is to guess the answer. There is no penalty for guessing the wrong answer.

Remember that success in any professional examination depends on several factors required of any student such as time management skills, preparation time and effort levels, education and experience levels, memory recall of the subject matter, state of the mind before or during the exam, and decision-making skills.

CIA Exam Content Specifications

Part 3 of the CIA Exam is called **Internal Audit Knowledge Elements** and the exam duration is 2.0 hours (120 minutes) with 100 multiple-choice questions. The following is a breakdown of topics in this Part.

Domain I: Governance and Business Ethics (5–15%)*

A. Corporate/organizational governance principles (A)**

B. Environmental and social safeguards (A)

C. Corporate social responsibility (A)

Domain II: Risk Management (10–20%)

A. Risk management techniques (A)

B. Organizational use of risk frameworks (A)

---

*Indicates the relative range of weights assigned to this topic area for both theory and practice sections in the CIA Exam.

**Indicates the level of difficulty for each topic in the CIA Exam expressed as (A) for Awareness and (P) for Proficiency. (A) = Candidates must exhibit awareness (i.e., knowledge of terminology and fundamentals) in these topic areas. (P) = Candidates must exhibit proficiency (i.e., thorough understanding and ability to apply concepts) in these topic areas.

Domain III: Organizational Structure, Business Processes, and Risks (15–25%)

A. Risk/control implications of different organizational structures (A)

B. Structure (e.g., centralized/decentralized) (A)

C. Typical schemes in various business cycles (e.g., procurement, sales, knowledge, and supply-chain management) (A)

D. Business process analysis (e.g., workflow analysis, bottleneck management, and Theory of Constraints) (A)

E. Inventory management techniques and concepts (A)

F. Electronic funds transfer (EFT) and electronic data interchange (EDI) (A)

G. Business development life cycles ((A)

H. The International Organization for Standardization (ISO) framework (A)

I. Outsourcing business processes (A)

Domain IV: Communication (5–10%)

A. Communication (e.g., the process, organizational dynamics, and impact of computerization) (A)

B. Stakeholder relationships (A)

Domain V: Management and Leadership Principles (10–20%)

A. Strategic management

- Forecasting (A)

- Quality management (e.g., TQM and Six Sigma) (A)

- Decision analysis (A)

B. Organizational behavior

- Organizational theory (A)

- Organizational behavior (e.g., motivation, impact of job design, rewards, and schedules) (A)

- Group dynamics (e.g., traits, development stages, organizational politics, and effectiveness) (A)

- Knowledge of human resource processes (e.g., individual performance management, supervision, personnel sourcing/staffing, and staff development) (A)

- Risk/control implications of different leadership styles (A)

C. Management skills

- Lead, inspire, and guide people, building organizational commitment and entrepreneurial orientation (A)

- Create group synergy in pursuing collective goals (A)

D. Conflict management

- Conflict resolution (e.g., competitive, cooperative, and compromise) (A)

- Negotiation skills (A)

- Conflict management (A)

- Added-value negotiating (A)

E. Project management and change management

- Change management (A)

- Project management techniques (A)

Domain VI: IT and Business Continuity (15–25%)

A. Security

- System security (e.g., firewalls and access controls) (A)

- Information protection (e.g., viruses and privacy) (A)

- Application authentication (A)

- Encryption (A)

B. Application development

- End-user computing (A)

- Change control (A)

- Systems development methodology (A)

- Application development (A)

- Information systems development (A)

C. System infrastructure

- Workstations (A)

- Databases (A)

- IT control frameworks (e.g., eSAC and COBIT) (A)

- Functional areas of IT operations (e.g., data center operations) (A)

- Enterprise-wide resource planning (ERP) software (e.g., SAP R3) (A)

- Data and network communications and connections (e.g., LAN, VAN, and WAN) (A)

- Servers (A)

- Software licensing (A)

- Mainframe (A)

- Operating systems (A)

D. Business continuity

- IT contingency planning (A)

Domain VII: Financial Management (13–23%)

A. Financial accounting and finance

- Basic concepts and underlying principles of financial accounting (e.g., statements, terminology, and relationships) (A)

- Intermediate concepts of financial accounting (e.g., bonds, leases, pensions, intangible assets, and research and development) (A)

- Advanced concepts of financial accounting (e.g., consolidation, partnerships, and foreign currency transactions) (A)

- Financial statement analysis (e.g., ratios) (A)

- Types of debt and equity (A)

- Financial instruments (e.g., derivatives) (A)

- Cash management (e.g., treasury functions) (A)

- Valuation models (A)

- Business valuation (A)

- Inventory valuation (A)

- Capital budgeting (e.g., cost of capital evaluation) (A)

- Taxation schemes (e.g., tax shelters and VAT) (A)

B. Managerial accounting

- Managerial accounting: general concepts (A)

- Costing systems (e.g., activity-based and standard) (A)

- Cost concepts (e.g., absorption, variable, and fixed) (A)

- Relevant cost (A)

- Cost-volume-profit analysis (A)

- Transfer pricing (A)

- Responsibility accounting (A)

- Operating budget (A)

Domain VIII: Global Business Environment (0–10%)

A. Economic/financial environments (A)

B. Cultural/political environments (A)

C. Legal and economics—general concepts (e.g., contracts) (A)

D. Impact of government legislation and regulation on business (e.g., trade legislation) (A)

CORPORATE/ORGANIZATIONAL GOVERNANCE PRINCIPLES

Corporate Governance Definition

Corporate governance refers to the method by which a firm is being governed, directed, administered, or controlled and to the goals for which it is being governed. It is concerned with the relative roles, rights, and accountability of such stakeholder groups as owners, boards of directors, managers, employees, and others who assert to be stakeholders.

Corporate Governance Principles

Principle I: Ensuring the Basis for an Effective Corporate Governance Framework

Principle II: The Rights of Shareholders and Key Ownership Functions

Principle III: The Equitable Treatment of Shareholders

Principle IV: The Role of Stakeholders in Corporate Governance

Principle V: Disclosure and Transparency

Principle VI: The Responsibilities of the Board

Corporate Governance Issues

- Components of corporate governance (i.e., shareholders, board of directors, management, and employees).
- Separation of ownership from control.
- Role of the board of directors.
- Need for board independence.
- Issues surrounding compensation. Major issues include CEO compensation (e.g., salaries, bonuses, stock options, and perks) and outside director compensation.
- Consequences of merger, acquisition, and takeover wave and divestiture of assets.
- Insider trading scandals.
- Board member liability.
- Lack of strong voice for board of directors due to their submissive behaviors
- Improving corporate governance: (1) changes in boards of directors to include more outside directors and (2) increased role of shareholders in the governance process.

Board of Directors' Duties

The board of directors has three fiduciary duties (1) duty of care (i.e., business judgment rule), (2) self dealing (i.e., fair to the company), and (3) corporate opportunities (e.g., mergers, acquisitions, and divestitures).

The business judgment rule is a legal presumption that the directors and officers of the corporation have exercised **duty of care** by acting on an informed basis, in good faith, and in the honest belief that their actions are in the best interests of the corporation. Unless a plaintiff can give persuasive evidence against at least one of the criteria, corporate directors and officers are insulated from liability for breach of the duty of care.

Regarding **self dealing**, corporate directors and officers may pursue business transactions that benefit themselves as long as they can prove the transaction, although self-interested, was nevertheless intrinsically "fair" to the corporation (i.e., the transaction is initiated and completed in an arms-length distance). A plaintiff must start by alleging the director or officer stood to gain a material economic benefit. The burden then shifts to the defendant to show the fairness of the transaction. The court considers both the terms and the process for the bargain (i.e., both a fair price and fair dealing). However, if the director shows that full disclosure was made to disinterested directors or disinterested shareholders, then the burden remains on the plaintiff.

As a part of fiduciary duties, it is acceptable for a director to inform one another of **corporate opportunities** which arise. Examples of these opportunities include identifying candidates for mergers, acquisitions, and divestitures; introducing new products, new suppliers, new customers, new contractors, new technologies, and new business ventures; and brining awareness of new laws and regulations.

Basic Ethical and Legal Principles for Managers, Executives, Officers, and Board of Directors

Basic ethical and legal principles guide managers, executives, officers, and board of directors in handling legal and ethical problems and issues on a day-to-day basis. When these principles are understood and implemented, they can reduce legal risks and ethical embarrassments, and protect reputation in the eyes of the general public. For example, officers and directors need to follow duty of due care, duty of loyalty, and duty of obedience, not duty of absolute care or duty of utmost care. Only reasonable and ordinary care is expected of the officers and the board of directors because no one can anticipate all problems or protect from all disasters or losses. Especially, officers and board of directors are expected to follow the highest levels of ethical and legal principles due to their fiduciary and governance responsibilities (i.e., duty of loyalty and duty of obedience).

Examples of basic ethical and legal principles follow:

Due process means following rules and principles so that an individual is treated fairly and uniformly at all times with basic rights protected. It also means fair and equitable treatment to all concerned parties so that no person is deprived of life, liberty, or property without due process of the law, which is the right to notice and a hearing. Due process means each person is given an equal and a fair chance of being represented or heard and that everybody goes through the same process for consideration and approval. It means all people are equal in the eyes of the law. Due law covers due care. Due process requires due care and due diligence. Two types of due process exist: procedural due process and substantive due process. Procedural due process ensures that a formal proceeding is carried out regularly and in accordance with the established rules and

Basic Ethical and Legal Principles for Managers, Executives, Officers, and Board of Directors (continued)

principles. Substantive due process deals with a judicial requirement that enacted laws may not contain provisions that result in the unfair, arbitrary, or unreasonable treatment of an individual. It protects personal property from governmental interference or possession.

Due care means reasonable care in promoting the common good, maintaining the minimal and customary practices, and following the best practices. Due care implies reasonable care and competence, not infallibility or extraordinary performance. Corporate directors and officers of a corporation must perform their duties in good faith and in a non-negligent manner. This requires due care and due diligence, which are part of due process.

Due law covers due process and due care. For example, it is the responsibility that managers and their organizations have a duty to provide for information security to ensure that the type of control, the cost of control, and the deployment of control are appropriate for the system being managed. Another related concept of due care is good faith, which means showing "honesty in fact" and "honesty in intent." Both due care and due diligence are similar to the "prudent man" or "reasonable person" concept.

Duty of due care is the legal obligation that each person has to others not to cause any unreasonable harm or risk of harm resulting from careless acts. A breach of the duty of due care is gross negligence, which means reckless behavior with willful intent to harm people and damage property. An example of duty of due care is that corporate directors and officers must use due care and due diligence when acting on behalf of a corporation. Duty of reasonable care is same as the duty of due care.

Basic Ethical and Legal Principles for Managers, Executives, Officers, and Board of Directors (continued)

The business judgment rule is a legal presumption that the directors and officers of the corporation have exercised due care by acting on an informed basis, in good faith, and in the honest belief that their actions are in the best interests of the corporation. Unless a plaintiff can give persuasive evidence against at least one of the criteria, corporate directors and officers are insulated from liability for breach of the duty of care. The concepts of due care and duty of care are similar in nature.

Due diligence reviews involve pre-assessment, examination, analysis, and reporting on major activities with due care before they are finalized or approved by management. Its purpose is to minimize potential risks from undertaking new businesses and ventures and involving in mergers, acquisitions, and divestitures. Due diligence requires organizations to develop and implement an effective system of controls, policies, and procedures to prevent and detect violation of policies and laws. It requires that the organization has taken minimum and necessary steps in its power and authority to prevent and detect violation of policies and laws. In other words, due diligence is the care that a reasonable person exercises under the circumstances to avoid harm to other persons or to their property. Due diligence is another way of saying due care. Both due care and due diligence are similar to the "prudent man" or "reasonable person" concept. A due diligence defense is available to a defendant in that it makes the defendant not liable if the defendant's actions are reasonable and they are proven.

Basic Ethical and Legal Principles for Managers, Executives, Officers, and Board of Directors (continued)

Examples of due care and due diligence include:

- Acquiring a business insurance policy to protect physical assets against theft, loss, or damage (due diligence).

- Training employees in information security to show that a standard of due care has been taken in protecting information assets (due care).

- Requiring acknowledgment statements that state employees have read and understood computer security requirements (due diligence).

- Maintaining good housekeeping in a computer data center to prevent accidents, damages, and disasters (due care).

Due professional care applies to professionals such as business managers and executives, accountants, auditors, engineers, lawyers, doctors, and others. Professionals should apply the care and skill expected of a reasonable prudent and competent person in the same or similar circumstances during their professional work. Due professional care does not imply infallibility. Having proper knowledge, skills, and abilities is the major issue here. Due professional care is related to due care and due diligence.

Basic Ethical and Legal Principles for Managers, Executives, Officers, and Board of Directors (continued)

For example, due professional care is exercised when internal audits are performed in accordance with the IIA *Standards*. The exercise of due professional care requires that: (1) internal auditors be independent of the activities they audit, (2) internal audits be performed by those persons who collectively possess the necessary knowledge, skills, and disciplines to conduct the audit properly, (3) audit work be planned and supervised, (4) audit reports be objective, clear, concise, constructive, and timely, and (5) internal auditors follow up on reported audit findings to ascertain that appropriate action was taken.

Duty of loyalty is expected of officers and board of directors of a corporation in that they have a duty not to act adversely to the interests of the corporation and not to subordinate their personal interests to those of the corporation and its shareholders. These adverse actions include self-dealing, taking personal advantage of a corporate opportunity, and competing with the corporation, thus creating conflict-of-interest situations. Under the duty of loyalty, a corporation can sue a director or an officer to recover the secret profit made on a business transaction.

Duty of obedience is expected of officers and directors of a corporation to act within the authority conferred upon them by the state corporation statutes, the articles of incorporation, the corporate bylaws, and the resolutions adopted by the board of directors.

Duty of reasonable care is same as the duty of due care. In this regard, business judgment rule says that directors and officers are not liable to the corporation or its shareholders for honest mistakes of judgment and for practicing the reasonable care as a prudent person would do under similar circumstances.

Basic Ethical and Legal Principles for Managers, Executives, Officers, and Board of Directors (continued)

Duty of slight care is a duty not to be grossly negligent in caring for something in one's responsibility. For example, it is a duty that common carriers (e.g., truckers and movers) owe that says if the goods are lost, damaged, destroyed, or stolen, the common carrier is liable even if it was not at fault for the loss.

Duty of ordinary care is the duty an owner owes an invitee or a licensee to prevent injury or harm when the invitee or licensee steps on the owner's premises. For example, banks for proper handling of checks, individual home owners for providing safe and secure premises, and commercial and office building owners for providing safe and secure premises come under the duty of ordinary care provision.

Duty of utmost care is a duty of care that goes beyond ordinary care that says common carriers (e.g., airlines, buses, taxies, and coaches) and innkeepers (e.g., hotels, motels, and resorts) have a responsibility to provide security to their passengers or guests.

Duties of principals and agents require duty to compensate of an agent, duty to reimburse the agent, duty to indemnify the agent, and duty to cooperate with the agent all are on the part of principals; and duty of performance to a principal, duty of notification to the principal, and duty of accountability to the principal all are on the part of agents. In addition, an agent should not involve in self-dealing, usurp an opportunity, compete with the principal, and misuse of confidential information, and should not maintain a dual agency relationship.

Summary of Ethical and Legal Principles Expected of Corporate Officers and Directors

- Due care (e.g., reasonable care, good faith, and prudent person).

- Duty of due care (e.g., no harm, nor risk, and no breach of duty).

- Due diligence (e.g., honesty in fact and honesty in intent).

- Duty of loyalty (e.g., no self-dealing, no stealing of company opportunities, no competition with the company, and no making of secret profits).

- Duty of obedience (e.g., comply with the state corporation statutes, the articles of incorporation, and the corporate bylaws).

Need for Board's Independence

Board independence from management is a crucial aspect of good corporate governance. It is here that the difference between inside directors and outside directors becomes most pronounced. Outside directors are independent from the firm and its top managers. In contrast, inside directors have some sort of ties to the firm. Sometimes they are top managers in the firm; other times insiders are family members or others with close ties to the CEO. To varying degrees, each of these parties is "beholden" to the CEO and, therefore, might be hesitant to speak out when necessary.

Another problem is managerial control of the board processes. CEOs often can control board perks, such as director compensation and committee assignments. Board members who rock the boat may find they are left out in the cold. Two issues surrounding compensation include (1) CEO compensation, which is very controversial and (2) director compensation, which is very subjective or can be interpreted as self-dealing.

Insider Trading Scandals

Insider trading is the practice of obtaining critical information from inside a company and then using that information for one's own personal financial gain, causing scandals. Not only are shareholders suspicious of what has been going on unbeknownst to them, but small investors and the general public have lost faith in what they thought was the stable and secure financial industry. When companies disclose meaningful information to shareholders and securities professionals, they must do so publicly so that small investors can enjoy a more level playing field as the large investors.

Board Member Liabilities

Many individuals do not want the board director positions. Concerned about increasing legal hassles emanating from stockholder, customer, and employee lawsuits, directors were quitting such positions or refusing to accept them in the first place. Although courts rarely hold directors personally liable in the hundreds of shareholder suits filed every year, over the past several years there have been a few cases in which directors have been held personally and financially liable for their decisions.

Roles of the Chief Executive Officer

The chief executive officer's (CEO's) management style, tone, and leadership skills set the stage for the entire corporation, which determines the ultimate success or failure of the organization. The CEO is the linchpin to the strategic management process in setting the overall direction for the organization and mobilizing resources to accomplish the organization mission, vision, goals, and objectives.

The CEO is the contact person for the stock markets, investment analysts, and the media along with the CFO in communicating financial and operational performance results. The CEO possesses more soft skills than hard skills. The other senior executives' management style and leadership skills should be compatible with that of the CEO to ensure goal congruence.

Improving Corporate Governance

Efforts to improve corporate governance may be classified into two major categories. First, changes could be made in the composition, structure, and functioning of boards of directors. Second, shareholders—on their own initiative or on the initiative of management or the board—could assume a more active role in governance.

Specifically, improving corporate governance requires (1) increased change in the composition of the directors between inside directors and outside directors, (2) increased role of shareholders with their initiatives to companies, (3) increased role of company initiatives to shareholders, and (4) increased obligation of companies to fully disclose vital information to shareholders.

Global Practices in Corporate Governance

Corporate governance practices differ considerably around the globe although there are some common practices. Regardless, most of the problems are rooted in poor governance policies and practices; fraudulent accounting practices; and executives' excessive and abusive behavior. Specific issues deal with ownership, board composition, influence, power, and control, as follows:

- Ownership is heavily dispersed in the United States but is much more concentrated in Canada, Germany, Japan, and China. High levels of influence and control over corporate affairs are associated with high concentration of ownership.

- National and state governments also own major stakes of public companies in Germany, Italy, Japan, and China.

- French and German companies have different types of owners than those found in the United States and the United Kingdom. In France, non-financial corporations and state government are the largest shareholders. In Germany, both banks and non-financial corporations are owners. In addition, German banks own both debt and equity in the same corporation; they have direct voting power and proxy voting positions from bank depositors.

- Most Chinese public firms' shares are controlled by state-owned or state-controlled shareholders and the remaining trading shares are owned by a combination of individual and institutional investors.

Global Practices in Corporate Governance (continued)

- In Brazil, China, France, and Russia, the government owns the largest companies in size.

- Owners and workers sit on the board in France, Germany, Japan, and China whereas outsiders and managers sit on the board in the United States, United Kingdom, and Canadian companies.

- CEOs have considerable power over the selection of board members in many U.S. corporations as well as in Canada and the United Kingdom. In France and Germany, owners nominate and elect the board members.

- In Japan, both supplier and customer organizations acquire financial interest and ownership in Japanese corporations and are represented on the corporate board (called Kiertsu).

Role of Internal Audit in Corporate Governance Process

The internal audit activity should assess and make appropriate recommendations for improving the governance process in its accomplishment of the following objectives:

- Promoting appropriate ethics and values within the organization.
- Ensuring effective organizational performance management and accountability.
- Effectively communicating risk and control information to appropriate areas of the organization.
- Effectively coordinating the activities of and communicating information among the board, external and internal auditors, and management.

The internal audit activity should evaluate the design, implementation, and effectiveness of the organization's ethics-related objectives, programs, and activities. Consulting engagement objectives should be consistent with the overall values and goals of the organization.

ROLES AND RESPONSIBILITIES OF THE AUDIT COMMITTEE

The audit committee's key responsibility—overseeing the process that produces reliable and credible financial statements while ensuring the company has effective internal controls—requires it to conduct activities that previously had been executed mostly by management. Today audit committees are also expected to retain and compensate the external auditors, grasp all of the key information included in a company's financial reporting, and oversee risk management and compliance with the laws and regulations affecting the company. This change is occurring in an environment that demands transparency. Responsibilities of the audit committee and its relationship with corporate management are:

- To ensure that published financial statements are not misleading.

- To ensure that internal controls are adequate.

- To follow up on allegations of material, financial, ethical, and legal irregularities.

- To ratify the selection of the external auditor.

- To press more and trust less with corporate management.

Types of Audits in Governance

Types of audits in governance include stakeholder audit, governance audit, strategic audit, and due diligence audit to monitor corporate governance policies, procedures, and activities.

BUSINESS ETHICS

Corporate business ethics play an important role in ensuring good corporate governance and better corporate management. Corporate ethics and corporate governance support corporate management. Ethical lapses and dilemmas are one of the root causes of many problems that corporate management are facing today.

Ethics can be defined broadly as the study of what is right or good for human beings. It attempts to determine what people ought to do or what goals they should pursue. Business ethics, as a branch of applied ethics, is the study and determination of what is right and good in business settings. Unlike legal analyses, analyses of ethics have no central authority, such as courts or legislatures, upon which to rely; nor do they follow clear-cut, universal standards. Nonetheless, despite these inherent limitations, it is still possible to make meaningful ethical judgments.

Scope of Ethics Management

The scope of ethics management is too broad as it includes several categories such as societal ethics, public ethics, personal ethics, business ethics, management ethics, professional ethics, Nation's ethics, government ethics, family ethics, environmental ethics and individual versus group ethics.

Interactions between Law, Ethics, and Economics

Business managers and executives can use the Venn diagram to understand the interactions (i.e., connections and disconnections) among law, ethics, and economics (profits). A firm's legal, ethical, and economic goals can be depicted in a Venn diagram showing how certain decisions address these goals.

Codes of Conduct

Corporate governance objectives are also formulated in voluntary codes and standards (i.e., codes of conduct) that do not have the status of law or regulation. While such codes play an important role in improving corporate governance arrangements, they might leave shareholders and other stakeholders with uncertainty concerning their status and implementation. When codes and principles are used as a national standard or as an explicit substitute for legal or regulatory provisions, market credibility requires that their status in terms of coverage, implementation, compliance, and sanctions is clearly specified.

The Codes of Conduct document should be distributed to all employees annually and acknowledging of receiving it, reading it, understanding it, and signing it stating that the employee will abide to the contents of this document.

World-class organizations have developed a "code of conduct" for their organizations, which should comply with the definition of a "code of ethics" set out in Section 406 (c) of the Sarbanes-Oxley Act of 2002. In addition, the code must provide for an enforcement mechanism and protection for persons reporting questionable behavior (i.e., whistleblowing). The board of directors must approve any waivers of the code for directors, executives, or officers of the organization.

Financial Disclosures

In the U.S. federal government, the Ethics in Government Act of 1978 requires financial disclosure reporting, which is intended to identify and deter conflicts of interest between federal employee duties and responsibilities and personal financial interests and activities. Depending on such matters as the position held or the amount of compensation, disclosure statements are either to be made available to the public or kept confidential.

Similarly, executives, board of directors, consultants, and contractors working for a private company are required to submit financial information such as stocks and bonds that they hold in the company. They also need to disclose any other conflicts of interest situations that can impair their independence and objectivity.

Key Ethical Principles

The Golden Rule. The golden rule states putting oneself in others' shoes. It includes not knowingly doing harm to others.

The Means-End Cycle. The means-end cycle states that when ends are of overriding importance, unscrupulous means may be used to reach the ends.

The Might-Equals-Right Principle. The might-equals-right principle states that justice is defined as the interest of the stronger, meaning that stronger people have an upper hand over the weaker people.

The Professional Principle. The professional principle states that a true professional will do things in such a way that he can explain them before a committee of peer professionals.

Goal Congruence Principle. The goal congruence principle states that actions, wills, and needs of employees should be subordinated to the greater good of the organization they work for. An employee should ask himself whether his goals are consistent with the organization's goals. This principle is similar to (1) the utilitarian ethic, meaning the greatest good should be done for the greatest number and (2) the organization ethic, meaning that employees do things for the good of the organization.

Prudent Person Concept. The prudent person, who is not infallible or perfect, has the ability to govern and discipline himself by the use of reason, does not neglect his duty, and applies his knowledge, skills, and sound judgment in the use of organization's resources. The prudent person concept is related to the goal congruence principle.

Types of Ethics

Basically, ethics can be of two types: the normative approach and the approach. Managers faced with tough ethical choices often benefit from a **normative approach**—one based on norms and values—to guide their decision making. Normative ethics are concerned with supplying and justifying a coherent moral system of thinking and judging. It asks a question "what ought to be"? Normative approach includes utilitarian, individualism, moral rights, and justice approaches. An application of the normative approach can occur when a decision is made to recruit, hire, train and promote both men and women equally.

The **descriptive approach** is concerned with describing, characterizing, and studying the morality of a people, a culture, or a society. It also compares and contrasts different moral codes, systems, practices, beliefs, and values. It asks a basic question 'what is." The business judgment rule is a legal presumption that the directors and officers of the corporation have exercised due care by acting on an informed basis, in good faith, and in the honest belief that their actions are in the best interests of the corporation. Unless a plaintiff can give persuasive evidence against at least one of the criteria, corporate directors and officers are insulated from liability for breach of the duty of care. A downside is that some people may adopt the view that "if everyone is doing it," it must be acceptable, which is not right. Examples include discrimination, speed driving a car, padding expense accounts, and deceptive advertising.

Normative Approach versus Descriptive Approach

- Normative approach deals with "what ought to be" or "what ought not to be" in the prevailing set of ethical standards.
- Descriptive approach focuses on "what is" in the prevailing set of ethical standards.
- One should compare "what ought to be" with "what is" to see what is going on in the real world.

Three major approaches to thinking about business ethics include conventional approach, principles approach, and ethical tests approach. The **conventional approach** to business ethics is essentially an approach whereby we compare a decision or practice with prevailing norms of acceptability. We call it the conventional approach because it is believed that this is the way that general society thinks.

The **principles approach** includes the utilitarian ethic, virtue ethics, and the Golden Rule, and augments the conventional approach to business ethics. The utilitarian ethics focuses on providing the greatest good for the greatest number. The Golden Rule includes not knowingly doing harm to others.

The **ethical tests approach** is based on practice while the principles approach is based on philosophy (e.g., servant leadership). Showing common sense, presenting one's best self, making something public, and ventilation are examples of the ethical test approach.

Models of Management Ethics

The **immoral management** model holds that management's motives are selfish and greedy and that it cares only about its own or its company's gains. For example, if Company A knowingly commits a wrongful act that is detrimental to Company B, Company A has exhibited an immoral type of management ethics. Immoral management decisions, behaviors, actions, and practices are discordant with ethical principles. It represents unethical behavior and follows exploiting strategy.

Moral management, as expected, exhibits ethical behavior and follows integrity strategy. It conforms to the highest standards of ethical behavior or professional standards of conduct. The six major elements or capacities that are essential to making moral judgments include: (1) moral imagination, (2) moral identification and ordering, (3) moral evaluation, (4) tolerance of moral disagreement and ambiguity, (5) integration of managerial and moral competence, and (6) a sense of moral obligation and integrity.

Amoral management can be intentionally amoral or unintentionally amoral. Intentionally amoral managers do not factor ethical considerations into their decisions, actions, and behaviors because they believe business activity resides outside the sphere to which moral judgments apply. They think that different rules apply in business than in other areas of life. Unintentionally amoral managers do not think about business activity in ethical terms. These managers are simply casual about the negative effects of their decisions on others. They lack ethical perception and moral awareness and do not stop to consider that their actions have ethical dimensions or consequences. Amoral management contains both intentional behavior and unintentional behavior, and follows compliance strategy.

Roles and Responsibilities of Gatekeepers

Gatekeepers include external auditors, attorneys, securities analysts, credit-rating agencies, and investment bankers, who inform and advise the board of directors and the shareholders, and the gatekeepers are not fulfilling their gatekeeper or agent role to its fullest extent. These gatekeepers should be serving investors, creditors, and stockholders by assuming independent monitor or watchdog role and by avoiding conflicts of interest situations that can compromise their independence and objectivity.

Gatekeepers are in a way policemen to prevent corporate wrongdoings. Some examples of corporate wrongdoings include manipulating earnings (earnings management), financial restatements, capitalizing expenses, deferring or misclassifying expenses, hiding liabilities, engaging in off-balance sheet transactions, and involving in other types of financial fraud to increase stock price and to receive big bonuses by corporate management.

Gatekeepers provide certification and verification services to investors and that they are hired and paid by the corporate managers that they are to watch. The impact of these services is to lower the cost of capital for a corporation, thereby increasing its stock price. Both shareholders and the board of directors are depending on gatekeepers for an unbiased flow of information that is not edited, filtered, or modified in favor of corporate management. Effective corporate governance requires a chain of actors including directors, managers, and

Roles and Responsibilities of Gatekeepers (continued)

gatekeepers, where the latter cannot become the weakest link. Taken to its extreme, the board of directors and the Securities and Exchange Commission (SEC) can also be viewed as gatekeepers.

Gatekeepers are not fulfilling their watchdog role in preventing and/or detecting fraud or other irregularities. Gatekeepers should not wear blinders; cannot ignore "red flags," cannot be indifferent to sins of omissions; and cannot do perfunctory audits or investigations. Gatekeepers should increase their positive reputational capital and decrease their negative reputational capital by exhibiting unbiased and professional behavior.

Ethics Audit

Specifically, the Chief Ethics Officer or his designee should perform an ethics audit as follows:

- Work with the internal audit department in developing audit plans and to identify areas of audit addressing ethical violations.
- Work with the legal department in pursuing cases that violated ethical principles either inside the company (e.g., employees and management) or outside (e.g., customers, suppliers, vendors, and contractors).
- Conduct ethics audits, special management reviews, and self-assessment reviews periodically and proactively to ensure continuous improvement in ethical matters.
- Encourage employees and others to report ethical violations through whistleblower telephone hotline, e-mail, or other means that will be kept confidential.
- Conduct training classes to managers and non-managers about ethical principles that include actions and consequences and referencing to all the applicable laws and regulations.
- Analyze outside-in views (i.e., views of stakeholders about company management) and inside-out views (i.e., views of company management about stakeholders) to identify disconnections between these views and to integrate them in a coherent manner.
- Issue an audit report describing significant findings and recommendations to management for corrective actions to take.

CORPORATE SOCIAL RESPONSIBILITY

Corporations have obligations to be good citizens of the local, national, and international communities in which they do business. Failure to meet these obligations can result in damage to the cooperation, both in immediate economic terms and in longer-term reputational value.

Definition of Corporate Social Responsibility

A corporation should be a good citizen and contribute to the communities in which it operates by making charitable contributions and encouraging its directors, manager, and employees to form relationships with those communities. A corporation also should be active in promoting awareness of health, safety, and environmental issues, including any issues that relate to the specific types of business in which the corporation is engaged. Organizations must alo comply with the ISO 26000 standard regarding social responsibility.

The social responsibility of business encompasses the economic, legal, ethical, and discretionary (philanthropic) expectations that society has of organizations at a given point in time.

Economic Responsibilities

The *economic responsibility* is required of business by society, and includes things such as (1) be profitable, (2) maximize sales, (3) minimize costs, (4) make sound strategic decisions, and (5) be attentive to dividend policy.

Legal Responsibilities

The *legal responsibility* is required of business by society, and includes things such as (1) obey all laws and adhere to all regulations,(2) obey U.S. Foreign Corrupt Practices Act, (3) obey U.S. Federal Securities Regulations, (4) obey U.S. Sarbanes-Oxley Act of 2002, (5) fulfill all contractual obligations, and (6) honor all warranties and guarantees given to customers/clients in acquiring products and services.

Ethical Responsibilities

The *ethical responsibility* is expected of business by society, and includes things such as (1) avoid questionable practices, (2) respond to spirit as well as letter of law, (3) assume law is a floor on behavior, (4) operate above minimum required, (5) do what is right, fair, and just, and (6) assert ethical leadership.

Philanthropic Responsibilities

The *philanthropic responsibility* is desired of business by society, and includes things such as (1) be a good corporate citizen, (2) make corporate contributions, (3) provide programs supporting community (e.g., education, health and human services, culture, arts, and civic duties), (4) provide for community development and betterment on a voluntary basis.

Social Audit

Social audit is a systematic analysis and testing of an organization's success in achieving its social responsibility. It is a systematic attempt to identify, measure, monitor, and evaluate an organization's performance with respect to its social efforts, goals, and programs. The social audit is a systematic and structured review of identifying issues and problems in the understanding and fulfilling of economic, legal, ethical, and philanthropic responsibilities, and making recommendations to resolve such issues and problems.

Pyramid Layers of Corporate Social Responsibility

A socially responsible firm should strive to:

- Be a good corporate citizen (top of the pyramid)

- Be ethical

- Obey the law

- Make a profit (base or bottom of the pyramid)

In summary, the total social responsibility of business entails the concurrent fulfillment of the firm's economic, legal, ethical, and philanthropic responsibilities. In equation form, this might be expressed as follows.

Total Corporate Social Responsibility = Economic Responsibilities + Legal Responsibilities + Ethical Responsibilities + Philanthropic Responsibilities

CORPORATE RISK MANAGEMENT

Risk is pervasive throughout an organization as it can arise from any business function or process at any time without warning. Because of this widespread exposure, no single functional department management, other than the board of directors, can oversee the enterprise-wide risk management program. This approach also supports the idea that risks cannot be identified, measured, and monitored on a piecemeal basis. A holistic approach is needed.

Risk Management Methodology

Risk management methodology encompasses three processes: risk assessment (risk analysis), risk mitigation, and risk monitoring (risk evaluation). Examples of risk mitigation options include risk rejection (risk ignorance), risk assumption (risk acceptance), risk avoidance, risk reduction (risk limitation), risk transfer, risk contingency, and risk compliance.

Various Types of Risks

Many organizations face various types of risks and exposures. Hence, the chief risk officer (CRO) must identify as many risk types as possible covering both current and potential risks. Each risk alternative for satisfying the business requirements must be evaluated for the selected risk types. The evaluator reviews each of these risks to determine the overall impact of significant variations from the original assumptions on which the expected success of the alternative is based.

Most of these risks are interrelated and interconnected, and have a magnifying effect. For example, legal risk and regulatory risk would magnify the reputation (image) risk of an organization. Some risks have a cascading effect, for example, non-compliance with contractual terms and conditions can lead to financial risk (i.e., loss of money due to payment of penalties) and legal risk (lawsuits resulting from violation of contractual rights). Therefore, all risk types should be viewed from a total business context, instead of a piecemeal basis.

Four common best practices that are applicable to each type of risk include (1) acquiring traditional and non-traditional insurance coverage to protect tangible and intangible assets, (2) conducting surveys of employees, customers, suppliers, and the industry, (3) performing benchmarking studies to understand existing and new risks better, and (4) keeping the chain of knowledge strong and current through continuously acquiring of knowledge, skills, and abilities (KSAs) for all employees.

Risk Management Tools

Measuring risk can be difficult, and in practice a variety of approaches are used ranging from simply adjusting costs up or benefits down, adjusting risk levels, dollar amounts, and probabilities to the use of statistical modeling and Monte Carlo simulation. A few of the more commonly used tools and techniques include business impact analysis; cost-benefit analysis; fit-gap analysis; option analysis; economic analysis; expected value analysis; sensitivity analysis; strengths, weaknesses, opportunity, and threat (SWOT) analysis (situation analysis); and subjective scoring. It is a good business practice to combine quantitative methods with the qualitative techniques to obtain broad perspectives and comprehensive picture of risks.

Examples of **quantitative methods** in risk management include single loss exposure value, annualized rate of occurrence, probability of loss, single loss exposure factor, and annualized loss expectancy.

Examples of **qualitative methods** in risk management include intuitive (gut feel) approach, checklists, self-assessments, focus groups, interviews, surveys, and Delphi technique. In the Delphi technique, subject matter experts (SMEs) present their own view of risks independently and anonymously, which are then centrally compiled. The process is repeated until consensus is obtained. The Delphi technique is a method used to avoid *groupthink*, as SMEs do not meet face-to-face to make decisions.

Best Practices in Managing Corporate Risks

- Manage existing safeguards and controls

- Periodically assess risks

- Mitigate risks by implementing and efficiently administering safeguards and controls

- Risk assessment and strategic planning

- Implement an enterprise risk management program

ENTERPRISE RISK MANAGEMENT

ERM Definition

An example of organizational use of risk frameworks is enterprise risk management (ERM), which is defined as a rigorous and coordinated approach to assessing and responding to all risks that affect the achievement of an organization's strategic and financial objectives. This includes both upside and downside risks. ERM risks are classified as financial risk, hazard risk, strategic risk, and operational risk.

Approaches and Dimensions to ERM

- The range of organization operations. This includes business units or locations, starting small as pilot projects and eventually rolling out to the entire enterprise (i.e., institutionalization).
- The sources of risk (e.g., hazard, financial, operational, and strategic). This may include property catastrophe risk and currency risk.
- The types of risk management activities or processes (i.e., risk identification, risk measurement, risk mitigation, and risk monitoring).

Alternative Risk-Transfer Tools

Five alternative risk-transfer tools, other than traditional insurance, include: (1) captive insurance firms, (2) financial insurance, (3) multiline/multiyear insurance, (4) multiple-trigger policies, and (5) risk securitization. Multiple-trigger policies and securitization tools are more commonly used.

Implementation of ERM

Senior management support and commitment is needed to properly implement the ERM program in the organization. A dedicated group of cross-functional staff is needed to push it through the organization. Most organizations are implementing the ERM program incrementally. Some are beginning by layering additional sources of risk, one at a time, into their exiting processes for risk assessment and risk mitigation. Some are embracing all sources of risk at the outset, but are tackling the processes one at a time, with most starting with risk assessment. Others are taking on all risk sources and all processes, but on a small, manageable subset of their operations as a pilot project.

Internal Auditing Role in ERM Implementation

The chief audit executive (CAE) is an ERM champion and should use risk-based audit plans that are consistent with the organization's goals. Internal auditing is the implementation arm of an ERM program. Internal auditors act as facilitators in cross-functional risk assessment workshops conducted in the business units.

RISK/CONTROL IMPLICATIONS OF DIFFERENT ORGANIZATIONAL STRUCTURES

Organization Defined

An organization is a system of consciously coordinated activities or forces of two or more persons. In other words, when people gather together and formally agree to combine their efforts for a common purpose or goal, an organization is the result. Organizations share four characteristics: (1) coordination of effort, (2) common goal or purpose, (3) division of labor, and (4) hierarchy of authority.

Classifying Organizations

Four categories of organizations exist, although some large and complex organizations have overlapping categories: (1) business organizations, (2) nonprofit service organizations, (3) mutual-benefit organizations, and (4) commonwealth organizations.

Theories of Organization

Two theories exist: the traditional view and the modern view. The traditional view has closed-system thinking, while the modern view incorporates open-system thinking.

Theories of Organizing

Several theories of organizing exist, including bureaucracy, administrative theory, scientific management theory, human relations theory, and contingency design theory.

TYPES OF ORGANIZATIONAL STRUCTURES

Contingency Design Alternatives

Contingency design requires managers to select from a number of situationally appropriate alternatives instead of blindly following fixed principles of organization. Design alternatives include span of control, centralization and decentralization, line and staff organizations, and matrix organization.

Span of Control

Narrow and Wide

The number of people who report directly to a manager represent that manager's span of control or span of management. The optimal size of a span of control in a work area is dependent upon (1) the department's function, (2) organizational levels, (3) changes in the nature of the work, and (4) the clarity of instructions given employees. The optimal span of control is not dependent upon the total number of employees in the department or company.

Tall and Flat

A tall organization has many levels of hierarchy and a narrow span of control. A flat organization structure is one with relatively few levels of hierarchy and is characterized by a wide span of management control.

Centralized and Decentralized Organizations

Two methods of organizing are centralized and decentralized. In a centralized organization, decisions are made at the higher levels of management. Decisions in a decentralized organization are made at the lower levels. Authority is delegated to lower levels of the organization.

Centralization is typically used in those organizations that emphasize coordination of decisions that must be applied uniformly to a set of known or common problems. In planning an audit of a highly decentralized operation, an auditor assumes that the authority to make significant risk decisions has been delegated to the unit managers.

Two approaches can be used to achieve decentralization: Functional and divisional. Functional decentralization occurs when related activities or functions are grouped within an organization. For instance, all functions relating to marketing are grouped under one head. The main advantage of functional decentralization is that it allows specialists to work in areas where they contribute the most to the firm. This is very important in industries that survive mainly because of technical expertise.

Divisional decentralization is the creation of units whose managers are in charge of producing and marketing a certain product, a group of related products, or activities for a geographic region. A division thus created will involve many if not all of the functions engaged in by the entire organization. Divisionalization results in many semi-independent units equivalent to small organizations within the larger parent.

Line and Staff Organizations

Line and staff organization structure is designed to maximize the unity-of-command principle by giving only the managers the authority to make decisions affecting those in the chain of command. There is no cross-over between line and staff organization structure since each structure has its own chain of command.

Line managers have the authority to make decisions and give orders to all subordinates in the chain of command. Staff authority is generally limited to subordinates within its department. There is a natural conflict between these two parties due to power differences and different backgrounds.

Matrix Organization

In a matrix organization, people with vertical (down) and horizontal (across) lines of authority are combined to accomplish a specific objective. This design is suitable to a project environment where the project manager is responsible for completing a project without a formal line authority. Under these conditions, project managers tend to use negotiation skills, persuasive ability, technical competence, and the exchange of favors to complete a project in order to compensate for their lack of formal authority.

Types of Departmentalization

Two common forms of integration are through the hierarchical chain of command and departmentalization. The chain of command refers to who is reporting to who in the chain of hierarchy, which is reflected in the organization chart. Some type of integration is needed to offset the negative effects of differentiation. It is through departmentalization that related jobs, activities, or processes are grouped into major organizational subunits such as departments, divisions, groups, or units. Four basic types of departmentalization include: (1) functional departments, (2) product-service departments, (3) geographic location departments, and (4) customer classification departments.

Functional Departments

In both profit and nonprofit organizations, functional departments categorize jobs according to the activity performed. Manufacturing, marketing, and finance are some examples of functional departments, and the structure is popular because it permits those with similar technical expertise to work in a coordinated subunit. It becomes unpopular when departmental concerns tend to override more important organizational concerns. Functional departments can encourage differentiation at the expense of integration. A small, single, standard product line may be organized as a functional department such as manufacturing, accounting, and sales. When organizational and reporting lines are unbroken, it is an indication of functional departmentalization.

Product-Service Departments

In the product-service department category, a product or service, rather than a functional category of work, is the unifying theme. Ideally, those working in a product-service department have a broad business orientation rather than a narrow functional orientation. One weakness of the product-service approach is that inefficient and costly duplication of effort may take place. A product departmentalization strategy may be good for a firm making multiple products. An example would be a computer manufacturer who organizes into mainframe computers, minicomputers, and personal computers.

Geographic Location of Departments

Geographic location dictates the structure and format of the organization and it emphasizes the concept that managers should be "closer to the action." Advantages include knowledge of local business and customers, and disadvantages include long lines of communication. The force behind the geographical lines is global competition. "Think globally and act locally" is the catchphrase for companies operating in a global market.

Customer Classification of Departments

Customers have different needs and are of different types (such as business versus residential, retail versus wholesale, industrial versus commercial). The rationale behind organizing the company into customer classification is to better service the distinctly different needs of each customer type.

New Organizational Configurations

New organizational configurations include hourglass organizations, cluster organizations, and network organizations.

Hourglass Organizations

The hourglass organization consists of three layers, with the middle layer distinctly pinched. The first layer is a strategic management who formulates a vision for the organization and makes sure it becomes a reality. The second layer is a shrunken middle management who carries out a coordinating function for diverse lower-level activities. These middle managers wear different hats all the time (i.e., they handle accounting problems one day, product design issues the other day, and marketing dilemmas the next day).

At the bottom of the hourglass is a broad layer of technical employees who act as their own supervisors much of the time. Consequently, the distinction between supervisors and rank-and-file employees is blurred. Employees at this operating level complain about a real lack of promotional opportunities. Management should try to keep them motivated with challenging work assignments, lateral transfers, skill training opportunities, and pay-for-performance schemes.

Cluster Organizations

Teams are the primary structural unit in the cluster organization. Employees are multi-skilled and move from team to team as projects dictate. Flexible work assignments are the norm. This structure promotes innovation and responsiveness. Pay for knowledge is a common practice. Motivation will be high, but so will stress levels. On the downside, job security is an issue due to constantly changing projects. Employees need to attend training programs in team building and communications.

Network Organizations

Network organizations do not produce what they sell and, hence, their only function is administrative oversight. For each organizational function (production, marketing), they have an independent contractor to handle business operations. In other words, network organizations buy a product with their own label on it and then hire other companies to distribute and sell the product.

Management Structures and Organization Systems

Two organization systems are closed system and open system, and two management structures are mechanistic and organic. A relationship between management structures and organization systems is established.

A closed system is independent of its external environment; it is autonomous, enclosed, and sealed off from the external environment. It focuses on internal systems only. Its external environment is simple, stable, and predictable. The major issue for management is to run the business efficiently with centralized decision making and authority. It represents a bureaucratic organization.

An open system is dependent on its environment to survive; it both consumes resources and exports resources to the external environment. It transforms inputs into outputs. It must continuously change and adapt to the external environment. Open systems are complex, unstable, and unpredictable and internal efficiency is a minor issue for management. It represents a modern organization.

A mechanistic management structure is characterized by rules, procedures, and a clear hierarchy of authority. Organizations are formalized and centralized and the external environment is stable.

An organic management structure is characterized by a fluid (looser) and free-flowing nature, which is adaptive to changes in the external environment with little or no written rules and regulations and operates without a clear hierarchy of authority. Organizations are informal and decentralized and responsibility flows down to lower levels. It encourages teamwork and problem solving by letting employees work directly with each other.

Criteria and Determinants of Organizational Effectiveness

- Effectiveness is a measure of whether or not organizational objectives are accomplished.
- Efficiency is the relationship between outputs and inputs.
- The effectiveness criteria is prescribed by society in the form of explicit expectations, regulations, and laws, and by stockholders in the form of profits, return on investment, and growth.
- Organizational effectiveness has a time dimension to it (i.e., near future, intermediate future, and distant future).
- Organizational decline results from management complacency (usually the primary culprit), unsteady economic growth, resource shortages, competition, and weak demand for products and services. It typically involves a reduction in the size or scope of the organization.

SCHEMES IN VARIOUS BUSINESS CYCLES

Sales Pricing Objectives and Policies

Pricing Objectives

Pricing decisions that integrate the firm's costs with its marketing strategy, business conditions, competition, consumer demand, product variables, channels of distribution, and general resources can determine the success or failure of a business. Pricing of products or services is the cornerstone of the marketing function. If the price is too high, buyers may purchase competitive brands leading to a loss of sales and profits. If the price is too low, profitability may suffer despite increases in sales.

General Pricing Decision Model

Pricing decisions require the consideration of many factors. A nine-step pricing decision model includes: (1) define target markets, (2) estimate market potential, (3) develop product positioning, (4) design the marketing mix, (5) estimate price elasticity of demand, (6) estimate all relevant costs, (7) analyze environmental factors, (8) set pricing objectives, and (9) develop the price structure.

Procurement and Supply Chain Management

The supply-chain or procurement (purchasing) process is seen as equivalent to an input-transformation-output system. In this context, both customer and supplier goodwill are to be viewed as key assets to an organization. The supply chain becomes a value chain when all of the transforming activities performed upon an input provide value to a customer. The real challenge is to ensure that value is added at every step of the chain to achieve customer satisfaction. Both purchasing and the supplier play a large role in the value chain.

Managing the supply base includes integration of suppliers, involvement of suppliers, supplier reduction strategies, supplier performance, and supplier certification. The purpose of managing the supply-base is to manage quality, quantity, delivery, price, and service.

Reverse Purchasing versus Reverse Marketing

In reverse purchasing, the buyer approaches the supplier to buy his materials. The buyer establishes prices, terms, and conditions. The buyer takes a proactive initiative in making the sourcing proposal to several suppliers in order to find a new supplier with better pricing, quality, and delivery. It is a reversal of the traditional buyer/supplier practice where a buyer goes to an existing supplier. Reverse purchasing is reverse marketing, which is also called supplier development.

Alternative Market Channels

It takes a considerable amount of time, money, and effort to set up channels of distribution. Because of this heavy commitment of resources, once decisions are made about the channel of distribution they are not easy to retract. Yet these decisions are very critical to the success of the firm. Decisions based on inaccurate or incomplete information can be very costly to the firm. Whether it is a consumer good or industrial good, channels of distribution provide the ultimate consumer or industrial user with time, place, and possession value (utility). Thus, an efficient channel is one that delivers the product when and where it is wanted at a minimum total cost. Marketing intermediaries exist to bring about product exchanges between buyers and sellers in a reasonably efficient manner.

Marketing Intermediaries

The primary role of intermediaries in marketing is to bring supply and demand together in an efficient and orderly manner.

Channels of Marketing Distribution

A channel of marketing distribution is the integration of intermediaries through which a seller markets his products to users or consumers. Agents, wholesalers, and retailers are called intermediaries. These intermediaries are also called middlemen. Channels with one or more intermediaries are referred to indirect channels. In addition, the choice of channels can be improved by considering distribution coverage required, degree of control desired, total distribution cost, and channel flexibility.

Selecting Marketing Intermediaries

The two basic methods of selecting intermediaries (middlemen) are pushing and pulling. Pushing a product through the channel means using normal promotional effort—personal skills and advertising—to help sell the whole marketing mix to possible channel members. This is a common approach with the producer working through a team to get the product to the user. By contrast, pulling means getting consumers to ask intermediaries for the product. This involves distributing samples and coupons to final consumers. If the promotion works, the intermediaries are forced to carry the product to satisfy their customer needs.

Managing Channels of Distribution

From a management point of view, entire channels of distribution should be treated as a social system since each party plays a defined role and each has certain expectations of the other. The interaction with each other is very critical for all parties involved and the behavioral implications are many.

Marketing Product Life Cycles

Product Strategy

Product strategy is a part of the marketing mix (i.e., product, price, place, and promotion). Other parts include promotion strategy, distribution strategy, and pricing strategy. There are many decision areas in product management, including product definition, product classification, product mix, and product line, and packaging and branding.

Product Definition

The way in which the product variable is defined can have important implications for the survival, profitability, and long-run growth of the firm.

Product Classification

A product classification is an analytical device to assist in planning marketing strategy and programs. A basic assumption underlying such classifications is that products with common attributes can be marketed in a similar manner. In general, products are classified according to two basic criteria: (1) end use or market and (2) degree of processing or physical transformation required.

Product Mix and Product Lines

The product mix is the composite of products offered for sale by the firm's product line. It refers to a group of products that are closely related in terms of use, customer groups, price ranges, and channels of distribution. There are three primary dimensions of a firm's product mix:

1. **Width.** Number of product lines in the firm
2. **Depth.** Average number of products in each line
3. **Consistency.** Similarity of product lines

Packaging and Branding

Distinctive or unique packaging is one method of differentiating relatively homogeneous products, such as toothpaste or soap. The design of packaging should focus on the size of the product, how easy it is to open, how strong the packaging should be in protecting the product, the attractiveness of the packaging, and costs.

Product Life-Cycle Concept

A firm's product strategy must consider the fact that products have a life cycle—phases or stages that a product will go through in its lifetime. This life cycle varies according to industry, product, technology, and market. In general, product growth follows an S-shaped curve due to innovation, diffusion of a new product, and changes in the product and the market. There are four phases that a typical product goes through including: (1) introduction, (2) growth, (3) maturation, and (4) decline. Some products skip a phase, such as introduction or maturity, while some products are revitalized after decline, thereby not going through the S-shaped pattern.

Product Audit

The product audit is a marketing management technique whereby the company's current product offerings are required to ascertain whether each product should be continued as is, improved, modified, or discontinued. The product manager, who is responsible for his product, should ensure that the product audit is performed at regular intervals as a matter of marketing policy. One of the major purposes of the product audit is to detect "sick" products for possible discontinuation. Some critical factors to be considered in this area are sales trends, profit contribution, and product life cycle. One of the objectives of the product audit is to determine whether to modify or improve the product or to leave things as they are (status quo).

New Product Development Steps

A company that can bring out new products faster than its competition enjoys many advantages and benefits. To increase speed in introducing new products, many companies are bypassing time-consuming regional tests in favor of national programs. The goal is to develop a new product right the first time. Marketing writers estimate that the primary reason for new product failure is the selling company's inability to match up its offerings to the needs of the customer. This inability to satisfy customer needs can be attributed to four main sources.

1. Inadequacy of up-front marketing intelligence efforts

2. Failure of the company to stick close to what it does best

3. The inability to provide better value than competing products and technologies

4. The inability to innovate new products coming from research and development (R&D) laboratories faster than competitors can

Traditional Innovation versus Reverse Innovation

- Traditional Innovation Approach → R&D Labs → Customers

- Reverse Innovation Approach → Customers → R&D Labs

Causes of New Product Failure

- Faulty estimates of new product potential.

- Unexpected reactions from competitors.

- Poor timing in the introduction of the product.

- Rapid change in the market (economy) after the product introduction was approved.

- Inadequate quality control.

- Faulty estimates in production costs.

- Inadequate expenditures on initial promotion programs.

- Faulty market testing.

- Improper channel of distribution.

New Product Policy

Developing a new product policy is a complicated matter since new products are the lifeblood of successful business firms. Thus, the critical product policy question is not whether to develop new products but in what direction to move. Marketing management needs to develop criteria (standards/norms) for success that new products must meet if they are to be considered candidates for launching. Possible areas for standards development include profits, costs, use of plant capacity, and market share.

Steps in the development of a new product policy are:

1. Prepare a long-range industry forecast for existing product lines.

2. Prepare a long-range profit plan for the company, using existing product lines.

3. Review the long-range profit plan.

4. Determine what role new products will play in the company's future.

5. Prepare an inventory of company capabilities.

6. Determine market areas for new products.

New Product Policy (continued)

7. Prepare a statement of new product objectives.

8. Prepare a long-range profit plan, incorporating new products.

9. Assign new product responsibility.

10. Provide for evaluation of new product performance.

Characteristics of Marketing Services

The service sector of the U.S. economy or in the world has grown to such an extent that it captures about 50 cents or more of the consumer's every dollar. The definition of what constitutes a service remains unclear. Both products and services have the following common variables that comprise the marketing mix:

- The product or service itself

- The price

- The distribution system

- Promotion

- Marketing research

Problems in Service Quality

Poor quality of service and non-performance are two major reasons, and high price is a minor reason for switching to the competition. Service quality is measured against performance, which can be very difficult to ascertain. In general, problems in the determination of good service quality are attributable to differences in the expectations, perceptions, and experiences regarding the encounter between the service provider and the service user.

It is easier and cheaper to keep an existing customer than to find a new one. Product quality can be measured against accepted standards, which is tangible, while service quality is measured against expected performance, which is intangible.

Overcoming the Obstacles in Service Marketing

In view of the size and importance of service economy, considerable innovation and ingenuity are needed to make high-quality services available at convenient locations for consumers. The actual services offered by service providers often fall behind the opportunities available due to the following obstacles: a limited view of marketing, a lack of competition, a lack of creative management, a concept of "no obsolescence," and a lack of innovation in the distribution of services.

BUSINESS PROCESS ANALYSIS

In a manufacturing company, the scope of process analysis starts from raw materials and ends up with finished goods shipping to customers. It includes all the transformation (processing) stages, inspection steps, and transportation stages. Similarly, in a service company the scope of process analysis starts, for example, with claims application and ends up with making payment to the claimant. The goal of process analysis is to facilitate change for improvement. This requires looking at not only the individual processes where problems exist but also the upstream and downstream processes that are related to the process in question. Process improvements can be made by rearranging equipment layout, plant layout, inspection points, and testing stages with the help of motion study, material study, time study, and material handling studies. In this effort, both product processes and service processes should be examined for waste, delays, and improvement.

Workflow Analysis

Workflow analysis looks at the overall flow of work to find ways of improving this flow. It can reveal value-added and non-value-added activities (e.g., waste and delays) and identify interdependence among departments. The outcome would be eliminating the non-value-added activities and waste and improving efficiency and effectiveness. Assembling tasks, whether subassembly or final assembly, and process time are value-added activities of a manufactured product, while other activities are non-value-added activities.

Bottleneck Management

Bottleneck is a constraint in a facility, function, department, or resource whose capacity is less than the demand placed upon it. For example, a bottleneck machine or work center exists where jobs where jobs are processed at a slower rate than they are demanded. Another example is where the demand for a company's product exceeds the ability to produce the product.

Theory of Constraints

Theory of constraints (TOC) is a manufacturing strategy that attempts to remove the influence of bottlenecks on a process. The TOC consists of three separate but interrelated areas: (1) logistics, (2) performance measurement, and (3) logical thinking.

Five Focusing Steps

The five focusing steps is a process to continuously improve organizational profit by evaluating the production system and the marketing mix to determine how to make the most profit using the system constraint. The five steps consist of: (1) Identifying the constraint to the system, (2) Deciding how to exploit the constraint to the system, (3) Subordinating all non-constraints to the system, (4) Elevating the constraint to the system, and (5) Returning to Step 1 if the constraint is broken in any previous step, while not allowing inertia to set in.

BUSINESS PROCESS REENGINEERING AND BUSINESS PROCESS IMPROVEMENT

Techniques such as business process reengineering (BPR) and business process improvement (BPI) are used to improve efficiency, reduce costs, and improve customer service. Information technology is an enabler of BPR and BPI, not a substitute for them. Specifically, BPR focuses on achieving dramatic improvements while BPI focuses on achieving incremental improvements.

BENCHMARKING

Benchmarking is the selection of best practices implemented by other organizations. Best practices are the best ways to perform a business process. Organizational change and improvement are the major elements of benchmarking. Benchmarks are the result of a study of organizational processes.

A company should benchmark for three reasons: (1) it wants to attain world-class competitive capability, (2) it wants to prosper in a global economy, and (3) it simply wishes to survive (desperation). A company can benchmark in six distinct ways: (1) internal benchmarking, (2) competitive benchmarking, (3) industry benchmarking, (4) best-in-class benchmarking, (5) process benchmarking, and (6) strategic benchmarking.

Specific benchmarking methods include:

- Internal benchmarking looks downward and inward.
- Competitive benchmarking looks outward.
- Industry benchmarking looks for trends. It provides a short-run solution and a quick fix to a problem.
- Best-in-class benchmarking looks for the best all around. It provides a quantum jump in improvement.
- Process benchmarking is specific to a production or service activity.
- Strategic benchmarking is broad with big impact and focuses in big picture.

PRODUCTION PROCESS FLOWS

Three operational process flow measures include flow time, inventory, and throughput and they are interrelated in that defining targets on any two of them defines a target for the third.

Inventory = Throughput × Flow time

The basic managerial levers for process improvement are:

- Decrease in flow time

- Increase in throughput

- Decrease in inventory and waiting time

- Control process variability

- Manage process flows and costs

DESIGN OF PERFORMANCE MEASUREMENT SYSTEMS

Performance measures should be accurately defined, analyzed, and documented so that all interested parties are informed about them. Performance standards should bring meaning to measurements. Employees who are being measured should feel that standards and specific performance measures are fair and achievable. Self-measurement may create confidence and trust, and permit fast feedback and correction from employees. But it can also lead to distortions, concealment, and delays in reporting.

One of the design objectives should be that the performance standards must be simple, meaningful, comparable, reproducible, and traceable given similar business conditions. Care should be taken to compare items that are alike in terms of units of measurements (pounds, grams, liters, or gallons), time frames (hours or days), quantity (volume in units or tons), and quality (meeting the requirements). The standards should match the objectives of the operation or function being measured.

Periodically, the performance measurements should be reviewed and updated to ensure their continued applicability to the situations at hand. Evaluations of performance measures should concentrate on the significant exceptions or deviations from the standards. Therefore, exception reporting is preferred. Significant variances (deviations) require analysis and correction of standards or procedures.

PERFORMANCE

Performance is the organization's ability to attain its goals by using resources in an efficient and effective manner. Productivity, in addition to efficiency and effectiveness, directly affects performance. Performance indicators include scorecards (e.g., strategy, stakeholder, key performance indicator, functional, dashboard, and balanced) metrics, cycle times, and standards (e.g., national, regional, international, organizational, industry, and professional), which are part of an organization's value chain.

PRODUCTIVITY

Productivity is the organization's output of goods and services divided by its inputs. This means productivity can be improved by either increasing the amount of output using the same level of inputs, or reducing the number of inputs required to produce the output.

Two approaches for measuring productivity are total factor productivity and partial productivity. Total factor productivity is the ratio of total outputs to the inputs from labor, capital, materials, and energy. Partial productivity is the ratio of total outputs to a major category of inputs (e.g., labor, capital, or material). Productivity measurement is used to indicate whether there is a need for any improvement in the first place. It is often a part of the improvement process itself, and is used to gauge whether improvement efforts are making any progress. Measurement alone has a dramatic impact on productivity since the effects of feedback are so powerful. Measurement helps diagnose productivity needs, and can be used to focus improvement resources on the most needed operations. Monitoring of performance, feedback, and regular consideration of performance peaks and valleys as indicated by measurement data are powerful stimuli for change.

Total factor productivity is a measure of the productivity of a department, plant, strategic business unit, or firm that combines the individual productivities of all its resources including labor, energy, capital, material, and equipment. For example, if material accounts for 50% of the cost of sales, labor 15% of the cost of sales, equipment 20% of the cost of sales, capital 10% of the cost of sales, and energy 5% of the cost of sales, the total factor productivity is as follows:

Total factor productivity = 0.50(material productivity) + 0.15(labor productivity) + 0.20(equipment productivity) + 0.10(capital productivity) + 0.05(energy productivity)

COMPONENTS OF PRODUCTIVITY MEASUREMENT

- Inputs

- Processes

- Interim outputs

- Final outputs from which all measures of productivity are built

CRITERIA FOR PRODUCTIVITY IMPROVEMENT

In addition to accuracy, four other criteria must be considered as part of the continuous process of productivity improvement: (1) quality, (2) mission and goals, (3) rewards and incentives, and (4) employee involvement.

Guidelines for Productivity Measurement

Productivity measurement occurs within a dynamic and complex organization. This means that the organization's culture, the values and experience of employees, and the political context all will have a greater impact on the measurement process. The ideal organization is the one that institutionalizes a productivity measurement system as a "way of doing business."

The traditional performance and productivity measurements such as time schedules, on-time delivery, and cost savings continue to be valid. However, new concepts such as benchmarking, continuous process improvement, concurrent engineering, quality circles, self-managed teams, statistical process control, and total quality management should be practiced and complemented with the traditional measurements.

Improving Productivity

When an organization decides that improving productivity is important, there are three places to look: Technological productivity, worker productivity, and managerial productivity. Increased technological productivity refers to the use of more efficient machines, robots, computers, and other technologies to increase outputs. Increased worker productivity means having workers produce more outputs in the same time period. This includes employees working harder, improving work processes, acquiring more knowledge, more resources, improved task or workplace design, and motivating employees. Increased managerial productivity simply means that managers do a better job of running the business. Often, the real reason for productivity problems is poor management.

Effectiveness, Efficiency, and Economy

Effectiveness is the degree to which an organization achieves a stated goal or objective. Efficiency is the use of minimal resources—raw materials, money, and people—to provide a desired volume of output. Economy means whether an organization is acquiring the appropriate type, quality, and amount of resources at an appropriate cost.

Effectiveness and efficiency are related to productivity measurement. Effective production is the process that produces the desired results. Efficient production means achieving the desired results with a minimum of inputs. Efficiency and effectiveness must go hand-in-hand in productive organizations. Organizations can temporarily survive without perfect efficiency; they usually die if they are ineffective.

BALANCED SCORECARD SYSTEM

Most businesses have traditionally relied on organizational performance based almost solely on financial or accounting-based data (e.g., return on investment and earnings per share) and manufacturing data (e.g., factory productivity, direct labor efficiency, and machine utilization). Unfortunately, many of these indicators are inaccurate and stress quantity over quality. They reward the wrong behavior; lack predictive power; do not capture key business changes until it is too late; reflect functions, not cross-functional processes; and give inadequate consideration to difficult-to-quantify resources such as intellectual capital. Most measures are focused on cost, not so much on quality.

Kaplan and Norton (*The Strategy-Focused Organization*, Harvard Business School Press, 2001) of Harvard Business School coined the term "balanced scorecard" in response to the limitations of traditional financial and accounting measures. They recommend that key performance measures should be aligned with strategies and action plans of the organization. They suggest translating the strategy into measures that uniquely communicate the vision of the organization. Setting targets for each measure provides the basis for strategy deployment, feedback, and review.

The balanced scorecard system (BSS) is a comprehensive management control system that balances traditional financial measures with nonfinancial measures (e.g., customer service, internal business processes, organization's capacity for innovation and learning, and manufacturing). This system helps managers focus on key performance measures and communicate them clearly throughout the organization.

BSS Measures

Measures should include both financial and nonfinancial. Financial measures include return on investment, residual income, earnings per share, profit, cost, and sales. Nonfinancial measures include customer measures, internal business process measures, innovation and learning measures, and manufacturing measures. Customer measures include satisfaction, perception, and loyalty. Internal business process measures include efficiency, quality, and time. Innovation and learning measures include research and development investment, research and development pipeline, skills and training for employees, and time to market a product or service. Manufacturing measures include factory productivity, direct labor efficiency, and machine utilization.

BSS Indicators

A good balanced scorecard system contains both leading and lagging indicators, and both financial and nonfinancial measures. For example, customer survey (performance drivers) about recent transactions might be a leading indicator for customer retention (a lagging indicator); employee satisfaction might be a leading indicator for employee turnover (a lagging indicator), and so on. These measures and indicators should also establish cause-and-effect relationships across all perspectives. The cause-and-effect linkages describe the path by which improvements in the capabilities of intangible assets (people) get translated into tangible customer satisfaction and financial outcomes.

BSS Perspectives

- The financial perspective is looking back.
- The internal process perspective is looking from inside out.
- The customer perspective is looking from outside in.
- The innovation and learning perspective is looking ahead.

INVENTORY MANAGEMENT TECHNIQUES AND CONCEPTS

From inventory management viewpoint, demand is of two types: independent demand and dependent demand. Independent demand inventory systems are based on the premise that the demand or usage of a particular item is independent of the demand or usage of other items. Examples include finished goods; spare parts; material, repair, and operating (MRO) supplies; and resale inventories.

Independent Demand Inventory Systems

Independent demand inventory systems are "pull" systems in that materials are pulled from the previous operation as they are needed to replace materials that have been used. An example: Finished goods are replaced as they are sold. These types of inventory systems answer the question of when to place the replenishment order and how much to order at one time. Reorder point models and fixed/variable order quantity models (e.g., economic order quantity [EOQ]) are examples of independent demand inventory systems as they do review inventory either continuously or periodically.

Dependent Demand Inventory Systems

Dependent demand inventory systems are based on the premise that the demand or usage of a particular item is dependent on the demand or usage of other items. Examples include raw materials, work-in-process inventories, and component parts.

Inventory Levels and Profit Levels

A company manages its inventory by using various methods and approaches (e.g., EOQ). Inventory consists of raw materials, work in process, and finished goods. Efficient inventory management is needed to support sales, which is necessary for profits. Benefits such as high turnover rate, low write-offs, and low lost sales can be attributed to efficient inventory management. These benefits, in turn, contribute to a high profit margin, a higher total asset turnover, a higher rate of return on investment, and a strong stock price. Inventory management is a major concern for product-based organizations (e.g., manufacturing and retail), since 20–40% of their total assets is inventory and as such, poor inventory control will hurt the profitability of the organization.

Investment in Inventory

Investment in inventory depends on the actual level of inventory carried. The relevant question is how many units of each inventory item the firm should hold in its stock. Two types of stock concepts must be understood: (1) working stock, and (2) safety stock. The actual level of inventories carried will equal the sum of the working stocks and safety stocks.

A working stock is needed to meet normal, expected production and sales demand levels. Producing more goods than are currently needed increases the firm's carrying costs and exposes it to the risk of obsolescence if demand should fall. Remember that demand for sales is uncertain. Economic order quantity (EOQ) establishes the working stock amount.

A safety stock is needed to guard against changes in sales rates or delays in production and shipping activities. Safety stock is additional stock beyond the working stock and satisfies when demand is greater than expected. The additional costs of holding the safety stock must be balanced against the costs of sales lost due to inventory shortages. Safety stock will not affect the reorder quantities.

Investment in inventory is not complete without discussing the various costs associated with inventories due to their direct relationships. The cost structure affects the amount and type of investment needed. Three types of inventory-related costs are: (1) carrying or holding costs, (2) ordering costs, and (3) stock-out costs.

Carrying or Holding Costs

The costs associated with carrying inventories, including storage, capital, and depreciation costs are known as carrying costs. Carrying costs rise in direct proportion to the average amount of inventory carried which, in turn, depends on the frequency with which orders are placed. That is, an increase in the frequency of inventory ordering will reduce total carrying costs.

Annual total carrying costs = $(C)(P)(A)$

Where C = Percentage cost of carrying inventory, that is, capital cost + storage cost + insurance + depreciation and obsolescence cost + property taxes divided by average inventory value. P = Percentage price per unit. A = Average number of units, i.e., (annual sales\number of orders) divided by 2. (P). (A) = Average inventory value.

Ordering Costs

The cost of placing and receiving an order is known as the ordering costs, which is fixed regardless of the average size of inventories.

Total ordering costs = $(F)(N)$ = $(F)(S\Q)$

Where F = Fixed costs associated with ordering inventories, N = Number of orders per year, S = Sales in units, and Q = Quantity ordered in units.

Total inventory cost = Total carrying cost + Total ordering cost

Stock-Out Costs

Safety stock reduces stock-out costs. The safety stock is useful in protecting against delays in receiving orders. However, safety stock has a cost. The increase in average inventory resulting from the safety stock causes an increase in inventory carrying costs.

Carrying Costs versus Ordering Costs versus Stock-out Costs

- The components of carrying costs, which increase in proportion to the average amount of inventory held, include the costs of capital tied up in inventory, storage, and handling costs, insurance premiums, property taxes, depreciation, and obsolescence cost.

- The components of ordering costs, which are fixed regardless of the average size of inventories, include the cost of placing orders including production setup and shipping and handling costs.

- The components of stock-out costs, which are costs of running short, include the loss of sales, the loss of customer goodwill, and problems or delays in production schedules.

Optimal Order Quantity

How many units should be ordered or produced at a given time is a major question faced by the inventory manager. Either too much or too little inventory is not good. An optimum inventory level is designed and is found through the use of the EOQ model. EOQ provides the optimal, or least-cost, quantity of inventory that should be ordered.

If Q is the order quantity, then the how-much-to-order decision involves finding the value of Q that will minimize the sum of holding and ordering costs.

$$Q = EOQ = \sqrt{\frac{2DCo}{Ch}}$$

Where D is annual sales demand in units, Co is cost of placing one order, and Ch is cost of holding (or carrying) one unit in inventory for the year.

Note that the data needed to calculate EOQ includes: the volume of product sales, the purchase price of the products, the fixed cost of ordering products, and carrying costs. It does not include: the volume of products in inventory, inventory delivery times, delays in transportation, or quality of materials.

Due to the square root sign, a given increase in sales will result in a less than proportionate increase in inventories, and the inventory turnover ratio will thus increase as sales grow.

Inventory Reorder Point

Another major problem facing the inventory manager is at what point inventory should be ordered or produced. The point at which stock on hand must be replenished is called the "reorder point." It is also the inventory level at which an order should be placed. The formula is

Reorder point = Lead time × Usage Rate

Where lead time is the time lag required for production and shipping of inventory. Usage rate is the usage quantity per unit of time. Note: the time period should be the same in both lead time and usage rate (i.e., days, weeks, or months).

A complication in the calculation of the reorder point arises when we introduce a concept of "goods-in-transit." This situation occurs when a new order must be placed before the previous order is received. The formula for a reorder point when goods-in-transit is considered is

Reorder point = (Lead time × Usage rate) − (Goods-in-Transit)

Inventory Management Decisions

Inventory managers face two decision rules in the management of inventories: "how-much-to-order" and "when-to-order" that will result in the lowest possible total inventory cost. The how-much-to-order decision rule can be satisfied with the use of an EOQ. This decision rule involves selecting an order quantity that draws a compromise between (1) keeping smaller inventories and ordering frequently (results in high ordering costs), and (2) keeping large inventories and ordering infrequently (results in high holding costs). The when-to-order decision rule can be satisfied with the use of a reorder point.

Calculating How Much to Order Using EOQ

The focus of the EOQ method is on the quantity of goods to order that will minimize the total cost of ordering and holding (storing) goods. EOQ is a decision model that focuses on the tradeoff between carrying costs and ordering costs. It calculates the order quantity that minimizes total inventory costs. Calculus is used in determining the EOQ. EOQ is appropriate for managing the finished goods inventories, which have independent demands from customers or from forecasts. The holding cost, the ordering cost, and the demand information are the three data items that must be prepared prior to the use of the EOQ model. If Q is the order quantity, then the how-much-to-order decision involves finding the value of Q that will minimize the sum of holding and ordering costs.

$$Q = EOQ = \sqrt{\frac{2DC_o}{C_h}}$$

Calculating How Much to Order Using EOQ (continued)

Where D is annual sales demand in units, Co is cost of placing one order, Ch is cost of holding (or carrying) one unit in inventory for the year.

EOQ Assumptions

Two major assumptions of EOQ include: (1) The demand for an item is constant. Since the constant demand assumption is not realistic, managers would have to be satisfied with the near-minimum-cost order quantity instead of a minimum-total-cost order quantity. (2) The entire quantity ordered arrives at one point in time.

EOQ Cost Characteristics

- The point at which the total cost curve is minimized represents the EOQ, and this, in turn, determines the optimal average inventory level. Here, total cost is the sum of ordering and carrying costs.

- Some costs rise with larger inventories whereas other costs decline.

- The average investment in inventories depends on how frequently orders are placed.

- Ordering costs decline with larger orders and inventories due to reduced order frequency.

Sensitivity Analysis and EOQ

It is good to know how much the recommended order quantity would change if the estimated ordering and holding costs had been different. Depending on whether the total annual cost increased, decreased, or remains the same, we can tell whether the EOQ model is sensitive or insensitive to variations in the cost estimates.

Calculating When to Order

The when-to-order decision rule is expressed in terms of a reorder point as follows:

$$r = d \times m,$$

Where r is reorder point, d is demand per day, m is lead time for a new order in days.

The cycle time answers how frequently the order will be placed, and it can be calculated as follows: cycle time is the number of working days in a year divided by the number of orders that will be placed in a year.

Safety Stock versus Stock-outs

Safety stock is the amount of extra stock that is kept to protect against stock-outs. Running out of an inventory item is called a stock-out situation. Safety stock is the inventory level at the time of reordering minus the expected usage while the new goods are in transit.

ABC Inventory Control System

ABC is a method of classifying and grouping on-hand inventory based on usage and value. It applies the Pareto principle consisting of 20% critical few items and 80% trivial many items in inventory. Expensive, frequently used, high stock-out cost items with long lead times are most frequently reviewed in an ABC inventory control system. Inexpensive and infrequently used items are reviewed less frequently. Group C items are low-dollar-value items and receive little or no management's attention. Group A items are high-dollar value items and receive a great deal of management's attention. Group B items fall in between Group A and C in terms of dollar-value and management's attention. Group A items are approximately 20% of stock items and represent approximately 80% of the total dollar usage. Group B and C items together are approximately 80% of stock items and represent approximately 20% of the total dollar usage.

JIT Strategy

Just-in-time (JIT) is a production strategy to continuously improve productivity and quality. It is based on the belief that small could be better, not "more" is better. An effective JIT strategy encompasses the entire product life cycle from the acquisition of raw materials to delivery of the end product to the final customer.

JIT is based on management principles such as eliminate waste; produce to demand and one-at-a-time; think long-term; develop, motivate, trust, and respect people; and achieve continuous improvement. This is made possible when the focus is "quality at the source" and the tools used are statistical process control methods, fail-safe methods, and problem-solving methods. Quality at the source means producing perfect parts every time and all the time. The major benefits of JIT strategy are improved productivity, quality, service, and flexibility and reduced costs, inventory investment, lead times, lot sizes, and physical space.

The scope of JIT strategy includes topics such as production, purchasing, (procuring), production processing, inventory, transportation, partnerships, quality, scheduling, and layout.

JIT Production

JIT production strategy is to continuously improve productivity and quality. It is based on the belief that "small could be better," not "more is better."

JIT Production versus Traditional Production

- The pull systems are the prothesis of JIT production.

- The pull system is based on a variable-flow manufacturing principle.

- The JIT (pull) production system has "no contingencies" (i.e., no safety stock) mentality.

- The push systems are the antithesis of JIT production.

- The push system is based on a fixed-flow manufacturing principle.

- The traditional (push) production system has a "contingency" (i.e., safety stock) mentality.

JIT Purchasing

JIT purchasing requires a partnership between a supplier and a customer, which is a major departure from the traditional purchasing. JIT supplier relations call for long-term partnerships with single source suppliers who provide certified quality while continuously reducing costs. The JIT supplier's manufacturing processes must be under statistical process control and their capability should be certified by the customer. The statistical process control charts serve as the documentation to assure that the process stayed in control during the time the parts were made.

Traditional Purchasing versus JIT Purchasing

- Traditional purchasing practices call for infrequent, large-lot shipments.
- JIT purchasing practices call for frequent, small-lot shipments.
- Traditional purchasing practices call for inspection, since they focus on continuous checking by the customer. These practices are reactive due to their focus on "after the fact."
- JIT purchasing practices call for no inspection, since they focus on continuous improvement (Kaizen) by the supplier. These practices are proactive due to their focus on "before the fact."

JIT Production Processing

JIT production processing requires setup reduction, focused factory, group technology, uniform scheduling and mixed model scheduling, and the pull system. The objective here is to produce many varieties of products in small quantities on short notice. Manufacturing flexibility is the hallmark of the JIT production processing strategy.

JIT Inventory

A misconception about JIT is that it is just a program to reduce inventory. Fortunately, JIT does more than that. JIT purchasing is called "stockless inventory" since the customer has no inventory to stock as it is used up in the production right after it was received. The major goal is to reduce or eliminate work in process inventory so that all raw materials are consumed in the production process.

JIT Transportation

While JIT purchasing is the starting point of a JIT cycle, the JIT transportation is the execution part of the JIT cycle. JIT transportation is the physical linkage between the inside and the outside processes. It is a process that starts at a supplier location and ends at a customer location. It requires the analysis of all transport events and eliminating the non-value-added events. The basic value-added events include: Move load to dock at a supplier location, load carrier, move load to customer location, return empty trailer to terminal, unload by the customer, and move load to assigned customer location.

JIT Partnerships

JIT partnerships are needed between suppliers and purchasers of raw materials, parts, and components to remove waste and to drive down costs for mutual benefits. Long-term partnerships are better than short-term, so few suppliers can invest money to improve quality.

JIT Quality

JIT quality is realized as JIT forces down inventory levels, meaning fewer bad units are produced which, in turn, means fewer units must be reworked, thus improving quality. As JIT shrinks queues and lead times, it creates an early warning system for quality problems and production errors. As JIT quality is increased, less need for safety stock (inventory buffers) to protect against unreliable quality levels and unpredictable customer demand levels.

JIT Scheduling

JIT scheduling improves the ability to meet customer order due dates, reduces inventory with smaller lot sizes, and reduces work-in-process. Two techniques include level schedules and Kanban. A level schedule means each day's production quantity meets the demand for that day, using frequent small batches. A Kanban system moves parts through production via a "pull" from a signal. Kanban uses a card system giving authorization for the next container of material to be produced.

JIT Layout

An efficient JIT layout reduces waste in the form of minimizing the movement of materials on a factory floor or paper in an office because these movements do not add value. The benefits of JIT facility include distance reduction, increased operational flexibility, employees working closer to each other, and reduced space and inventory.

JIT and Lean Operations

Lean operations means identifying customer value by analyzing all the activities required to produce a product and then optimizing the entire process to increase value from the customers' perspective. The highlights of lean operations include understanding what the customer wants and ensuring that the customer input and feedback are obtained to increase value to that customer. Lean operations adopt a philosophy of minimizing waste by striving for perfection through continuous learning, creativity, and teamwork, which can be equally applied to manufacturing and service industries.

Both JIT and Toyota production system (TPS) have an internal focus on jobs, employees, work practices, materials, and training. Lean operations have an external focus on the customer. Lean operations need both JIT and TPS techniques and more.

Materials Requirements Planning

Materials requirements planning (MRP) is suitable for managing raw materials, components, and subassemblies, which have dependent demands that may be calculated from the forecasts and scheduled production of finished goods. In other words, the order for component inventory is placed based on the demand and production needs of other items that use these components.

Normal Inventory Deduction versus Backflush Inventory Deduction

- In a normal inventory deduction method, the amount of component parts used in an assembly operation is deducted from its inventory records based on planned or scheduled production count of end products. MRP system uses this method by exploding the bill of materials list for planning purposes.

- In a backflush inventory deduction method, the amount of component parts used in an assembly operation is deducted from its inventory records based on actual count of end assemblies produced. This method works backward from end products to raw materials or component parts; and uses the bill of materials list for explosion into individual items.

Kanban Production and Inventory Systems

Working under a "pull" system, production procedures and work instructions are communicated by a system of signals sent among workers through the use of a series of cards called Kanbans. The JIT production system and Kanban inventory system work together. In Kanban, the last workstation is informed of the day's production needs; all other workstations respond to the Kanban cards and containers, that is, all other workstations are pulled in.

After the Kanban system informs the final assembly production needs, each workstation then "orders" products or parts from the preceding workstation. This chain moves back to the point of purchasing raw materials. A condition is that a workstation cannot produce unless an order has been placed.

Two kinds of Kanban cards are used for posting and tracking inventory activity and to communicate among workers at the workstation: (1) move card and (2) production card.

The move card allows the worker to take one standard container of a specific part from one work center to another. The production card tells another production work center to produce the number of parts that will fit a standardized container. There is only one card with each container at any point in time. The following formulas can be used to calculate the number of Kanban containers:

Number of Kanban containers = (Demand during production lead time + Safety stock)/Container size

Where production lead time = wait time + material handling time + processing time and demand during production lead time = daily demand × the production lead time.

Kanban Production and Inventory Systems (continued)

MRP is a widely used computerized system that operates under the "push" principle, while Kanban represents the "pull" system. The newer version of MRP is MRP II, which takes the bill of materials for the products to be produced, calculates all subassembly and raw materials needed by time and quantity. Then the workstations are informed as to the number of units to be produced. This method is equated to the "push" system where the work is pushed through the plant.

Benefits of Kanban Inventory Systems

- Paperwork-free system
- Product is made to order
- Diminished need to take physical inventory for income determination purposes
- Lower finished goods inventory amounts
- Simple procedures for taking physical inventory, when needed
- Lower work in process inventory amounts
- Zero or fewer defective products

Kanban Production and Inventory Systems (continued)

Traditional Production Systems versus MRP versus JIT versus Kanban Systems

- Traditional manufacturing system practices a "push" production system.

- MRP systems operate under "push" production system.

- JIT manufacturing system practices a "pull" production system.

- Kanban manufacturing system practices a "pull" production system since it responds to the JIT production plan.

Quick Response Retail Systems

Quick response (QR) retail systems or efficient consumer response (ECR) systems collect customers' data at point-of-purchase terminals and then transmit this data back through the entire marketing channel to enable efficient production and distribution scheduling. These QR and ECR systems integrate data from sales, production, and logistics systems based on consumer/customer actions.

Distribution Systems

Inventory in a distribution system can be managed through the use of independent demand models such as continuous and periodic review models. The continuous review model can be a single order point system or double order point system.

Continuous Review: Single Order Point System

The single order point system basically ignores the fact that the order takes place in a chain and assumes that each element in the distribution system is independent of all other components. This independent behavior can cause large swings caused by a phenomenon called "lumpy demand" at the next level down in the distribution chain. The lumpy demand comes from the lack of communication and coordination between factories, warehouses, distributors, and retailers.

Continuous Review: Double Order Point System

The double order point system considers two levels down in the distribution system, hence the name "double." For example, if a distributor is quoted a lead time from the factory warehouse of two weeks and it takes the factory warehouse three weeks to have stock replenished, the reorder point is set based on the demand for a five-week period. It does not produce lumpy demand, as does the single order point system. An advantage is that it reduces the risk of stock-outs. Increasing the safety stock is its disadvantage.

Periodic Review System

In a periodic review system, orders are placed on a predetermined time schedule. The advantage is that the order times can be staggered throughout the chain to smooth the demand at each point in the distribution chain. This reduces peaks and valleys caused by several customers ordering at the same time.

Sales Replacement System

In the sales replacement system, the supplier ships only what the customer used or sold during the period. The objective is to maintain a stable inventory level in the system. This does require having enough inventory to cover the potential demand during the replenishment cycle. In essence, the sales replacement system is a periodic review model with variable order quantities.

Distribution Requirements Planning

Distribution requirements planning (DRP) is an application of the time-phasing logic of MRP applied to the distribution system. The purpose of DRP is to forecast the demand by distribution center to determine the master production scheduling needs. It uses forecasts and known order patterns from customers in the distribution chain to develop the demand on the master schedule.

Inventory Distribution Methods

The functions of warehouse distribution, production, and purchasing are closely interrelated and constantly interacting with each other in a manufacturing firm. The decision problems considered during inventory distribution strategy are when, what, and how much of it to ship to a warehouse; when, what, and how much of it to produce at the factory, with what size workforce; and when, what, and how much of it to purchase as inputs to the factory warehouse system.

Warehouse Inventory Control

Warehouses usually stand in a distribution system between a factory and final customers or other warehouses. Warehouse inventory controls include shipments and costs.

Warehouse Shipments

Warehouses usually stock a very large number of products—the larger the shipment size, the more products are involved, and the greater are the problems of controlling the inventories of different products jointly. These are some of the considerations involved in decisions to order shipment to warehouses. Two basic types of shipments can take place: (1) periodic shipments based on time intervals, and (2) trigger shipments based on action or event.

Costs of Alternative Shipping Carriers

In estimating the cost of alternative shipping carriers, the cost of having valuable inventory tied up while the vehicle is in transit should be considered. While this cost will usually not be large, taking it into account will systematically lower the costs of using faster rather than slower carriers. Another economy associated with fast shipments that may be overlooked is the fact that time in transit is one component of the lead-time. Shortening the lead-time allows a reduction in the inventory buffers, and hence a decrease in inventory holding costs.

Forward Logistics versus Reverse Logistics

In forward logistics, raw materials and finished products are moved from upstream suppliers to downstream customers. In reverse logistics, already sold finished products are moved from the downstream customers to upstream suppliers and eventually to manufacturers for returns and repairs.

ELECTRONIC DATA SYSTEMS

Electronic Commerce

E-Commerce Security Issues

Electronic commerce (e-commerce) is defined as a place where buyers and sellers are connected using computers and networks (the Internet) to buy and sell goods and services. The term electronic business (e-business) is much broader than e-commerce because the former includes distribution of information and customer support, which are lacking in the latter. In other words, e-commerce is a subset of e-business.

E-commerce can be grouped into three models: business to business (B2B), business to consumer (B2C), and government to citizen (G2C). On-line stores selling goods directly to consumers is an example of the B2C model. EDI is a critical component of the sales process for many online retailers. B2B e-commerce involves "Internet-enabling" of existing relationships between two companies in exchanging goods and services. EDI is the underlying technology enabling online catalogs and continuous stock replenishment programs. In the G2C model, the federal government is using the Internet to reach its citizens for a variety of information-dissemination purposes and transactions (e.g., Internal Revenue Service, U.S. Postal Service, and Social Security Administration). A value chain is created in e-commerce between demand planning, supply planning, and demand fulfillment. The demand planning consists of analyzing customer buying patterns and developing customer demand forecasts. The supply planning consists of supply allocation, inventory planning, distribution planning, procurement

E-Commerce Security Issues (continued)

planning, and transportation planning. The demand fulfillment consists of order capturing, customer verification, order promising, backlog management, and order fulfillment.

E-Mail Security Issues

The use of e-mail to carry business-critical communications is growing exponentially. While e-mail provides a low-cost means of communication with customers, suppliers, and partners, a number of security issues are related to the use of e-mail. The security issues include: Internet e-mail addresses are easily spoofed. It is nearly impossible to be certain who created and sent an e-mail message based on the address alone, E-mail messages can be easily modified. Standard SMTP mail provides no integrity checking, there are a number of points where the contents of an e-mail message can be read by unintended recipients, and there is usually no guarantee of delivery.

EDI Security Issues

Traditional electronic data interchange (EDI) systems allow pre-established trading partners to electronically exchange business data through VANs. The Internet can provide the connectivity needed to support EDI at a substantial cost savings over VAN. However, the Internet does not provide the security services (integrity, confidentiality, and nonrepudiation) required for business EDI. Similar to e-mail, EDI transactions are vulnerable to modification, disclosure, or interruption when sent over the Internet. The use of cryptography to provide the required security services has changed this; consequently many companies and government agencies are moving to Internet-based EDI.

Information Transactions Security Issues

Providing information (e.g., stock quotes and news) is a major and costly element of commerce. Using the Internet to provide these services is substantially less expensive than fax, telephone, or postal mail services. Integrity and availability of the information provided are key security concerns that require security controls and policy.

Financial Transactions Security Issues

Computer networks have been used to process financial transactions such as checks, debit cards, credit cards, and EFT. Similar to EDI over value-added networks (VANs), the connectivity options have been limited, and the leased lines are expensive. The Internet provides an opportunity for cost savings in electronic financial transactions. The use of the Internet to carry these types of transactions replaces the physical presentation or exchange of cash, checks, or debit/credit cards with the electronic equivalent. Each of these forms of transactions involves the use of cryptography to provide for integrity, confidentiality, authentication, and nonrepudiation. For example, a standard known as secure electronic transactions (SET) is used for processing credit card transactions over public networks. The use of SET involves three-way transactions between the buyer, the seller, and a financial institution (a bank).

E-Commerce Software

E-commerce software should support the following tasks: catalog management, product configuration, shopping cart facilities, e-commerce transaction processing, and Web traffic data analysis.

E-Commerce Infrastructure

Key technology infrastructure for e-commerce applications include Web server hardware, server operating system, server software, e-commerce software, virtual private network (VPN), VAN, and the Internet, intranet, or extranet. Strategies for successful e-commerce include: developing an effective Web site that creates an attractive presence and that meets the needs of its visitors (customers), contracting out with Web site hosting service providers or storefront brokers, building traffic into the Web site through meta tag, which is a special HTML tag that contains keywords about the Web site, and analyzing Web site traffic to identify which search engines are effective for your business.

Mobile Commerce

Scope of M-Commerce

M-commerce or mobile commerce is conducted using mobile devices such as smartphones, digital tablets, digital phones, personal digital assistants (PDAs), and mobile computers, requiring a connection to the Internet. Consumers use these devices from any location to research product information, compare prices, make purchases, and communicate with customer support. Retailers can use these devices for tasks such as price checks, inventory inquiries, and payment processing.

Cyber Threats to Mobile Devices Used in M-Commerce

A multitude of threats exist for mobile devices such as application of social engineering methods (i.e., using deceptive marketing practices on system users by creating illegal and unethical Web sites, emails, text messages, facsimiles, and voice mails); exploitation of social networking media due to blind sharing of information from unauthenticated users; use of mobile botnets controlling computers remotely; spreading of mobile malware such as viruses and worms; exploitation of mobile applications (e.g., creating fraudulent banking apps for checking balances, pay bills, transfer funds, or locate nearby ATMs and banking centers); and exploitation of day-to-day m-commerce work using illegal mobile devices and apps.

Risks to M-Commerce

Several risks exist in m-commerce, similar to e-commerce. For example, smartphones' credit card reader functionality has the potential risk to enable criminal activity such as skimming and carding. Skimming is the theft of credit card information using card readers, or skimmers, to record and store victim's data, which is accomplished with legitimate transactions. Carding is the process of testing the validity of stolen credit card numbers, which can be done on Web sites that support real-time transaction processing to determine if the credit card information can be successfully processed.

Electronic Data Interchange

Electronic data interchange (EDI) systems provide computer-to-computer communication. EDI systems are becoming a normal way of exchanging or transmitting documents, transactions, records, quantitative and financial information, and computer-related messages from one computer to another. Some examples of transactions and documents involved are as follows: purchase orders, invoices, shipping notices, receiving advice, acknowledgements, and payments. When payment is involved, the EDI system can be referred to as an electronic funds transfer (EFT) system.

Workings of an EDI System

- The buyer identifies the item to be purchased. Data are entered into the purchasing application system. Translation software creates an EDI purchase order, which is sent electronically to the supplier. The same order is sent to the buyer's accounts payable and goods receiving system.

- A functional acknowledgment, indicating receipt of the order, is automatically generated and electronically transmitted to the buyer.

- The supplier's computer sends the order information to his shipping and invoicing systems.

- Upon receipt by the buyer of the ship notice, the data are electronically entered into the receiving system file.

- The receipt notice is electronically transmitted to the accounts payable application system.

- The ship notice is electronically transmitted to the invoicing application system.

- An invoice is electronically generated and transmitted to the buyer. The same information is sent to the supplier's accounts receivable system.

- The invoice is received by the buyer's computer and is translated into the buyer's format. The invoice, receiving notice, and purchase order are electronically matched and reconciled.

- The buyer electronically transmits payment to the supplier's bank through their bank. An electronic remittance advice is transmitted to the supplier.

Workings of an EDI System (continued)

- Upon receipt of the remittance and notice of payment, the data are transmitted into accounts receivable system, and the buyer account is updated. The buyer is given credit for payment.

Components of an EDI System

The components of an EDI system include standards, software, and networks. The EDI standards consist of formatting standards and communication standards. Formatting standards deal with the type, sequence, and content of an electronic document. Communication standards cover baud rate, protocols, electronic envelopes, and message transmission times. Standards provide a set of common rules, in terms of syntax and formatting, for the development of electronic communications.

In terms of software, a translation program is needed to translate company-specific data to EDI standard format for transmission. A reverse translation is performed when data arrive at the organization from external sources.

In terms of networks, there are two approaches in common use. In a direct network the computers of the trading partners are linked directly, usually through dial-up modems. A direct network is effective for a limited number of trading partners. As the number of trading partners increases, it is difficult to maintain open lines for all trading partners. The second choice is to use a third-party network, also known as a value-added network (VAN) that acts as an intermediary between trading partners. A VAN maintains a mailbox for both the sender and the receiver.

Benefits of EDI

A major benefit of EDI is being able to load data, without rekeying, from various formats and placing it where it is needed in a different format for further processing. Besides savings due to reductions in document mailing and processing costs, decreases in data entry personnel costs, and reductions in inventory stock levels, organizations are realizing other significant benefits.

BUSINESS DEVELOPMENT LIFE CYCLES

The business development life cycle refers to the recurrent ups and downs in the level of economic activity that extends over time. Economists suggest four phases of the business cycle: peak, recession, trough, and recovery. The duration and strength of each phase is variable. Some economists prefer to talk of business fluctuations rather than cycles, because cycles imply regularity while fluctuations do not.

Causes Behind the Business Cycles and Business Activity

- Innovations (e.g., computers, drugs, synthetic fibers, and automobiles) have greater impact on investment and consumer spending, and therefore upon output, employment, and the price level. This innovation is not regular and continued.

- Political and random events such as war have a major impact on increasing employment and inflation followed by slump when peace returns.

- Monetary policy of the government has a major impact on business activity. When government creates too much money, inflation results. When government restricts money supply, it results in lower output and unemployment.

- The level of total expenditures has a major impact on the levels of output and employment.

- Many businesses such as retail, automobile, construction, and agriculture are subject to seasonal variations (e.g., pre-Christmas and pre-Easter).

- Business activity is also subject to a secular trend. The secular trend of an economy is its expansion or contraction over a long period of time (i.e., 25 or more years). Both seasonal variations and secular trends are due to noncyclical fluctuations.

Consumer Durable Goods

Those industries producing heavy capital goods and consumer durables (e.g., household appliances and auto-mobiles), called "hard goods" industries, are highly sensitive to the business cycle. Both production and employment will decline during recession and increase during recovery.

Consumer Nondurable Goods

Output and employment in nondurable consumer goods industries are less sensitive to the business cycle. This is because food and clothes, which are examples of the consumer nondurable industry, are simply neces-sities of life. These are called "soft good" industries. Because it is a highly competitive and low concentration industry, prices will be cut instead of production. Production and employment decline would be modest, even if it occurs.

Growth Concepts in Business Cycles

Four growth concepts in business cycles emerge: (1) supernormal growth, (2) normal growth, (3) zero growth, and (4) negative growth.

INTERNATIONAL ORGANIZATION FOR STANDARDIZATION FRAMEWORK

ISO Framework

The ISO 9000 standards consists of a series of generic standards with appropriate guidelines published by the International Organization for Standardization (called ISO) for vendor certification programs. The ISO 9000 addresses quality system processes, not product performance specifications. In other words, it covers how products are made, but not necessarily how they work. The ISO 9000 standards focus on processes, not on products or people. It is based on the concept that one will fix the product by fixing the process. The ISO 9000 is a standard to judge the quality of suppliers. It assumes that suppliers have a sound quality system in place and it is being followed. The ISO 9000 standards can be used as a baseline quality system to achieve total quality management (TQM) objectives.

ISO Certification Process

To earn ISO 9000 certification, a company must set up and document all procedures that relate to the process to be certified. These procedures can include everything from procuring and storing raw materials, to designing products, to issuing change orders on designs, to controlling inventory, to answering customer phone calls.

Benefits of ISO 9000 Standards

- Products from ISO 9000-certified suppliers are likely to be more reliable.

- When every step of a manufacturing process is documented, it is easier to spot problems and trace them back to an exact point in the manufacturing line. Problem tracking is facilitated.

- Its document-it-all approach makes it easier for users to evaluate products and services and to anticipate potential problems.

- Costs will be lower for both the manufacturer and the customer due to efficient operations. Lower design costs translate to lower product costs, which should mean lower prices for users.

- Buying products from ISO-certified suppliers can save customers the time and expense of conducting on-site visits of manufacturing facilities.

- It saves time and money by not having to test incoming parts from ISO-certified suppliers because its suppliers' procedures include testing.

ISO Standards in Quality Management

The ISO standard 8402 presents vocabulary for quality management and quality assurance.

The ISO standard 9000 presents quality management and quality assurance standards. It serves as an introduction to the other standards in the series.

The ISO standard 9001 addresses quality systems. It is the most comprehensive model for quality assurance in design, development, production, installation, and servicing.

The ISO standard 9002 addresses quality systems and it is a model for quality assurance in production, installation, and servicing.

The ISO standard 9003 addresses quality systems and it is a model for quality assurance in final test and inspection.

The ISO standard 9004 deals with quality management and quality system elements. It consists of four parts:

Part 1 provides general guidelines for most of the quality system elements contained in ISO 9001, 9002, and 9003 in greater detail.

Part 2 provides guidelines for services.

ISO Standards in Quality Management (continued)

Part 3 provides guidelines for processed materials.

Part 4 provides guidelines for quality improvement.

The ISO standard 10005 deals with quality management providing guidelines for quality plans.

The ISO standard 10012 deals with quality assurance requirements for measuring equipment. It assumes that quality depends upon accurate measurements.

The ISO standard 10013 deals with guidelines for developing quality manuals. It describes the development and control of quality manuals, tailored to the specific user needs.

The QS-9000 standard provides guidelines that make it easier for suppliers to do business with auto manufacturers and other original equipment manufacturers for quality management.

Other ISO Standards

The ISO standard 10007 provides guidelines for software configuration management.

The ISO standard 15026 addresses software assurance in terms of managing risks and assuring safety, security, and dependability within the context of system and software life cycles. This standard is applicable to systems and software and is intended for use by:

- Definers of integrity levels such as industry and professional organizations, standards organizations, and government agencies

- Users of integrity levels such as developers and maintainers, suppliers and acquirers, users, assessors of systems or software, and for the administrative and technical support of systems and/or software products

The ISO standard 17025 addresses independent testing of software using either white box testing method or black box testing method. This standard specifies the general requirements for the competence to carry out tests and/or calibrations, including sampling. It covers testing and calibration performed using standard methods, non-standard methods, and laboratory-developed methods.

The ISO standard 19011 provides guidelines for auditing quality systems. Part 1 deals with auditing and includes first-, second-, and third-party audits. Part 2 covers qualification criteria (education, training,

Other ISO Standards (continued)

and experience) for quality systems auditors. Part 3 addresses management of an audit from initial planning to the closing meeting.

The ISO standard 27003 deals with information technology security techniques regarding system implementation guidance in accordance with ISO 27001 standard.

The ISO standard 27004 deals with information technology security techniques regarding measurement of controls in accordance with ISO 27001 standard.

The ISO standard 27005 deals with information technology security techniques regarding risk management in accordance with ISO 27001 standard.

The ISO standard 27007 deals with information technology security techniques regarding systems auditing in accordance with ISO 19011 standard.

Other ISO Standards (continued)

The ISO standard 90003 deals with software engineering guidelines for the application of ISO 9001:2000 to computer software. This standard provides guidance for organizations in the application of ISO 9001:2000 to the acquisition, supply, development, operation, and maintenance of computer software and related support services. This standard does not add to otherwise change the requirements of ISO 9001:2000. These guidelines are not intended to be used as assessment criteria in quality management system's registration or certification. The application of ISO 90003 is appropriate to software that is:

- Pat of a commercial contract with another organization

- A product available for a specific market sector

- Used to support the processes of an organization

- Embedded in a hardware product

- Related to software services

Most Popular ISO Standards

- ISO 9000—Quality Management

- ISO 14000—Environmental Management

- ISO 17021—Conformity Assessment

- ISO 21500—Project Management

- ISO 22000—Food Safety Management

- ISO 22301—Business Continuity Management

- ISO 26000—Social Responsibility

- ISO 27001—Information Technology Security Techniques—Requirements of Information Security Management Systems

- ISO 27002—Information Technology Security Techniques—Code of Practice for Information Security Management

- ISO 28000—Security Management Systems for the Supply Chain

- ISO 31000—Risk Management

- ISO 50001—Energy Management

OUTSOURCING BUSINESS PROCESSES

Scope of Outsourcing

Outsourcing means an organization goes "outside" for the knowledge and experience required to do a specific job. In simpler terms, it means subcontracting or farming out for business functions, systems, and services. The scope of outsourcing includes human resources, tax, legal, help-desk services, technical support, telecommunications and network, facilities (computer center) management, disaster recovery services, education and training, ongoing hardware maintenance, data center design and construction, equipment relocation services, systems integration, application development and maintenance, and other services. The scope is broad and could include all or part of any function, service, process, or system operation.

Examples of IT operations frequently outsourced by financial organizations include: the origination, processing, and settlement of payments and financial transactions; information processing related to customer account creation and maintenance; as well as other information and transaction processing activities that support critical banking functions, such as loan processing, deposit processing, fiduciary and trading activities; security monitoring and testing; system development and maintenance; network operations; help desk operations; and call centers.

Examples of Sourcing

- Outsourcing is acquiring non-core products or services from external sources.
- Insourcing is keeping core products or services in-house.
- Cosourcing is having one or two suppliers for an item. Sometimes, one supplier works as a backup for the other.
- Multiple sourcing is more common in the supply-chain environment where there are several suppliers in the chain. However, too many suppliers are not good due to problems in communication and coordination, which is in conflict with the goal of reducing the supply base. Few strong and stable suppliers with long-term commitment are better than too many weak and unstable suppliers with short-term commitments.
- Offshoring is moving a business function or process to a foreign country but retaining control of it in the home country.
- Nearshoring is choosing an outsource provider located either in the home country or in a nearby foreign country.
- Backsourcing is the return of a business activity to the original firm in the home country.

Reasons for Outsourcing

- To gain operational or financial efficiencies
- To increase management focus on core business functions
- To refocus limited internal resources on core functions
- To obtain specialized expertise
- To increase availability of services
- To accelerate delivery of products or services through new delivery channels
- To increase ability to acquire and support current technology and avoid obsolescence
- To conserve capital to invest in other business ventures

Outsourcing of business or technology-related services may improve quality, reduce costs, strengthen controls, and achieve any of the objectives listed previously. Ultimately, the decision to outsource should fit into the organization's overall strategic plan and corporate objectives.

Before considering the outsourcing of significant functions, an organization's directors and senior management should ensure such actions are consistent with their strategic plans and should evaluate proposals against well-developed acceptance criteria. The degree of oversight and review of outsourced activities will depend on the criticality of the service, process, or system to the organization's operation as well as quality of service and quality of protection.

Risks in Outsourcing

Organizations should have a comprehensive outsourcing risk management process to govern their business or technology service provider relationships. The process should include risk assessment, selection of service providers, contract review, and monitoring of service providers. Outsourced relationships should be subject to the same risk management, security, privacy, and other policies that would be expected if the organization were conducting the activities in-house.

According to neoIT.com, IT offshore outsourcing comes with risk, including cultural compatibility, legal framework, technical infrastructure, geopolitical risks, and security and privacy risks. Security concerns over the IT outsourced vendor include:

- Business continuity and disaster recovery, which includes risk assessments, restoration process, testing of backup systems, audits, ongoing monitoring, managing the alternate site, key resources, and post disaster communication

- Information protection, which includes vulnerability assessment and penetration studies (technical and non-technical), data access, data audits, data security, data transmission, data storage, and virus management

- Data backup and recovery, which includes scheduled backups, data recovery, non-storage of production code and data in an offshore location, and disposal of sensitive data

Risks in Outsourcing (continued)

- Insurance coverage, which includes protection over buildings, equipment, personnel, and electronic information

- Intellectual property rights protection, which includes agreements, country laws, data security, physical security, legal obligations, compliance to international security and data privacy standards (e.g., European Union, OECD, ISO 27002, Safe Harbor, ITIL, and COBIT), logging and auditing, employee contract, and security management training

- Network security, which includes dedicated infrastructure, network security, and network device security

- Personnel security, which includes background checks, reference checks, integrity checks, non-disclosure and confidentiality agreements, Internet usage, suppliers' access to hardware, usage of mobile commuting, and housekeeping

- Physical security, which includes access control, limited access, camera surveillance, and fire safety

Benefits of Outsourcing

Organizations turn to outsourcing to improve performance (system and people) and to reduce operating costs. From a positive side, outsourcing offers solutions when there is a shortage of in-house skills, when a high-risk and high-overhead project needs to be managed, and when there is an unacceptable lead time to complete a project using company personnel.

The benefits from outsourcing usually focus on performance improvements and/or cost reduction. Another benefit is that it allows internal management's time and resources to be devoted more to the core business and the company's future. Outsourcing prevents hiring additional employees to meet temporary needs. However, outsourcing does not mean surrendering control and internal management responsibility of subcontracted functions and projects to outside vendors.

Some of the organization's IT employees could work for the outsourcing vendor. The key point here is to monitor the performance of the outsourced vendor during the contract period. Selection of an outsourcing vendor is no different from selecting other types of vendors. Selection factors such as proximity of the vendor, attitude of the vendor's personnel, vendor's reputation and knowledge, and the vendor's financial condition and management's integrity are important to consider.

The fixed-price service contract is best for the user organization because the amount is known in advance. However, the fixed-price contract may not be feasible in all situations especially when cost variables are uncertain and vendors may overbid because of perceived risk and because they have never done this kind of work before. An alternative is incentive contract where (1) attainable targets are communicated to the

Benefits of Outsourcing (continued)

contractor and (2) incentive arrangements are designed to motivate contractor efforts that might not otherwise be emphasized and discourage contractor inefficiency and waste. Another type of contract is share-in-savings arrangement which includes not only sharing in costs and savings but also providing training and education to the supplier.

The contract should spell out vendor performance-level guarantees, the remedies for nonperformance, and the right to audit clause. Contractual risks can be addressed or mitigated through terms and conditions, vendor certifications, evaluation factors for award, and risk mitigation requirements included in the statement of work.

From the economics point of view, the outsourcing approach provides an option to buy IT or business services from outsiders, rather than from the organization's IT or other departments. Users can perform "make-or-buy" analysis.

Outsourced Vendor Governance

Outsourcing vendor governance requires a vendor to establish written policies, procedures, standards, and guidelines regarding how to deal with its customers or clients in a professional and business-like manner. It also requires establishing an oversight mechanism and implementing best practices in the industry. Customer (user) organizations should consider the following criteria when selecting potential hardware, software, consulting, or contracting vendors.

- **Experience** in producing or delivering high quality security products and services on-time and all the time
- Track-record in responding to security flaws in vendor products, project management skills, and cost and budget controls
- Methods to handle software and hardware maintenance, end-user support, and maintenance agreements
- Vendor's long-term financial, operational, technical, and strategic viability
- Adherence to rules of engagement during contractual agreements, procurement processes, and product/ service testing

Service-Level Agreements for Outsourced Vendors

Contractual agreements in procurement processes for outsourced vendors should include a service-level agreement (SLA). For example, the SLA represents the understanding between the cloud subscriber and cloud provider about the expected level of service to be delivered and, in the event that the provider fails to deliver the service at the level specified, the compensation available to the cloud subscriber. The overall scope of service contract or service agreement includes the SLA, licensing of services, criteria for acceptable use, service suspension and termination, liabilities, guarantees, privacy policy, and modifications to the terms of service.

SLA is a better way for computer center management to improve the quality of computing services to system users. The computer center management must define a set of user service levels or service objectives that describe application systems, transaction volume, processing windows, online system response times, and batch job turnaround times. Without well-defined service levels to monitor against actual performance determined in the resource utilization function, a computer system's capacity limit is difficult to identify.

Without service levels, the computer center management will consider computer capacity at its limit when users begin to complain about computer performance. By monitoring performance against service levels, computer center management can identify approaching problems in meeting service objectives. In order to achieve these goals, computer center management needs to develop service level objectives for internal use.

COMMUNICATION SKILLS

One thing that is common to all four functions of management (i.e., planning, organizing, directing, and controlling) is communication. Surveys have shown that 80% of a manager's time is spent on communication and 20% on other activities. Communication involves two or more people. The effectiveness of organizational communication can be increased with clear verbal and written messages with little or no noise. Communication as a chain is made up of identifiable links—sender, encoding, medium, decoding, receiver, and feedback. The communication chain is only as strong as its weakest link. The following are the identifiable links in the communication chain:

- Sender conveys the message to a receiver.
- Encoding translates the message from sender.
- Medium is the vehicle to send or receive a message.
- Decoding translates the message from sender to receiver.
- Receiver gets the message.
- Feedback means the receiver acknowledges the message.

Sender

The sender is an individual or a group of people whose goal is to convey or transmit the message to a receiver in the best possible media and in the fastest way.

Encoding

The objective of encoding is to translate internal thought patterns into a language or code that the intended receiver of the message will be able to understand. Words (written or oral), numbers, gestures, or other symbols are used in encoding. The purpose of the message affects the medium of encoding. For example, if a manager were proposing a new employee benefit plan, which is a sensitive program, a meeting with emotional appeal and gestures would have a bigger impact than a normal written (cold) report. A meeting conveys personal interest and empathy, unlike the report.

Medium

Many types of media exist to send and receive a message, including, face-to-face communications, telephone calls, regular meetings and electronic meetings (video-conferencing), memos, letters, reports, facsimiles, bulletin boards, newsletters, and others. Each media type varies in richness from high rich to low rich. Media richness is described as the capacity of a given medium to convey information properly and promote learning. *The goal is to match media richness with the situation. Otherwise, mismatching occurs, which can lead to confusion and embarrassment.*

Examples of high-rich media include face-to-face conversation, telephone, or video-conferencing, since they provide multiple information cues (e.g., message content, tone of voice, and facial expressions), facilitate immediate feedback, and are personal in focus. High-rich media is good for discussing non-routine issues and problems. Examples of low-rich or lean media include bulletin boards, reports, memos, and letters. These media provide a single cue, do not facilitate immediate feedback, and are impersonal. Low-rich media is good for discussing routine problems.

Decoding

Decoding is the translation of the transmitted message from the sender's language and terminology to that of the receiver's. Effective decoding requires that these be the same between the sender and the receiver. The receiver's willingness to receive the message is a primary criterion for successful decoding.

Receiver

The receiver is an individual or a group of people whose goal is to acknowledge and receive the intended message sent by a sender. The receiver will take an action based on the message received.

Feedback

The communication process is not complete until the receiver acknowledges the message (via verbal or non-verbal feedback) to the sender. Without feedback, the sender is not sure whether the receiver has received his message. Feedback affects follow-up: If the receiver does not understand the message, follow-up meetings should be scheduled.

Factors in the Communication Process

- **Noise.** Noise is not part of the chainlike communication process. It is any interference with the normal flow of understanding of a message from one person to another. Examples of noise include misperception, illegible print, speech impairment, and garbled computer data transmission. Understanding has an inverse relationship with noise—the higher the noise, the less the understanding. We all need to identify the sources of noise and reduce it for effective communication to take place between and among people. Greater amounts of noise in communication not only waste resources (time and money) but also create frustration between the sender and the receiver.

- **Perception.** Perception is a process of giving meaning to one's environment, and is a vital link in the communication process. It consists of three subprocesses: (1) selectivity, (2) organization, and (3) interpretation. Selectivity is sensory screening and a sorting out process. Organization is mentally creating meaningful patterns from disorganized thoughts. Interpretation is how people understand a message, which is often different for different people.

- **The Grapevine.** A grapevine is the unofficial and informal communication system. It sometimes conflicts with the formal system and complements and reinforces it at other times. The grapevine will remain in organizations as long as people are working in a group environment. It has both positive and negative sides. From a positive side, the grapevine can help management learn how employees truly feel about policies, procedures, and programs—a type of feedback mechanism. However, a negative consequence to the grapevine is rumors.

Formal and Informal Communications

Formal communication channels are those that flow within the chain of command and outside the chain of command, and include downward, upward, horizontal communication, and diagonal communication.

- *Downward communication* refers to the messages and information sent from a higher-level to a lower-level in the management hierarchy (e.g., goals, strategies, mission, vision, directives, policies, procedures, and performance feedback).

- *Upward communication* refers to the messages and information transmitted from a lower-level to a higher-level in the management hierarchy (e.g., grievances and disputes, routine progress and performance reports, suggestions for improvement, and problems and exceptions).

- *Horizontal communication* refers to the lateral or diagonal exchange of messages and information among peers or coworkers, occurring within or across departments (e.g., intradepartmental problem solving requests, interdepartmental coordination on joint projects, and use of task forces and committees). Horizontal communication is important in learning organizations with teams solving problems.

- *Diagonal communication* refers to the exchange of messages and reports from a lower-level employee in one department to a higher-level employee in another department. This communication occurs only when the manager of the lower-level employee is fully informed and gives permission to initiate such communication. The diagonal communication occurs when the higher-level employee requests special studies and

Formal and Informal Communications (continued)

projects from the lower-level because the latter has the necessary skills and knowledge to conduct such special studies and projects. This diagonal communication can take place in both directions between lower-level employees and higher-level employees and vice versa.

Informal communication channels exist that do not consider the organization's formal hierarchy of authority and chain of command. Examples include management by wandering around and the grapevine. Management by wandering around means higher-level employees (e.g., executives and senior managers) talk directly with lower-level employees (e.g., hourly workers at factory, office, or warehouse) to learn about problems and issues confronting them, as well as to share their key ideas and values. These meetings are informal and unannounced.

Barriers to Communication

It is false to assume that if a person can talk, he can communicate. Talking is different from communicating. There are many barriers that exist between all people, making communication much more difficult than most people seem to realize. The auditor needs to know all the barriers that exist that can block effective communication. The negative effect of roadblocks to communication include diminishing of self-respect in others, triggering defensiveness, resistance, and resentment. They can also lead to dependency, withdrawal, and feelings of defeat or of inadequacy.

Organizational Dynamics in Communication

- **Individual dynamics**. Individual dynamics deal with how an individual's needs and wants are satisfied at the workplace. Managers should understand Maslow's hierarchy of needs, which help to explain the actions of employees at the workplace.

- **Group dynamics**. Group dynamics deal with how group members interact with each other at the workplace and how managers resolve group problems. Each member of the group plays an expected role, and the group has its own biases, values, and beliefs. Another dimension affecting group dynamics is conflicts among departments or functions within an organization.

- **Work-related environmental dynamics**. The environment—physical and social—is part of the situational context of human behavior. We are affected not only by our relationships with others, but by the places and spaces in which we interact. The science of transactions between human behavior and the environment is called environmental psychology.

STAKEHOLDER RELATIONSHIPS

Scope of Stakeholder Relationships

Stakeholder types include shareholders, investors, creditors, stock markets, investment analysts, employees, labor unions, regulators and government authorities (e.g., SEC, FTC, and IRS), supplier, vendors, contractors, customers, and the public community in general. Each of these stakeholder types requires a different way of handling due to their different objectives.

Initiatives of Shareholders and Corporations

Examples of shareholder initiatives include (1) Increase in filing of shareholder lawsuits against directors especially with respect to buyout offer price, (2) Increase in shareholder activist groups through organizing and exercising power over company management, and (3) Increase in filing of shareholder resolutions at annual meetings through booklets of shareholder questions.

Examples of corporation initiatives include (1) Increasing amounts of full disclosure of information to investors that affects their investment decisions, (2) showing full accountability and transparency to shareholders about business activities, financial condition, and tender offers made during mergers and acquisitions, (3) avoiding conflict of interest situations by board members and executives, (4) avoiding the use of insider information for personal gain by board members and executives, and (5) avoiding personal use of company assets and taking personal loans by directors and executives.

Shareholder Lawsuits

Shareholder activist groups are increasingly suing companies for several major or minor reasons, and most of them were settled out of court. Examples of major reasons include paying a high price for the acquisition of new assets and receiving a low price for the divestiture of existing assets. The U.S. Private Securities Litigation Reform Act of 1995 was issued to curb the filing of frequent and frivolous class-action lawsuits in federal courts. A loophole in the 1995 Act diverted the cases which increased the filings of such lawsuits in state courts and decreased the filings such cases in federal courts. Later, the U.S. Securities Litigation Uniform Standards Act of 1998 was issued to plug that loophole, which says that state court filings will be referred to the federal district courts for the district in which the action is pending. This means all lawsuits must be filed in federal courts, which will come under the provisions of the 1995 Act.

In addition, shareholders can file **derivative lawsuits** on behalf of a corporation against an offending party for damages caused to the corporation when the corporation fails to bring such a lawsuit against the offending party. Here, the shareholder's goal is to recover the damages due the corporation in which the recovered money is deposited into the company's treasury account.

Protecting Employees from Whistleblowing Actions

Handling employees is a sensitive matter because people are the most valuable asset of an organization. Management needs to be familiar with applicable laws and regulations in this matter. In a high-performing workplace, employees must be able to pursue the missions of their organizations free from discrimination and should not fear or experience retaliation or reprisal for reporting—blowing the whistle on—waste, fraud, and abuse. Laws should protect employees from discrimination based on their race, color, sex, religion, national origin, age, or disability, as well as retaliation for filing a complaint of discrimination. Employees break the code of silence rules when they report on whistleblower actions.

Whistleblower reprisal is generally defined as employers' taking or threatening to take personnel action against employees for reporting a violation of law, rule, or regulation; or gross mismanagement; gross waste of funds, abuse of authority, or a substantial and specific danger to public health or safety. Under the U.S. Whistle-blower Protection Act of 1994 and the Notification and Federal Employee Anti-discrimination and Retaliation Act of 2001 (No FEAR Act), federal agencies are responsible for the prevention of reprisal to their employees.

Private sector organizations, similar to public sector organizations, should develop policies and procedures to protect whistleblowing employees and to prevent the reprisal to their employees.

Possible management's negative actions if employees report misconduct:

- Deny expected cash award or bonus
- Deny expected promotion

Protecting Employees from Whistleblowing Actions (continued)

- Dismissal

- Duties or responsibilities reduced or lowered

- Harassment

- Lower next performance appraisal

- Reassignment of work location

- Social isolation by peers

- Reassignment of work schedule

Possible management's positive actions if employees report misconduct:

- Positive recognition by management

- Positive support by peers

- Promotion

- Employee self-satisfaction

Dealing with Purchasing Agents, Buyers, or Commodity/Service Experts

Corporate management can reduce unethical or illegal behavior of purchasing agents, buyers, or commodity/service experts, and salespeople with a policy and codes of conduct statement combined with appropriate punishment to those who conduct themselves improperly.

Purchasing managers, more than any other management group within an organization, face enormous pressure to act in unethical way. This occurs for several reasons. First, purchasing has direct control over large sums of money. A buyer responsible for a multi-million dollar contract may find sellers using any means available to secure a favorable position. The very nature of purchasing means that a buyer must come in contact with outside, and occasionally, unethical sellers. A second reason is due to the pressure placed on many salespeople. A seller who must meet aggressive sales goals might resort to questionable sales practices which, in turn, influences the buying practices.

Three rules must be understood as part of the purchasing buyer behavior. First, a buyer must commit his attention and energies for the organization's benefit rather than personal enrichment at the expense of the organization, Ethical buyers do not accept outside gifts or favors that violate their company's ethical policy. Ethical buyers are also not tempted or influenced by the unethical practices of salespeople and do not have personal financial arrangements with suppliers. Second, a buyer must act ethically toward suppliers or potential suppliers. This means treating each supplier professionally and with respect. Finally, a buyer must uphold the ethical standards set forth by his profession. A code of professional ethics usually formalizes the set of ethical standards.

Dealing with Purchasing Agents, Buyers, or Commodity/Service Experts (continued)

Organizations must do the following to enhance the ethical behavior of their purchasing personnel:

- Install buying teams to evaluate potential suppliers across different performance categories or selection criteria. Using a team approach to evaluate a supplier's capabilities limits the opportunity for unethical behavior.
- Develop a formal ethics policy defining the boundaries of ethical behavior, such as accepting gifts and receiving other favors.
- Communicate top management's message to buyers about whether or not unethical behavior is tolerated.
- Develop systems for internal reporting of unethical behavior such as a fraud hotline.
- Rotate buyers among different purchasing items or commodities to prevent a buyer from becoming too comfortable with any particular group of suppliers. This is to prevent collusion between buyers and vendors, suppliers, and contractors.
- Develop a policy to limit a buyer's authority for awarding purchase contracts, say, to amounts of $10,000 or less. Contracts greater than $10,000 requires a manager's signature, and the signature chain continues up the management hierarchy with the increased purchase contract amounts.
- Provide ethical training.

Dealing with Marketing and Salespeople

A policy should be established prohibiting marketing and salespeople to distribute gifts and favors in the process of acquiring new customers and retaining current customers. This policy should be consistent with the policy prohibiting purchasing personnel from accepting gifts and favors from new suppliers as well as current suppliers. Other illegal and unethical practices that should be prohibited include price discrimination, misleading advertising, defrauding customers with false claims, unfair credit practices, price collusion with competing firms, and sexual harassment. This policy should be referred and linked to the company's codes of conduct statement.

Handling Related Parties and Third Parties

It is important for the market to know whether the company is being run with due regard to the interests of all its investors. To this end, it is essential for the company to fully disclose material related party transactions to the market, either individually or in a grouped basis, including whether they have been executed at arms-length and on normal market terms. In a number of jurisdictions this is indeed already a legal requirement. Related parties can include entities that control or are under common control with the company, significant shareholders including members of their families and key management personnel.

Examples of Related-Party Transactions

- Misreported sales between affiliates
- Unspecified intercompany transactions
- Failure to disclose and account for a compensation arrangement with a former CEO
- Personal loans to current CEO or other executives

Transactions involving the major shareholders (e.g., close family and relations) either directly or indirectly, are potentially the most difficult type of transactions. In some jurisdictions, shareholders above a limit as low as five percent (5%) shareholdings are obliged to report transactions. Disclosure requirements include the nature of the relationship where control exists and the nature and amount of transactions with related parties, grouped as appropriate. Given the inherent opaqueness of many transactions, the obligation may need to be placed on the beneficiary to inform the board about the transaction, which in turn should make a disclosure to the market. This should not absolve the company from maintaining its own monitoring, which is an important task for the board members.

Handling Business Mergers, Acquisitions, and Divestitures

In some countries, companies employ anti-takeover devices or tactics during business mergers and acquisitions. However, both investors and stock exchanges have expressed concern over the possibility that widespread use of anti-takeover devices may be a serious impediment to the functioning of the market for corporate control. In some instances, takeover defenses can simply be devices to shield the management or the board from shareholder monitoring. In implementing any anti-takeover devices and in dealing with takeover proposals, the fiduciary duty of the board to shareholders and the company must remain paramount. Shareholder lawsuits are possible when a company is paying a high price for the acquisition of new assets and receiving a low price for the divestiture of existing assets when compared to what shareholders think the correct price should be.

STRATEGIC MANAGEMENT

Strategic Management Process

Strategic management is the set of decisions and actions used to formulate and implement strategies that will provide a competitively superior fit between the organization and its environment so as to achieve organizational goals. Managers ask questions such as, "What changes and trends are occurring in the competitive environment? Who are our customers? What products or services should we offer? How can we offer those products and services most efficiently?" Answers to these questions help managers make choices about how to position their organization in the environment with respect to rival companies. Superior organizational performance is not a matter of luck. It is determined by the choices that managers make. Top executives use strategic management to define an overall direction for the organization, which is the firm's grand strategy. The strategic management process is defined as a series of activities, such as grand strategy, strategy formulation, strategy implementation, and strategic control.

Grand Strategy

Grand strategy is the general plan of major action by which a firm intends to achieve its long-term goals. Grand strategies can be defined for four general categories: (1) growth, (2) stability, (3) retrenchment, and (4) global operations.

Strategy Formulation

The overall strategic management process begins when executives evaluate their current position with respect to mission, goals, and strategies. They then scan the organization's internal and external environments and identify strategic factors that might require change. Internal or external events might indicate a need to redefine the mission or goals or to formulate (plan) a new strategy at either the corporate, business, or functional level. The next stage is implementation of the new strategy. The final stage is strategic control to keep strategic plans on track.

Strategy formulation (planning) includes the planning and decision making that lead to the establishment of the firm's goals and the development of a specific strategic plan. Strategy formulation may include assessing the external environment and internal problems and integrating the results into goals and strategy. This is in contrast to strategy implementation, which is the use of managerial and organizational tools to direct resources toward accomplishing strategic results. Strategy implementation is the administration and execution of the strategic plan. Managers may use persuasion, new equipment, changes in organization structure, or a reward system to ensure that employees and resources are used to make formulated strategy a reality.

Strategy Implementation

Some people argue that strategy implementation—how strategy is put into action—is the most difficult and important part of strategic management. No matter how creative the formulated strategy, the organization will not benefit if it is incorrectly implemented. In today's competitive environment, there is an increasing recognition of the need for more dynamic approaches to formulating as well as implementing strategies. Strategy is not a static, analytical process; it requires vision, intuition, and employee participation. Many organizations are abandoning central planning departments, and strategy is becoming an everyday part of the job for workers at all levels. Strategy implementation involves using several tools—parts of the firm that can be adjusted to put strategy into action. Once a new strategy is selected, it is implemented through changes in leadership, structure, information and control systems, and human resources. For strategy to be implemented successfully, all aspects of the organization need to be in congruence with the strategy. Implementation involves regularly making difficult decisions about doing things in a way that supports rather than undermines the organization's chosen strategy.

Strategic Control

A formal control system can help keep strategic plans on track. A control system (e.g., reward systems, pay incentives, budgets, IT systems, rules, policies, and procedures) should be proactive instead of reactive. Control should not stifle creativity and innovation since there is no tradeoff between control and creativity. Feedback is part of control.

The goal of a control system is to detect and correct problems in order to keep plans on target. This means negative results should prompt corrective action both at the steps immediately before and after the problem identification. Some examples of corrective actions include updating assumptions, reformulating plans, rewriting policies and procedures, making personnel changes, modifying budget allocations, and improving IT systems.

STRATEGIC PLANNING PROCESS

Strategic planning process consists of defining organizational mission, objectives, strategies, and portfolio plan.

Organizational Mission

Every organization exists to accomplish something and the mission statement is a reflection of this. The mission statement of an organization should be a long-term vision of what the organization is trying to become, the unique aim that differentiates the organization from similar ones. It raises questions such as "What is our business?" and "What should it be?" In developing a statement of mission, management must take into account three key elements:

1. The organization's history
2. The organization's distinctive competencies
3. The organization's environment

Organizational Objectives

An organization's mission is converted into specific, measurable, and action-oriented commitments and objectives. These objectives, in turn, provide direction, establish priorities, and facilitate management control. When these objectives are accomplished the organization's mission is also accomplished. Peter Drucker advises at least eight areas for establishing objectives, including: (1) market standing, (2) innovations, (3) productivity, (4) physical and financial resources, (5) profitability, (6) manager performance and responsibility, (7) worker performance and attitude, and (8) social responsibility.

Organizational Strategies

Organizational strategy involves identifying the general approaches a business should take in order to achieve its objectives. It sets the major directions for the organization to follow. Specific steps include understanding and managing the current customer and current products and identifying new customers and new products. Mission and objectives lead an organization where it wants to go. Strategies help an organization to get there.

Organizational Portfolio Plan

An organization can be thought of as a portfolio of businesses (i.e., combination of product lines and divisions, and service lines and divisions). It is understandable that some product lines will be more profitable than others. Management must decide which product lines or divisions to build, maintain, add, or eliminate.

GLOBAL ANALYTICAL TECHNIQUES

Structural analysis of industries include threat of new entrants, rivalry among existing firms, pressure from substitute products or services, bargaining power of buyers, and bargaining power of suppliers.

Threat of New Entrants

New entrants to an industry bring new capacity, the desire to gain market share, and they often also bring substantial resources. As a result, prices can be low, cost can be high, and profits can be low. There is a relationship between threat of new entrants, barriers to entry, and reaction from existing competitors. For example,

- If barriers and reaction are high, then the threat of entry is low.

- If barriers are low and reaction is low, then the threat of entry is high.

There are seven major barriers to entry including: (1) economies of scale, (2) product differentiation, (3) capital requirements, (4) switching costs, (5) access to distribution channels, (6) cost disadvantages independent of scale, and (7) government policy.

Rivalry Among Existing Firms

Rivalry tactics include price competition, advertising battles, new product introduction, and increased customer service or product/service warranties. Competitors are mutually dependent in terms of action and reaction, moves and countermoves, or offensive and defensive tactics. Intense rivalry is the result of a number of interacting structural factors, such as numerous or equally balanced competitors, slow industry growth, high fixed costs or storage costs, lack of differentiation or switching costs, capacity increased in large increments, diverse competitors, high strategic stakes, and high exit barriers. Porter referred to the "advertising slugfest" when describing the scrambling and jockeying for position that often occurs among fierce rivals within an industry.

Pressure from Substitute Products or Services

In a broad sense, all firms in an industry are competitors with industries producing substitute products. Substitutes limit the potential returns of an industry by placing a ceiling on the prices firms can profitably charge. The more attractive the price-performance alternative offered by substitutes, the stronger or firmer the lid on industry profits. Substitute products that deserve the most attention are those that are subject to trends improving their price–performance tradeoff with the industry's product or produced by industries earning high profits.

Bargaining Power of Buyers

Buyers compete with the industry by forcing down prices, bargaining for higher quality or more services, and playing competitors against each other—all at the expense of industry profits. A buyer group is powerful if the following circumstances hold true: it is concentrated or purchases large volumes relative to seller sales, the products it purchases from the industry represent a significant fraction of the buyer's costs or purchases, the products it purchases from the industry are standard or undifferentiated, it faces few switching costs, it earns low profits, buyers pose a credible threat of backward integration, the industry's product is unimportant to the quality of the buyers' products or services, and the buyer has full information about demand, prices, and costs. Informed customers (buyers) become empowered customers.

Bargaining Power of Suppliers

Suppliers can exert bargaining power over participants in an industry by threatening to raise prices or reduce the quality of purchased goods or services. The conditions making suppliers powerful tend to mirror those making buyers powerful. A supplier group is powerful if the following apply: it is dominated by a few companies and is more concentrated than the industry it sells to, it is not obligated to contend with other substitute products for sale to the industry, the industry is not an important customer of the supplier group, the suppliers' product is an important input to the buyer's business, the supplier group's products are differentiated or it has built up switching costs, and the supplier group poses a threat of forward integration.

PORTER'S COMPETITIVE STRATEGIES

Michael E. Porter (*Competitive Strategy*, Free Press, 1980) introduced a framework describing three generic competitive strategies (i.e., differentiation, low-cost leadership, and focus) to outperforming other firms in an industry. The focus strategy, in which the organization concentrates on a specific market or buyer group, is further divided into focused low cost and focused differentiation. To use the Porter model, managers evaluate two factors: competitive advantage and competitive scope.

With respect to **competitive advantage**, managers determine whether to compete through lower cost or through the ability to offer unique or distinctive products and services that can command a premium price. Managers then determine whether the organization will compete on a broad **competitive scope** (competing in many customer segments) or a narrow scope (competing in a selected customer segment or group of segments). These choices determine the selection of strategies.

The **differentiation** strategy involves an attempt to distinguish the firm's products or services from others in the industry. An organization may use advertising, distinctive product features, exceptional service, or new technology to achieve a product that is perceived as unique. This strategy usually targets customers who are not particularly concerned with price; therefore it can be quite profitable. The differentiation strategy can be profitable because customers are loyal and will pay high prices for the product. Companies that pursue a differentiation strategy typically need strong marketing abilities, a creative flair, and a reputation for leadership.

A differentiation strategy can reduce rivalry with competitors and fight off the threat of substitute products because customers are loyal to the company's brand. However, companies must remember that successful

PORTER'S COMPETITIVE STRATEGIES (CONTINUED)

differentiation strategies require a number of costly activities such as product research and design and extensive advertising.

With a **low-cost leadership** strategy, the organization seeks efficient facilities, pursues cost reductions, and uses tight cost controls to produce products more efficiently than competitors. A low-cost position means that the company can undercut competitors' prices and still offer comparable quality and earn a reasonable profit.

Being a low-cost producer provides a successful strategy to defend against the five competitive forces mentioned earlier. The low price acts as a barrier against new entrants and substitute products.

The low-cost leadership strategy tries to increase market share by emphasizing low cost compared to competitors. This strategy is concerned primarily with stability rather than taking risks or seeking new opportunities for innovation and growth.

With Porter's third strategy, the **focus** strategy, the organization concentrates on a specific regional market or buyer group. The company will use either a differentiation or low-cost approach, but only for a narrow target market. Managers think carefully about which strategy will provide their company with its competitive advantage. Without a strategic advantage, businesses earned below-average profits compared with those that used differentiation, cost leadership, or focus strategies.

Competitive Analysis

The objective of a competitive or competitor analysis is to develop a profile of the nature and success of the likely strategy changes, each competitor's response to the strategic moves, and each competitor's probable reaction to the industry changes. A series of "what if" questions must be raised and answered here.

There are four diagnostic components to a competitor analysis: (1) future goals, (2) current strategy (either explicit or implicit), (3) assumptions, and (4) capabilities (strengths and weaknesses). Both future goals and assumptions jointly answer the question "what drives the competitor"? Both current strategy and capabilities jointly answer the question "what is the competitor doing and what can he do?"

Market Signals

A market signal is any action or indirect communication by a competitor that provides a direct or indirect indication of its intentions, motives, goals, or internal situation. The behavior of competitors provides several signals such as bluffs, warnings, and earnest commitments. Market signals, either conscious or unconscious, can aid in competitor analysis and strategy formulations, where they add greatly to the firm's base of knowledge about competitors.

Industry Evolution

Analyzing industry evolution can increase or decrease the basic attractiveness of an industry as an investment opportunity, and it often requires the firm to make strategic adjustments. Structural analysis of industries is the starting point for analyzing industry evolution. Most of all, industry evolution should not be viewed as a fait accompli to be reacted to, but as an opportunity to explore.

Some analytical techniques that will aid in anticipating the pattern of industry changes include product life cycle; initial structures (the entry barriers, buyer power, and supplier power); incentives or pressures for change; potential structures; long-run changes in industry growth; changes in buyer segments; buyers' knowledge about a product or service; high degree of experimentation due to reduction of uncertainty about market size, optimal product configuration, and nature of buyers; diffusion of proprietary technology (patents); accumulation of experience (learning curve); expansion or contraction in scale; changes in input costs such as wages, materials, cost of capital, media, and transportation; innovations in product, marketing, and process management; entry and exit barriers; structural changes in adjacent industries; and changes in government policy.

The industry evolution is similar to a product life cycle (the grandfather concept), where industry growth follows an S-shaped curve due to innovation. The industry evolution has four stages such as introduction, growth, maturity, and decline.

INDUSTRY ENVIRONMENTS

Competitive Strategies Related to Fragmented Industries

A fragmented industry is defined as an industry where there is no single firm with a significant market size, where there are large numbers of small and medium-sized firms, and where there are no market leaders with the power to shape the industry events. These industries range from high-tech to low-tech, providing differentiated to undifferentiated products.

Although there is no fundamental economic basis for fragmentation, the following are underlying economic causes for fragmentation: Low entry barriers, absence of economies of scale or experience curve, high transportation costs, high inventory costs, no significant bargaining power between buyers and suppliers, diverse market needs, economic and managerial exit barriers, new industry, local regulations, and government prohibition of concentration.

The strategic analyst should note the following red flags (traps) during the analysis of strategic alternatives: Seeking dominance, lack of strategic discipline, over-centralization, incorrect assumptions about competitors' overhead costs and objectives, and overreactions to new products that result in increasing overall costs and overhead costs.

Competitive Strategies Related to Emerging Industries

Emerging industries (e.g., video games, solar heating, and fiber optics) are defined as newly formed or reformed industries that have been created by technological innovations, shifts in cost structures, new consumer needs, and redefining the business due to growth in scale. There are no rules of the game to follow therefore they must be established. The absence of rules is both a risk and opportunity which must be managed and explored, respectively.

The emerging industries, though small in size and new to the industry, possess common structural characteristics, such as technological and strategic uncertainty, high initial costs with steep learning curve, first-time buyers with the possibility of inducing substitution, short-term horizon to develop products and customers, and subsidization to early entrants from government and nongovernment sources.

Emerging industries usually face problems in getting the industry off the ground. These problems include: inability to obtain raw materials and components; period of rapid escalation of raw materials' prices; absence of infrastructure such as distribution channels and service facilities; absence of product or technological standardization; perceived likelihood of obsolescence; customers' confusion; erratic product quality; image and credibility difficulties with the financial community; regulatory approval delays; high unit costs; and response of threatened entities such as labor unions or distribution channels.

Competitive Strategies Related to Declining Industries

Declining industries are defined as those industries experiencing an absolute decline in unit sales over a long period. The decline cannot be due to changes in business cycles or short-term problems such as strikes or material shortages. Declining industries are characterized by shrinking sales and profit margins, pruning product lines, falling research and development efforts, reduced advertising budgets, and diminishing number of competitors. The decline phase of an industry is different from and more complex than the decline phase of a product life cycle. Industries differ markedly in the way competition responds to decline; some industries age gracefully and some engage in bitter warfare, all leading to prolonged excess capacity and heavy operating losses. Mergers and acquisitions can reduce the excess capacity and wipe out the obsolete capacity. End-game strategies must be developed for declining industries. Four alternative strategies exist for declining industries: leadership, niche, harvest, and quick divestment.

When the industry structure is favorable for decline because of low uncertainty and low exit barriers for competitors, the firm should use (1) the leadership or niche strategies if it has strengths relative to its competitors or (2) the harvest or divest quickly strategies if it lacks strengths relative to its competitors.

When the industry structure is unfavorable for decline because of high uncertainty and high exit barriers for competitors, the firm should use (1) niche or harvest strategies if it has strengths relative to its competitors or (2) the divest quickly strategy if it lacks strengths relative to its competitors.

A firm should prepare for the decline phase by taking the following steps during the maturity phase: (1) minimize investments that raise exit barriers, (2) emphasize market segments that will be favorable under decline conditions, and (3) create high switching costs in these segments.

Sources and Impediments to Global Competition

Sources of global competitive advantage include comparative advantage; economies of scale in production, logistics, marketing, and purchasing areas; global experience; product differentiation; proprietary product technology; and mobility of production. Note that all the sources of advantage also create mobility barriers for global firms.

Impediments to achieving the global competitive advantage include economic impediments such as transportation and storage costs, differing product needs, sales force, distribution channels, local repair, sensitivity to lead times, complex price–performance tradeoffs among competing brands, and lack of worldwide demand. Global competitive advantage can also be affected by managerial impediments, such as differing marketing tasks; intensive local services; rapidly changing technology; government impediments (including tariffs, duties, quotas, and local content requirements) and policies related to tax, labor, and bribery; and resource impediments, such as building world-scale facilities or start-up investments.

EVOLUTION OF GLOBAL MARKETS

Many industries slowly evolve into global industries over time. To create a global industry, a firm needs more sources of global competitive advantage or fewer impediments to global competition.

Environmental triggers to globalization include increased economies scale economies, decreased transportation or storage costs, increased factor costs (e.g., labor, energy, and materials), and reduced government constraints (e.g., tariffs, quotas, duties, taxes, and local content requirements).

Strategic Alternatives to Compete Globally

A firm must make a choice about whether it must compete globally or compete in one or a few national markets. The alternatives include broad-line global competition with full product line, global focus (low cost or differentiation), national focus (low cost or differentiation), and protected niche such as requiring high local content in the product and high tariffs. A better approach is to form transnational coalitions or cooperative agreements between firms in the industry that are located in different home countries.

STRATEGIC DECISIONS

Analysis of Integration Strategies

Vertical integration is defined in terms of a firm exercising full control over the entire supply chain, that is, from purchasing of raw materials to production, distribution, and selling of goods or services. Vertical integration can occur in three ways: full integration (the entire supply chain done internally), partial (tapered) integration (part internally and part externally with independent contractors), and quasi integration (alliances or partnerships with other firms in the supply chain using debt or equity investment without full ownership). A firm can integrate either in forward or backward direction where the upstream firm is the selling firm and the downstream firm is the buying firm. It has been said that doing all of the vertical integration tasks internally is less costly, less risky, and easier to coordinate.

Capacity Expansion

Capacity for a manufacturing company is defined as the ability to produce quantity of goods as the market demands it. Increasing capacity requires large amounts of capital investment, involves longer lead times, and is a complex decision-making process. Often capacity decisions are irreversible and can be compared to an economic "oligopoly" situation where firms are mutually dependent. Usually, overbuilding (over-capacity) is a problem, not under-capacity. Prior to increasing capacity, a firm must have a clear expectation of future demand and competitors' behavior. However, the latter is difficult to predict.

Over-capacity means supply is more than demand, while under-capacity means demand is greater than supply. Thus, capacity expansion deals with the uncertainty about future demand, which requires a systematic process. When the future demand is fairly certain, the capacity expansion process becomes a game of preemption. The risk of overbuilding is most severe in commodity-type businesses due to cyclical demand and undifferentiated products. Mergers and acquisitions can reduce the excess capacity and wipe out the obsolete capacity.

Entry into New Businesses

Three strategies exist to enter a new business: (1) entry through internal development, (2) entry through acquisition, and (3) sequenced entry.

PORTFOLIO TECHNIQUES OF COMPETITIVE ANALYSIS

Portfolio strategy pertains to the mix of business units and product lines that fit together in a logical way to provide synergy and competitive advantage for the corporation. For example, an individual might wish to diversify in an investment portfolio with some high-risk stocks, some low-risk stocks, some growth stocks, and perhaps a few income bonds. In much the same way, corporations like to have a balanced mix of business divisions called **Strategic Business Units (SBUs)**. An SBU has a unique business mission, product line, competitors, and markets relative to other SBUs in the corporation. Executives in charge of the entire corporation generally define the grand strategy and then bring together a portfolio of strategic business units to carry it out.

BCG Matrix Model

The Boston Consulting Group (BCG) matrix model organizes businesses along two dimensions—business growth rate and market share. Business growth rate pertains to how rapidly the entire industry is increasing. Market share defines whether a business unit has a larger or smaller share than competitors. The combinations of high and low market share and high and low business growth provides four categories for a corporate portfolio.

The BCG matrix model utilizes a concept of experience curves, which are similar in concept to learning curves. The experience curve includes all costs associated with a product and implies that the per-unit cost of a product should fall, due to cumulative experience, as production volume increases. The manufacturer with the largest volume and market share should have the lowest marginal cost. The leader in market share should be able to underprice competitors and discourage entry into the market by potential competitors. As a result, the leader will achieve an acceptable return on investment.

GE Model

The General Electric (GE) model is an alternative to the BCG model and it incorporates more information about market opportunities (industry attractiveness) and competitive positions (company/business strength) to allocate resources. The GE model emphasizes all the potential sources of business strength and all the factors that influence the long-term attractiveness of a market. All SBUs are classified in terms of business strength (i.e., strong, average, or weak) and industry attractiveness (i.e., high, medium, or low).

FORECASTING

The simplest form of forecasting is the projection of past trends called extrapolation. Model-building activities are examples of analytical techniques. A model breaks down a major problem into parts or subproblems and solves it sequentially. Models require a set of predetermined procedures. If there are no well-ordered and fully-developed procedures, there is no need to model. That is, no procedure, no model.

A key concept in all forecasting models dealing with probabilities is the expected value. The expected value equals the sum of the products of the possible payoffs and their probabilities.

Time-Series Analysis

Time-series analysis is the process by which a set of data measured over time is analyzed. Decision makers need to understand how to analyze the past data if they expect to incorporate past information into future decisions. Although the factors that affect the future are uncertain, often the past offers a good indication of what the future will hold. The key is to know how to extract the meaningful information from all the available past data.

Regression Analysis

Regression analysis is a statistical technique used to measure the extent to which a change in the value of one variable, the independent variable, tends to be accompanied by a change in the value of another variable, the dependent variable.

Most measures of associations are non-directional, that is, when calculated, it is not necessary to indicate which variable is hypothesized to influence the other. Measures of association show to what degree, on a zero-to-one scale, two variables are linked.

Sensitivity Analysis

Sensitivity analysis is an evaluation of how certain changes in inputs results in what changes in outputs of a model or system.

Changes in inputs Lead to ⟶ Changes in outputs

The primary reason that sensitivity analysis is important to managers is that real-world problems exist in a dynamic environment. Change is inevitable. Prices of raw materials change as demand fluctuates, changes in the labor market cause changes in production costs. Sensitivity analysis provides the manager the information needed to respond to such changes without rebuilding the model. For example, bank management can use the sensitivity analysis technique to determine the effects of policy changes on the optimal mix for its portfolio of earning assets.

Simulation Models

The primary objective of simulation models is to describe the behavior of a real system. A model is designed and developed and a study is conducted to understand the behavior of the simulation model. The characteristics that are learned from the model are then used to make inferences about the real system. Later, the model is modified (asking "what if" questions) to improve the system's performance. The behavior of the model in response to the "what if" questions is studied to determine how well the real system will respond to the proposed modifications. Thus, the simulation model will help the decision maker by predicting what can be expected in practice. A key requisite is that the logic of the model should be as close to the actual operations as possible. In most cases, a computer is used for simulation models.

Computer simulation should not be viewed as an optimization technique, but as a way to improve the behavior or performance of the system. Model parameters are adjusted to improve the performance of the system. When good parameter settings have been found for the model, these settings can be used to improve the performance of the real system.

QUALITY MANAGEMENT

Total Quality Management (TQM) is a strategic, integrated management system for achieving customer satisfaction. It involves all managers and employees and uses quantitative methods to continuously improve an organization's processes. It is not an efficiency (cost-cutting) program, a morale-boosting scheme, or a project that can be delegated to operational managers or staff specialists.

Elements of TQM

Three essential requirements or principles of TQM are: (1) the pursuit of complete customer satisfaction by (2) continuously improving products and services, through (3) the full and active involvement of the entire workforce.

What Is Different about TQM?

- Process management

- Quality teams

- Quality councils

- Ongoing training

Areas of Agreement on Quality

- Producing a quality product costs less because there is less waste.

- Preventing quality problems is better than detecting and correcting them.

- Statistical data should be used to measure quality.

- Managers need to take a leadership role in improving quality.

- Managers and employees need training in quality improvement.

- Companies need to develop a quality management system.

Areas Needing Improvement in Quality

- Many managers encourage employee involvement and empowerment, but few organizations adopt the specific practices that bring them about, such as reliance on teams of employees to identify and resolve specific operating problems. Where teams are used, few have been delegated sufficient authority to make changes or have been trained to use the full array of TQM tools.

- Although many organizations recognize the importance of measurement and analysis to decision-making, many measure the wrong things. Also, few organizations focus on internal processes across functions in order to assure that quality is built into the production and service system on a continuing basis.

- Many organizations have in place a system they call "Quality Assurance," but these systems are often designed to check for adherence to quality standards at the end of the production process. TQM creates procedures for assuring quality throughout the production and service process.

- Many organizations claim to serve the customer first, but few systematically and rigorously identify the needs of customers, both internal and external, and monitor the extent to which those needs are being met.

Definitions and Criteria of Quality

Judgment-based criteria is synonymous with superiority or excellence, which is abstract and subjective, and difficult to quantify.

Product-based criteria assume that higher levels or amounts of product characteristics are equivalent to higher quality and that quality has a direct relationship with the price.

User-based criteria define that quality is fitness for intended use or how well a product performs its intended function. It is basically dictated by user wants and needs.

Value-based criteria focus on the relationship of usefulness or satisfaction of a product or service to price. This means a customer can purchase a generic product at a lower price if it performs the same way as the brand-name product.

Manufacturing-based criteria mean conformance to specifications (e.g., engineering or manufacturing) that are important to customers. Taguchi opposes the manufacturing-based definition of quality due to built-in defects to be produced at a higher cost.

Customer-driven quality is meeting or exceeding customer expectations. This definition is simple and powerful; and hence most companies use it.

What Is the Difference between Big Q and Little q in Quality?

- **Big Q** and **little q** are two contrasting terms in quality.
- **Big Q** focuses on all business products and processes in the entire company.
- **Little q** focuses on all or parts of products and processes in one factory or plant.

Examples of Quality Drivers

Drivers of quality include customers; suppliers/vendors; employees; products; services; organizational culture; organizational policies, procedures, and standards; total organizational focus; and management commitment.

Quality Assurance, Quality Control, Quality Audit, Quality Circles, and Quality Councils

- **Quality assurance** focuses on the front end of processes, beginning with inputs, rather than the traditional controlling mode of inspecting and checking products at the end of operations, after errors are made.

- **Quality control** is an evaluation to indicate needed corrective action, the act of guiding, or the state of a process in which the variability is attributable to a constant system of chance causes. Quality control includes the operational techniques and activities used to fulfill requirements for quality. Often, quality assurance and quality control are used interchangeably, referring to the actions performed to ensure the quality of a product, service, or process.

- **Quality audit** is a systematic, independent examination and review to determine whether quality activities and related results comply with planned arrangements, and whether these arrangements are implemented effectively and are suitable to achieve the objectives.

- **Quality circles** refer to teams of employees (6 to 12) voluntarily getting together periodically to discuss quality-related problems and issues and to devise strategies and plans to take corrective actions.

- Establishment of a **quality council** is a prerequisite of implementing a TQM program in the organization. The quality council is similar to an executive steering committee.

Concurrent Engineering

- Improved quality of design, leading to a reduction in change orders
- Reduction in product cycle time as a result of using concurrent design, rather than sequential design
- Reduction in manufacturing costs as a result of using multifunction teams to integrate product and process
- Reduction in scrap and rework as a result of product and process design optimization
- Concurrent engineering is an improvement over sequential engineering

Cost of Quality

The Cost of Quality (COQ) measurement identifies areas for process improvement. The focus of this measurement is to express quality in terms of quantitative and financial language, that is, costs, return on investment, cost of poor quality, cost of rework, and so on.

The COQ definition includes the following three items:

1. COQ is the cost of making a product conform to quality standards (i.e., quality goods).

2. COQ is the cost of not conforming to quality standards (i.e., waste, loss).

3. COQ is a combination of item 1 and 2.

   COQ = The cost of conformance (A) + The cost of nonconformance (B)

   Where (A) includes cost to prevent and detect a failure and (B) includes cost to correct a failure.

Prevention Costs

These costs are associated with all the activities that focus on preventing defects. It is the cost of conformance to quality standards.

Appraisal Costs

These costs are associated with measuring, evaluating, or auditing products to assure conformance with quality standards and performance requirements.

Failure Costs

These costs are associated with either correcting or replacing defective products, components, or materials that do not meet quality standards. Failure costs can be either internal failure costs that occur prior to the completion or shipment of a product or the rendering of a service, or external failure costs that occur after a product is shipped or a service is rendered.

Quality Metrics

Quality metrics can be developed for the cost of quality measurement to help managers monitor quality.

- The total cost of quality as percentage of revenue by year
- The cost of conformance as percentage of total cost of quality
- The cost of nonconformance as percentage of total cost of quality

Quality Tools

Either an auditor or auditee can use quality tools. The seven old and new quality tools can be used to analyze processes, prioritize problems, report the results, and to evaluate the results of a corrective action plan.

Old seven quality control tools are traditional:

1. **Check sheets** are used for collecting data in a logical and systematic manner.

2. A **histogram** is a frequency distribution diagram in which the frequencies of occurrences of the different variables being plotted are represented by bars.

3. A **scatter diagram** is a plot of the values of one variable against those of another variable to determine the relationship between them. These diagrams are used during analysis to understand the cause and effect relationship between two variables. Scatter diagrams are also called correlation diagrams.

4. A **Pareto diagram** is a special use of the bar graph in which the bars are arranged in descending order of magnitude. The purpose of Pareto analysis, using Pareto diagrams, is to identify the major problems in a product or process, or more generally, to identify the most significant causes for a given effect. This allows a developer to prioritize problems and decide which problem area to work on first.

5. A **flowcharting** tool can be used to document every phase of a company's operation, for example, from order taking to shipping in a manufacturing company. It will become an effective way to break down a

Quality Tools (continued)

process or pinpoint a problem. Flowcharting can be done at both the summary level and the detailed level serving different user needs.

6. One form of a **cause-and-effect (C&E) diagram** is used for process analysis when a series of events or steps in a process creates a problem and it is not clear which event or step is the major cause of the problem. Each process or subprocess is examined for possible causes; after the causes from each step in the process are discovered, significant root causes of the problem are selected, verified, and corrected.

7. A **control chart** assesses a process variation. The control chart displays sequential process measurements relative to the overall process average and control limits. The upper and lower control limits establish the boundaries of normal variation for the process being measured.

New seven quality management tools are modern:

1. An **affinity diagram** is a data reduction tool in that it organizes a large number of qualitative inputs into a smaller number of major categories. These diagrams are useful in analyzing defect data and other quality problems, and used in conjunction with cause-and-effect diagrams or interrelationship digraphs.

2. A **tree diagram** can be used to show the relationships of a production process by breaking it down from few larger steps into many smaller steps. The greater the detail of steps, the better simplified they are. Quality improvement actions can start from the right—most of the tree to the left-most.

Quality Tools (continued)

3. A **process decision program chart** is a preventive control tool in that it prevents problems from occurring in the first place and mitigates the impact of the problems if they do occur. From this aspect, it is a contingency planning tool. The objective of the tool is to determine the impact of the "failures" or problems on project schedule.

4. A **matrix diagram** is developed to analyze the correlations between two groups of ideas with the use of a decision table. This diagram allows one to systematically analyze correlations. Quality function deployment (QFD) is an extension of the matrix diagram.

5. An **interrelationship digraph** is used to organize disparate ideas. Arrows are drawn between related ideas. An idea that has arrows leaving it but none entering is a "root idea." More attention is then given to the root ideas for system improvement. The digraph is often used in conjunction with affinity diagrams.

6. **Prioritization matrices** are used to help decision-makers determine the order of importance of the activities being considered in a decision. Key issues and choices are identified for further improvement. These matrices combine the use of a tree diagram and a matrix diagram.

7. **Activity network diagrams** are project management tools to determine which activities must be performed, when they must be performed, and in what sequence. These diagrams are similar to PERT and CPM, the popular tools in project management. Unlike PERT and CPM, activity network diagrams are simple to construct and require less training to use.

Plan-Do-Check-Act Cycle

Deming's plan-do-check-act (PDCA) cycle, which consists of four phases, is a core management tool for problem solving and quality improvement. It can be used for planning and implementing quality programs. The "plan" phase calls for developing an implementation plan for initial effort followed by organization-wide effort. The "do" phase carries out the plan on a small-scale using a pilot organization, and later on a large-scale. The "check" phase evaluates lessons learned by pilot organization. The "act" phase uses the lessons learned to improve the implementation.

Quality Models and Awards

A system should be put in place to allow the organization to determine systematically the degree to which product and services please customers, and focus on internal process improvement. Data should be collected on features of customer satisfaction such as responsiveness, reliability, accuracy, and ease of access. The measurement systems should also focus on internal processes, especially on processes that generate variation in quality and cycle time.

Deming Quality Model

According to Deming, good quality does not necessarily mean high quality. It is, rather, a predictable degree of uniformity and dependability, at low cost, and suited to the market.

Juran Quality Model

According to Jospeh M. Juran, there are two kinds of quality: fitness for use and conformance to specifications. To illustrate the difference, he says a dangerous product could meet all specifications, but not be fit for use. He pointed out that the technical aspects of quality control had been well covered, but that firms did not know how to manage for quality. He identified some of the problems in quality as organizational, communication, and coordination of functions—in other words, the human element. He coined the term "quality trilogy" consisting of quality planning (developing the products and processes required to meet customer needs), quality control (meeting product and process goals), and quality improvement (achieving unprecedented levels of performance). The trilogy is a three-pronged approach to managing for quality.

Crosby Quality Model

According to Philip B. Crosby's definition, quality is conformance to requirements, and it can only be measured by the cost of nonconformance. "Don't talk about poor quality or high quality. Talk about conformance and non-conformance," he says. This approach means that the only standard of performance is zero defects. Crosby encourages prevention (perfection) as opposed to inspection, testing, and checking.

U.S. Malcolm Baldrige National Quality Award

The Malcolm Baldrige National Quality Award is an annual award to recognize U.S. companies that excel in quality management and quality achievement. The award promotes:

- Awareness of quality as an increasingly important element of competitiveness
- Understanding of the requirements for quality excellence
- Sharing of information on successful quality strategies and the benefits derived from implementation of these strategies

European Quality Award

The European Quality Management Association has set up a European equivalent to the U.S. Baldrige program, the European Quality Award (EQA). Quality measures for EQA include: leadership, information and analysis, strategic quality planning, human resource development and management, management of process quality, quality and operational results, customer focus and satisfaction, financial results, and environmental concerns.

Six Sigma Quality Program

Six Sigma is an approach to measuring and improving product and service quality. In Six Sigma terminology, a defect (nonconformance) is any mistake or error that is passed on to the customer. It redefines quality performance as defects per million opportunities (dpmo), as follows:

dpmo = (Defects per unit) $\times$ 1,000,000/opportunities for error where defects per unit
     = Number of defects discovered/Number of units produced

Six Sigma represents a quality level of at most 3.4 defects per million opportunities. Its goal is to find and eliminate causes of errors or defects in processes by focusing on characteristics that are critical to customers.

Six Sigma Tools

Six Sigma tools can be categorized into eight general groups, which will integrate the tools and the methodology into management systems across the organization.

1. Elementary statistical tools include basic statistics, statistical thinking, hypothesis testing, correlation, and simple regression.

2. Advanced statistical tools include design of experiments, analysis of variance, and multiple regression.

3. Product design and reliability tools include quality function deployment (QFD) and failure mode and effects analysis (FMEA).

4. Measurement tools include process capability and measurement systems analysis.

5. Process improvement tools include process improvement planning, process mapping, and mistake-proofing (Poka-Yoke).

6. Implementation tools focus on organizational effectiveness and facilitation of meetings and communication.

7. Teamwork tools focus on team development and team assessment.

8. Process control tools include quality control plans and statistical process control (SPC).

Six Sigma Players

Several Six Sigma players exist in the planning and implementation of Six Sigma programs in an organization, including white belts (at the bottom), green belts, black belts, master black belts, project champions, and senior champions (at the top) in the Six Sigma hierarchy. All these players assume defined roles and responsibilities and need specific training with varying lengths to make the Six Sigma program a success.

White belts are hourly employees needing basic training in Six Sigma goals, tools, and techniques to help green belts and black belts on their projects.

green belts are salaried employees who have a dual responsibility in implementing Six Sigma in their function and carrying out their regular duties in that function. They gather and analyze data in support of a black belt project, and receive a simplified version of black belt training. Yellow belts are seasoned salaried employees who are familiar with quality improvement processes.

Black belts are salaried employees who have a full-time responsibility in implementing Six Sigma projects. They require hard-skills and receive extensive training in statistics and problem-solving and decision-making tools and techniques, as they train green belts. Black belts are very important to Six Sigma's success.

Master black belts are salaried employees who have a full-time responsibility in implementing Six Sigma projects. They require soft skills, need some knowledge in statistics, and need more knowledge in problem-solving and decision-making tools and techniques, as they train black belts and green belts.

Senior champions are sponsors and executives in a specific business function and manage several project champions at the business unit level who, in turn, manage specific projects. Senior champions develop plans, set

Six Sigma Players (continued)

priorities, allocate resources, and organize projects. Project champions deploy plans, manage projects that cut across the business functions, and provide managerial and technical guidance to master black belts and black belts. All champions require soft skills.

Which Six Sigma Player Does What?

- White belts help green belts and black belts.
- Green belts help black belts.
- Black belts help master black belts.
- Master black belts help project champions.
- Project champions help senior champions.
- Senior champions decide "what gets done" while project champions, master black belts, and black belts decide "how to get it done."

DECISION ANALYSIS

Problem Solving

A problem exists when there is a gap between "what is" and "what should be." Individuals recognize a problem when they feel frustrated, frightened, angry, or anxious about a situation. Organizations recognize problems when outputs and productivity are low; when quality of products and services is poor; when revenues are decreasing and expenses are increasing; when market share is decreasing; when stock price is decreasing; when most employees have several motivational issues; when most employees are not cooperating, sharing information, or communicating; or when there is a dysfunctional degree of conflict among employees in various departments.

Problem-Solving Process

Problem-solving is a systematic process of bringing the actual situation or condition closer to the desired condition. There are many ways to handle problems. The correct sequence of problem-solving steps is:

Step 1: Identifying the problem (what is)

Step 2: Generating alternative solutions

Step 3: Selecting a solution

Step 4: Implementing and evaluating the solution (what should be)

Impediments to Problem Solving

Business problems are solved either by individuals or by groups. The most neglected area of problem solving is human resources, the people who participate in the problem-solving group. The group leader can encourage new ideas and creativity in group members by following these guidelines.

- Practice effective listening because people think much more rapidly than they speak. Effective listening is the best way to gather information. Try not to be distracted.

- Practice "stroking," a concept borrowed from transactional analysis. A stroke is a unit of recognition. Provide recognition to people and ideas. Positive stroking makes people more important and secure and invites more ideas and creativity.

- Discourage "discounting" (i.e., not paying attention), another concept borrowed from transactional analysis. When discounting is high, group members will feel reluctant to respond to questions and will be constantly ready to attack or retreat. This is not a healthy climate for successful problem solving, and it encourages dysfunctional behavior and uncooperative attitudes among the members of the group.

- Keep the group members informed about progress and what is expected of them.

Problem Solving and Creativity

The reorganization of experience into new configurations is called "creativity." The best argument in favor of creativity is that environmental changes make creativity essential for long-term survival. Stagnation can lead to organizational failure or demise. Creativity is not easy to get or to manage, as it requires hiring intelligent people and motivating them to deliver to the fullest extent of their skills.

Reasons Why Individuals Solve Problems Differently

Problem-solving skills are different with different people. Five factors have a major play in a person's problem-solving capabilities: (1) Value system, (2) Information filtration, (3) Interpretation, (4) Internal representation, and (5) External representation.

Prospective and Retrospective Methods in Problem Solving

Often management asks auditors to deal with forward-looking, future-oriented problems or questions. Collectively they are referred to as prospective methods to distinguish them from approaches designed to answer questions about what is happening now or what has happened in the past—that is, retrospective methods. An auditor's problem-solving skill set should address both of these methods. Conducting a repeat audit of accounts payable is an example of a retrospective method. Performing a due diligence review is an example of a prospective method of problem solving.

Tools and Techniques for Problem Solving

Many tools and techniques are available for the problem solver to handle problems. They include brainstorming, synectics, nominal group technique, force-field approach, systems analysis, and others. Differences exist among the problem-solving methods, and all of them do not work equally well in different situations. In any given situation, one or two methods might have a greater probability of leading to the desired outcomes. Specific tools and techniques for problem solving include:

○ **Imagineering**. Imagineering involves the visualization of a complex process, procedure, or operation with all waste eliminated. The imagineer assumes the role of dreamer, realist, and critic. The steps in imagineering consist of taking an action, comparing the results with the person's imagined perfect situation, and making mental correction for the next time. This approach will eventually improve the situation and bring it to the desired level. Imagineering is similar to value-analysis.

○ **Value analysis**. Value analysis is a systematic study of a business process or product with a view to improving the process or product and reducing cost. Creative skills are required while doing value analysis. Its goal is to ensure that the right activities are performed in the right way the first time. Industrial engineering techniques, such as work measurement and simplification methods, can be used to achieve the goals.

○ **Leapfrogging**. Leapfrogging is taking a big step forward in thinking up idealistic solutions to a problem. For example, leapfrogging can be applied to value-analyzing comparable products to identify their best features and design. These ideas are then combined into a hybrid product that, in turn, can bring new superior products to enter a new market.

Tools and Techniques for Problem Solving (continued)

○ **Blasting, creating, and refining.** Blasting, creating, and refining are used when a completely new way of thinking or speculation is required or when answering a question such as "What else will do the job?" Blasting is good when the group members are free to speculate and come up with totally new ideas that were never heard of or thought about before. Creativity comes into full play.

○ **Attribute listing.** Attribute listing emphasizes the detailed observation of each particular characteristic or quality of an item or situation. Attempts are then made to profitably change the characteristic or to relate it to a different item.

○ **Edisonian.** Edisonian, named after Thomas Edison, involves trial-and-error experimentation. This method requires a tedious and persistent search for the solution.

○ **Investigative questions.** The scope includes asking six investigative (journalism) questions: who, what, when, where, why, and how—to understand the root causes of issues and problems better.

○ **Cause and effect diagrams.** Cause and effect (C&E) diagrams (also called Ishikawa or fishbone diagrams) can be used to identify possible causes for a problem. The problem solver looks for the root causes by asking the "why" five or six times to move from broad (possible) causes to specific (root) causes. The idea is that by repeating the same question "why," the true source of a problem is discovered. This process will help identify the real problem. Then the problem solver chooses the most likely cause for further review. Brainstorming can be used in developing the C&E diagrams.

○ **Pareto charts.** Pareto charts can be drawn to separate the vital few from the trivial many. They are based on the 80/20 rule, that is, 20% of items contribute to 80% of problems.

Tools and Techniques for Problem Solving (continued)

○ **Psychodramatic approaches**. These approaches involve role-playing and role-reversal behavior. In psychodrama, the attempt is made to bring into focus all elements of an individual's problem; in sociodrama, the emphasis is on shared problems of group members.

○ **Checklists**. Checklists focus one's attention on a logical list of diverse categories to which the problem could conceivably relate.

○ **General semantics**. These include approaches that help the individual to discover multiple meanings or relationships in words and expressions.

○ **Morphological analysis**. This is a system involving the methodical interrelating of all elements of a problem in order to discover new approaches to a solution.

○ **Panel consensus technique**. This technique is a way to process a large number of ideas, circumventing organizational restraints to idea creation, using extensive participation and emphasizing methods for selecting good ideas.

○ **Delphi technique**. This technique is a method used to avoid groupthink. Group members do not meet face-to-face to make decisions. Rather, each group member independently and anonymously writes down suggestions and submits comments, which are then centrally compiled. The compiled results are then distributed to the group members who, independently and anonymously, write additional comments. These comments are again centrally compiled and the process repeated until consensus is obtained. The Delphi technique is a group decision-making method.

○ **Work measurement**. This industrial engineering program applies some of the general principles of creative problem solving to the simplification of operations or procedures.

Tools and Techniques for Problem Solving (continued)

○ **Storyboards.** Storyboarding is a group problem-solving technique to create a picture of relevant information. A storyboard can be created for each group that is making decisions. A positive outcome of storyboarding is that it takes less time than interviewing, and many employees can get involved in problem solving, not just the managers.

○ **Humor.** In addition to being a powerful tool to relieve tension and hostility, humor is a problem-solving tool. When correctly executed, it opens the mind to seeking creative solutions to the problem. Humor can be in the form of detached jokes, quips, games, puns, and anecdotes. Humor gives perspective and solves problems. Stepping back and viewing a problem with a certain level of detachment restores perspective. A sense of humor sends messages of self-confidence, security, and control of the situation. However, humor should not be sarcastic or scornful.

○ **Operations research.** Operations research is a management science discipline attempting to find optimal solutions to business problems using mathematical techniques, such as simulation, linear programming, statistics, and computers.

○ **Intuitive approach.** The intuitive approach is based on hunches (gut feelings). It does not use a scientific approach and uses subjective estimates or probabilities, which are difficult to replicate.

○ **T-Analysis.** T-analysis is a tabular presentation of strengths on one side and weaknesses on the other side of the letter "T." The goal is to address the weaknesses (problems).

○ **Closure.** Closure is a perceptual process that allows a person to solve a complex problem with incomplete information. It is the last step in problem solving.

Tools and Techniques for Problem Solving (continued)

○ **TRIZ**. TRIZ (a Russian acronym) is a theory of solving inventive problems. It supports the idea that unsolved problems are the result of contradicting goals (constraints) and nonproductive thinking. It suggests to break out of nonproductive thinking mold by reframing the contradicting and competing goals in such a way that the contradictions disappear.

○ **Stratification**. Stratification is a procedure used to describe the systematic subdivision of population or process data to obtain a detailed understanding of the structure of the population or process. It is not to be confused with a stratified sampling method. Stratification can be used to break down a problem to discover its root causes and can establish appropriate corrective actions, called counter-measures. Failure to perform meaningful stratification can result in the establishment of inappropriate countermeasures, which can then result in process or product deterioration in quality.

Considerations of Problem Solving: Traits and Behaviors

All auditors should be familiar with certain traits and behaviors during problem solving. While certain problem-solving behaviors, such as conjecturing, predicting, and drawing conclusions, can be learned and taught, the other behaviors and problem-solving traits, such as self-reliance, risk taking, creative thinking, and interacting, are examples of affective-related behaviors that are fostered through individual encouragement.

DECISION MAKING

Decision making is a process of choosing among alternative courses of action. The correct sequence of decision-making steps is:

Step 1. Identifying the right information.

Step 2. Identifying an acceptable level of risk.

Step 3. Identifying alternative courses of actions.

Step 4. Making a timely decision.

Note the difference between problem-solving and decision-making steps. Identifying an acceptable level of risk (Step 2) does not enter into the problem-solving process. Risk is unique to decision making and is an integral part of it. Decision making reduces or increases the risk depending on the quality of the decision making and the level of uncertainty.

The process of management is fundamentally a process of decision making. The functions of management (i.e., planning, organizing, directing, and controlling) all involve the process of initiating, selecting, and evaluating courses of action. Therefore, decision making at the center of the functions comprises the management process.

DECISION MAKING (CONTINUED)

The manager makes decisions in establishing objectives; he makes planning decisions, organizing decisions, motivating decisions, and control decisions.

Professor Igor Ansoff (*Corporate Strategy*, McGraw-Hill, 1965) classifies the organizational decisions into three categories: (1) strategic decisions, (2) administrative decisions, and (3) operating decisions.

Many Facets of Decision Making

Managers and leaders make decisions. The type of decision made depends on the level of that manager in the organization hierarchy. Facets of decision making include sequential versus non-sequential, static versus dynamic, structured versus unstructured, programmed versus non-programmed, and routine versus non-routine.

Senior-level managers make non-programmed (non-routine) decisions for strategic management purposes. Programmed (routine) decisions address lower-level and highly repetitive tasks, as they are fully programmed. Clerks and computers are involved in routine, programmed decisions such as production scheduling and machine loading. Programmed decisions serve the needs of operating management. However, there is an overlap with semi-programmed decisions in the sense that such decisions are made by both higher-level managers as well as middle-level managers.

Routine decisions involve structured and programmed tasks. Non-routine decisions involve unstructured and non-programmed tasks. Higher levels of management deal with non-routine decision making while lower-level management handles routine decisions.

Decision-Making Models

Models are predetermined procedures that specify the step-by-step actions to be taken in a particular situation. Two types of decision models exist: normative and empirical models. Normative models prescribe the decision-making process—what should be. These models do not describe actual management practice in decision making. Instead, they describe how a decision procedure should be followed.

Empirical decision models do not describe how a decision maker should go about making a decision. Instead, they describe the actual decision processes followed by a decision maker—what is. A decision process is any interrelated set of activities leading to a "decision"—a commitment of resources. Reconciliation is needed between the normative and empirical results in order to develop theories and hypotheses about how managers make use of information. When there is no set of procedures for a decision process, then by definition there is no "model" for it. (e.g., crisis handling and leadership situations)

Normative models are programmed decisions. They help lower-level operating management to implement programs such as production scheduling or inventory control. Empirical models are non-programmed decisions. They help middle to senior management in making strategic decisions such as pricing and new product introduction.

Types of Data Used in Decision Making

Decision making is a process that incorporates the estimating and predicting of the outcome of future events. When specific events are known with certainty, the decision maker does not use probabilities in the evaluation of alternatives. When specific events are uncertain, the decision maker uses probabilities in the evaluation of alternatives. The decision maker often uses the most likely outcome stated in deterministic format rather than incorporating all outcomes in a probabilistic (stochastic) format.

A decision maker uses two types of data: **deterministic data** and **probabilistic data**. Deterministic data are known and not subject to any error or distribution of error. They are based on historical data; their environment is stable and predictable. Decision results will be certain with a single unique payoff. There is only a single outcome for each possible action. Probabilistic data is used to evaluate decisions under situations of risk and uncertainty. The environment is characterized as unstable and unpredictable since each event is assigned a probability of occurrence. Probabilistic data allow for better risk evaluation since sensitivity analysis can be performed on each action to measure the material impact of the various events. An estimated payoff table or decision tree can be developed for analysis. A drawback of using the probabilistic data is the availability and integrity of data to determine multiple courses of action.

Types of Decisions

Decision making is a frequent and important human activity and is especially a managerial activity. Decisions are not all of one kind. The procedure for making one decision, such as buying a home, is entirely different from making another decision, such as taking a CIA examination.

Decision making is related to risk levels. With respect to risk, individuals act differently, and can be grouped into three categories: risk takers, risk neutral, and risk averters. When contrasted with a risk-taking entrepreneur, a professional manager (or an auditor) is likely to be more cautious than a risk taker (i.e., either risk neutral or risk averter). Another factor is that risks are related to returns. The higher the risk, the greater the return, and vice versa. Also, controls are related to risks. The higher the risk, the greater the need for controls, and vice versa. Controls reduce or eliminate risks and exposures.

Four general types of decisions exist that require different decision procedures: (1) decisions under certainty, (2) decisions under risk, (3) decisions under uncertainty, and (4) decisions under conflict or competition.

Pure Strategy and Mixed Strategy in Decision Making

A pure strategy exists if there is one strategy for player X and one strategy for player Y that will be played each time. The payoff, which is obtained when each player pays the pure strategy, is called a **saddle point**. The saddle point represents an equilibrium condition that is optimum for both competitors.

The **Wald criterion**, which is a variant of decision making under uncertainty, is a useful technique to determine if a pure strategy exists. A saddle point can be recognized because it is both the smallest numerical value in its row and largest numerical value in its column. Not all two-person zero-sum games have a saddle point. When a saddle point is present, complex calculations to determine optimum strategies and game values are unnecessary.

When a pure strategy does not exist, a fundamental theorem of game theory states that the optimum can be found by using a mixed strategy. In a mixed strategy, each competitor randomly selects the strategy to employ according to a previously determined probability of usage for each strategy. Using a mixed strategy involves making a selection each time period by tossing a coin, selecting a number from a table of random numbers, or by using some probabilistic process.

Tools and Techniques for Decision Making

- **Differential analysis**. Differential analysis is a technique to compare differences in revenues or costs of two or more alternatives.

- **Decision table**. A decision table is a tool that documents rules used to select one or more actions based on one or more conditions. These conditions and their corresponding actions can be presented either in a matrix or tabular form.

- **Flowcharts**. Flowcharts help a decision maker in analyzing a large, complex problem. Flowcharts and decision trees both show flow or sequencing. Unlike the flowchart, a decision tree shows outcome probabilities.

- **Discriminant analysis**. Discriminant analysis is a qualitative, subjective tool to differentiate between effective and ineffective procedures or actions.

- **Management science**. Operations research or management science provides management an approach that focuses on decision making and reliance on formal mathematical models.

- **Decision trees**. A decision tree is a graphical representation of possible decisions, events, or states of nature resulting from each decision with its associated probabilities, and the outcomes of the events or states of nature. The decision problem displays the sequential nature of the decision making situation.

Tools and Techniques for Decision Making (continued)

The decision tree has nodes, branches, and circles to represent junction boxes, connectors between the nodes, and states-of-nature nodes, respectively.

- **Payoff table.** A payoff table is a tabular representation of the payoffs for a decision problem. It shows losses and gains for each outcome of the decision alternatives.

- **Cost-benefit analysis.** Cost-benefit analysis is a decision procedure in which we compare the expected costs and benefits of alternative actions. We choose the action for which the expected value of the benefits minus the expected value of the costs is greatest. The expected value is the desirability of alternative multiplied by the probability of success. The likelihood of an occurrence that is derived mathematically from reliable historical data is called objective probabilities. However, subjective probabilities do not have mathematical reliability since they are derived from intuition and "gut feel" of the decision maker.

- **Success-failure analysis.** Success-failure analysis is a qualitative approach to brainstorm conditions for both success and failure. A T-column can be used with headings "What will guarantee success" and "What will guarantee failure."

- **Devil's advocate technique.** In the devil's advocate technique, the decision maker is focusing on failures and identifies ways an action or an alternative can be less than successful.

Tools and Techniques for Decision Making (continued)

- **Reality check**. The reality check decision is tested in the pseudo–real-world conditions. A T-column is used with headings "Our expectations" and "Our concerns" to facilitate the analysis.

- **Risk analysis**. Risk analysis is the analysis of possible risks to be encountered and the means to handle them that can be performed. A T-column can be used with headings "Anticipated risks" and "Actions to overcome risks."

- **Activity analysis**. All current activities can be labeled as either value-added or nonvalue-added using a T-account diagram. The goal is to eliminate or reduce nonvalue-added activities since they are adding little or no value to the process at hand. Decisions affecting costs incurred for nonvalue-added activities can then be challenged or revisited by performing a detailed analysis of all tasks and activities with the purpose of eliminating or reducing them. A T-column can be used with headings "Value-added activities" and "Nonvalue-added activities" to facilitate the activity analysis.

Decision Making versus Problem Solving

Decision-making and problem solving are not the same—they have two different time dimensions. The basic difference is that decision making is future-oriented and problem solving is past-oriented. Decision making deals with risk, while problem solving does not.

Decision-making is the probability of success. Examples of decision-making situations include investing in a new product line, buying new equipment, and selecting an employee for a key position. Examples of problem-solving situations include handling a tardy employee, correcting a poor-quality production, and working with a slow-paying customer.

ORGANIZATIONAL BEHAVIOR

Organizational Theory

Basically two organizational theories exist: the traditional view and the modern view. The traditional view has closed-system thinking, while the modern view incorporates open-system thinking.

The **traditional view** assumes that the surrounding environment is fairly predictable and that uncertainty within the organization can be eliminated through proper planning and strict control. The primary goal is economic efficiency. All goal-directed variables are known and controllable.

The **modern view** assumes that both the organization and its surrounding environments are filled with variables that are difficult to predict or control. The organization interacts continuously with an uncertain environment. The primary goal is survival in an environment of uncertainty and surprise. The modern view deals with more variables that cannot be controlled or predicted.

Motivation Defined

The term motivation refers to the psychological process that gives a purpose and direction to human behavior. Motivation theories are generalizations about the "why" and "how" of purposeful behavior. The goal is to move individual employees toward achieving organizational objectives, including job performance.

Motivation Theories: Maslow's Needs Hierarchy Theory

Maslow's theory focuses on five needs structured as a hierarchy, from bottom to top, and includes physi- ological, safety, love, esteem, and self-actualization needs. Individuals proceed up the hierarchy of needs, one level at a time. Higher needs emerge as lower needs are met. A fulfilled need does not motivate an individual. Needs are related to motivation in that unsatisfied needs motivate behavior. Maslow's esteem needs are most closely associated with Herzberg's concept of job enrichment.

Motivation Theories: Herzberg's Two-Factor Theory

Herzberg's theory was based on employee satisfaction in that a satisfied worker is motivated from within to work harder and that a dissatisfied employee is not self-motivated. Herzberg's two factors are satisfiers and dissatisfiers. Dissatisfaction is associated with complaints about the job context or factors in the immediate work environment.

Motivation Theories: Expectancy Theory

Individual perception, though secondary in the Maslow and Herzberg models, is central to expectancy theory. The expectancy theory is based on the assumption that motivational strength is determined by perceived probabilities of success. The term "expectancy" refers to the subjective probability (or expectation) that one thing will lead to another. The focus of this model is as follows: One's motivational strength increases as one's perceived effort–performance and performance–reward probabilities increase. This theory has received empirical support from researchers, and is based on common sense since Effort ⟶ Performance ⟶ Reward. Employees tend to work harder when they believe they have a good chance of getting personally meaningful rewards. The relationship is:

Effort ⟶ Performance ⟶ Reward

Motivation Theories: Goal-Setting Theory

Goal setting is the process of improving individual or group job performance with clear objectives and high standards. Management by objectives (MBO) is an example of goal-setting theory.

Using MBO, organizational goals can be better achieved if the goals of superiors and subordinates are integrated with organizational goals. All levels of management should be involved in setting the objectives of the organization in working toward the common goals.

Motivation Strategies: Motivation through Job Design

○ Motivation through job design deals with two specific strategies: (1) fitting people to jobs and (2) fitting jobs to people.

○ The strategy of fitting people to jobs includes job previews and job rotation. Job previews deal with audiovisual previews about the job and written descriptions in booklet form. Surveys have shown that those who were given realistic job previews tended to have lower initial expectations, greater organizational commitment and job satisfaction, and a lower turnover rate. However, the impact of realistic job previews on job performance was mixed. Job rotation involves periodically moving people from one specialized job to another. It permits employees to rotate among several job positions. Job rotation provides for the continual development of managerial skills. Limited exposure deals with limiting the individual's exposure to tedious and highly fragmented jobs. This technique is called "earned time off," which involves establishing a challenging yet fair daily performance standard, and letting employees go home when the standard is reached.

○ The strategy of fitting jobs to people includes job enlargement and job enrichment. Job enlargement is the process of combining two or more specialized tasks in a work flow sequence into a single job. It adds width to a job. Job enrichment is redesigning a job to increase its motivating potential. Job enrichment adds depth to a job and increases the challenge of one's work by reversing the trend toward greater specialization. Unlike job enlargement, which merely combines equally simple tasks, job enrichment builds more complexity and depth into jobs by introducing planning, decision making, and responsibility normally carried out at higher levels. Job enrichment may motivate employees because it addresses the work itself instead of trying to change the workers to fit the jobs.

Motivation Strategies: Motivation through Rewards

Every employee expects to be rewarded in some way for work performed. Rewards may include material and psychological payoffs for performing tasks in the workplace. Managers have found that job performance and satisfaction can be improved by properly administered rewards. Two types of rewards exist: (1) extrinsic rewards, which are payoffs granted to the individual by other people (e.g., money, employee benefits, promotions, recognition employee of the month, status symbols, and praise) and (2) intrinsic rewards, which are self-granted and internally experienced payoffs (e.g., sense of accomplishment, self-esteem, and self-actualization). An intrinsic reward is an internally generated benefit or satisfaction resulting from good work performed.

Motivation Strategies: Motivation through Employee Participation

Participative management is defined as the process of empowering employees to assume greater control of the workplace. Employees may participate in setting goals, making decisions, solving problems, and designing and implementing organizational changes. Employee participation will not work if individual values and attitudes are not in tune with it. Organizational factors such as job design and corporate culture can also help or hinder the process. Environmental factors such as technological change and competition also affect the participation process.

Motivation Strategies: Motivation through Work Schedules and Services

New approaches such as flexible work schedules, family support services, and sabbaticals are aimed at enhancing employee motivation and increasing job performance. While employees liked the flexible work schedules, employers did not like it because of greater administrative expense, supervisory resistance, and inadequate coverage of jobs. Alternative approaches were invented such as compressed workweeks (40 hours fewer than 5 days), permanent part-time jobs (workweeks with fewer than forty hours), and job sharing (complementary scheduling that allows two or more part-timers to share a single full-time job).

GROUP DYNAMICS

How Groups Think and Make Decisions

Groups or committees make many decisions in organizations. There is a link between communication concepts and the subject of group decision making. Since messages are transmitted between members of the group, the effectiveness of this communication process will have a greater impact on the quality of the group's decisions.

Groups offer an excellent vehicle for performing many of the steps in the decision-making process. They are a source of both breadth and depth of input for information gathering. If the group is composed of individuals with diverse backgrounds, the alternatives generated should be more extensive and the analysis more critical. When the final solution is agreed upon, there are more people in a group decision to support and implement it. These pluses, however, can be more than offset by the minuses—time consumed by group decisions, the internal conflicts they create, and the pressures they generate toward conformity.

Group Behaviors

Group psychology studies have revealed that various groups produced contradictory behavior. Sometimes, people did better at their tasks when there were other people around and sometimes they did worse.

Groupthink, groupshift, and group polarization are the three byproducts of group decision making, all of which have the potential to affect the group's ability to evaluate alternatives objectively and arrive at quality decision solutions.

Factors Affecting Group Decisions

Many factors affect group decisions, including ownership of the problem, nature of the problem, structure of the problem, nature of the group, maturity level of the group, the size of the group, and the climate of the group.

Stages of Group Development

Effectiveness and efficiency increase as the group matures. Similarly, immature groups are ineffective and inefficient. A significant benefit of group maturity is that a person's individuality strengthens. Also, members of mature groups tend to be emotionally mature. Six stages include:

Stage 1: Orientation. Group members give the impression to managers and leaders that they want permanent control expressed through wants and needs.

Stage 2: Conflict and change. Group members struggle for control by suggesting alternative courses of action and strive to clarify and reconcile their roles. Many groups do not continue past this stage because they get bogged down due to emotionalism and political infighting. An "I" feeling is dominant at this stage for power and authority.

Stage 3: Cohesion. A "we" feeling becomes apparent at this stage as everyone becomes truly involved in the project and any differences over power and authority are resolved.

Stage 4: Delusion. Issues and problems are dismissed or treated lightly. Group members work in participation and promote harmony at all costs.

Stages of Group Development (continued)

Stage 5: Disillusion. Disillusion sets in as unlimited goodwill wears off and disenchantment grows. Some members will prevail by showing their strengths while others hold back. Tardiness and absenteeism are the norm, which is symptomatic of diminishing cohesiveness and commitment.

Stage 6: Acceptance. Some group members move from conflict to cohesion and act as group catalysts as their expectations are more realistic. Power and authority structure is accepted. Consequently, the group members tend to be highly effective and efficient.

Organizational Politics

Organizational Politics (OP), impression management, focuses on self-interest in response to opposition at the workplace. Many employees feel that "freedom from office politics" is important to their job satisfaction. Positive aspects of OP include exchanging favors, forcing coalitions, and seeking sponsors at upper levels of the organization. Negative aspects of OP include whistleblowing, revolutionary coalitions, threats, and sabotage.

Criteria and Determinants of Group Effectiveness

A group is defined as two or more freely interacting individuals who share a common identity and purpose. Individuals join groups for various reasons to satisfy their personal and professional goals. Two kinds of groups exist, including informal and formal groups. An informal group is a collection of individuals seeking friendship while a formal group is a collection of individuals doing productive work. Individuals can be subjected to ostracism, which is rejection from a group.

Two criteria for group effectiveness are attractiveness and cohesiveness. Attractiveness has the outside-looking-in view, while the cohesiveness has the inside-looking-out view. Cohesive group members tend to stick together as they focus on "we" instead of "I." An individual's perception and frames of reference have a lot to do with how groups can be attractive or cohesive.

HUMAN RESOURCE MANAGEMENT

Purpose of Policies

A policy is a statement of how an organization intends to handle an issue or a situation. A policy statement can be brief or expanded. A key element of a policy is that it is a predetermined guideline providing a specified course of action for dealing with prescribed circumstances. Some organizations operate without written policies because they want to handle issues on a case-by-case basis. Employees may see this as a way to show favoritism or discrimination. Unwritten practices tend to become informal policies causing confusion and chaos.

Two choices are available for companies who want to develop written policies: (1) develop policies on a department level or (2) an organization level. Policies developed at the individual department level could create conflicting practices for common items such as attendance, promotions, vacations, sick leave, and employee discipline, leading to low productivity and high morale problems.

Policies developed on an organization level would provide: consistency in handling similar issues, improved communication of policy issues, control over personnel costs, prevention or response to administrative claims and litigations, compliance with government laws and regulations, and delegation of routine personnel decisions to supervisors and managers.

Recruiting Policy

A human resource policy on recruiting will guide managers to hire the right person for the job. The primary purpose of the recruiting policy is to attract qualified candidates at a minimum cost and time. A recruiting policy will also enable the organization to contact a diverse variety of recruiting resources, which helps to avoid charges of bias in recruiting practices.

Employee Selection Policy

Careful employee selection is an important activity because capable, hardworking employees affect the productivity and profitability of the organization. This involves employee screening, testing, physical exam, and orientation. Costs are incurred during selection, termination, and rehiring.

Equal Employment Opportunity Policy

A policy statement asserting equal employment opportunity, by itself is not enough to prevent discriminatory practices. Since equal employment laws cover all employment decisions, specific guidelines are needed to guide managers in effectively implementing this policy.

A policy on equal employment opportunity must accomplish a variety of purposes. It must identify protected class employees, specify covered employment decisions, outline guidelines for managers, provide a mechanism for individuals to present claims, and define procedures for resolution of those claims.

Transfers and Promotions Policy

Employee transfers can occur between jobs, work locations, operating shifts, or departments. Transfers may be initiated by the organization to move an employee to another assignment in response to staffing requirements. Employees may also request transfers. Transfers may be temporary or permanent.

Performance Appraisals Policy

A performance appraisal is a structured discussion between employee and supervisor. It provides an opportunity for the supervisor to recognize an employee's achievements, offer suggestions for improvement when needed, discuss job responsibilities, define job objectives, counsel on career advancements, and justify a pay adjustment.

A policy on performance appraisals provides guidelines for managers to conduct effective performance appraisal. The policy can identify when performance appraisals should be scheduled, who is responsible for preparation of the appraisal, how the appraisal influences pay adjustments, and how to prepare for and conduct performance appraisals.

Pay Administration Policy

A pay administration policy provides instructions to aid supervisors in understanding the organization's compensation philosophy, formulating pay offers, and having salary adjustments. Further, it can define guidelines which allow supervisors to make pay decisions within prescribed limits. Exceptions to pay policy can be referred to human resources management for approval.

Bonus Incentives Policy

Many organizations have considered bonus or incentive pay plans as a way to stimulate desired improvements in productivity and quality levels. The goal of a bonus incentive plan is to reward employees for achievement of specified performance results. It is a win-win situation—the employees benefit from higher compensation based upon their attainment of plan objectives. The employer benefits because increased productivity (or lower costs) promotes higher profits. A good bonus plan should pay for itself.

Varieties of incentive pay plans follow. Premium pay is used by some firms to provide an incentive for certain kinds of work. Premium pay is added to the employee's base pay when certain specified conditions are met. Piece rate is often used in manufacturing firms where employee productivity is measured by the number of pieces produced. Many sales people are compensated on a commission basis. The commission is a designated percent of the selling price or profits on the items sold. Bonus incentives can be an informal payout to employees after a profitable year based on management discretion.

Wage Garnishments Policy

Wage garnishments are a court-ordered process for an employer to withhold a portion of an employee's earnings for payment of a debt. Therefore, the garnishments impose a legal obligation upon the employer. An employer's failure to withhold monies as directed could create financial obligations on the company. Further, failure to properly handle deductions can create legal liabilities for the firm. For these reasons, it is important to define a policy to guide the handling of wage deduction orders.

There are a variety of wage deduction orders: tax liabilities (back taxes) to tax authorities, spouse or dependent (child) support payments, and creditors based on wage assignment agreement when granting credit.

The U.S. Consumer Credit Protection Act is one law that defines employer obligations relating to wage garnishments. The Act prohibits employers from discharging an employee whose earnings have been subjected to any indebtedness. Further the law limits the amount of an employee's wages that can be subject to garnishments.

The U.S. Hatch Act, amended in 1994, requires federal agencies to honor court orders for withholding amounts of money from an employee's wages, and to make payment of that withholding to another person or organization for the specific purpose of satisfying a legal debt of the employee. The total debt can include recovery of attorney's fees, interest, or court costs.

Records Retention Policy

The U.S. federal government's labor laws, wage hour laws, and many similar state laws specify certain minimum records that must be maintained by employers. These laws define minimum records retention requirements. Some states have laws that deal with the issues of personnel records privacy and employee access to personnel files.

Safety Policy

Firms that have successful safety programs typically share three common characteristics: a management commitment to safety, active employee participation in safety activities, and thorough investigation of accidents. Successful safety programs reduce accidents. Fewer accidents mean less work interruptions, fewer worker's compensation claims, and lower insurance costs.

The U.S. Occupational Safety and Health Administration (OSHA) is the federal government agency responsible for defining and enforcing job standards. The OSHA law covers all employers engaged in a business affecting commerce, but excludes self-employed individuals, family firms, and workplaces covered by other federal safety laws. Employers covered by OSHA have a general duty to maintain a safe and healthful workplace. The general duty requirements mean that the employer must become familiar with safety standards that affect the workplace, educate employees on safety, and promote safe practices in the daily operation of the business.

RISK/CONTROL IMPLICATIONS OF DIFFERENT LEADERSHIP STYLES

The leadership styles have a significant impact on risks and controls. The control environment has a pervasive influence on the way business activities are structured, objectives are established, and risks are assessed. It also influences control activities, information and communication systems, monitoring activities, and leadership styles.

Control Environment Factors

- Integrity and ethical values
- Commitment to competence
- Board of directors or audit committee
- Management's philosophy and operating style
- Organizational structure
- Assignment of authority and responsibility
- Human resource policies and practices

Incentives and Temptations for Engaging in Illegal and Improper Acts

Incentives cited for engaging in fraudulent or questionable financial reporting practices and, by extension, other forms of unethical behavior are:

- Pressure to meet unrealistic performance targets, particularly for short-term results.
- High performance-dependent rewards.
- Upper and lower cutoffs on bonus plans.

Temptations for employees to engage in improper acts include:

- Nonexistent or ineffective controls, such as poor segregation of duties in sensitive areas, that offer temptations to steal or to conceal poor performance.
- High decentralization that leaves top management unaware of actions taken at lower organizational levels and thereby reduces the chances of getting caught.
- A weak internal audit function that does not have the ability to detect and report improper behavior.
- An ineffective board of directors that does not provide objective oversight of top management.
- Penalties for improper behavior that are insignificant or unpublicized and thus lose their value as deterrents.

Employee Empowerment

There is a tendency to push authority downward to bring decision making closer to front-line personnel. An entity may take this tact to become more market-driven or quality focused—perhaps to eliminate defects, reduce cycle time, or increase customer satisfaction.

MANAGEMENT SKILLS

Management Skills Defined

Management skills can be broadly classified as conceptual, human, and technical. These skills are not exhibited equally across management levels. They vary with the nature of the job, the level of decision making, and the type of interaction with people.

Management Functions

Management is the attainment of organizational goals in an effective and efficient manner through planning, organizing, leading, and controlling organizational resources. There are two important ideas in this definition: (1) the four functions of planning, organizing, leading (directing), and controlling and (2) the attainment of organizational goals in an effective and efficient manner. Managers use a multitude of skills to perform these functions.

Management Types

Managers use conceptual, human, and technical skills to perform the four management functions of planning, organizing, leading, and controlling in all organizations. But not all managers' jobs are the same. Managers are responsible for different departments, work at different levels in the hierarchy, and meet different requirements for achieving high performance. Two management types include (1) vertical differences (i.e., top, middle, and front-line managers) and (2) horizontal differences (i.e., functional and general managers).

Managerial Roles

Henry Mintzberg studied what managers do by focusing on the key roles they play. He then isolated ten roles he believed are common to all managers. These ten roles have been grouped into three major categories: (1) interpersonal (i.e., figurehead, leader, and liaison), (2) informational (i.e., nerve center, disseminator, and spokesperson), and (3) decisional roles (i.e., entrepreneur, disturbance handler, resource allocator, and negotiator).

Manager's Information-Processing Styles

The quality of a decision is a direct reflection of how the decision-maker processes information. Managers approach decision making and problem solving in very different ways, depending on their information-processing styles. Their approaches, perceptions, and recommendations vary because their minds work differently. Researchers have identified two general information-processing styles: (1) the thinking (analytical) style and (2) the intuitive (creative) style. One is not superior to the other. In practice, many managers process information through a combination of analytic and intuitive styles.

Leadership Theories

The evolution of leadership theory can be presented in four ways: (1) trait theory, (2) behavioral style theory, (3) situational theory, and (4) transformational theory.

Leadership Categories

Leadership is of two categories: (1) good and bad leaders and (2) formal and informal leaders. Effective leadership is associated with both better performance and more ethical performance.

Big Five Personality Factors for Leaders

Big five personality factors or dimensions for leaders include a leader's extroversion, agreeableness, conscientiousness, emotional stability, and openness to experience.

Role of Leaders in Employee Development

Concepts such as coaching, mentoring, training, counseling, job rotation, and delegation are a part of employee development program. All these concepts have similar purpose of learning and growing personally and professionally with the advice and experience of others.

Coaching is the responsibility of the immediate supervisor, who provides assistance, much like a mentor. Coaching is more direct and occurs more often than mentoring.

Mentoring is advising, coaching, and nurturing a protégé to enhance his career development. The mentor can be anywhere in the same organization as the protégé or may work in another organization or another industry. The mentor or the sponsor could be the same or different gender as the protégé. Sometimes, a protégé may have more than one mentor to learn the unwritten rules to make it to the top. Mentoring is a relationship in which experienced managers aid employees in the earlier stages of their careers. Such a relationship provides an environment for conveying technical, interpersonal, and organizational skills from the more-experienced to the less-experienced person. Not only does the inexperienced employee benefit, but also the mentor may enjoy the challenge of sharing his wisdom and knowledge. Mentoring is of two types: normal mentoring and reverse mentoring.

Implications of Mentoring

- Mentoring can break the glass-ceiling obstacle facing women and minorities.

- Research has shown that women who have women mentors have done well in enhancing their careers.

Role of Leaders in Employee Development (continued)

- Research has shown that African-American women who have more than one mentor are **more likely** to get promoted.
- Research has shown that African-American women who have more than one mentor are **most likely** to get promoted.

Reverse mentoring is where older employees learn from younger ones because the latter group has some special skills that the former group does not have. This approach will keep the older employees more productive with special skills, thus more useful to the company.

Normal Mentoring → More Experienced Managers → Less Experienced Employees

Reverse Mentoring → Less Experienced Employees → More Experienced Employees

Although mentoring and coaching concepts sound good in theory, there are some practical problems in selecting and pairing the right mentor and the right protégé, the amount of attention given by the mentor to the protégé, the temperament of the both parties, interpersonal skills of each party, and the personality conflicts between the two parties.

Delegation is the process of assigning various degrees of decision-making authority to subordinates. It is not an all-or-nothing proposition. Authority may be passed along to subordinates; ultimate responsibility cannot be passed along. Thus delegation is the sharing of authority, not the abdication of responsibility.

Role of Leaders in Employee Development (continued)

Delegation is a higher-level management right to transfer authority and responsibility to a lower-level management, where the latter group develops managerial skills such as problem-solving and decision-making, and learns how to take responsibility and accountability for achieving results. As a part of the employee development program, delegation involves developing and empowering the lower-level management. Although supervisors and managers are encouraged to delegate, they often find it difficult to do so due to lack of confidence in employees and in themselves, and due to mistrust of people in general. Experts say that it is good to delegate those activities the manager knows best.

TEAM BUILDING

Role of Worker as Individual or Team Member

Every worker has a dual role: as an individual and as a member of a **group**. A group is defined by functional qualities, not physical properties. A group consists of a minimum of two or more people who interact, communicate with, and influence each other for a period of time. To comprise a group, a collection of people must share more than circumstances. They must share perceptions and goals. Group members must be aware of each other, interact with each other, and exert influence on each other. To communicate with each other, they must both send and receive messages. And they must be engaged in these processes for more than a few moments.

Individuals in Group Context

People do not inevitably lose their individuality in groups, although groups may help lessen self-awareness and produce a state of de-individuation. In fact, group membership can heighten certain aspects of individual experience. Three important effects of the group on the individual are (1) Identity, (2) deviance, and (3) social impact.

Group Structures

Groups have tasks such as solving problems and making decisions (task agenda) and meeting the emotional needs and social roles of the group's members (social agenda). Groups meet these two agendas through several key processes and structures: Norms, roles, and cohesiveness.

Methods Used in Team Building

After a team has been created, there are distinct stages through which it develops. New teams are different from mature teams. The challenge for leaders is to understand the stage of the team's development and take action that will help the group improve its functioning.

Research findings suggest that team development is not random, but evolves over definitive stages. One useful model for describing these stages contains five phases:

1. The **forming** stage of development is a period of orientation and getting acquainted.
2. During the **storming** stage, individual personalities emerge.
3. During the **norming** stage, conflict is resolved, and team harmony and unity emerge.
4. During the **performing** stage, the major emphasis is on problem solving and accomplishing the assigned task.
5. The **adjourning** stage occurs in committees, task forces, and teams that have a limited task to perform and are disbanded afterward.

The five stages of team development typically occur in sequence. In teams that are under time pressure or that will exist for only a short period of time, the stages may occur quite rapidly. The stages may also be accelerated for virtual teams. For example, bringing people together for a couple of days of team building can help virtual teams move rapidly through the forming and storming stages.

Assessing Team Performance

Another important aspect of the team process is cohesiveness. **Team cohesiveness** is defined as the extent to which members are attracted to the team and motivated to remain in it. Members of highly cohesive teams are committed to team activities, attend meetings, and are happy when the team succeeds. Members of less cohesive teams are less concerned about the team's welfare. High cohesiveness is normally considered an attractive feature of teams.

Characteristics of team structure and context influence cohesiveness. First is team interaction. The greater the contact among team members and the more time spent together, the more cohesive the team. Through frequent interactions, members get to know one another and become more devoted to the team. Second is the concept of shared goals. If team members agree on goals, they will be more cohesive. Agreeing on purpose and direction binds the team together. Third is personal attraction to the team, meaning that members have similar attitudes and values and enjoy being together.

Two factors in the team's context also influence group cohesiveness. The first is the presence of competition. When a team is in moderate competition with other teams its cohesiveness increases as it strives to win. Finally, team success and the favorable evaluation of the team by outsiders add to cohesiveness. When a team succeeds in its task and others in the organization recognize the success, members feel good, and their commitment to the team will be high.

The outcome of team cohesiveness can fall into two categories—morale and productivity. As a general rule, morale is higher in cohesive teams because of increased communication among members, a friendly team

Assessing Team Performance (continued)

climate, maintenance of membership because of commitment to the team, loyalty, and member participation in team decisions and activities. High cohesiveness has almost uniformly good effects on the satisfaction and morale of team members.

With respect to the productivity of the team as a whole, research findings suggest that cohesive teams have the potential to be productive, but the degree of productivity depends on the relationship between management and the working team.

How Many Teams Are There?

- **Formal teams** are created by the organization as part of the formal organization structure. Two common types of formal teams are vertical and horizontal, which typically represent vertical and horizontal structural relationships.

- A **vertical team** is composed of a manager and his or her subordinates in the formal chain of command. Sometimes called a functional team or a command team, the vertical team may in some cases include three or four levels of hierarchy within a functional department.

- A **horizontal team** is composed of employees from about the same hierarchical level but from different areas of expertise. A horizontal team is drawn from several departments, is given a specific task, and may be disbanded after the task is completed. The two most common types of horizontal teams are task forces and committees.

- A **virtual team** is made up of geographically or organizationally dispersed members who are linked primarily through advanced information and telecommunications technologies. Although some virtual teams may be made up of only organizational members, virtual teams often include contingent workers, members of partner organizations, customers, suppliers, consultants, or other outsiders.

- **Global teams** are cross-border work teams made up of members of different nationalities whose activities span multiple countries. Generally, global teams fall into two categories: intercultural teams, whose

How Many Teams Are There? (continued)

members come from different countries or cultures and meet face to face, and virtual global teams, whose members remain in separate locations around the world and conduct their work electronically.

- **Special-purpose teams,** sometimes called project teams, are created outside the formal organization structure to undertake a project of special importance or creativity. Special-purpose teams focus on a specific purpose and expect to disband once the specific project is completed.

- **Problem-solving teams** typically consist of five to twelve hourly employees from the same department who voluntarily meet to discuss ways of improving quality, efficiency, and the work environment. Recommendations are proposed to management for approval. Problem-solving teams usually are the first step in a company's move toward greater employee participation. The most widely known application is quality circles, in which employees focus on ways to improve quality in the production process.

- In **self-directed teams,** employee involvement through teams is designed to increase the participation of low-level workers in decision making and the conduct of their jobs, with the goal of improving performance. Employee involvement started out simply with techniques such as information sharing with employees or asking employees for suggestions about improving the work. Gradually, companies moved toward greater autonomy for employees, which led first to problem-solving teams and then to self-directed teams.

How Many Teams Are There? (continued)

- The scope of **self-managing teams** includes not only the normal work routine but also some of the traditional managerial tasks. Employees are assigned to self-managed teams. Team members get rotated for cross-training purposes. The manager's role becomes more of a facilitator rather than the traditional supervisor role.

- **Venture teams** (V-teams) are groups of employees working together focusing exclusively on the development of a new product or acquisition of a new business.

- **Training teams** (T-teams) are groups of employees participating in the basic skills training and development sessions away from the workplace.

- A **focus group** is a team representation of individuals, either inside or outside of a firm, who are solicited to share their opinions (likes and dislikes) about a specific product, service, or process for its improvement under the direction of a trained moderator. Focus groups are used for several purposes in various functions such as marketing, operations, and finance.

How Many Committees Are There?

People join various groups or committees to reach decisions and solve problems. An **ad hoc committee** is formed for a short period with a specific purpose and is disbanded after the purpose is accomplished. The members of the ad hoc committee will come from functional departments such as manufacturing, human resources, law, and marketing.

A **steering committee** is a long-term group of people focusing on a specific area of an organization such as information systems and new product development. A **standing committee** exists indefinitely. An **executive committee** is created when there is a large number of members on the board. A **nominating committee** is responsible for the nomination of the board members, including the chairperson. A **corporate governance committee** is responsible for approving the guidelines about how the board of directors should operate and oversee the company. A **compensation committee** determines the amount and type of compensation given to executives and other senior managers. A **succession committee** is responsible for selecting replacements for senior management positions. An **audit committee** is responsible for monitoring the internal operations and evaluating the financial statements of a company. A **finance committee** is responsible for raising the financial capital and reviewing alternative financial and investment plans. An **employee benefits committee** is responsible for overseeing pension funds and retirement benefits. **Special committees** are responsible for specific topics such as ethics, privacy, safety, piracy, and information technology security (e.g., cyber threats and attacks) issues using task forces, special studies, and focus groups.

NEGOTIATION AND CONFLICT MANAGEMENT

Negotiating Skills

Negotiation is a decision-making process among different parties with different preferences. Two common types of negotiation include two-party (buyer and seller) and third-party (buyer, seller, and agent). Traditionally, negotiation takes a win–lose attitude, which is based on power, position, and competition. Here, one person's success is achieved at the expense of the success of others. It takes something from the other party. However, win–win attitude is based on high principles and cooperativeness among parties. Here, one person's success is not achieved at the expense of the success of others. Every party gets something.

Process of Negotiation

A negotiation is more than an exchange of material objects and words. It is a way of acting and behaving that can foster understanding, belief, acceptance, respect, and trust between two or more parties. It is the manner of your approach, the tone of your voice, the attitude you convey, the methods you use, and the concern you exhibit for the other side's feelings and needs. All these things comprise the process of negotiation. Hence, the way you go about trying to achieve your objective may, in and of itself, meet some of the other party's needs.

The prerequisite to negotiation is a conflict situation. Conflict is an unavoidable part of life. It occurs when the goals of each party are in opposition. But conflict can arise even if both parties are in agreement about what they want—sometimes the conflict may be centered around how to get it (or the means used). Conflict may arise from differences in experiences, information, or attitudes about the different roles of the negotiators.

What Is Negotiation?

Negotiation is gaining the favor of people from whom we want things such as money, justice, status, and recognition. People with technical experience, such as accountants and auditors, are often frustrated because they lack the negotiating skills needed to sell their ideas and audit findings to auditees and management alike. Auditors also need negotiating skills to obtain help from and support of colleagues, supervisors, peers, auditees, and even friends and family members.

Why Opposition to Negotiation?

Opposition to negotiation is essential because it results in growth and progress. People who are dissatisfied with the status quo generate tension with their different ideas, which often leads to a creative solution. Thus, opposition is the foundation of progress and growth.

Elements of Negotiation

- **Power**. The other side always seems to have more power and authority than you think you have.

- **Time**. The other side does not seem to be under the same kind of organizational pressure and time constraints you feel you are under.

- **Information**. The other side seems to know more about you and your needs than you know about them and their needs.

Modes of Negotiations

Two modes of negotiating behavior/conflict resolution exist: (1) the competitive strategy and (2) the collaborative (cooperative) strategy.

Competitive strategy focuses on getting what you want and defeating an opponent (I win, you lose). This may range from intimidation to manipulation. People applying competitive strategy often start with tough demands, get red-faced, raise their voices, act exasperated, delay making any concession, tend to be patient, and ignore deadlines.

When the other party is focusing on competitive strategy, it is better to switch to collaborative (cooperative) strategy. **Collaborative strategy** shifts the effort from trying to defeat an opponent to trying to defeat a problem and to achieve a mutually accepted outcome. With this method, all parties work together to find an acceptable solution or common ground that will meet the needs of both sides.

Accomplishing mutual satisfaction using the collaborative win-win style involves emphasis on three important activities.

1. Building trust
2. Gaining commitment
3. Managing opposition

Compromise versus Collaboration in Negotiations

Compromise is not synonymous with collaboration. Compromise results in an agreement in which each side gives up something it really wanted. Compromise is an outcome where no one's needs are fully met. This is because the strategy of compromise rests on the faulty premise that your needs and the other party's needs are always in opposition. With this thinking, it is never possible for mutual satisfaction to be achieved. Each party starts out with greater (extreme) demands, hoping to compromise at a midpoint. This is not to say that compromise is always a poor choice. Often the strategy of compromise may be appropriate, depending on the particular circumstances.

Successful collaborative negotiations depend upon finding out what the other side really wants and showing them a way to get it, while still getting what you want. It is the definition of win-win. Auditors should practice successful collaborative negotiations to reach a win-win situation.

Best Alternative to a Negotiating Agreement

Each party (buyer and seller) in the negotiation process should have its own best alternative to a negotiating agreement (BATNA), which is a settlement amount (bottom line) if negotiations do not produce the desired outcome. Also, each party should estimate the BATNA for the other party. BATNA is the standard; it can protect both parties from accepting terms that are too unfavorable and from rejecting terms that are too favorable. A realistic BATNA is good insurance against the three decision-making traps—framing error, escalation of commitment, and overconfidence. Each party should also identify the bargaining zone, which is the gap between the two parties' BATNAS. This gap is the area of overlapping interests where agreement is possible.

Added-Value Negotiating

Added-value negotiating (AVN) is a value-added process (win-win) involving development of multiple deals with multiple outcomes as opposed to traditional (win-lose) negotiating, which is based on a single outcome with a single winner.

Specific Steps to Achieve AVN

Step 1. Clarify interests. Both parties jointly identify subjective and objective interests so that a common goal is found.

Step 2. Identify options. A variety of choices are developed to create value for both parties.

Step 3. Design alternative deals. Multiple win-win offers are designed to promote creative agreement.

Step 4. Select a deal. Each party selects a mutually acceptable deal after testing the various deals for value, balance, and fit.

Step 5. Perfect the deal. Unresolved details are openly discussed and agreements are put in writing, which strengthens the relationship for future negotiations.

Conflict Management

Conflict management involves accepting or even encouraging constructive conflict as necessary. The key point is to minimize the destructive form of conflict.

Conflict is the medium by which problems are recognized and solved. Conflict is closely related to change and interpersonal dealings. It refers to all kinds of opposition or antagonistic interaction. Not all conflict is bad. Conflict is based on scarcity of power, availability of resources, social position, and difference in value structure between individuals or groups involved in the situation. Conflict is divided into two types:

1. **Functional conflict.** The organizational benefits of functional (constructive) conflict are increased effort and improved performance, enhanced creativity, and personal development and growth. It is like expressing anger in a constructive manner, without actually showing the anger. Functional conflict is always encouraged for obvious reasons.

2. **Dysfunctional conflict.** The signs and symptoms of dysfunctional (destructive) conflict include indecision, resistance to change, destructive emotional outbursts, apathy, and increased political maneuvering. The goal of management is to resolve or neutralize dysfunctional conflict, which is always discouraged, for obvious reasons.

Three kinds of conflict exist, such as (1) conflict of emotions, (2) value conflicts, and (3) conflict of needs.

Personal Conflict Prevention and Control Methods

Although it is impossible to totally eradicate conflict, personal conflict prevention and control can avert much needless strife (unrealistic conflict). Both individuals and institutions need to develop prevention and control methods.

Group or Organizational Conflict Prevention and Control Methods

Individual actions alone are not enough. Group and/or organizational actions are needed to prevent and control the conflict that occurs in the workplace. The way an organization is structured has a bearing on the amount of conflict generated in it. The potential for conflict tends to be greater in centralized, bureaucratic organizations than in decentralized organizations. The more rigid institutions have less effective communication and are less adept at managing conflict constructively than are the organizations at the other end of the continuum.

Conflict Triggers

A conflict trigger is a factor or circumstance that increases the chances of intergroup or interpersonal conflict. It can stimulate either functional or dysfunctional conflict, where the former should be continued and the latter should be removed or corrected.

Conflict Resolution Choices and Techniques

Managers have two choices in resolving conflict: do nothing, which is not a good strategy, or try one or more of the following five conflict resolution techniques, such as (1) problem solving, (2) superordinate goals, (3) compromise, (4) forcing, or (5) smoothing.

Ways to Implement the Conflict Resolution Methods

- Speak in a non-inflammatory way.
- Explain the method by role playing.
- Approach it in a calm and peaceful manner.
- Play a third-party role.

Collaborative Problem Solving in Conflict

In collaborative problem solving, once the people discover they have conflicting needs, they join together to find a solution acceptable to both. It entails redefining the problem, discovering alternatives, and focusing on overlapping interests. In this process, neither person capitulates to or dominates the other. Because no one loses, no one gives up or gives in, and because all parties benefit, this is often called a win-win way of dealing with conflicting needs. Collaborative problem solving is usually the most desirable way to resolve the conflicts of needs that occur between people. This is different from other ways that can occur such as win-lose, lose-lose, mini-lose–mini-lose.

Alternatives to Collaborative Problem Solving

There are four fairly common alternatives to collaborative problem solving: (1) denial, (2) avoidance, (3) capitulation, (4) and domination. Excessive, repeated use of any of these options leads to predictable negative consequences.

What Is the Solution for Interpersonal Differences Causing Conflict?

Accommodation and **compromise** are good solutions for solving interpersonal differences in conflict situations. Accommodation is the intention of one party to sacrifice for others. One party places the opponent's interests above his own in the interest of maintaining good relations. Supporting others' opinions and forgiving others for an infraction are examples of accommodation.

Compromise is consent reached by mutual concessions. It takes into account the needs and fears of both parties. In a world of conflicting needs, wants, and values, compromise does have its place. However, when used exclusively, it can lead to very undesirable results. This is because with compromise, each party settles for something less than its full needs and desires (the mini-lose–mini-lose method). Each side gives something up to end the conflict or solve the problem. Again, although this is perfectly acceptable in some negotiations, it is not ideal for all situations.

PROJECT MANAGEMENT AND CHANGE MANAGEMENT

Project Management Techniques

In order for projects to be successfully implemented, they must be well managed. Many organizations apply a variety of project management techniques to optimize project success and enhance the likelihood of meeting project-specific as well as organization-wide goals. These techniques include monitoring project performance, establishing incentives to meet project goals, and developing a project management team with the right people and the right skills. This can help avert cost overruns, schedule delays, and performance problems common to many organizations.

It is important to develop **performance measures** and link project outcomes to business unit and strategic goals and objectives. The key is monitoring project performance and establishing incentives for account-ability, and using cross-functional teams to involve those with the technical and operational expertise necessary to plan and manage the project.

Project Management's Basic Guidelines

- Define the objective(s) of the project.

- Establish a project organization.

- Install project controls.

Project Controls

In any project, there will be at least four types of controls applied: (1) time control, (2) cost control, (3) quality control, and (4) value control using earned value management method. Sometimes, other types of controls are also used (e.g., logs, checklists, and status reports).

Project Organization

Project organization is where the reporting relationships and the work location rest predominantly with the project manager. Three common types of project organization include traditional structure, matrix organization, and hybrid form.

Problems in Project Management

Project managers face unusual problems in trying to direct and harmonize the diverse forces at work in the project situation. Their main difficulties arise from three sources: (1) organizational uncertainties, (2) unusual decision pressure, and (3) inadequate senior management support.

Project Scheduling Techniques

Six project scheduling techniques include program evaluation and review techniques (PERT), critical path methods (CPM), line-of-balance (LOB) method, graphical evaluation and review techniques (GERT), work breakdown structure (WBS), and Gantt chart. When PERT is used on a project, the three time estimates (optimistic, most likely, and pessimistic) are combined to determine the expected duration and the variance for each activity.

PERT Approach

The status of a project at any time is a function of several variables such as resources, performance, and time. Resources are in the form of dollars, or what "dollars" represent—manpower, materials, energy, and methods of production; and technical performance of systems, subsystems, and components. An optimum schedule is the one that would properly balance resources, performance, and time.

Information concerning the inherent difficulties and variability in the activity being estimated are reflected in the three numbers: the optimistic, most likely elapsed time, and pessimistic estimates should be obtained for each activity. The purpose of the analysis is to estimate, for each network event, the expected times (mean or average) and calendar time of occurrence (TE).

When PERT is used on a project, the three time estimates (optimistic, most likely, and pessimistic) are combined to determine the expected duration and the variance for each activity.

- **Optimistic.** An estimate of the minimum time an activity will take. This is based on everything "going right the first time." It can be obtained under unusual, good luck situations.

- **Most likely.** An estimate of the normal time an activity will take, a result which would occur most often if the activity could be repeated a number of times under similar circumstances.

- **Pessimistic.** An estimate of the maximum time an activity will take, a result that can occur only if unusually bad luck is experienced.

PERT Approach (continued)

The expected times determine the critical path, and the variances for the activities on this path are summed to obtain the duration variance for the project. A probability distribution for the project completion time can be constructed from this information. However, the variances of activities, which do not lie on the critical path are not considered when developing the project variance, and this fact can lead to serious errors in the estimate of project duration.

An estimate of the length of an activity is an uncertain one. A stochastic model can be used to reflect this uncertainty. This model measures the possible variation in activity duration. This may take the form of a distribution showing the various probabilities that an activity will be completed in its various possible completion times. Alternatively, this may be non-distribution such as range or standard deviation.

The expected time $= 1/6(a + 4m + b)$

Where a is optimistic time, m is most likely time, and b is pessimistic time.

The expected activity time derived from a three-estimate, PERT-type calculation provides a more accurate estimate and allows the activity time variance to be calculated and included in the estimates of project duration.

PERT Time Dimensions

ES = Earliest start time for a particular activity

EF = Earliest finish time for a particular activity

EF = ES + t, where t is expected activity time for the activity

LS = Latest start time for a particular activity

LF = Latest finish time for a particular activity

LS = LF + t, where t is expected activity time for the activity

Total slack time (TS) = LS − ES or LF − EF

Free slack time (FS) = EF − ES

Project Governance Mechanisms

Project governance mechanisms include establishing a project steering committee and project oversight board and conducting a project management audit.

The project steering committee is a high-level committee to integrate several functions of the organization. The project oversight board is similar to steering committee except that it is focused on a specific project at hand. The board:

- Reviews the project request and scope

- Assesses the project impact

- Approves the project funding

- Challenges the costs, schedules, and benefits

- Monitors the project progress

- Reviews project deliverables

- Solves the project-related problems

Regarding the project scope, the board determines what is in scope and what is out of scope so that scope creep does not happen. Any changes in project scope are controlled by change management procedures.

Project Management Audit

The scope of project management audit consists of reviewing project planning, organizing, staffing, leading, and controlling tasks for effectiveness and efficiency and determining whether the project objectives and goals are achieved.

The major objective of the project management process, a part of software assurance process, is to establish the organizational structure of the project and assign responsibilities. The process uses the system requirements documentation and information about the purpose of the software, criticality of the software, required deliverables, and available time and other resources, to plan and manage the software development and maintenance processes. The project management process begins before software development starts and ends when its objectives have been met. The project management process overlaps and often reiterates other software assurance processes. It establishes/approves standards, implements monitoring and reporting practices, develops high-level policy for quality, and cites laws and regulations for compliance.

CHANGE MANAGEMENT TECHNIQUES

Agents of Change

Organizations must change to survive in a competitive environment. This requires everyone in the organization believing in and accepting the change. Ideally, managers need to be architects or agents of change rather than the victims of change. When managers are acting as agents of change, their company will be much more responsive, flexible, and competitive. In addition to managers, internal auditors can act as change agents due to the nature of their work. Auditors facilitate change through their recommendations to management. Each recommendation auditors make requires some change in the existing policies, procedures, and practices or the creation of new ones.

How to Change

A corporation can change by reengineering business policies, processes, jobs, and procedures; outsourcing nonstrategic activities; partnering with major suppliers and customers; implementing total quality management programs; redesigning the organizational structure to fit the business strategy; renovating physical plants and facilities; installing computer-based systems and technologies; understanding one's own products, services, markets, and customers as well as those of competitors; and installing performance measurement methods and reward systems.

Types of Organizational Change

- Anticipatory change
- Reactive change
- Incremental change
- Strategic change

Resistance to Organization Change

Organizational change comes in all forms, sizes, and shapes, and with varying degrees of impact and consequences for employees. Among the most common reasons for resistance to change are: surprise, inertia, misunderstanding, emotional side effects, lack of trust, fear of failure, personality conflicts, lack of tact, threat to job status or security, and breakup of work groups. Management faces the challenge of foreseeing and neutralizing resistance to change, as the resistance is both rational and irrational.

Factors in the Change Process

Internal auditors should consider the following factors of change process during their audit work: paradigm shift, motivating stakeholders, grapevine, employee empowerment, barriers to change, departmental border-crossing, performance measurement system, and cultural differences in the workplace.

Organizational Development as a Change Program

Organizational development (OD) is a systematic approach to planned change programs intended to help employees and organizations function more effectively. OD combines the knowledge from various disciplines, such as behavioral science, psychology, sociology, education, and management. OD is a process of fundamental change in an organization's culture. For OD programs to be effective, not only must they be tailored to unique situations, but they also must meet the seven common objectives in order to develop trust:

1. Deepen the sense of organizational purpose and align individuals with that purpose.

2. Strengthen interpersonal trust, communication, cooperation, and support.

3. Encourage a problem-solving rather than a problem-avoiding approach to organizational problems.

4. Develop a satisfying work experience capable of building enthusiasm.

5. Supplement formal authority with authority based on personal knowledge and skill.

6. Increase personal responsibility for planning and implementing.

7. Encourage personal willingness to change.

SECURITY

Information Security Objectives

There are five information security objectives, such as confidentiality, integrity, availability, accountability, and assurance. However, information systems literature primarily focuses on three security objectives or attributes such as confidentiality, integrity, availability. These three objectives (i.e., confidentiality, integrity, and availability) form the three legs of the *CIA* **triad**.

○ **Confidentiality.** Confidentiality of data and information is the requirement that private or confidential information not be disclosed to unauthorized individuals. Confidentiality protection applies to data is in storage, during processing, and while in transit. Confidentiality is the preservation of authorized restrictions on information access and disclosure, including means for protecting personal privacy and proprietary information. Thus, confidentiality is related to privacy.

○ **Integrity.** Integrity of system and data is required as protection against intentional or accidental attempts to violate either (1) data integrity—the property that data has not been altered in an unauthorized manner while in storage, during processing, or while in transit, or (2) system integrity—the quality that a system has when performing the intended function in an unimpaired manner, free from unauthorized manipulation. In other words, integrity is lack of improper modification, alteration, or destruction.

Information Security Objectives (continued)

○ **Availability.** Availability of system and data is a requirement intended to assure that systems work promptly and service is not denied to authorized users. This objective protects against (1) intentional or accidental attempts to either perform unauthorized deletion of data or otherwise cause a denial of service/data, and (2) attempts to use system or data for unauthorized purposes. Availability is continually and reliably accessible and usable in a timely manner, including the ability to share.

Accountability

Accountability is the requirement that actions of an entity may be traced uniquely to that entity. Accountability (i.e., taking responsibility for one's own actions and inactions) is dependent on confidentiality and integrity. If confidentiality or integrity is lost, accountability and accountability share the same concerns and controls. Accountability is often an organizational policy requirement and directly supports non-repudiation, deterrence, fault isolation, intrusion detection and prevention, and after-action recovery and legal action (e.g., audits, investigations, and courts). Here accountability is at the individual level. Accountability is the ability to associate actors with their acts and to include non-repudiation (i.e., ensuring that actors are unable to deny (repudiate) an action).

Assurance

Assurance is the basis for confidence that the security measures, both technical and operational, work as intended to protect the system and the data it processes. Assurance verifies that the other four security objectives (i.e., confidentiality, integrity, availability, and accountability) have been adequately met by a specific implementation. Adequately met refers to the following (1) required functionality is present and performs correctly, (2) there is sufficient protection against unintentional errors (by users or software), and (3) there is sufficient resistance to intentional penetration or bypass. Assurance is the basis for confidence that the security measures, both technical and operational, work as intended to protect the system and the data it processes. Assurance is addressing the question of the amount of uncertainty one should have in software system.

Information Security Controls

Information security controls can be classified from a technical viewpoint and according to their action such as preventive controls, detective controls, and recovery controls. **Preventive controls** include identification, authentication, authorization, access control enforcement, cryptographic key management, non-repudiation, system protections, transaction privacy, protected communications, and security administration. **Detective controls** include audit, audit trails, checksums, intrusion detection and containment, proof-of- wholeness, and virus detection and eradication. **Recovery controls** include backups, check-points, contingency plans, and controls to restore a system to its secure state.

Information Security Policies

Effective information security policies and procedures are the first step or the first line-of-defense to ensure secure systems and networks. To make the security policy effective, it must be practical and enforceable, and it must be possible to comply with the policy. The policy must not significantly impact productivity, be cost pro-hibitive, or lack support. This delicate balance is best accomplished by including both functional management and information security management in the policy development process.

Four basic types of security policies exist: program policy, issue-specific policies, system-specific policies, and acceptable use policies. In addition to security policies, rules of behavior and rules of engagement must be considered to exact proper behavior from employees and outside contractors and vendors.

Rules of behavior describe the rules established and implemented concerning use of, security in, and acceptable level of risk of the system. Rules will clearly delineate responsibilities and expected behavior of all individuals with access to the system. The organization establishes and makes readily available to all infor-mation system users a set of rules that describes their responsibilities and expected behavior with regard to information system usage.

Rules of engagement provide detailed guidelines and constraints regarding the execution of information security testing. The rules of engagement are established before the start of a security test. It gives the test team authority to conduct the defined activities without the need for additional permissions. Rules of engagement are aimed at outside contractors and vendors before performing their work for an organization.

Security Impact Analysis

An impact in an information system is the magnitude of harm that can be expected to result from the consequences of unauthorized disclosure of information, unauthorized modification of information, unauthorized destruction of information, loss of information, or loss of information system availability.

Impact levels are categorized as high, moderate, or low, which classify the intensity of a potential impact that may occur if the information system is jeopardized or compromised.

- A **high-impact system** is an information system in which at least one security objective (i.e., confidentiality, integrity, or availability) is assigned a potential impact value of high.

- A **moderate-impact system** is an information system in which at least one security objective (i.e., confidentiality, integrity, or availability) is assigned a potential impact value of moderate and no security objective is assigned a potential impact value of high.

- A **low-impact system** is an information system in which all three security objectives (i.e., confidentiality, integrity, or availability) is assigned a potential impact value of low.

- A **potential-impact** considers all three levels of impact regarding the loss of confidentiality, integrity, or availability. It could be expected to have (i) a limited adverse effect (low), (ii) a serious adverse effect (moderate), or (iii) a severe or catastrophic adverse effect (high) on organizational operations, systems, assets, individuals, or other organizations.

Key Concepts to Remember in Information Security

Implementing the following can provide reasonable security mechanisms over computer systems and networks:

- Implement access controls, firewalls, routers, sensors, hardware and software guards, and demilitarized zones to protect computer systems and networks from attacks.

- Build security into a system, not add-on later because it is too late, costly, and risky. It requires the integration of security principles, standards, policies, procedures, controls, safeguards, and mechanisms into all phases or processes of a system development lifecycle (i.e., from beginning to the end).

- Keep security as simple as possible because complexity leads to design, development, and implementation problems thus making a system unusable, unstable, unmanageable, and uncontrollable, and even vulnerable to threats.

- Avoid single point-of-failure situations, which are security risks due to concentration of risk in one place, system, process, or with one person. Causes leading to these situations include placement of Web services, and domain name system (DNS) servers; use of primary telecommunication services without backups; use of centralized identity management; use of central certification authority; password synchronization problems; use of single sign-on systems, use of firewalls, use of Kerberos, use of converged networks with voice and data; use of cloud storage services, and system administrators.

Key Concepts to Remember in Information Security (continued)

- Fix security problems and issues correctly and timely as soon as possible. Practice separation of duties, whether manual or electronic. Require mandatory vacations for all employees. Practice rotation of job duties. Practice the principle of least privilege with secure defaults. Fail securely in a known, safe, and secure state. The efficiency and effectiveness of access control policy and its implementation depends on the *system state* and *secure state* in which the system is in at any point in time and the use of fail-safe defaults. A secure state is a condition in which no subject can access any object in an unauthorized manner.

- Implement system-hardening techniques to make computer systems and networks more robust. These include (1) removing all non-essential and unnecessary computer programs and their associated utility program to prevent or eliminate backdoor or trapdoor attacks, and (2) implementing security engineering principles, which are fully discussed in the application development section of this domain.

- Implement secure coding principles, which include minimizing attack surface, establishing secure defaults; implementing the principle of least privilege, deploying defense-in-depth principle, failing securely in a known system state, avoiding security by obscurity, keeping security simple, minimizing programming errors that lead to software vulnerabilities, and implementing secure coding standards.

Key Concepts to Remember in Information Security (continued)

- Balance the costs, risks, and benefits equation, because one should not spend $10 on controls to protect an asset, information, or a risk costing $1. Costs should not exceed benefits.

- A tradeoff exists in security: Pay now or pay later.

SYSTEM SECURITY

Access is the ability to make use of any information system's resource. Subjects (e.g., an individual, process, or device) access objects (e.g., programs, files, records, tables, processes, domains, devices, directories, and Web pages) on a computer system or network. Subject is an activity entity that causes information to flow among objects or changes to the system state and object is a passive entity that contains or receives information.

Access Controls

Access controls provide several purposes such as (1) identifying and authenticating users to prevent unauthorized access, (2) enforcing the principle of least privilege to ensure that authorized access was necessary and appropriate, (3) establishing sufficient boundary protection mechanisms, (4) applying encryption to protect sensitive data on networks and portable devices, and (5) logging, auditing, and monitoring security-relevant events.

Access control is the process of granting or denying specific access requests. Access controls are of two types: physical and logical. Examples of **physical access controls** include keys, visitor logs, physical and electronic locks, security guards, gates and guns, security cameras, smart cards and PINs, access codes, dual control, employee rotation of duties, biometrics, motion detectors with sensors and alarms, and physical tokens. Examples of **logical access controls** include passwords, passphrases, PINs, firewalls, routers, sensors (intrusion detection systems), hardware/software guards, demilitarized zones, memory/smart cards, and hardware tokens.

Preventive, detective, corrective, and recovery controls are needed to control unauthorized or illegal access to objects by subjects, as follows:

Examples of preventive controls include access control and accountability policies and procedures; access rules; account management; identification and authentication techniques for internal users, external users, cryptographic modules, and mobile and non-mobile devices; identifier management; authenticator management; session lock; access control enforcement by checking identity and requested access

Access Controls (continued)

against access control lists (ACLs) and file encryption; information flow enforcement; separation of duties principle; least privilege principle; permitted actions without identification or authentication for emergencies and accessing public websites; security labels, attributes, tags, and markings; trust relationships in using external information systems; allowed and disallowed access to remote networks; usage restrictions for wireless access; restrictions in sharing information with business partners; separating public information from nonpublic information (e.g., personnel privacy and vendor proprietary data); information system monitoring for information disclosure; time stamps; protection of audit-related information; audit record retention and storage capacity; security advisories and directives; information input restrictions; predictable failure prevention; security functionality verification; malicious code protection, including spam; trustworthy communications in distributed systems; intrusion prevention system; single-sign-on, reduced sign-on, and single-logout; Web content filtering software; application content filters; security policy filters; blacklisting of user IDs and IP addresses; and security banners on computer screens.

Examples of detective controls include unsuccessful login attempts; system use notification; previous access logon notification to detect false logons; concurrent session control; system logs; session audit; audit review, analysis, and reporting; security alerts; error handling; proof-of-wholeness; and intrusion detection system.

Access Controls (continued)

Examples of corrective controls include authenticator feedback; response to audit-related data processing failures; audit reports; and error correction.

Examples of recovery controls include fail in a known secure state; recover/restore to a known secure state; flaw remediation; information output handling and retention; and audit recovery from security breaches

Access Control Principles

Access control principles include need-to-know principle, least privilege principle (e.g., need-to-withhold and access safety), and static/dynamic separation of duties principle.

Access Rights and Permissions

Access control policies should deal with access rights in terms of file permissions, program permissions, and data permissions.

Access Control Policies

Access control is exercised through procedures and controls to limit or detect access to critical information resources. This control can be accomplished through software, biometrics devices, or physical access to a controlled area. Access control policy is the set of rules that define the conditions under which an access may take place.

Discretionary access control (DAC) policy leaves certain amount of access control to the discretion of the object's owner or anyone else who is authorized to control the object's access. DAC is known as surrogate access control. DAC is generally used to limit a user's access to a file; it is the owner of the file who controls other users' accesses to the file. Only those users specified by the owner may have some combination of read, write, execute, and other permissions to the file. DAC policy tends to be very flexible and is widely used in the private and public sectors. DAC policy is often referred to as identity-based controls, apply the need-to-know principle, and use ACLs, but not capability lists, for implementation. DAC also uses a combination of access mechanisms for individual owners, groups, and other categories. Four basic models for DAC control exist: hierarchical, concept of ownership, laissez-faire, and centralized. DAC is a means of optionally restricting access to objects (programs and files) based on the identity of subjects (users and devices), the groups to which they belong, or both of these criteria. Access controls are discretionary in the sense that a subject with a particular access right can pass that access to any other subject. The user has control and ownership of access privileges over the items that he creates.

Access Control Polices (continued)

Non-discretionary access control (NDAC) policy includes all access control policies other than the DAC policy. NDAC policy has rules that are not established at the discretion of the user. This policy establishes access controls that cannot be changed by users, but only through administrative action. NDAC policies may be employed in addition to the use of DAC policies.

Mandatory access control (MAC) policy is a means of restricting access to system resources based on the sensitivity (as represented by a security label) of the information contained in the system resource and the formal authorization (i.e., security clearance) of users to access information of such sensitivity. Users cannot change the privileges, except by system administrators. MAC is often referred to as rule-based controls, apply marking (label) principle, and use security clearances for implementation. MAC policy establishes coverage over all subjects and objects under its control to ensure that each user receives only that information to which the user is authorized access based on classification of the information, and on user clearance and formal access authorization. The information system assigns appropriate security attributes (e.g., labels/security domains/types) to subjects and objects, and uses these attributes as the basis for MAC decisions.

Role-based access control (RBAC) policy supports higher-level organizational policies and access control mechanisms, and they are natural to the way the enterprises typically conduct their business. RBAC policy establishes coverage over all users and resources to ensure that access rights are grouped by role name, and access to resources is restricted to users who have been authorized to assume the associated role.

Access Control Polices (continued)

In the RBAC method, the role of a requester is the key determinant for access. The RBAC method better supports the implementation of *least privilege and separation of duties* but does not scale well similar to the IBAC method. In the commercial world, RBAC is the de facto access control implementation at the enterprise level because RBAC is what most solutions support. In fact, a role-based implementation security policy is the only logical choice for an organization that experiences a large turnover of personnel. RBC is the privilege to use computer information in some manner based upon an individual's role (i.e., teller or doctor).

Summary of Specific Access Control Policies and Techniques

- Three primary access control policies are DAC, MAC, and RBAC.

- DAC was developed originally to implement controlled sharing and to enforce the need-to-know principle. This is done with the maximum efficiency of system data and resource administration while retaining protection effectiveness.

- Both DAC and MAC policies are not well suited for private and public sectors processing unclassified but sensitive information. In these environments, security objectives often support higher-level organizational policies derived from existing policies, laws, ethics, regulations, or generally accepted practices. Such environments usually need to control the individual's actions, beyond the individual's ability to access information, according to how that information is labeled, based on its sensitivity.

- Both DAC and MAC support lower-level organizational policies and access control mechanisms and they are unnatural to the way the enterprises typically conduct their business.

- RBAC is an improvement compared to DAC and MAC, but it ties users to roles and privileges toward objects.

- DAC policy implements the need-to-know principle.

- RBAC policy better supports the implementation of least privilege and separation of duties.

 Focus on: **Information Technology and Business Continuity (15–25%)**   289

Summary of Specific Access Control Policies and Techniques (continued)

- DAC and identity-based access control (IBAC) policies are considered equivalent.

- MAC and rule-based access control (RuBAC) policies are considered equivalent.

- High-latency based transaction policy deals with provisions, prerequisites, and obligations.

- Access control lists (ACLs), but not capability lists, are used to implement DAC, IBAC, and RuBAC policies.

- RBAC is a composite policy because it is a variant of both IBAC and RuBAC.

- RuBAC and RBAC policies can be combined so that rules can either replace or complement roles.

- Three basic access control policies are RBAC, ABAC, and IBAC. Whatever access control can be defined with IBAC or RBAC can also be defined with attribute-based access control (ABAC). In addition, the ABAC method can provide more complex access control than can be accomplished with IBAC or RBAC. However, this complexity comes with the additional administrative and managerial burdens. With the ABAC method, the policies to be supported must be known in order to assess the tradeoff between capability and complexity.

- International access control policy standards do not use the U.S. based MAC or DAC policies; instead they use IBAC or RuBAC policies.

Summary of Specific Access Control Policies and Techniques (continued)

- Structured query language (SQL) database incorporates many aspects of RBAC and RuBAC policies.

- Non-discretionary access control (NDAC) policies include RBAC, RuBAC, ABAC, UDAC, MAC (most mentioned NDAC policies), and temporal constraints, where the latter covers workflow policy and Chinese wall policy. UDAC is user-directed access control.

- ABAC or RBAC policy is used to implement separation of domains.

- AuBAC = ABAC + RuBAC where AuBAC is authority-based access control.

- RBAC and RuBAC policies are used to achieve static separation of duty.

- Workflow and Chinese wall policies are used to achieve dynamic separation of duty.

- Workflow policy is applied to organize tasks based on process rules.

- The Chinese wall policy addresses the conflict-of-interest issues arising in specific workplaces.

- Temporal constraints are related to history-based access control policies such as Workflow and Chinese wall policies.

Summary of Specific Access Control Policies and Techniques (continued)

- Note that although a person may be free to read sensitive information under the Chinese wall policy, he may be restricted from reading such information with respect to a MAC policy.

- RBAC, not ABAC, implements privilege management capabilities.

- No access control policy is better or worse than any other; each has its own place and should be adopted according to its suitability for a particular set of requirements and circumstances after analyzing its strengths and weaknesses.

FIREWALLS

Firewall Purpose

A firewall is a network connectivity device that mediates all traffic between two computer networks and protects one of them or some part thereof against unauthorized access. Generally, the protected network is a private, internal network. A firewall may permit messages or files to be transferred to a high-security workstation within the internal network, without permitting such transfer in the opposite direction.

Many enterprise networks employ firewalls to restrict connectivity to and from the internal networks used to service more sensitive functions, such as accounting or personnel. By employing firewalls to control connectivity to these areas, an organization can prevent unauthorized access to its systems and resources. Inclusion of a proper firewall provides an additional layer of security. Organizations often need to use firewalls to meet security requirements from regulatory mandates.

Enclave boundary protection takes the form of firewalls and virtual private networks (VPNs). While these technologies offer perimeter and access controls, authorized internal and external (remote) users can attempt probing, misuse, and malicious activities within an enclave. Firewalls do not monitor authorized users' actions, nor

Firewall Purpose (continued)

do they address internal (insider) threats. Firewalls also must allow some degree of access, which may open the door for external vulnerability probing and the potential for attacks.

Configuration management activities can be extended to firewalls using a firewall ruleset, which is a table of instructions that the firewall uses for determining how network packets or data packets should be routed between firewall's interfaces.

Firewall Technology

Firewall technologies include packet filtering, stateful inspection, application firewalls, application-proxy gateways, dedicated proxy servers, and personal firewalls or personal firewall appliances, as follows:

Packet Filtering

The most basic feature of a firewall is the packet filter (also known as stateless inspection firewall), operating at the network layer does not keep track of the state of each flow of traffic that passes though the firewall; this means, for example, that they cannot associate multiple requests within a single session to each other. The following are the characteristics of packet filters:

- Packet filters are not concerned about the content of packets

- Rulesets govern the access control functionality of packet filters

- Packet-filtering capabilities are built into most operating systems and devices capable of routing; the most common example of a pure packet filtering device is a network router that employs access control lists.

   Stateless packet filters are generally vulnerable to attacks and exploits that take advantage of problems within the TCP/IP specification and protocol stack.

Stateful Inspection

Stateful inspection improves on the functions of packet filters by tracking the state of connections and block-ing packets that deviate from the expected state. This is accomplished by incorporating greater awareness of the transport layer. As with packet filtering, stateful inspection intercepts packets at the network layer and inspects them to see if they are permitted by an existing firewall rule, but unlike packet filtering, stateful inspection keeps track of each connection in a state table. While the details of state table entries vary by firewall product, they typically include source IP address, destination IP address, port numbers, and con-nection state information.

Application Firewalls

A newer trend in stateful inspection is the addition of a *stateful protocol analysis* capability, referred to by some vendors as *deep packet inspection*. Stateful protocol analysis improves upon standard stateful inspec-tion by adding basic intrusion detection technology—an inspection engine that analyzes protocols at the application layer to compare vendor-developed profiles of benign protocol activity against observed events to identify deviations. This allows a firewall to allow or deny access based on how an application is running over the network.

Application-Proxy Gateways

An application-proxy gateway is a feature of advanced firewalls that combines lower-layer access control with upper-layer functionality. These firewalls contain a proxy agent that acts as an intermediary between two hosts that wish to communicate with each other, and never allows a direct connection between them. Each successful connection attempt actually results in the creation of two separate connections—one between the client and the proxy server, and another between the proxy server and the true destination. The proxy is meant to be transparent to the two hosts—from their perspectives there is a direct connection. Because external hosts only communicate with the proxy agent, internal IP addresses are not visible to the outside world. The proxy agent interfaces directly with the firewall rule-set to determine whether a given instance of network traffic should be allowed to transit the firewall.

In addition to the ruleset, some proxy agents have the ability to require authentication of each individual network user. This authentication can take many forms, including user ID and password, hardware or software token, source address, and biometrics.

Dedicated Proxy Servers

Dedicated proxy servers differ from application-proxy gateways in that while dedicated proxy servers retain proxy control of traffic, they usually have much more limited firewalling capabilities. They have a close relationship to application-proxy gateway firewalls. Many dedicated proxy servers are application-specific, and some actually perform analysis and validation of common application protocols such as HTTP. Because these servers have limited firewalling capabilities, such as simply blocking traffic based on its source or destination, they are typically deployed behind traditional firewall platforms. Typically, a main firewall could accept inbound traffic, determine which application is being targeted, and hand off traffic to the appropriate proxy server (e.g., e-mail proxy). This server would perform filtering or logging operations on the traffic, and then forward it to internal systems. A proxy server could also accept outbound traffic directly from internal systems, filter or log the traffic, and pass it to the firewall for outbound delivery. An example of this is an HTTP proxy deployed behind the firewall—users would need to connect to this proxy en route to connecting to external Web servers. Dedicated proxy servers are generally used to decrease firewall workload and conduct specialized filtering and logging that might be difficult to perform on the firewall itself.

Personal Firewalls or Personal Firewall Appliances

Securing PCs at home or remote locations is as important as securing them at the office; many employees telecommute or work at home and use an organization's data. *Personal firewalls* usually do not offer protection to other systems or resources. They do not provide controls over network traffic that is traversing a computer network because they protect only the computer system on which they are installed.

Personal firewall appliances are similar to traditional firewalls in that they are designed to protect small networks such as networks that might be found in home office. These appliances run on specialized hardware and integrate some other forms of network infrastructure components in addition to the firewall itself. These components include broadband modem wide-area network (WAN) routing, local-area network (LAN) routing with dynamic routing support, network hub, network switch, dynamic host configuration protocol (DHCP), simple network management protocol (SNMP) agents, and application-proxy agents.

Although both personal firewalls and personal firewall appliances address connectivity concerns associated with telecommuters or branch offices, most organizations are employing them on their intranet, practicing a layered defense strategy.

Limitations of Firewalls

Firewalls can only work effectively on traffic that they can inspect. Regardless of the firewall technology chosen, a firewall that cannot understand the traffic flowing through it will not handle that traffic properly—for example, allowing traffic that should be blocked. Many network protocols use cryptography to hide the contents of the traffic [e.g., IPsec, TLS, secure shell [SSH], and secure real-time transport protocol [SRTP]). Firewalls also cannot read application data that is encrypted, such as e-mail that is encrypted using the S/MIME or Open-PGP protocols, or files that are manually encrypted. Another limitation faced by some firewalls is understanding traffic that is tunneled, even if it is not encrypted. For example, IPv6 traffic can be tunneled in IPv4 in many different ways. The content may still be unencrypted, but if the firewall does not understand the particular tunneling mechanism used, the traffic cannot be interpreted.

Firewall Management

Managing the firewall solution involves maintaining firewall architecture, policies, software, and other components of the solution chosen to be deployed, as follows:

- Test and apply patches to firewall devices

- Update policy rules as new threats are identified and requirements change, such as when new applications or hosts are implemented within the network, and should also be reviewed periodically to ensure they remain in compliance with security policy.

- Monitor the performance of firewall components to ensure that potential resource issues are identified and addressed before components become overwhelmed.

- Monitor logs and alerts continuously to identify threats—successful and unsuccessful—that are made to the system.

- Perform periodic testing to verify that firewall rules are functioning as expected.

- Backup the firewall policies and rule-sets regularly.

- Conduct penetration testing to assess the overall security of their network environment. This testing can be used to verify that a firewall rule-set is performing as intended by generating network traffic and monitoring how it is handled by the firewall in comparison with its expected response. Penetration testing should be employed in addition to, rather than instead of, a conventional audit program.

Advantages of Firewalls

- Protection from vulnerable services
- Controlled access to site systems
- Concentrated security
- Enhanced privacy
- Logging and statistics on network use, misuse
- Policy enforcement

Disadvantages of Firewalls

- Restricted access to desirable services such as TELNET, FTP, X Windows, and NFS.

- Large potential for back doors due to unrestricted modem access.

- Little protection from insider attacks such as copying the data onto a tape and taking it out of the facility.

- World Wide Web (www), gopher, and WAIS do not work well with firewalls.

- Firewalls do not protect against user downloading virus-infected PC programs from Internet archives or transferring such programs in attachments to e-mail. Antiviral controls are needed.

- Firewalls represent a potential bottleneck in throughput since all connections must pass through the firewall.

- Security is concentrated in one spot as opposed to distributing it among systems (i.e., putting all eggs in one basket, leading to a single point of failure situation).

ROUTERS

Router Purpose

A router is a network connectivity device that establishes a path through one or more computer networks. Routers offer a complex form of interconnectivity. The router keeps a record of node addresses and current network status. Routers are known to the end-stations, as they are device dependent. Local-area networks (LANs) connect personal computers, terminals, printers, and plotters within a limited geographical area. An extended LAN is achieved through the use of bridges and routers. In other words, the capabilities of a single LAN is extended by connecting LANs at distant locations. A router operates in the network layer of the OSI Reference Model.

Routers convert between different data link protocols and re-segment transport level protocol data units (PDUs) as necessary to accomplish this. These PDUs are reassembled by the destination end point transport protocol entity. There are several routing protocols in common use. Routers must have more detailed knowledge than bridges about the protocols that are used to carry messages through inter-network. When routers are used to connect fiber distributed data interface (FDDI) to other networks, it is important to be certain that the routers support the needed network level protocols.

Router Accounts and Passwords

Restricting access to all routers is critical in safeguarding the network. In order to control and authorize access, an authentication server that provides extended user authentication and authority levels will be implemented.
For router accounts and passwords, the router administrator will ensure:

- An authentication server is used to gain administrative access to all routers

- When an authentication server is used for administrative access to the router, only one account is defined locally on the router for use in an emergency (i.e., authentication server or connection to the server is down)

- Each user has their own account to access the router with username and password

- All user accounts are assigned the lowest privilege level that allows them to perform their duties

- Immediately remove accounts from the authentication server or router that are no longer required

- A password is required to gain access to the router's diagnostic port (management port used for troubleshooting)

- The enable secret password does not match any other username and passwords, enable password, or any other enable secret password

- Passwords are not viewable when displaying the router configuration.

Routing Table Integrity

A rogue router could send a fictitious routing table to convince a site's premise router to send traffic to an incorrect or even a rogue destination. This diverted traffic could be analyzed to learn confidential information of the site's network, or merely used to disrupt the network's ability to effectively communicate with other networks.

Router Packet Filtering and Logging

Access control lists (ACLs) are used to separate data traffic into that which it will route (permitted packets) and that which it will not route (denied packets). Secure configuration of routers makes use of ACLs for restricting access to services on the router itself as well as for filtering passing through the router.

Router Configuration Management

Configuration management activities can be extended to routers using rulesets, similar to firewalls. The ruleset can be a file that the router examines from top to bottom when making routing decisions, using routing tables.

SENSORS

Sensors are intrusion detection systems (IDSs) and are composed of monitors and scanners, and they fill the gap left by firewalls. *Monitors* are of two types: network monitors and host monitors. Both monitors perform intrusion detection and malicious code detection. *Scanners* are of two types: network scanners and host scanners. Network scanners provide vulnerability scanning and war dialing. Host scanners provide vulnerability scanning and file integrity checking. Both monitors and sensors must have detect and respond capabilities.

IDSs are hardware and software products that gather and analyze information from various areas within a computer or network to identify possible security breaches. These breaches include intrusions from outside the organization and misuses from within the organization. An IDS is a system to detect, report, and provide limited response to an activity that may be harmful to an information system. Some IDSs can even prevent the intrusion activities. Tools to complement the IDSs include anti-malware products (i.e., antivirus software, anti-spyware software), firewalls, routers, honeypots, honeynets, padded cell systems, and canaries.

HARDWARE AND SOFTWARE GUARDS

Guards Purpose

Hardware and/or software guards enable users to exchange data between private and public networks, which is normally prohibited because of information confidentiality. A combination of hardware and/or software guards is used to allow to secure local-area network (LAN) connectivity between enclave boundaries operating at different security classification levels (i.e., one private and the other public).

A guard is a device used to defend the network boundary by employing the following functions and properties: (1) typically subjected to high degree of assurance in its development, (2) supports fewer services (3) services are at the application level only, (4) may support application data filtering review, (5) may support sanitization of data, and (6) typically used to connect networks with differing levels of trust (i.e., provides re-grading of data).

Guard Technology

Guard technology can bridge across security boundaries by providing some of the interconnectivity required between systems operating at different security levels. Several types of guard exist. These protection approaches employ various processing, filtering, and data-blocking techniques in an attempt to provide data sanitization (e.g., downgrade) or separation between networks. Some approaches involve human review of the data flow and support data flow in one or both directions. Information flowing from public to private networks is considered an upgrade. This type of transfer may not require a review cycle, but should always require a verification of the integrity of the information originating from the public source system and network. Guards can be used to counteract attacks made on the enclave.

The guard is designed to provide a secure information path for sharing data between multiple system networks operating at different security levels. The guard system is composed of a server, workstations, malicious code detection, a firewall, and/or filtering routers all configured to allow transfer of information among communities of users operating at different security levels.

Guard Implementations

Most guard implementations use a dual network approach, which physically separate the private and public sides from each other. Guards are application specific; therefore, all information will enter and exit by first passing through the Application Layer, Layer 7 of the open system interconnection (OSI) model. In addition, most guard processes are high-assurance platforms that host some form of trusted operating system and trusted networking software.

Attacks on Guards

Enclave boundaries need protection from the establishment of unauthorized network connections. The focus is on attacks into an enclave by malicious e-mail transfer, file transfer, or message transfer. Guards can be implemented to provide a high level of assurance for networks by preventing certain types of malicious messages from entering the enclave.

DEMILITARIZED ZONES

DMZ Purpose

A demilitarized zone (DMZ) is an interface on a routing firewall that is similar to the interfaces found on the firewall's protected side. Traffic moving between the DMZ and other interfaces on the protected side of the firewall still goes through the firewall and can have firewall protection policies applied.

A DMZ is a separate network subnet designed to expose specific services to a larger, untrusted network. The subnets are used in large corporations or organizations to safely expose functions to the Internet, such as Web or database applications. DMZs also are used internal to networks to facilitate secure data transfer from a high security network zone to a zone with lower security. A DMZ uses explicit access control and contains computer hosts that provide network services to both low-security and high-security network zones. DMZ networks are usually implemented with a firewall or other traffic routing network device. It can be split into several sub-DMZ networks with specific functional groupings for the computers such as Web servers, timeservers, or FTP repositories. Having multiple DMZs protects the information resources from attacks using virtual-LAN hopping and trust exploitation, thus providing another layer to the defense-in-depth strategy.

DMZ Architecture

A possible architecture for a DMZ is to use firewalls with the ability to establish a DMZ between two networks. The use of a DMZ-capable firewall allows the creation of an intermediate network. Creating a DMZ requires that the firewall offer three or more interfaces, rather than the typical public and private interfaces. If a patch management server, a Web server, an authentication server, a system log (syslog) server, a remote access server, a DNS server, an antivirus server, or a VPN server is to be used for a network, it should be located directly on the DMZ. *Limitations of DMZ* include that it cannot work all by itself and it needs to work with a firewall or router.

INFORMATION PROTECTION

Risks to Data and Information

Data is a collection of facts and figures, and it is usually expressed as numbers. Information is data that is computed using mathematical equations and formulas; aggregated or summarized in a designated way; combined with several data items in different ways; compared and contrasted in some manner; analyzed and reported in some manner; arranged or sorted either in ascending or descending order; or otherwise manipulated or massaged in different ways. In other words, data is raw data and information is processed data. Data by itself is meaningful to some whereas information is meaningful to many, because information is derived from data. Most people use the data and information terms interchangeably and loosely.

Possible risks for data and information include destruction, loss, damage, or stealing credit and debit card information and social security numbers, disclosure to unauthorized parties, which lead to privacy issues and legal disputes.

Specifically, these vital assets are easily and constantly exposed to greater risks from insiders (current employees, disgruntled, employees, and previous employees) and outsiders (e.g., attackers, hackers, adversaries, suppliers, vendors, customers, contractors, and business partners) for their personal and financial gains, including intelligence gathering purpose for competitive reasons.

Risks to Data and Information (continued)

Data and information are spread out everywhere in an organization and in all organizations. Because of this, most people want them since they have intrinsic and extrinsic value. These vital assets, such as data and information, are the major targets of insiders and outsiders alike. For example, insiders (managers and executives) want them for decision-making and to run business operations. Outsiders (e.g., attackers, adversaries, competitors, consultants, contractors, suppliers, and vendors) want them for personal gain, financial benefit, competitive advantage, grudge, revenge, and even fun. Therefore, data and information must be protected at all times and with whatever means.

Threats and Vulnerabilities in Data and Information

Two important, complicated, and related terms exist in information security: threats and vulnerabilities. A **threat** is any circumstance or event with a potential to adversely impact an organization's operations (e.g., mission, functions, image or reputation), assets, information, or individuals through an information system via unauthorized access, destruction, disclosure, modification of information, and/or even denial of service. Also, a potential for a threat-source can exploit a particular system's vulnerability. The presence of a threat-event does not mean that it will necessarily cause actual harm or loss. To become a risk, a threat must take advantage of vulnerabilities in system security features and controls.

A **vulnerability** is a weakness or a security hole in a system's functions and operations, security procedures, and design and implementation of internal controls that could be exploited or triggered by a threat source.

A relationship exists between vulnerabilities, threats, risks, and controls, as follows:

Vulnerabilities → Threats → Risks → Controls

Controls reduce risks. Lack of adequate and/or inappropriate controls often increase the vulnerabilities in a system and, therefore one needs to focus on vulnerabilities first, threats next.

Many **threat-events** are looming around over in all organizations, including business corporations; governmental agencies, including defense; industrial control systems; electric power grid systems; railroad company's computer systems; gas utility company's systems; water purification and pumping station's

Threats and Vulnerabilities in Data and Information (continued)

computer systems; oil refinery company's computer systems; and individual's personal computer systems, to name a few.

Many **threat-sources** exist, including malware and malicious code (e.g., viruses, worms, logic bombs, time bombs, and Trojan horses), mobile code on mobile devices (e.g., mobile botnets, mobile applications, exploitation of mobile commerce, exploitation of social media networks, and social engineering), Web browser-based attacks (e.g., browser session hijacking, applets, flash, Active X, Java, plug-ins, cookies, JavaScript, and VBScript), eavesdropping (e.g., packet snarfing), masquerading (i.e., impersonating, spoofing, and mimicking) attacks.

Summary of Information Protection Methods

- **Deploy a defense-in depth strategy**. It is securing data/information and computer systems against the full spectrum of threats requires the use of multiple, overlapping protection approaches addressing the people, technology, and operational aspects of IT. This is due to the highly interactive nature of the various systems and networks, and the fact that any single system cannot be adequately secured unless all interconnecting systems are also secured.

  By using multiple, overlapping protection approaches, the failure or circumvention of any individual protection approach will not leave the system unprotected. Through user training and awareness, well-crafted policies and procedures, and redundancy of protection mechanisms, layered protections enable effective protection of IT assets for the purpose of achieving its objectives. The concept of layered protections is called security-in-depth.

  The defense-in-depth strategy recommends several information assurance principles. These include (1) defense in multiple places and (2) layered defenses:

  - *Defense in Multiple Places*. Given that adversaries can attack a target from multiple points using either insiders or outsiders, an organization needs to deploy protection mechanisms at multiple locations to resist all classes of attacks. As a minimum, these defensive focus areas should include (1) defend the networks and infrastructure by (i) protecting the local and wide area communications networks from denial-of-service attacks, (ii) providing confidentiality and integrity protection for data transmitted over

Summary of Information Protection Methods (continued)

these networks by using encryption and traffic flow security measures to resist passive monitoring, (2) defend the enclave (envelope) boundaries by deploying firewalls and intrusion detection mechanisms to resist active network attacks, and (3) defend the computing environment by providing access controls on hosts and servers to resist insider, close-in, and distribution attacks.

- *Layered Defenses*. In no time, adversaries find an exploitable vulnerability. An effective countermeasure is to deploy multiple defense mechanisms between the adversary and his target. Each of these mechanisms must present unique obstacles to the adversary. Further, each mechanism should include both protection and detection measures. These help to increase risk of detection for the adversary while reducing his chance of success or making successful penetrations unaffordable. Deploying nested firewalls, each coupled with intrusion detection, at outer and inner network boundaries is an example of a layered defense. The inner firewalls may support more granular access control and data filtering.

- **Deploy a defense-in breadth strategy.** It is a planned, systematic set of multidisciplinary activities that seek to identify, manage, and reduce risk of exploitable vulnerabilities at every stage of the system, network, or sub-component lifecycle (system, network, or product design and development; manufacturing; packaging; assembly; system integration; distribution; operations; maintenance; and retirement). It is a strategy dealing with scope of protection coverage of a system. It is also called supply chain protection control. It supports agile defense strategy and is same as security-in-depth.

Summary of Information Protection Methods (continued)

- **Deploy a defense-in-technology strategy**. It is a strategy dealing with diversity of information technologies used in the implementation of a system. Complex technologies can create complex security problems.

- **Deploy a defense-in-time strategy**. It is a strategy dealing with applying controls at the right time and at the right geographic location. It considers global systems operating at different time zones.

- **Deploy agile defenses with the concept of information system resilience**. *Agile defense* assumes that a small percentage of threats from cyberattacks will be successful by compromising information systems through the supply-chain by defeating the initial security controls implemented by organizations or by exploiting previously unidentified vulnerabilities for which protections are not in place. In this scenario, adversaries are operating inside the defensive parameters established by organizations and may have substantial or complete control of systems.

    Information system resilience is the ability to quickly adapt and recover from any known or unknown changes to the system environment through holistic implementation of risk management, contingency mechanisms, and continuity planning.

    Agile defense employs the concept of information system resilience, that is, the ability of systems to operate while under attack, even in a degraded or debilitated state, and to rapidly recover operational capabilities for essential functions after a successful attack. The concept of system resilience can be applied not only to cyber attacks, but also to environmental disruptions and human errors of omission or

Summary of Information Protection Methods (continued)

commission. The agile defense and system resilience concepts should be combined with defense-in-depth and defense-in-breadth strategies to provide a stronger protection against attacks.

- **Install several lines-of-defense.** The lines-of-defense are security mechanisms for limiting and controlling access to and use of computer system resources. They exercise a directing or restraining influence over the behavior of individuals and the content of computer systems. They can be grouped into four categories - first, second, last, and multiple—depending on their action priorities. A first line-of-defense is always preferred over the second or the last. If the first line-of-defense is not available for any reason, the second line-of-defense should work. These lines-of-defense form a core part of defense-in-depth strategy or security-in-depth strategy. If the second line-of-defense is not available or does not work, then the last line-of-defense must work. The term "multiple defenses" here denotes more than one control, device, policy, layer, factor, mode, or level acting together in concert providing greater synergy, strength, and security to a system.

  Multi-user, multi-platform, remote access, resource-sharing, and data-sharing computer systems require different and stronger controls than single-user, single-platform, and local access systems. For a multi-user environment, a minimum security requirement should be provided as a "reasonable first-line of defense" against an unauthorized user's attempt to gain access to the system or against an authorized user's inadvertent attempt to gain access to information for which he has not been granted access.

- **Implement traditional backup methods** to protect data files, computer programs, and computer systems with full back ups, incremental backups, differential backups, and hybrid backups (e.g., a full backup on the

Summary of Information Protection Methods (continued)

weekend and differential backup in each evening). These backup methods are good for disks and tapes. Remember that "no backup means no recovery" from disasters and damages to organization's assets.

- **Implement zero-day backup method**, which is similar to traditional or full backup where it archives all selected files and marks each as having been backed up. An advantage of this method is the fastest restore operation because it contains the most recent files. A disadvantage is that it takes the longest time to perform the backup.

- **Deploy advanced backup methods** on large storage media using disk arrays (e.g., redundant array of independent disk [RAID] technology), which are a cluster of disks used to backup data onto multiple disk drives at the same time, to provide data protection, data availability, and data reliability.

- **Defend attack-in-depth strategies and zero-day attacks**. Malicious code attackers use an *attack-in-depth strategy* in order to carry out their goals. Single-point solutions will not be able to stop all of their attacks because a single countermeasure cannot be depended on to mitigate all security issues. In addition, a single-point solution can become a single-point of failure (or compromise) that can provide extended access due to pre-existing trust established among interconnected resources. A *zero-day attack* or threat is a computer threat that tries to exploit computer application vulnerabilities that are unknown to others, undisclosed to the software vendor, or for which no security fix is available.

Summary of Information Protection Methods (continued)

Attack-in-depth strategy can create advanced persistent threats where an adversary that possesses sophisticated levels of expertise and significant resources which allow it to create opportunities to achieve its objectives by using multiple attack vectors such as cyber, physical, logical, and deception. Advanced persistent threats can be mitigated with agile defenses combined with boundary protection controls. Agile defense employs the concept of information system resilience.

    Multiple countermeasures against attack-in-depth strategy include agile defenses, boundary protection controls (e.g., firewalls, routers, and software/hardware guards), defense-in-depth strategy, and defense-in-breadth strategy because they can disseminate risks over an aggregate of security mitigation techniques.

- **Protect Web browsers** from attacks by (1) disabling mobile code on websites that you are not familiar with or do not trust, (2) disabling options to always set cookies, and (3) setting the security levels for trusted websites (i.e., websites that you most often visit and trust) to the second highest level. At the highest level, some websites may not function properly.

- **Implement strong password methods** such as passphrases, encrypted passwords, and dynamic pass-words with challenge-response protocols to protect against attacks such as brute-force password attacks.

    Password management may seem simple, but it is not especially when doing business on the Internet. One should not think that some passwords are less important than others because all passwords are important to hackers. Some hackers can piece together password-related information stored online and

Summary of Information Protection Methods (continued)

shared on social media networks. Another risk is that some commercial websites give customers the ability to store billing and shipping addresses along with their credit/debit card information, social security numbers, bank account numbers, system-user identification numbers, and passwords. This could lead to *identity theft*, which involves stealing personal information mostly financial) and using it illegally and is a form of phishing attack.

The following are some guidelines to protect from identity theft:

- *Never provide your personal information in response to an unsolicited request*, whether it is over the phone or over the Internet. E-mails and Internet pages created by phishers may look exactly like the real thing. They may even have a fake padlock icon that ordinarily is used to denote a secure site. If you did not initiate the communication, you should not provide any information.

- *If you believe the contact may be legitimate, contact the financial institution yourself.* You can find phone numbers and websites on the monthly statements you receive from your financial institution, or you can look the company up in a phone book or on the Internet. The key is that you should be the one to initiate the contact, using contact information that you have verified yourself.

- *Never provide your password over the phone or in response to an unsolicited Internet request or phone request.* A financial institution would never ask you to verify your account information online. Thieves armed with this information and your account number can help themselves to your savings.

Summary of Information Protection Methods (continued)

- **Review your bank account statements regularly to ensure all charges are correct.** If your account statement is late in arriving, call your financial institution to find out why. If your financial institution offers electronic account access, periodically review activity online to catch suspicious activity.

The following is a list of three common mistakes most users do with passwords and their remedies:

Mistake #1: Using a weak password such as common phrase, dictionary term, name, or birthday.

Remedy #1: Use a passphrase that is long, is not a common phrase, includes numbers, lowercase and uppercase letters, and special characters (e.g., punctuation, a dollar sign, or pound sign).

Mistake #2: Using the same password for every account.

Remedy #2: Use a different password for each website with password manager software, which is an encrypted database.

Mistake #3: Exposing passwords to others, such as logging in from a public computer, keeping a note with passwords written on it where it can be found or sharing passwords with others.

Remedy #3: Avoid the use of public computers and public access networks, if possible. If there is a need to use them, do not send or receive private, sensitive, or confidential information, and change the password afterward. Store passwords in an encrypted file or password manager and avoid sharing passwords.

Summary of Information Protection Methods (continued)

- **Install software patches, updates, and hot fixes** in a timely manner to close security holes and potential vulnerabilities. The goal is to implement a robust software patch management process which is important in reducing vulnerabilities in an information system. As patches greatly impact the secure configuration of an information system, the patch management process should be integrated into configuration management at a number of points, as follows.

    - Perform security impact analysis of patches

    - Test and approve patches as part of the configuration change control process

    - Update baseline configurations to include current patch level

    - Assess patches to ensure they were implemented properly

    - Monitor systems/components for current patch status

- **Understand zero-day exploits and zero-day incidents (attacks).** *Zero-day exploits* (i.e., actual code that can use a security vulnerability to carry out an attack) are used or shared by attackers before the software vendor fixes those exploits. A *zero-day attack* or threat is a computer threat that tries to exploit computer application vulnerabilities that are unknown to others, undisclosed to the software vendor, or for which no security fix is available. This is a timing game played by sophisticated attackers on user organizations. This is an unfortunate situation for most organizations because they are helpless.

Summary of Information Protection Methods (continued)

- **Protect data on storage media with sanitization methods** such as overwriting (i.e., clearing), degaussing (i.e., purging) and physical destruction (i.e., disintegration, pulverization, melting, incineration, shredding, sanding, and acid solutions). Overwriting, not erasing, is an effective method for clearing data from magnetic media because the deleted data cannot be retrieved later on. The same thing cannot be said for the erasing. Note that destruction is a strong form of sanitization and disposal in a waste container is a weak form of sanitization. The goal is to ensure that there is no residual data on the storage media because attackers can target it for personal gain. Remember that residual data is residual risk for the user organization.

- **Sanitize computer memory,** whether it is volatile memory or non-volatile memory to prevent memory leakage to attackers. The contents of volatile memory found in random access memory (RAM) chips can be sanitized by removing the electrical power from the chip because it requires power to maintain its content. On the other hand, the contents of non-volatile memory as found in programmable read-only memory (PROM) flash memory is permanent until reprogrammed; and it can be sanitized using ultraviolet light, overwriting, and physical destruction.

- **Protect data-at-rest with cryptographic mechanisms,** which are discussed in the encryption section of this domain. The scope of data-at-rest, data-in-storage, or data-on-a-hard-drive includes protecting the confidentiality, integrity, and availability of data residing on servers, workstations, computers, storage/disk arrays (e.g., RAID), network attached storage appliances, disk drives, tape drives, and removable media such as flash drives, thumb drives, and pen drives.

Summary of Information Protection Methods (continued)

- **Protect data-in-transit with cryptographic mechanisms**, which are discussed in the encryption of this domain. The scope of data-in-transit, data-in-flight, or data-on-the-wire includes protecting the confidentiality, integrity, and availability of data as they are transferred across the storage network, the LAN, and the WAN.

- **Protect from dumpster-diving risk** by shredding sensitive or confidential documents and not disposing or recycling them because it is a high risk.

- **Protect from hardware-based and software-based key logger attacks**, which are spyware attacks. Hardware devices usually slip inline between the keyboard cable and computer, which is difficult to do because it requires a physical access to the cable and computer. Software key loggers capture keyboard events and record the keystroke data before it is sent to the intended application for processing. As a remedy, install anti-spyware programs.

- **Protect configuration data by creating a gold disk (i.e., master disk)**, which contains a baseline configuration data about an operating system so that the systems software, ports, system services, and login credentials are run in a safe and efficient manner, using the gold disk. The gold disk is a master disk containing all the necessary information about configuration in one place, instead of several places. Ensure that the gold disk does not contain guest accounts and unnecessary user accounts, and that it contains only the least amount of privileges. Because of this approach, the gold disk increases the security posture and lowers the attack surface. Even with the gold disk, misconfiguration is possible, which is a security risk

Summary of Information Protection Methods (continued)

leading to a security breach, and as such it should be managed well. Misconfiguration means that initial configuration settings are established incorrectly and inappropriately, or implemented ineffectively, and that changes to configuration data are incorrectly made. Misconfiguration leads to vulnerability. Configuration management is fully discussed in the application development section of this domain.

- **Implement fault-tolerance mechanisms** such as fail-stop processors and redundancy mechanisms with fault detection, error recovery, and failure recovery abilities. Refer to the business continuity section of this domain for full details.

- **Control superusers, special privileged users, privileged programs, guest accounts, and temporary accounts.** A superuser is a user who is authorized to modify and control IT processes, devices, networks, and files. Special privileged users are given permissions to access files, programs, and data beyond normal users, thus creating a security risk. Privileged programs are those programs that if unchecked could cause damage to computer files (e.g., some utility programs).

- **Install antivirus software** to control viruses and other forms of malware.

- **Install spam-filtering software.** Web content filtering software, Bayesian spam filters, whitelists, and blacklists to control spamming attacks.

- **Implement anti-spoofing methods** to prevent the unauthorized use of legitimate identification and authentication data

Summary of Information Protection Methods (continued)

- **Install anti-spyware software** to detect both malware and non-malware forms of spyware.

- **Install anti-jam methods** to control jamming attempts, which ensures that transmitted information can be received despite deliberate jamming attempts. Jamming is attack in which a device is used to emit electromagnetic energy on a wireless network's frequency to make it unstable.

- **Install Web content filtering software to control Web bugs**. A Web bug is a tiny image of a malicious code, invisible to a user, placed on Web pages, websites, or Web browsers, to enable third parties to track use of Web servers and collect information about the user, including IP address, host computer name, browser type and version, operating system name and version, and cookies. Web content filtering software is a program that prevents access to undesirable websites, typically by comparing a requested website address to a list of known bad websites. In general, content filtering is the process of monitoring communications such as e-mail and Web pages, analyzing them for suspicious content, and preventing the delivery of suspicious content to users.

- **Implement Kerberos authentication protocol** to provide authentication and authorization of users and systems on the network because it uses symmetric cryptography

- **Implement digital signatures, digitized signatures, electronic signatures, and digital certificates** to verify the identity of originators and receivers of electronic messages and signatures.

Privacy Management

Privacy deals with balancing individual rights in a society. Two definitions exist: (1) the individual right to determine the degree to which he is willing to share information about himself that may be compromised by unauthorized exchange of such information among other individuals or organizations and (2) the individual and organizational rights to control the collection, storage, and dissemination of their information.

Privacy is the right of an individual to limit access to information regarding that individual. Privacy refers to the social balance between an individual's right to keep information confidential and the societal benefit derived from sharing information, and how this balance is codified to give individuals the means to control personal information. Confidentiality refers to disclosure of information only to authorized individuals and entities.

Privacy means that the rights of the accused (suspect) cannot be violated during the investigation. The accused can use protective orders if his privacy rights are ignored or handled improperly. If the accused can prove that evidence brought against him would do more harm to him than good, the courts will favor the accused in suppressing such evidence from being presented.

With respect to information systems, privacy deals with the collection and use or misuse of personal data. The issue of privacy deals with the right to be left alone or to be withdrawn from public view. Privacy at work creates conflict between employers wanting to monitor their employees' work activities and the employees who resent such monitoring. For example, computer workstation software can track employee keystrokes made at the PC keyboard. Another privacy issue is e-mail at work. Courts have ruled that a privileged communication does not

Privacy Management (continued)

lose its privileged character if it is communicated or transmitted electronically. E-mail is a controversial topic where many state and federal laws have been passed in this area.

Another area of privacy concern is the Internet, where a website collects personal information (e.g., cookies) when potential or actual customers are buying or selling goods or services or simply inquiring. Individuals should protect their personal information by finding out what data is stored and how it is used, not using a work e-mail system to send personal e-mails, and not sharing personal information without written consent.

Privacy Risks

Privacy risk originates from divulging or releasing personal financial information, personal medical information, trade secret formulas, and other sensitive information (e.g., salaries) about an individual to unauthorized parties.

Best practices to reduce privacy risks include (1) installing a privacy officer or its equivalent, (2) developing and communicating privacy policies that contain consequences for not complying with the policy, (3) understanding privacy laws and regulations, (4) implementing policies and procedures for controlling and releasing personal information to third parties, (5) providing employee orientation classes by the human resources department at the time of hiring, and (6) conducting privacy audits, special management reviews, and privacy self-assessment reviews periodically and proactively to reduce privacy risks.

Privacy Impact Assessments

Organizations should conduct privacy impact assessments (PIAs), which is a process for examining the risks and ramifications of collecting, maintaining, and disseminating information in identifiable form in an electronic information system. The assessment also includes the means for identifying and evaluating protections and alternative processes to mitigate the impact to privacy of collecting information in identifiable form.

Compliance with Privacy Laws and Information Protection Laws and Regulations

Many laws and regulations apply to privacy of information and information protection both inside the U.S and outside the U.S. and these include the U.S. Privacy Act of 1988, the U.S. Computer Security Act of 1987, the U.S. Fair Credit Reporting Act, the U.S. Gramm-Leach-Bliley Financial Modernization Act of 1999, the U.S. Health Insurance Portability and Accountability Act (HIPAA) of 1996, the U.S. Federal Trade Commission, the European Unions (EU's) directives, and the Europe's Organization for Economic Co-operation Development (OECD) guidelines.

IDENTIFICATION AND AUTHENTICATION

Identification is establishing the identity of a user, process, or device prior to authentication. It is the means by which a user provides a claimed identity to the system. Authentication is verifying the identity of a user, process, or device, often as a prerequisite to allowing access to system resources. It is the means of establishing the validity of this claim. Authorization is the process of defining and maintaining the allowed actions. Accountability is making individuals responsible for their actions and inactions equally, and it supports the identification, authentication, and audit requirements, non-repudiation, deterrence, fault isolation, intrusion prevention and detection, and after-action recovery and legal action. Accountability should be reflected in audit trails. Access rules support accountability.

Identification and authentication (I&A) establishes the basis for accountability and the combination of all three enables the enforcement of identity-based access control. The correct sequence of actions taking place in an access control mechanism is as follows:

Identification $\rightarrow$ Authentication $\rightarrow$ Authorization $\rightarrow$ Accountability

Note that identification comes before authentication, authorization comes after authentication, and accountability comes after authorization.

Basic I&A Mechanisms

- Knowledge-based I&A techniques (e.g., *what you know* using passwords, user IDs, usernames, pass-phrases, and personal identification numbers, PINs).

- Token-based I&A techniques (e.g., *what you have* using memory card, smart card, personal identification verification (PIV) card, hardware token, non-cryptographic key, and digital certificate).

- Physical location-based I&A techniques (e.g., *where you are* using global positioning system and wireless sensor network).

- Biometrics-based I&A techniques (e.g., *what you are* using fingerprints, iris recognition, and dynamic biometrics such as handwriting and voice recognition).

Examples of Weak and Strong I&A Methods

Examples of weak I&A methods include user IDs, PINs, and reusable (static and simple) passwords.

Examples of strong I&A methods include dynamic passwords (i.e., one-time passwords using challenge-response protocols), hardware tokens, passphrases, encrypted time-stamps, smart cards, location-based authentication, memory cards, multiple factors of authentication, biometrics, and public key infrastructure (PKI) systems such as digital signatures and digital certificates.

Principal Forms of Authentication

Static authentication reuses a specific authenticator (e.g., static password) where an attacker cannot obtain this authenticator. The strength of the authentication process is highly dependent on the difficulty of guessing or decrypting the authentication value.

Dynamic authentication uses cryptography to create one per-session authenticator and it changes with each authentication session between a claimant and verifier.

Multiple factor authentication requires two or more types of authentication techniques. It can include both static and dynamic authentication mechanisms. One example is the user of a password along with a smart card token.

Authorization Mechanisms

Local authorization is performed for each application and computer to which a user requires access. The local operating system and applications are employed to setup and maintain the authorizations for that computer or application.

Network authorization is performed at a central, authorization server, providing access to a user's account from one or more workstations on the network, and giving access to a single user account or multiple accounts. Security tokens (e.g., memory cards, flash memory, USB tokens, and smart cards) are used to allow access first to a computer and then to a network.

Single sign-on (SSO) employs a central authorization server to enable a user to authenticate once and then access all the resources that the user is authorized to use. This achieves access to multiple applications, computers, workstations, and domains operating with a variety of authentication mechanisms (e.g., a Kerberos implementation used within a heterogeneous network). The central server establishes and maintains the authorization at each application, workstation, computer, or domain that the user is allowed to access.

Authorization Mechanisms (continued)

Reduced sign-on (RSO) is a technology that allows a user to authenticate once and then access many, but not all, of the resources that the user is authorized to use.

Single log-in is similar to single sign-on, and it eliminates the need for authorization at each resource and for individual authentications to each resource.

Single log-out is closing all open programs, files, functions, sessions, and screens with one system command so no computer resource is vulnerable to attackers.

Application Authentication Techniques for System Users

Organizational users include employees and outsiders such as contractors. Users must uniquely be identified and authenticated for all accesses. Unique identification of individuals in group accounts (e.g., shared privilege accounts) may need to be considered for detailed accountability of activity. Authentication of system user identities is accomplished through the use of passwords, tokens, biometrics, or in the case of multifactor authentication, some combination thereof.

Access to systems is defined as either local or network. Local access is any access to an organizational information system by a user (or process acting on behalf of a user) where such access is obtained by direct connection without the use of a network. Network access is any access to an organizational information system by a user (or process acting on behalf of a user) where such access is obtained through a network connection. Remote access is a type of network access which involves communication through an external network (e.g., the Internet). Internal networks include local area networks, wide area networks, and virtual private networks that are under the control of the organization. For a virtual private network (VPN), the VPN is considered an internal network if the organization establishes the VPN connection between organization-controlled endpoints in a manner that does not require the organization to depend on any external networks across which the VPN transits to protect the confidentiality and integrity of information transmitted.

Application Authentication Techniques for Devices

An information system should uniquely identify and authenticate specific types of devices before establishing a connection. Devices include mobile devices (e.g., USB memory sticks, external hard disk drives, notebook/laptop computers, cellular/mobile telephones, digital cameras, audio recording devices, and personal digital assistants) and mobile ID devices (used to acquire fingerprint, face, and iris images in personal identify verification program). These devices can use either shared known information (e.g., media access control [MAC] or transmission control protocol/internet protocol [TCP/IP] addresses) for identification or authentication solution (e.g., IEEE 802. 1x and Extensible Authentication Protocol, RADIUS server with EAP-Transport Layer Security authentication, or Kerberos) to identify and authenticate devices on LANs, WANs, and wireless networks. The required strength of the device authentication mechanism is determined by the security categorization of the information system.

Identity Management and Privilege Management

Identity Management

Identity management is the comprehensive management and administration of user permissions, privileges, and profiles. It provides a single point of administration for managing the lifecycle of accounts and profiles. Identity is the distinguishing character or personality of an individual based on a set of physical and behavioral characteristics by which that individual is uniquely recognized.

Access control ensures that only authorized access to resources occurs and it helps protect confidentiality, integrity, and availability and supports the principles of legitimate use, least privilege, and separation of duties. Access control simplifies the task of maintaining enterprise network security by reducing the number of paths that attackers might use to penetrate system or network defenses. Identity and access management ensures that adequate safeguards are in place to secure authentication, authorization, and other identity and access management functions.

In the past, users typically subscribe to each system or resource separately, as needed for their job functions, by undertaking multiple systems and user registration processes. This results in users having to manage multiple security credentials (i.e., certificates, usernames, and passwords). This arrangement is tedious, expensive, time-consuming, unattractive, and frustrating for users, as it scales poorly as the number of resources increases.

Identity Management (continued)

In light of these problems, a single solution is needed that allows user management processes to be efficiently and effectively leveraged and reused across trust domains, thereby facilitating interoperability between various information systems. This solution is accomplished through an access lifecycle consisting of five phases such as provisioning, permissioning, credentialing, analyzing, and revoking, as follows:

- **Provisioning (vetting)** is a procedure for enabling end users to access and use system services. It involves creating for each user an account in a directory service and populating the account with the user-specific information needed by each service. It asks a question: What can you access?

- **Permissioning** is the authorization given to users that enables them to access specific resources on the network, such as data files, applications, printers, and scanner. User permissions also designate the type of access such as read only (view) or update only (read/write). It asks a question: What can you access?

- **Credentialing** involves a certification authority issuing a certificate after validating an applicant that is requesting the access. It asks a question: How do I know it is you?

Identity Management (continued)

- **Analyzing** is reviewing current accounts, old accounts, expired accounts for correctness and appropriateness against their access rights and permissions.

- **Revoking** includes canceling user accounts, expired accounts, illegal accounts, and decertifying users that are no longer valid, appropriate, or correct.

In addition, identity binding and identity proofing are required. Identity binding is binding of the vetted claimed identity according to the credential issuing authority, perhaps through biometrics. Identity proofing is the process by which a credential issuing authority validates sufficient information (e.g., source documents, credentials, personal identification cards, and photo IDs) and validating them to uniquely identify an individual.

Major benefits of identity and access management include providing single sign-on (SSO), reduced sign-on (RSO), and single logout (SLO) capabilities to end users for accessing multiple online systems and services. This will eliminate the need for registering end user identity information in multiple systems and services. This is supported by several basic security technologies, including cryptographic trust model, identity management standards and middleware, and a metadata model for securely exchanging information about users.

Although the SSO system is designed for user convenience, cost savings, and efficiency, it can be subjected to a single point of failure due to concentration of risks in one place and at one time. This means, if the SSO system is compromised all the connected multiple systems can be compromised too.

Privilege Management

Privilege management creates, manages, and stores the attributes and policies needed to establish criteria that can be used to decide whether an authenticated entity's request for access to some resource should be granted. Enterprise-level privilege management fits under the umbrella of enterprise-level access control. At the enterprise level, access management encompasses all the practices, policies, procedures, data, metadata, and technical and administrative mechanisms used to manage access to the resources of an organization. Access management includes access control, privilege management, and identity management, as below:

Access Management = Access Control + Privilege Management + Identity Management

Access control ensures that resources are made available only to authorized users, programs, processes, or systems by reference to rules of access that are defined by attributes and policies. In *Privilege management*, resources can be both computer-based objects (e.g., files and Web pages) and physical objects (e.g., buildings and vault safes). The entities requesting access to resources can be users (people) and processes running on a computer, application, or system. *Identity management* deals with identification and authentication, authorization, decision, and enforcement processes.

Integrating Identification and Authentication Methods

One-Factor Authentication Method

Any one of the following can represent a one-factor authentication method, which is not strong and secure:

- Something you have (e.g., photo ID, memory card, smart card, personal identity verification (PIV) card with PIN for swiping into a reader with photo, decal mounted onto a motorized vehicle, transponder mounted on a motorized vehicle used for operating an automated entry point, visitor badge without name and photo, physical key, digital certificate, hardware token, and mobile ID device).

- Something you know (e.g., password or PIN; shared or unshared combination such as electronic safe, cipher lock, PIN pad combination, and digital certificate).

- Something you are (e.g., photo ID, PIV card with PIN or photo, fingerprint identification (one-to-many), fingerprint verification (one-to-one), hand geometry (one-to-many), iris scan (one-to-many), colleague (peers and co-workers) recognition, and user (peers or security guards) recognition). Colleague and user recognition are considered as attended access.

- Somewhere you are (e.g., geodetic location such as a building, city, state, or country using a global positioning system) for employees traveling to and from the company's remote location or to and from the vendor/customer location.

Two-Factor Authentication Methods

Any one of the following can represent a two-factor authentication method. Note that there are many combinations due to use of several authentication devices:

- Combination of something you have and something you know (e.g., digital certificate where digital signature is used with PIN to unlock the private key; cryptographic hardware token with one-time password device and PIN; and PIV card with PIN or password for after-hours entry without after-hour attendant).

- Combination of something you have and something you are (e.g., verified digital or optical photo ID with drivers' license and personal identity card with photo or attended/unattended access, and hardware tokens with biometrics).

- Combination of something you know and something you are (e.g., User ID, PIN, password, and biometric sample).

- Combination of something you have, something you know, and something you are (e.g., personal identity card with attended access and PIN). It is an attended or two-person access control method using the card and the PIN, and is not the strongest two-factor authentication because of the attendant.

- Combination of (1) something you have, (2) something you have, which is the same as in (1), and (3) something you know (e.g., PIV card and digital certificate). This option illustrates that multiple instances of

---

Two-Factor Authentication Methods (continued)

the same factor (i.e., using the same "something you have" two times) is counted as one-factor, and when this is combined with "something you know" results in a two-factor authentication. However, this implementation represents a higher level of assurance than other normal instances of two-factor authentication (e.g., something you have and something you know). Two-factor is better than one-factor.

Three-Factor Authentication Methods

Combination of something you have (i.e., PKI keys or a hardware token), something you know (i.e., PIN or password), and something you are (i.e., comparing the cardholder to his biometric image stored on the biometric database and/or on the access card) represents the strongest three-factor authentication. A hardware token can be used in support of this level of assurance in logical access control. Three-factor is better than one-factor and two-factor methods.

Four-Factor Authentication Methods

Combination of something you have (i.e., card, key, or mobile ID device), something you know (i.e., PIN or password), something you are (i.e., fingerprint or signature), and something about where you are (i.e., building or company/remote location, or vendor/customer location) represents the strongest and highest form of all authentication methods.

ENCRYPTION

Foundational Concepts

Cryptography is the science of transforming data so that it is interpretable only by authorized persons, and it involves encryption and decryption methods in transforming such data. Encryption is disguising plaintext results in ciphertext (i.e., encrypted data). Decryption is the process of transforming ciphertext back into plaintext (i.e., unenrypted data). This means, original process is encryption and the reverse process is decryption. Cryptography and encryption are related in that encryption technologies are used in the cryptographic transformation of plaintext data into ciphertext data to conceal the data's original meaning to prevent it from being known or used. When interception, theft, or destruction is a likely threat to information, encryption provides an additional layer of protection.

The relationship between cryptology, cryptography, and cryptanalysis is as follows:

Cryptology = Cryptography + Cryptanalysis

Cryptology is the field that encompasses both cryptography and cryptanalysis. It is the science that deals with hidden, disguised, or encrypted communications. It embraces communications security and communication intelligence.

Cryptography relies upon two basic components: an algorithm and a key. *Algorithms* are complex mathematical formulae, and *keys* are strings of bits used in conjunction with algorithms to make the required

Foundational Concepts (continued)

transformations. For two parties to communicate, they must use the same algorithm(s) that are designed to work together. In most cases, algorithms are documented, and formulae are available to all users although the algorithm details are sometimes kept secret. Some algorithms can be used with keys of various lengths. The greater the length of the key used to encrypt the data, the more difficult it is for an unauthorized person to use a trial-and-error approach to determine the key and successfully decrypt the data.

Cryptanalysis is the steps and operations performed in converting encrypted messages into plaintext without initial knowledge of the key employed in the encryption algorithm.

Encryption or cryptography is a method of converting information to an unintelligible code. The process can then be reversed, returning the information to an understandable form. The information is encrypted (encoded) and decrypted (decoded) by what are commonly referred to as "cryptographic keys." These "keys" are actual values used by a mathematical algorithm to transform the data. The effectiveness of encryption technology is determined by the strength of the algorithm, the length of the key, and the appropriateness of the encryption system selected.

Because encryption renders information unreadable to any party without the ability to decrypt it, the information remains private and confidential, whether transmitted or stored on a computer system. Unauthorized parties will see nothing but an unorganized assembly of characters. Furthermore, encryption technology provides data integrity assurance as some algorithms offer protection against forgery and tampering. The technology's ability to protect information requires that authorized parties properly manage the encryption and decryption keys.

Methods of Encryption

In general, the encryption mechanism effectively seals the information within an object inside an additional (logical) container. Used primarily to provide confidentiality, general encryption can be used to ensure the detection of integrity violations and to otherwise hinder integrity attacks. Encryption is not absolute protection, as the sealing process may only be as safe as the encryption key. Also, encryption of an object does not in and of itself prevent damage to its integrity. However, encryption does provide an additional level of protection that must be circumvented in order to violate protection policies or to succeed at making violations without detection. Distinct advantages of encryption are (1) its flexibility of use, which are its ability to be used either as blanket protection or "on demand" and (2) its applicability to a wide array of object types. For example, digital signatures are intended to produce the desired effect as a real signature, an unforgeable proof of authenticity.

The three major methods of encryption include one-time pads, substitution ciphers, transposition ciphers, and substitutions and permutations.

Types of Encryption

There are at least three types of encryption: stream ciphers, block ciphers, and product ciphers.

Modes of Encryption

There are basically two modes of encryption in a network, namely link (online) encryption and end-to-end encryption (offline) encryption. It is possible to combine both modes of encryption.

Link encryption encrypts all of the data along a communications path (e.g., a satellite link, telephone circuit, or T1 line), including headers, addresses, and routing information. Since link encryption also encrypts routing data, communications nodes need to decrypt the data to continue routing.

Link encryption provides good protection against external threats such as traffic analysis because all data flowing on links can be encrypted, thus providing traffic-flow security. Entire packets are encrypted on exit from, and decrypted on entry to, a node. Link encryption also protects against packet sniffing and eavesdropping threats. Link encryption is easy to incorporate into network protocols.

However, link encryption has a major disadvantage: a message is encrypted and decrypted several times. If a node is compromised, all traffic flowing through that node is also compromised. A secondary disadvantage is that the individual user loses control over algorithms used. Another disadvantage is that key distribution and management is more complex.

In **end-to-end encryption**, a message is encrypted and decrypted only at endpoints, thereby largely circumventing problems that compromise intermediate nodes. However, some address information (data link headers and routing information) must be left unencrypted to allow nodes to route packets. Although data remains encrypted when being passed through a network, header and routing information remains visible. High-level network protocols must be augmented with a separate set of cryptographic protocols.

Alternatives to Encryption

Full disk, virtual disk and volume, and file/folder encryption technologies are used for storage encryption on end user devices. Many other acceptable alternative methods to encryption are available to achieve the same objective and include:

- Using backup utility programs to encrypt backups

- Using compression utility programs to encrypt archives

- Using cryptographic hashes of passwords instead of regular passwords

- Using digital rights management (DRM) software to restrict access to files

- Using a virtual machine (VM) to access and store sensitive information

Sometimes, the best way to address the problem of protecting sensitive information on end user devices is not to store the information on higher-risk devices (e.g., mobile devices or removable media) and to remove unneeded sensitive information from files or databases. If certain network traffic does not need to be encrypted or should not be encrypted, then other security controls such as IDS sensors can monitor the contents of traffic.

Alternatives to Encryption (continued)

Other alternative approaches to encryption include the following:

- Using a *thin client* solution, such as terminal services, a thin Web-based application, or a portal, to access the information, and configuring the thin client solution to prohibit file transfers of the sensitive information to the end user device.
- Configuring the organization's devices, including desktop computers, to prevent writing sensitive information to removable media (e.g., compact disks, flash drives, thumb drives, or pen drives) unless the information is properly encrypted.

Basic Types of Cryptographic Key Systems

Cryptography relies upon two basic components: an algorithm and a key. Algorithms are complex mathematical formulae and keys are strings of bits. For two parties to communicate, they must use the same algorithm(s). In some cases, they must also use the same key. Most cryptographic keys must be kept secret; sometimes algorithms are also kept secret.

There are two basic types of cryptographic key systems: secret key or private key systems (also called symmetric key systems) and public key systems (also called asymmetric key systems). Often, the two are combined to form a hybrid system to exploit the strengths of each type. Which type of key is needed depends on security requirements and the operating environment of the organization. See Exhibit 6.1 for basic types of cryptographic key systems.

Basic Types of Cryptographic Key Systems (continued)

Secret (private) key system (uses a single key, shared by parties, also called symmetric key system (e.g., DES, 3DES, and AES))
Public key system (uses two keys, both private and public, not shared by parties, also called asymmetric key system (e.g., RSA, DSS, and DH))
Hybrid key system (combines the best of secret and public key systems)

Exhibit 6.1   Basic types of cryptographic key systems

Basic Uses of Cryptography

Cryptography creates a high degree of trust in the electronic world. Cryptography is used to perform five basic security services such as confidentiality, data integrity, authentication, authorization and non-repudiation.

Digital Signatures

A digital signature is an electronic analogue of a hand written signature in that it can be used to prove to the recipient, or a third party, that the originator in fact signed the message. Digital signatures are also generated for stored data and programs to verify the integrity of data and programs at any time later.

Digital signatures authenticate the integrity of the signed data and the identity of the signatory. Digital signatures verify to a third party that data were actually signed by the generator of the signature. Digital signatures are used in electronic mail, electronic funds transfer, electronic data interchange, software distribution, data storage, and other applications requiring data integrity assurance and data origin authentication. Digital signatures can address potential threats such as spoofing, masquerading, replay attacks, and password compromise. They can-not address denial-of-service attacks.

The security of a digital signature system is dependent on maintaining the secrecy of users' private keys. Users must, therefore, guard against the unauthorized acquisition of their private keys. A digital signature can also be used to verify that information has not been altered after it was signed; this provides message integrity. A simpler alternative to a digital signature is a hash function.

Digitized Signatures

Digital signatures offer protection not available by alternative signature techniques. One such alternative is a digitized signature. Converting a visual form of a handwritten signature to an electronic image generates a digitized signature. Although a digitized signature resembles its handwritten counterpart, it does not provide the same protection as a digital signature. Digitized signatures can be forged as well as duplicated and appended to other electronic data. Digitized signatures cannot be used to determine whether information has been altered after it is signed.

Electronic Signatures

An electronic signature is a cryptographic mechanism that performs a similar function to a handwritten signature. It is used to verify the origin and contents of a message.

Electronic signatures are very difficult to forge, although handwritten signatures are easily forged. In general, electronic signatures have received the same legal status as that of written signatures. Cryptography can provide a means of linking a document with a particular person, as is done with a written signature. If a cryptographic key is compromised due to social engineering attack, then the electronic originator of a message may not be the same as the owner of the key. Trickery and coercion are problems for both electronic and handwritten signatures (i.e., social engineering attacks).

Digital Certificates

Digital certificates are basically containers for public keys and act as a means of electronic identification. The certificate and public keys are public documents that, in principle, anyone can possess. An associated private key, possessed only by the entity to which the certificate was issued, is used as a means of binding the certification to that entity. Users not possessing this private key cannot use the certificate as a means of authentication. Entities can prove their possession of the private key by digitally signing known data or by demonstrating knowledge of a secret exchanged using public-key cryptographic methods. A digital certificate is a password-protected and encrypted file. It should not contain any owner-related information that changes frequently. In practice, anyone can generate public-private key pairs and digital certificates; consequently, it is necessary to determine whether the certificate holder is trustworthy.

Cryptographic Mechanisms to Protect Data-at-Rest

The scope of data-at-rest, data-in-storage, or data-on-a-hard-drive includes protecting the confidentiality, integrity, and availability of data residing on servers, workstations, computers, storage/disk arrays (e.g., RAID), network attached storage appliances, disk drives, tape drives, and removable media such as flash drives, thumb drives, and pen drives.

The need for encrypting the storage media is increasing, and selecting an encryption algorithm with the right strength is important to protect the media from internal and external attacks. Use of encryption algorithms (e.g., DES and 3DES) and hashing algorithms (e.g., MD5 and SHA-1) are considered to be no longer secure. Encrypting the storage media with AES-256 and providing end-to-end security is advised due to its strong and secure algorithm. When using the AES-256, do not store the encryption keys in clear-text and leave them in an open operating system because the keys can be compromised.

Cryptographic mechanisms to protect data at rest include storage encryption technologies such as full (whole) disk encryption, virtual disk encryption, volume encryption, file encryption, and/or folder encryption. Information stored on end-user devices can be encrypted in many ways. For example, an application that accesses sensitive information could be responsible for encrypting that information. Applications such as backup programs might also offer encryption options. Another method for protecting files is digital rights management software.

Technologies such as firewalls, intrusion prevention systems, and virtual private networks seek to secure data by protecting the perimeter of the network. Unfortunately, these technologies do not adequately secure data in storage, as data is still stored in clear text, thus open to a wide range of internal and external attacks.

Cryptographic Mechanisms to Protect Data-at-Rest (continued)

Encrypting data-at-rest on tape and disk will mitigate such attacks and secure data while maintaining the current service levels.

Adding encryption to data-at-rest poses some challenges such as changing the application code, data compression problems, slow response time, user unfriendliness, complexity, and additional cost to storage systems. The other challenge includes the impact of encryption on cryptographic key management, such as the following:

- Keys can be lost resulting in loss of data
- Keys need to be kept secure but should be available
- Keys have to be retained until the data is retained
- Keys need to be created, changed, or destroyed
- Keys need to be managed without excessive operational and administrative complexity

Cryptographic Mechanisms to Protect Data-at-Rest (continued)

Storage encryption can be applied as a part of data-at-rest solution in several places, as follows:

- Encryption in the application

- Encryption in the file system or operating system

- Encryption in the device driver or network interface

- Encryption on the network

- Encryption in the storage controller

- Encryption in the storage device using a single-factor authentication (e.g., password, user ID, or, hardware token) and multiple-factor authentication (e.g., password, user ID, smart card, or cryptographic token)

Cryptographic Mechanisms to Protect Data-in-Transit

The scope of data-in-transit, data-in-flight, or data-on-the-wire includes protecting the confidentiality, integrity, and availability of data as they are transferred across the storage network, the LAN, and the WAN.

Cryptographic mechanisms in controlling data in transit through remote access to an information system include (1) using encryption with a strong key in relation to the security categorization of the information, (2) restricting execution of privileged commands, (3) using standard bulk or session layer encryption such as Secure Shell (SSH) and virtual private networks (VPNs) with blocking mode enabled, (4) routing all remote accesses through a limited number of managed access control points, and (5) not using Bluetooth and peer-to-peer networking protocols because they are less secure.

Alternatives to Cryptography

Steganography

Steganography deals with hiding messages and obscuring who is sending or receiving them. Steganography (concealed writing) is the art and science of writing hidden messages in such a way that no one, apart from the sender and intended recipient, suspects the existence of the message, a form of security through obscurity.

Steganography includes the concealment of information within computer files. In digital steganography, electronic communications may include steganographic coding inside of a transport layer, such as a document file, image file, program or protocol.

The advantage of steganography, over cryptography alone, is that messages do not attract attention to themselves. Plainly visible encrypted messages—no matter how unbreakable—will arouse suspicion, and may be incriminating in countries where encryption is illegal. Therefore, whereas cryptography protects the contents of a message, steganography can be said to protect both messages and communicating parties. Media files are ideal for steganographic transmission because of their large size and changes are so subtle that someone not specifically looking for it is unlikely to notice it.

Digital Watermarking

Digital watermarking is a type of marking that embeds copyright information about the copyright owner. Digital watermarking is the process of irreversibly embedding information into a digital signal.

Steganography is sometimes applied in digital watermarking, where two parties communicate a secret message embedded in the digital signal. Annotation of digital photographs with descriptive information is another application of invisible watermarking. While some file formats for digital media can contain additional information called metadata, digital watermarking is distinct in that the data is carried in the signal itself.

A digital watermark is called robust with respect to transformations if the embedded information can reliably be detected from the marked signal even if degraded by any number of transformations. Typical image degradations are JPEG compression, rotation, cropping, additive noise and quantization. For video content temporal modifications and MPEG compression are often added to this list.

A digital watermark is called imperceptible if the cover signal and marked signal are indistinguishable with respect to an appropriate perceptual metric. In general it is easy to create robust or imperceptible watermarks, but the creation of robust and imperceptible watermarks has proven to be quite challenging. Robust and imperceptible watermarks have been proposed as a tool for the protection of digital content, for example as an embedded 'no-copy-allowed' flag in professional video content.

Reversible Data Hiding

Reversible data hiding is a technique, which enables images to be authenticated and then restored to their original form by removing the watermark and replacing the image data, which had been overwritten. This would make the images acceptable for legal purposes.

Summary of Encryption Methods

- In link encryption, all data including addresses flowing on links can be encrypted.
- In end-to-end encryption, a message is encrypted and decrypted only at endpoints by hardware and software techniques.
- Bulk (trunk) encryption is simultaneous encryption of all channels of a multi-channel telecommunications trunk. No bulk encryption is needed when a public key cryptographic keys is used to distribute keys since the keys are generally short.
- Session encryption is used to encrypt data between applications and end users. It is effective in preventing an eavesdropping attack from remote access to firewalls. A secure server supports server authentication and session key encryption.
- Stream encryption encrypts and decrypts arbitrarily sized messages.
- Line encryption protects data in transfer, which can be used to achieve confidentiality.
- File encryption protects data in storage. It is the process of encrypting individual files on a storage medium and permitting access to the encrypted data only after proper authentication is provided.
- Field-level encryption is stronger than file-, record-, and packet-level encryption.
- + Folder encryption is the process of encrypting individual folders on a storage medium and permitting access to the encrypted files within the folders only after proper authentication is provided.

Summary of Encryption Methods (continued)

- Full (whole) disk encryption is the process of encrypting all the data on the hard drive used to boot a computer, including the computer's operating system, and permitting access to the data only after successful authentication with the full disk encryption product is made.

- Virtual disk encryption is the process of encrypting a container, which can hold many files and folders, and permitting access to the data within a container only after proper authentication is provided.

- Volume encryption is the process of encrypting an entire volume and permitting access to the data on the volume only after proper authentication is provided.

- Multiple (e.g., triple) encryption is stronger than single encryption, but costs may increase and system performance may decrease.

- NULL encryption is used when integrity protection is required for an (Internet Protocol security (IPsec) system, not for confidentiality.

- Super-encryption is a process of encrypting information that is already encrypted. It occurs when a message, encrypted offline, is transmitted over a secured, online circuit, or when information encrypted by the originator is multiplexed onto a communications trunks, which is then bulk encrypted. In other words, super-encryption is encryption plus encryption.

APPLICATION DEVELOPMENT

Traditional Approaches to Develop or Acquire Systems

Two approaches or methodologies exist to develop or to acquire information systems or application systems: traditional approaches and alternative approaches. The traditional approach requires a systematic and disciplined work using a system development life cycle (SDLC) methodology with phases to ensure consistency and quality of work. Five phases of SDLC include planning/initiation, development/acquisition, implementation/ assessment, operation/maintenance, and disposal/decommissioning. Usually, the traditional approach combined with the SDLC methodology is used in developing custom software.

Phase 1: Planning/Initiation. *System-related activities* include understanding functional user's request for a new system; conducting feasibility study (i.e., costs and benefits); performing high-level needs assessment; doing a preliminary risk assessment; and using decision tables, flowcharts, data-flow diagrams, and finite-state-machine models to express user needs and system requirements.

Security-related activities include developing security-planning document, sensitivity assessment, and security assurance (cost driver). The security-planning document contains several elements, such as security awareness and training plans, rules of behavior, risk assessment, configuration management plan, contingency plan, incident response plan, system interconnection agreements, security tests and evaluation

Traditional Approaches to Develop or Acquire Systems (continued)

results, and plan of actions and milestones. However, the security-planning document does not contain request for proposal, vendor contract plans, and statement of work, as they are related to project management, not to security management.

Phase 2: Development/Acquisition. System-related activities include performing an in-depth analysis of user needs; performing general and detailed system design work; developing computer programs; conducting unit and system testing; planning desk reviews, mutation analysis, sensitivity analysis for analyzing changes, boundary-value analysis, and error seeding methods during testing; performing quality assurance (QA) and quality control (QC) reviews; and doing a detailed risk assessment. During this phase, the system is designed, purchased, programmed, developed, or otherwise constructed.

Security-related activities include (1) determining security features, controls, assurances, and operational practices, (2) incorporating these security requirements into security design specifications, (3) actually building or buying these security requirements into the system, (4) conducting design reviews through walkthroughs, (5) preparing test documents with test cases and test procedures with formal specific programming languages, and (6) conducting certification and accreditation activities. Possible security threats or vulnerabilities that should be considered during this phase include Trojan horses, incorrect/incomplete program code, poorly functioning software development tools, manipulation of program code, and malicious insiders.

Traditional Approaches to Develop or Acquire Systems (continued)

Phase 3: Implementation/assessment. *System-related activities* include providing training to end-users and system-users; conducting acceptance testing for end users; converting old system into new system; developing instruction manuals for system use; and performing QA and quality control QC reviews. After acceptance testing and conversion, the system is installed or fielded with a formal authorization from management to put into production status.

Security-related activities include installing or turning on security controls, performing security tests (e.g., functional tests, penetration tests), and security evaluation report and accreditation statement.

Phase 4: Operation/Maintenance. *System-related activities* include doing production operations and support work, performing a post-implementation review; undertaking system maintenance and modification work; and monitoring the system's performance. During this phase, the system is fully operational and doing its work as intended and planned. The system is frequently modified by the addition of new hardware and software and by new functional requirements. Configuration management process is implemented with baselines and change controls.

Security-related activities include security operations and administration (e.g., performing backups, manag-ing cryptographic keys, setting user access accounts, and updating security software), operational assurance (e.g., conducting system audits and continuous monitoring), and periodic reaccreditation when security is insuf-ficient and when the changes made are significant.

Traditional Approaches to Develop or Acquire Systems (continued)

Phase 5: Disposal/decommissioning. System-related activities include system retirement or replacement plans and media sanitization procedures. The computer system is disposed of (terminated) once the transition to a new computer system is completed.

Security-related activities include (1) disposition of information (i.e., data sanitization), hardware, and software, (2) moving information to archives after considering legal and audit requirements for records retention and the method of retrieving the information in the future, (3) disposition of software after considering licensing terms and agreements (site-specific) with the developer, if the agreement prevents the software from being transferred, and (4) taking appropriate steps to ensure secure long-term storage of cryptographic keys and for the future use of data if the data has been encrypted.

Some organizations may not have software disposal or decommissioning policies and procedures while others might have been overlooked. Software acquirers' should ensure that such policies and procedures are developed and followed to ensure the safe and secure disposal or decommissioning of software, along with ensuring data are destroyed or migrated safely and securely. When a software-intensive system is retired or replaced, the data must be migrated by validated means to the new software-intensive system or unreadable before disposal. Note that encrypted data may not be adequately protected if it is weakly encrypted. *Simply stated, residual data is residual risk.*

Another consideration in this phase is storage devices used in virtualization process. Before a device using virtualization process permanently leaves an organization (such as when a leased server's lease expires or when

Traditional Approaches to Develop or Acquire Systems (continued)

an obsolete PC is being recycled), the organization should remove any sensitive data from the host. Data may also need to be wiped if an organization provides "loaner" devices to teleworkers, particularly for travel. Note that sensitive data may be found nearly anywhere on a device because of the nature of virtualization. Because of this, an organization should strongly consider erasing all storage devices completely.

Another related concern in this phase is removing or destroying any sensitive data from the system basic input output system (BIOS) to reduce the chances of accidental data leakage. The configuration baseline should be reset to the manufacturer's default profile; in particular, sensitive settings such as passwords should be deleted from the system and cryptographic keys should also be removed from the key store.

Software Acquisition Methodology

Some organizations develop all application systems in-house while others develop only unique, one-of-a-kind systems in-house. These are often supplemented by acquiring software packages for normal, standard, or common systems from software vendors.

Software Package Acquisition Guidelines

- Develop software requirements.

- Establish software selection criteria.

- Identify several suitable software packages.

- Develop request for proposal document.

- Assess software packages for user functions.

- Assess software vendors and conduct outside user survey.

- Assess software packages for system/technical functions to assure testability, maintainability, and portability.

- Assess vendor-supplied documentation.

- Assess software packages for security, audit, and control features.

- Perform a cost-benefit analysis.

- Select a software package.

- Develop a software contract.

Software Package Modification Alternatives

User organizations have three alternatives regarding software adaptation or modification:

1. Modify/change the vendor-supplied basic software.

2. Adapt/change user and IS organization's manual and/or automated operating methods and procedures.

3. A combination of the above.

Models in Information System Development

Several models exist to either develop or acquire information systems, and each model may be suitable to a particular environment. In practice, a combination of these models may be deployed considering the time, cost, and skills constraints and tradeoffs.

- The *waterfall model* takes a linear, sequential view of the software engineering process, similar to a SDLC model.

- The *rapid application development (RAD) model* is quite opposite to the waterfall model. That is, it is good when requirements are not fully understood by both parties. It uses integrated computer-aided software engineering (I-CASE) tools and fourth general programming languages (4GLs) to quickly prototype an information system. Often, software is reused in RAD.

- Although the *incremental development model* and the evolutionary development models are better than the waterfall model, they are not as good as rapid prototyping in terms of bringing the operational viewpoint to the requirements specification. Successive versions of the system are developed reflecting constrained technology or resources.

- The *spiral model* is another type of evolutionary model. It has been developed to provide the best feature of both the classic life cycle approach and prototyping.

Models in Information System Development (continued)

- The *rapid prototyping model* is a process that enables the developer to create a model of the software built in an evolutionary manner. Rapid prototyping uses special software and special output device to create prototype to design and test a system in three dimensions.

- The *object-oriented development model* is applied once the design model has been created, the software developer browses a library, or repository that contains existing program components to determine if any of the components can be used in the design at hand. If reusable components are found, they are used as building blocks to construct a prototype of the software.

Tools for Information Systems Development

Prototyping

Definition of software requirements is the biggest and most troublesome area to handle and control for functional users, IT staff, and auditors. Yet, it is the foundation upon which the entire applications software system is built. It is a very simple concept to grasp. If software requirements are incompletely defined and documented, the final product will be incomplete.

Prototyping is one way of dealing with the uncertainty, impreciseness, inconsistency, difficulty, and ambiguity involved in defining software requirements and design work. User requirements are not frozen; in fact, changing of user mind is welcomed. Prototyping assures that system requirements are adequately defined and correct through actual user experience in using the model. Prototyping also addresses the question of timely delivery of completed systems. It is especially useful to develop unstructured application systems.

How Prototyping is Done

A prototyped system is developed to address partial or full system functions, or to build the final (real) system to operate in a production environment.

Using Software Prototyping Results

- Discard the prototype.

- Move the prototype into production operations as is.

- Use the prototype as a starting point for the full-scale design work.

Cleanroom Software Engineering

The primary goal of software quality assurance is to enhance the quality of software. Cleanroom process or cleanroom software engineering, is deployed to ensure software quality. With cleanroom process, programmers do not compile their code. Instead they spend more time on design, using a "box structure" method, and on analyzing their own work. When the programmers are confident of their work, it is submitted to another group, who then compiles and tests the code. Cleanroom experiments have shown that a lower error rate in the finished software product and an increase in productivity across a system's life cycle are possible.

Cleanroom software engineering, which is a concept borrowed from cleanroom hardware engineering, is the result of combined effect of statistical quality control and proof-of-correctness principles. The first priority of the cleanroom process is defect prevention, not defect removal with the understanding that any defects not prevented should be removed. This priority is achieved through human verification procedures to assure proof of correctness, instead of program debugging to prepare the software for system test. The next priority is to provide quality assurance, which is measured in terms of mean-time-to-failure (MTTF). Both of these priorities eventually reflect in lowering the number of defects per thousand lines of code before the first executable tests are conducted.

Computer-Aided Software Engineering

Computer-aided software engineering (CASE) tools, compilers, and assemblers are used to expedite and improve the productivity of software developers' work. The CASE tools provide a 4GL or application generator for fast code writing, flowcharting, data-flow diagramming, data-dictionary facility, and word-processing in order to develop and document the new software. The CASE tools are used in prototyping the system by developing online screens and reports for the end user to view and change, as needed. Modern CASE tools are often called integrated CASE (I-CASE) tools due to integration of several tools.

Alternative Approaches to Develop or Acquire Software

- *Commercial-off-the shelf* (COTS) is a term for proprietary software products (including software appliances) that are ready-made and available for sale to customers

- *Custom software* is developed for either a specific organization or function that differs from other already available software such as COTS. It is generally not targeted to the mass market but is usually created for interested organizations.

- *Modifiable-off-the shelf* (MOTS) software is typically a COTS product whose source code can be modified. The product may be customized by the purchaser, by the vendor, or by another party to meet the requirements of the customer.

- *Government-off-the shelf* (GOTS) software products are typically developed by the internal IT staff of a specific government agency and can be used by other agencies. GOTS can sometimes be developed by an external contractor, but with funding and product specification from the agency.

- *Mobile code software* modules are obtained from remote systems, transferred across a network, and then downloaded and executed on local systems without explicit installation or execution by the recipient. Mobile code is risky because it is passed from one system to another and is used to describe applets within Web browsers.

- *Freeware* is copyrighted software that is available for use free of charge for an unlimited time.

Alternative Approaches to Develop or Acquire Software (continued)

- *Shareware* is a marketing method for commercial software, whereby a trial version is distributed in advance and without payment, as is common for proprietary software. Shareware software is typically obtained free of charge and is also known as "try before you buy," demo-ware, and trial-ware. Although it is typically obtained free of charge, a payment is often required once a set period of time has elapsed after installation.

- *Open-source software* is computer software whose source code is available under a copyright license that permits users to study, change, and improve the software, as well as to redistribute it in modified or unmodified form. Usually, it is not obtained by a contract but a fee may be charged for use.

Possible risks from the use of open-source software can include (1) not knowing whether the software is original source or modified version because the modified software can introduce malicious code or other vulnerabilities, (2) not knowing whether the software infringes upon any copyright or patent, (3) not knowing whether the software validates (e.g., filter with whitelisting) inputs from untrusted sources before being used, (4) not knowing whether the software is designed to execute within a constrained execution environment (e.g., virtual machine, sandbox, chroot jail, single-purpose pseudo-user, and system isolation), (5) not knowing whether the software was measured or assessed for its resistance to identified relevant attack patterns, (6) not knowing whether the software was subjected to thorough security testing with results posted, (7) not knowing whether patches are distributed or whether patches can be uninstalled, and (8) not knowing whether the vendor practices version management.

Alternative Approaches to Develop or Acquire Software (continued)

- *Embedded software* is part of a larger physical system and performs some of the requirements of that system (e.g., software used in an automobile, rapid transit system, traffic control system, or aircraft system) and may or may not provide an interface with the user. Embedded software is internally built within the physical system.

- *Integrated software* results from when there is a prime contractor with multiple subcontractors, as in a supply-chain environment. Each subcontractor provides a specific piece of software product and /or service for the software-intensive system. The prime contractor is responsible for integrating all the pieces into a whole software-intensive system or he may hire a separate contractor to integrate it for him. The supply-chain environment can increase security risks to user organizations due to multiple contractors and sub-contractors involved since they can bring new risks to the system.

- If a supplier is acting as an *application service provider* (ASP) and offering to provide software as a service, instead of a standalone software package product, software acquirers should consider the governance of these services. Here, governance refers to the computer programs, processes, and procedures that the ASP organization puts in place to ensure that things are done right in accordance with best practices and principles. The ASP should provide appropriate access controls, audit, monitoring, and alerting activities. Note that with the ASP, a user organization is acquiring services, not products.

Alternative Approaches to Develop or Acquire Software (continued)

When considering the above alternative approaches to software, application owners and acquirers should seek to reduce or manage the risks because each alternative can introduce its own, new risks. Applying due care principles and performing due diligence reviews are highly recommended here to reduce such risks.

Specifically, application owners and acquirers should perform the following analysis to reduce risks:

- Evaluate alternatives for treatment of risks (i.e. accept, mitigate, avoid, transfer, or share with a third-party supplier)
- Identify protection strategies (i.e., security objectives and security controls) that reduce risks to levels within acceptable tolerance
- Identify potential tradeoffs between decreased risks, increased costs, and decreased operational effective-ness and efficiency
- Identify approaches for managing residual risks that remain after protection strategies are adopted

Due Care and Due Diligence Reviews in Software Development and Acquisition

Regardless of the software alternative selected, due care and due diligence reviews are required because each software source can introduce its own risks. This is because there are many parties involved (e.g., integrators, suppliers, prime contractors, and subcontractors) in the development, maintenance, and distribution of software chain, which is a risky to manage.

Due care means reasonable care that promotes the common good. It is maintaining minimal and customary practices, and/or following the best practices. It is the responsibility that managers and their organizations have a duty to provide for information security to ensure that the type of control, the cost of control, and the deployment of control are appropriate for the system being managed. Another related concept of due care is good faith, which means showing "honesty in fact" and "honesty in intent." Both due care and due diligence are similar to the "prudent man" concept.

Due diligence requires organizations to develop and implement an effective system of controls, policies, and procedures to prevent and detect violation of policies and laws. It requires that the organization has taken minimum and necessary steps in its power and authority to prevent and detect violation of policies and laws. In other words, due diligence is the care that a reasonable person exercises under the circumstances to avoid harm to other persons or to their property. Due diligence is another way of saying due care. Both due care and due diligence are similar to the "prudent man" concept. Note that due-diligence defense is available to a defendant in a legal case in that the defendant is not liable when he follows all the prescribed legal procedures.

Due Care and Due Diligence Reviews in Software Development and Acquisition (continued)

Some examples of applications of due diligence reviews include:

- When an information security team is reviewing policies, procedures, and controls during acquisition and divestiture of security-related products and services, including initial screening of vendors and suppliers, performing make or buy or lease or purchase analysis, understanding contracts, and negotiating with suppliers and contractors.

- When a software acquirer is requiring potential software suppliers to be evaluated in a qualitative and quantitative manner to ensure software quality prior to contract negotiations in order to make a go/no-go decision in selecting suppliers

- When auditing suppliers that provide computer products and services for regulated pharmaceutical operations

- When software suppliers claiming mature process capabilities prove their software assurance practices

- When selecting the appropriate set of security controls to adequately mitigate risk and in protecting the confidentiality, integrity, and availability of data/information and information systems

- When a user organization decided to outsource media sanitization work with a contractual agreement

- When using encryption mechanisms for Web sessions whenever a rented application requires the confidentiality of application interactions with other applications, data transfers, and data storages

Software Assurance, Safety, Security, and Quality

Software security is directly related to software assurance, software safety, and quality assurance. Critical software is software the failure of which could have an impact on security, safety, privacy, or could cause large financial loss, property loss, human loss, or social loss. It is also referred to as high consequence software and software-intensive system. A software-intensive system is a system in which the majority of components are implemented in or by software and the functional objectives are achieved through software components.

Security controls over the critical software include defensive design and programming techniques; robust identity and authentication methods; resilient/robust/trustworthy software; agile defenses to protect supply chain software and advanced persistent threats using boundary protection mechanisms and information system resilience concepts; built-in-software defenses; defense-in-depth strategies; defense-in-breadth strategies; defense-in-technology strategies; and defense-in-time strategies.

The scope of a secure software environment consists of software safety and software quality because security of an information system depends on both safety and quality elements of the system. An information system should have the right amounts security controls, software safety functions, and software quality features.

Software Assurance

Software assurance is related to reducing the level of uncertainty in software in terms of estimation, prediction, information, inference, or achievement of a specific goal. Such a reduction can provide an improved basis for justified confidence in software.

Contrast software assurance to information assurance where the latter is related to measures that protect and defend information and information systems by ensuring their availability, integrity, authentication, confidentiality, and non-repudiation. These measures include providing for restoration of information systems by incorporating protection, detection, and reaction capabilities.

Software Safety

Software safety is important, since lack of safety considerations in a computer-based application system can cause danger or injury to people, damage to equipment and property. It could also create financial or other loss to people using the system or people affected by the system. For example, an incorrectly programmed and incompletely tested medical diagnostic and treatment prescription system could kill a patient or injure people receiving the treatment. Another example is a process control system in a pharmaceutical company where drugs are incorrectly formulated by a computer system could kill or injure patients due to errors in software. Similarly, incorrect and obsolete documentation, especially after a program change was made, could lead to improperly functioning software, loss of life, failed missions, and lost time.

Software needs to be developed using specific software development and software assurance processes to protect against or mitigate failure of the software. A complete software safety standard references other standards that address these mechanisms and includes a software safety policy identifying required functionality to protect against or mitigate failure.

As software is included in more and more critical systems (e.g., medical devices, nuclear power plants, and transportation systems) the need for software safety programs becomes crucial. These software safety programs should consist of not only software safety analyses, but methodologies that assist in the assurance of developing quality software.

Software safety should not be confused with software reliability. Reliability is the ability of a system to perform its required functions under stated conditions for a specified period of time. Safety is the probability that conditions

Software Safety (continued)

(hazards) that can lead to a mishap do not occur, whether or not the intended function is performed. Reliability concerns all possible software errors, while software safety is concerned only with those errors that cause actual system hazards. Software safety and software reliability are part of software quality. Quality is the degree to which a system meets specified requirements and customer or user needs or expectations.

Software Quality Assurance

Software quality assurance (SQA) is a planned systematic pattern for all actions necessary to provide adequate confidence that the product, or process by which the product is developed, conforms to established requirements.

The primary *goal* of SQA is to enhance the quality of software. The thrust of SQA is product of service assurance. Quality of process is related to the quality of product. New software quality assurance focuses on evaluating the processes by which products are developed or manufactured.

The major *objectives* of the SQA process are to ensure that the software development and software assurance processes comply with software assurance plans and standards, and to recommend process improvements. The process uses the system requirements, and information about the purpose and criticality of the software to evaluate the outputs of the software development and software assurance processes. It begins before the software requirements process and ends when its objectives have been met. A software quality assurance plan and review/audit reports are produced during the SQA process.

Software Testing Objectives, Approaches, Methods, and Controls

Several *testing objectives* exist to test either developed or acquired information systems, and each objective may be suitable to a specific program, module, subsystem, or the entire system. In practice, compatible test objectives should be combined after considering the time, cost, and skills constraints (e.g., recovery test, security test, and configuration test). Testing is important to ensure that security-related functions and business-related functions work correctly.

Several *testing approaches* include big-bang, top-down, bottom-up, and sandwich. The big-bang testing approach puts all the units or modules together at once, with no stubs or drivers. In it, all the program units are compiled and tested at once. Top-down testing approach uses stubs. The actual code for lower level units is replaced by a stub, which is a throwaway code that takes the place of the actual code. Bottom-up testing approach uses drivers. Units at higher levels are replaced by drivers that emulate the procedure calls. Drivers are also a form of throwaway code. Sandwich testing approach uses a combination of top-down (stubs) and bottom-up (drivers) approaches.

Several *testing methods* are available to test computer programs at detailed level each with a different focus. The following is a list of specific and detailed application software testing methods with their objectives:

- **Resiliency test**: To measure durability of a system in withstanding system failures.

- **Conformance test:** To determine if a product satisfies the criteria specified in standard documents.

- **Conversion test**: To determine whether old data files and record balances are carried forward accurately, completely, and properly to the new system.

Software Testing Objectives, Approaches, Methods, and Controls (continued)

- **Interface test:** To demonstrate that all systems work in concert. Input/output description errors are detected in the interface testing phase.

- **Recovery test:** To determine whether the system can function normally after a system failure, error, or other malfunction and to determine the ability to operate within the fallback and recovery structure.

- **Security test:** To determine whether unauthorized people can use computer resources using red team and blue team testing approaches.

- **Configuration test:** To verify that the product can be installed and operated in different hardware and software environments without using vendor default settings.

- **Integration test:** To test a group of programs to see that a transaction or data passes between programs. It is least understood by software developers and end users due to lack of specification documents and the variety of testing methods used. A formal change control mechanism should start after completion of integration test.

- **Regression test:** To verify that changes do not introduce new errors. A significant amount of repetition of testing occurs by design.

- **Stress test:** To verify boundary conditions of a program.

Software Testing Objectives, Approaches, Methods, and Controls (continued)

- **Parallel test**: To verify test results, two systems are compared with each other.

- **Performance test**: To measure resources required (e.g., memory and disk) and to determine online system response time and batch job throughput.

- **Interoperability test:** To ensure that two or more communications products (e.g., hosts or routers) can interwork and exchange data.

- **Network security test:** To ensure that network protection devices (e.g., firewalls and intrusion detection systems) selectively block packet traffic based on application system configurations.

- **Production acceptance test**: To test operational preparedness of a new system prior to moving from the testing to production environment. This performed by IT production staff.

- **Pilot test**: To test a new system in one department or division at a time until enough experience is gained prior to launching an all out implementation throughout the organization.

- **Program unit/module test**: To test individual programs, modules, subroutines, or sub-programs to verify their functionality.

Software Testing Objectives, Approaches, Methods, and Controls (continued)

- **Systems test**: To test the entire system to prove the validity of the software requirements definition and design specifications including its interfaces. It should include a representative sample of data for both valid and invalid conditions using test data or copies of live data not real live data.

- **User acceptance test**: To test software functions and features, to determine if the system meets business needs and user needs, and to see if the system was developed according to end user requirements. The end user must accept the system before moving it into the production environment. This performed functional user staff.

- **Load/volume test**: To test whether simultaneous users can overload the system.

- **Concurrency test**: To test whether multiple users can create system deadlocks or damage each other's work.

- **Quality assurance test**: To make sure the software product fails.

- **Function test**: To verify that each required capability and system operation is implemented correctly.

- **End-to-end test**: To verify that a defined set of interrelated systems, which collectively support an organizational core business area or function, interoperate as intended in an operational environment (either actual or simulated). This test is conducted extensively when an internal system exchanges data with an external system.

Software Testing Objectives, Approaches, Methods, and Controls (continued)

In addition, five broad testing methods include black box testing, gray box testing, white box testing, and independent testing, as discussed below.

Black box testing is a basic test methodology that assumes no knowledge of the internal structure and implementation detail of the assessment object. It examines the software from the user's viewpoint and determines if the data are processed according to the specifications, and it does not consider implementation details. It verifies that software functions are performed correctly and that advertised security mechanisms are tested under operational conditions. It focuses on the external behavior of a system and uses the system's functional specifications to generate test cases. It ensures that the system does what it is supposed to do and does not do what it is not supposed to do. It is also known as generalized testing or functional testing, and should be combined with white box testing for maximum benefit because neither one by itself does a thorough testing job. Black box testing is functional analysis of a system.

Gray box testing is a test methodology that assumes some knowledge of the internal structure and implementation detail of the assessment object. It is also known as focused testing.

White box testing is a test methodology that assumes explicit and substantial knowledge of the internal structure and implementation detail of the assessment object. It focuses on the internal behavior of a system (program structure and logic) and uses the code itself to generate test cases. The degree of coverage is used as a measure

Software Testing Objectives, Approaches, Methods, and Controls (continued)

of the completeness of the test cases and test effort. White box testing is performed at individual components level, such as program or module, but not at the entire system level. It is also known as detailed testing or logic testing, and should be combined with black box testing for maximum benefit because neither one by itself does a thorough testing job. White box testing is structured testing since it focuses on structural analysis of a system and as such it is also called glass-box testing because the tester can see the inside of a system through a glass. *Independent testing* is conducted by an independent accredited software testing organization as per the ISO/IEC 17025 standard to verify that it meets both functional requirements and software quality assurance requirements. The testing organization can use either a white box or black box scenario depending on the need.

Software testing controls bring discipline and structure to the testing process. The following are examples of controls to be exercised during application software testing:

- Activity logs, incident reports, and software versioning are the controls used during testing

- There is a tendency to compress system initiation, requirements definition, design, programming, and training activities. However, the testing activities should not be compressed for quality assurance and security reasons.

- The correct sequence of tests is unit test, integration test, system test, and acceptance test

- The correct sequence of test tasks is prepare, execute, and delete

Software Reviews, Inspections, Traceability Analysis, and Walkthroughs

Reviews, inspections, traceability analysis, and walkthroughs are examples of quality assurance (QA) and quality control (QC) tools used during the SDLC to ensure a safe, secure, and quality product.

Reviews are conducted in a meeting at which the requirements, design, code, or other products of software development project are presented to the user, sponsor, or other interested parties for comment and approval, often as a prerequisite for concluding a g\iven phase of the software development process. Reviews are more formal than walkthroughs.

Inspections are evaluation techniques in which software requirements, design, code, or other products are examined by a person or group other than the author to detect faults, violations of development standards, and other problems. The type of errors detected in inspections includes incomplete requirements errors, infeasible requirements errors, and conflicting requirements errors. Inspections are more formal than walkthroughs.

Traceability analysis is the process of verifying that each specified requirement has been implemented in the design or code, that all aspects of the design or code has their basis in the specified requirements, and that testing produces results that are compatible with the specified requirements. Traceability analysis is more formal than walkthroughs.

Software Reviews, Inspections, Traceability Analysis, and Walkthroughs (continued)

A **walkthrough** is an evaluation technique in which a designer or programmer leads one or more other members of the development team through a segment of design or code, while the other members ask questions and make comments about technique, style, and identify possible errors, violations of development standards, and other problems. Walkthroughs are similar to reviews, but are less formal.

Categories of Malware Inserted During Software Development and Maintenance Work

Malware is referred to as malicious software or malicious code, which is designed to deny, destroy, modify, or impede the software's logic, configuration settings, data, or program library routines. Malware can be inserted during software's development, preparation for distribution, deployment, installation, and or update. It can be planted manually or through automated means and it can also be inserted during a system's operation. Regardless of when in the software lifecycle the malware is embedded, it effectively becomes part of the software and can present substantial dangers and risks. Malware has become the most significant external threat to most systems, causing widespread damage and disruption, and necessitating extensive recovery efforts within user organizations.

There are several ways in which malware is likely to be inserted during software development or maintenance through back door or trapdoor, time bomb, logic bomb, and software holes. This malware is introduced into a system due to unnoticed, forgotten, or neglected functions, or when unnecessary functions are disregarded, and can be discovered through table-top reviews, periodic assessments, war-dialing, war-driving, wireless-scanning, and penetration testing. Not having a source code escrow is a risk by itself.

Categories of Malware Planted on Operational Systems

There are several ways in which malware is likely to be planted on operational systems, including viruses, worms, Easter egg viruses, Trojan horses, zombies, cross-site scripts, botnets, rootkits, cookies, adware, spyware, active content, electronic dumpster diving, and buffer overflow.

Categories of Non-Malware Deployed on Operational Systems

Sometimes malware is combined with non-malware deceptive practices such as social engineering techniques to accomplish complex attacks on unsuspecting users. Three major categories of social engineering attacks include pre-texting, spamming, phishing, or pharming.

Program Change Management and Control

Change Management. A formal change management program should be established and procedures used to insure that all modifications to a computer system or network meet the same security requirements as the original components identified in the asset evaluation and the associated risk assessment and mitigation plan. The change control procedures for a software-intensive system should ensure that software assurance requirements are not compromised when changes are requested. Each change control request should include a specific section that addresses the impact of the requested change on software assurance requirements.

Risk assessment should be performed on all changes to the system or network that could affect security, including configuration changes, the addition of network components, and installation of software. Changes to policies and procedures may also be required. The current network configuration must always be known and documented. For example, in the object-oriented database management system model, *version management* is a facility for tracking and recording changes made to data over time through the history of design changes. The version management system tracks version successors and predecessors. When objects constituting a portion of the design are retrieved, the system must ensure that versions of these objects are consistent and compatible.

Difference Between Version Control and Version Management

- Version control involves controlling the different versions of software, uniquely identifying versions and configurations, and providing version change history to ensure stability, traceability, and repeatability.

- Version management system tracks version successors and predecessors.

- Both version control and version management ensure that all versions are consistent and compatible with each other.

Configuration Management

The three essential features of configuration management (CM) include stability, traceability, and repeatability.

- Stability means that an information system will not crash, shut down, or fail. Even if it fails, it fails in a known secure state.
- Traceability means that one can follow the change activities from origin to destination and in between.
- Repeatability is the ability to reproduce any version of the software at any given time.

The correct sequence of CM activities is item identification, change control, item status accounting, and audit.

- **Configuration item identification.** A methodology for selection and naming of configuration items that need to be placed under CM
- **Configuration change control.** A process for managing updates to the baselines for the configuration items
- **Configuration item status accounting.** It consists of recording and reporting of information needed to manage a configuration effectively.
- **Configuration audit.** It consists of periodically performing a review to ensure that the CM practices and procedures are rigorously followed. CM answers the following two questions: (1) what constitutes a software product at any point in time and (2) what changes have been made to the software product.

Configuration Control

Configuration control is the process of controlling modifications to hardware, firmware, and software, and documentation to protect the information system against improper modification prior to, during, and after system implementation. Change control is related to configuration control.

Access Controls over Changes

The information security management defines, documents, approves, and enforces physical and logical access restrictions associated with changes to the information system.

Any changes to the hardware, software, and/or firmware components of the information system can potentially have significant effects on the overall security of the system. Accordingly, only qualified and authorized individuals are allowed to obtain access to information system components for purposes of initiating changes, including upgrades and modifications. Additionally, maintaining records of access is essential for ensuring that configuration change control is being implemented as intended and for supporting after-the-fact actions should the organization become aware of an unauthorized change to the information system. Access restrictions for change also include software libraries.

Examples of access restrictions include, for example, physical and logical access controls, workflow automation, media libraries, abstract layers (e.g., changes are implemented into a third-party interface rather than directly into the information system component), change windows (e.g., changes occur only during specified times and making unauthorized changes outside the change window for easy discovery), authorizations to make changes to the information system, auditing changes, and retaining and review records of changes.

Check-In and Check-Out Procedures

Check-in and check-out procedures, as they relate to a configuration item (CI), are expressed in terms of a state-transition diagram where it deals with events, transitions, and actions. System requirements and analysis is the major emphasis in processing a request for change. The following events and actions (i.e., initial, check-out, modify, and check-in) take place when the CIs are checked in and out:

- **Initial.** The initial state assumes that the CI is checked into the CM workspace and locked without a flag.

- **Check-out.** The action here is to copy the CI to the software developer's workspace in the unlocked state. The CI is flagged as out and locked.

- **Modify.** The action is to modify the contents of the developer's workspace.

- **Check-in.** The action is to copy the modified CI to the CM workspace, remove the flag in the CM workspace, and delete the CI from the developer's workspace.

System Stages

Whether database or non-database, there should be four stages a new system goes through during its development. These stages include development, testing, staging (quality assurance), and production libraries, and they all require the same security controls, especially the staging library because the staging library is often copied into production library. Non-production environments pose a security risk due to the use of production data without masking. Therefore, non-production environments should be treated with the same care as the production environment. The sequence of stages is as follows:

Development → Testing → Staging → Production

Application Software Maintenance Controls

The scope of application software maintenance controls includes controls used to monitor the installation of and updates to application software to ensure that the software functions as expected and that a historical record is maintained of application system changes. Such controls also help to ensure that only authorized software is allowed on the system. These controls may include software configuration policy that grants managerial approval to modification and then documents the changes. They may also include some products used for virus protection.

Change Control Board

Installing a change control board or committee is an example of best practices to review and approve the initial change requests, fund the approved change requests, and approve the final changes after they are successfully changed and tested prior to their implementation.

End-User Computing

Scope of EUC

The scope of end-user computing (EUC) can be limited or extended; limited means end-user systems are developed to automate an individual's day-to-day work functions using small computer programs or spreadsheet applications, which is a low risk. But the risk is high with extended systems when these end-user systems are uploading or downloading end-user data files back and forth to local-area network systems or mainframe computer systems in order to exchange and share data between these systems.

This is because end-user systems, by definition, often have inadequate and incomplete application-based controls and lack effective security controls, thus compromising data integrity in all connected systems. Usually, end users deploy personal computers (PCs) and/or desk top computers to facilitate their work and as such seek help through help-desk staff and IT technical support staff for assistance.

The ideal EUC system is a system that is well confined to its scope and contained within its boundary. When this is not possible, end users should obtain design and development assistance either from internal IT staff or external contractors.

Audit Challenges of EUC

According to the IIA study results, the following are the audit challenges in EUC. Organizations and auditors must: (1) understand the present use or impact of EUC; (2) need to link EUC activities with business objectives; (3) coordinate potentially synergistic EUC activities; (4) ensure connectivity and interoperability; (5) assist end-user department managers and staff to identify business risks, control points, and benefits for adopting application-based controls and security controls; (6) implement the application selection and development methodologies; and (7) expand audit programs to include EUC when significant financial or operational issues exist.

Audit and Control Risks Over EUC

The following is a list of audit and control risks in end user–developed systems:

- Information (audit) trails, controls, and security features may not be available in the end user–developed application systems.
- Data storage and file retention, backup, purging, archiving, and rotating procedures may not be available or adequate.
- Documentation may not be available or it is inadequate or incorrect.
- Backup and recovery procedures may not be available or effective in the application systems developed by end users.
- Program change controls may not be available or effective.

Suggested Controls Over EUC

Lack of adequate separation of duties is a potential control weakness in end-user systems. Direct supervision, training, and frequent work reviews should be conducted to balance the control weaknesses.

When uploading data from a PC to a host computer, the data conversion programs residing on the host computer should reject inaccurate or incomplete data before updating any host-resident data files. Control totals should be developed between the PC and the host computer and reconciled automatically by the program. Uploading is one source of computer viruses, and its effects on other programs and data files are unknown.

Knowledge-Based Systems

Artificial Intelligence Technology

Artificial intelligence (AI) includes many disciplines such as operations research and expert system technology. AI involves the creation of computer software that emulates the way humans solve problems. Fifth-generation programming languages such as PROLOG and LISP are used in developing computer systems based on artificial intelligence technology. AI is the enabling technology for parsers, neural networks, expert systems, knowledge bases, object formation, and intelligent editors. The objective of AI is to get the computer to think like a person.

Parsers

Parsing is the procedure of (1) breaking the program code, comments, or sentences into logical parts and then (2) explaining the form, function, and interaction of these parts. Parsers (either self-generated or user-loaded) recognize syntactic and semantic constructs in the source code and load them as object-oriented representations into a repository.

Neural Network Systems

Neural networks are artificial intelligence systems built around concepts similar to the way the human brain's web of neural connections—known as synapses—is believed to work to identify patterns, learn, and reach conclusions.

Neural networks have the ability to learn and to utilize accumulated experience to make decisions that rival those of human beings. Neural networks have nothing to do with telecommunications-related networks.

Neural network systems are particularly apt for risk management and forecasting activities, in which the ability to identify intricate patterns is crucial to making predictions. In theory, a neural network can be put to work in any application in which substantial amounts of data are used to predict an outcome.

Some examples of applications of neural networks are:

- To trade securities and options

- To identify fraudulent use of credit cards

- To decide whether to approve a mortgage application

A neural network develops the ability to decide and then learns to improve its performance through massive trial-and-error decision making. A neural network is trained by being supplied with key data from a sample group of transactions. The neural network is able to use fuzzy or incomplete data successfully and to discover patterns in decision making that conventional rule based systems would not pick up.

Expert Systems

Expert systems (also known as knowledge-based systems) use artificial intelligence programming languages to help human beings make better decisions. In the business world, managers at all levels make decisions based on incomplete data and ambiguous information and under uncertain conditions. Expert systems are built by a knowledge system builder, a knowledge engineer, a human expert in the subject matter based on rules-of-thumb, facts, and an expert's advice. The knowledge system builder is like a programmer and the knowledge engineer is similar to a systems analyst in a conventional systems development environment. The human expert is a person knowledgeable in the subject matter located either inside the organization or outside. More than one expert can participate in an expert system project to develop the knowledge base.

Expert systems have an inference engine, which decides how to execute an application or how the rules are fired. The inference methods include forward and backward chaining (or reasoning). In the forward chaining, the data is subjected to rules to achieve system goals, whereas in backward chaining the system starts with goals and works backward through the rules to determine what data is required. Facts (data) and rules are stored in the knowledge base of the system and are used in the question and answer session with the end user. The system can be designed with a multiple-choice question format with a list of alternatives provided, and the end user chooses one. In a way, the expert system becomes a personal consultant or guide to the end user in solving problems.

Difference Between Conventional Systems and Expert Systems

- Conventional systems are aimed at problems that can be solved using a purely algorithmic approach but can be solved using a SDLC methodology

- Expert systems are aimed at problems that cannot be solved using a purely algorithmic approach but can be solved using a heuristic methodology

Safety and Security Risks in Expert Systems

- If the rules in the expert systems are not formulated properly and tested correctly, the outcomes could lead to loss of life or damage to property in medical and military systems

- Use of too many rules in the expert systems can complicate the programming work and access control decisions thus compromising the system's security

The operation of an expert system can be viewed in terms of the interaction of distinct components such as the *knowledge base, inference engine, and end-user interface.* The knowledge base stores knowledge about how to solve problems. Inference procedures are executed by a software module called the inference engine. If the user of the expert system is a person, communications with the end user are handled via an end-user interface.

SYSTEM INFRASTRUCTURE

Information Technology Control Frameworks

Information technology (IT) control frameworks provide overall guidance to user organizations as a frame of reference for security, governance, and for implementation of security-related controls. Several organizations within the U.S. and outside the U.S. provide such guidance.

Summary of Information Technology Control Frameworks

- **The IIA's electronic systems assurance and control (eSAC)** sets the stage for effective technology and risk management by providing a framework for evaluating the e-business control environment.

- The **IT Governance Institute's Control Objectives for Information and Related Technology (COBIT)** states that control objectives make a clear and distinct link to business objectives in order to support significant use outside the audit community. Control objectives are defined in a process-oriented manner following the principle of business reengineering. COBIT focuses on processes and process ownership, looks at fiduciary, quality, and security needs of enterprises, and provides seven information criteria in terms of what a business requires from IT, including effectiveness, efficiency, availability, integrity, confidentiality, reliability, and compliance.

- **ISACF's Control Objectives for Net Centric Technology Framework** focuses on intranet, extranet, internet; data warehouses; and online transaction processing systems.

- **AICPA/CICA SysTrust Principles and Criteria for Systems Reliability** provide guidance on information security in terms of principles, standards, management, assurance, and measurement.

- **IFAC's managing security of information** states that the objective of information security is to protect the interest of those relying on information, and the information systems and communications that deliver the information, from harm resulting from failures of availability, confidentiality, and integrity.

Summary of Information Technology Control Frameworks (continued)

- **Information Security Forum (ISF) Standard** divides security into five component areas: (1) security management, (2) critical business applications, (3) computer installations, (4) networks, and (5) system development.

- **The U.S. Department of Homeland Security's** task force on corporate governance calls upon all organizations to make information security governance a corporate board-level priority.

- **The European Union's (EU's) Security Directives** cover information security, attacks against information systems, legal aspects of electronic commerce, access to electronic communications networks, protection of personal data, safer Internet plus program, unfair commercial practices, copyrights in the information society, and international safe harbor privacy principles.

- The **OECD's Guidelines for the Security of Information Systems** cover data collection limitations, quality of data, limitations on data use, IT security safeguards, accountability of the data controller, trans-border data flow dealing with personal data, cross-border threats, privacy laws, cryptography guidelines, anti-spam regulations, electronic authentication guidelines and cross-border cooperation in the enforcement of laws protecting privacy.

- **The International Common Criteria (CC)** is a product evaluation model, which represents the outcome of efforts to develop criteria for evaluation of IT security. These criteria will be used throughout the international community.

Summary of Information Technology Control Frameworks (continued)

- **The International Organization and Standardization (ISO) Standards** issues several standards to business, government, and society for economic, environmental, and social development throughout the world. The two popular ISO standards related to IT include ISO 27001, which provides guidelines on Information Security Management—Requirements and ISO 27002, which addresses the Code of Practice for Information Security Management and has three major components such as confidentiality, integrity, and availability.

- The **minimum security requirements** are expressed in terms of management, operational, and technical controls. Summary of management controls include risk assessment; planning; systems and services acquisition; certification, accreditation, and security assessments.

  Summary of operational controls include personnel security; physical and environmental protection; contingency planning; configuration management; maintenance; system and information integrity; media protection; incident response; and awareness and training. Summary of technical controls include identification and authentication; access control; audit and accountability; and system and communications protection.

- The **Canadian Institute of Chartered Accountants (CICA) and Information Technology Control Guidelines (ITCG)** provides security guidelines.

- **The U.K. Office of Government Commerce (OGC) and Information Technology Infrastructure Library ITIL)** provides security management guidelines.

 Focus on: **Information Technology and Business Continuity (15–25%)**   415

Operating Systems, Mainframe Computers, Terminals, Workstations, and Servers

Operating Systems

An operating system (OS) is an integrated collection of software routines that service the sequencing and processing of computer programs by a computer, and is often called systems software. Many control operations are concentrated in systems software, which is defined as a collection of programs or systems that help interconnect and/or control the elements of input devices, computer processing operations, output devices, data files, application programs, and hardware. Typically, systems software is provided by outside vendors.

The OS may provide many services such as computer resource allocation, computer job scheduling, input/output control, and data management. The OS software controls the allocation and usage of hardware resources such as memory, computer processing unit (CPU) time, disk space, and peripheral devices. The OS is often called the "brain" of a computer, whether it is a mainframe computer, personal computer, desktop computer, palm top computer, notebook computer, lap top computer, tablet computer, and mobile devices (e.g., Smartphones, digital pads and tablets, and personal digital assistants). The operating system is the foundation software on which applications software depends. Popular operating systems for workstations include Windows, Mac OS, Linux, and UNIX. Network connectivity devices such as routers have their proprietary OSs, personal digital assistants (PDAs) often run on specialized OSs, and many embedded systems such as cellular phones, digital cameras, and audio players also use OSs. Although operating systems are predominantly software-based, partial or full implementations can be made in hardware in the form of firmware.

Operating Systems (continued)

OS is a program that runs on a computer and provides a software platform on which other programs can run. In addition, an OS is responsible for processing input commands from a user, sending output to a display, interacting with storage devices to store and retrieve data, and controlling peripheral devices such as printers and modems.

OS data exists in both non-volatile and volatile states. Non-volatile data is data that persists even after a computer is powered down, such as a filesystem stored on a hard drive. Volatile data is data on a live system that is lost after a computer is powered down, such as the current network connections to and from the system. Both types of data are useful to internal auditors when they perform IT system audits.

Mainframe Computers, Terminals, and Workstations

Operating system software, mainframe computers, personal computers, terminals, workstations, and servers are highly connected in a network and they work in a harmonious ways in handling computing jobs and services.

Mainframe Computers

Mainframe computers are big computers in terms of their memory, size, speed, and processing power. They are suitable to handling heavy-duty computing tasks required in databases and complex networks. They have the ability to support many users connected to the computer by terminals. Other computers such as personal computers and terminals are connected to the mainframe computers to share resources and computing power.

Terminals

A terminal is a networking device consisting of a video adapter, a monitor, and a keyboard. It is capable of sending and/or receiving information over a communications channel. A terminal does little no or no computer processing on its own; instead, it is connected to a computer with a communications link over a cable.

Workstations

A workstation is a hardware device and is defined in several ways depending on its configuration. Several variations of configurations include (1) it is a combination of input, output, and computing hardware that can be used for work by an individual, (2) it is a powerful stand-alone computer used in computer-aided design wok requiring heavy-duty calculations and graphics, (3) it is a personal computer or terminal connected to a network, (4) it provides operator-system interface, and (5) it may not require external access.

Servers

A server is a host computer that provides one or more services for other hosts over a network as a primary function. A server is deployed in several ways, including (1) it is a computer or device on a network that manages network resources such as files, programs, and data; (2) it is a computer program that provides services to other computer programs in the same or another computer; (3) it is a computer program running a server program and is based on client/server architecture where the server software receives requests from the client, processes the request, and returns data to the client; and (4) it is a computer running administrative software that controls access to the network and its resources, such as printers and disk drives, and provides resources to computers functioning as workstations on the network.

One of the most common motivations for using a server is resource sharing. The goal is to provide transparent access to organization-wide data distributed across personal computers (PCs) and mainframe computers while protecting the security and integrity of that data.

The database management system handles the logical organization of the data and communicates with the server operating system to access the data storage devices. Servers can be either a local-area network (LAN) database server or a host database accessed via a gateway. The network operating system provides software connectivity between the server database management systems software and the local-area network (LAN).

Servers (continued)

There are many servers and each server has its own specific purpose and they pose specific risks due to concentration of data in one place. For example, a file server is a computer and storage device dedicated to storing files, a Web server for access to Web content, a domain name system (DNS) server for domain name services, a database server for access to relational tables, and an e-mail server for access to e-mail services.

Today, servers are very powerful and fast, and perform diverse functions such as transferring files, storing data, communicating outside the network, and processing databases. Because a LAN server is charged with moving large quantities of data from disk and memory onto the network, it is by nature I/O-bound rather than computer-bound, resulting in degraded performance. One way to curb memory operations is with caching, a performance-enhancing technique that establishes a small, very-high-speed static RAM cache (or buffer) between main memory and the processor. This approach frees the LAN server from repeated calls to memory. The next time the processor goes looking for data, it will first try to retrieve it from cache memory.

Server Types

Basically, servers are of two types: dedicated and non-dedicated. The choice depends on the significance and risk level of the work done on the network.

In a **dedicated server**, the computer running the server software cannot be used as a workstation, hence the name dedicated. *Advantages* of a dedicated server include (1) it is easier to manage because all data is in one place, and (2) it is faster to run because servers do not have a local user to serve. *Disadvantages* of a dedicated server include (1) it is harder to make resources available on an ad-hoc basis because setting up a server is more difficult and time-consuming, and (2) if the server fails, all users are forced to discontinue their work because all resources are centralized, that is, all users either work or don't work.

A **non-dedicated server** can work as both a computer and a workstation. *Advantages* of a non-dedicated server include (1) it allows flexibility to users because users can make resources available on their computers as necessary, and (2) it makes users LAN-literate, requiring them to take some administrative responsibilities for system backup and security. This item (2) can be viewed as either an advantage or a disadvantage, because the user now can be a network administrator. Convenience is the advantage and unlimited access to system resources is the disadvantage of being a network administrator.

Disadvantages of non-dedicated servers include (1) servers can suffer some performance degradation when being used simultaneously as a workstation and as a computer, and (2) users must be LAN-literate, requiring them to back up the shared data, set up security, and establish access rights to the system.

Server Types (continued)

Specific types of servers include file servers, database servers, print servers, communication (terminal) servers, facsimile servers, image servers, network servers, mail servers, application servers, redundant servers, X Window servers, video servers, Web servers, authentication servers, remote access servers/network access servers, quarantine servers, virtual servers, domain name system servers, transport layer security proxy servers, network time protocol servers, system log servers, management servers, dynamic host configuration protocol servers, anonymizer servers, Warez servers, Kerberos security servers, socket servers, and load balancing servers.

Server-Based Threats

Server-based threats occur due to poorly implemented session-tracking, which may provide an avenue of attack. Similarly, user-provided input might eventually be passed to an application interface that interprets the input as part of a command, such as a Structured Query Language (SQL) command. Attackers may also inject custom code into the website for subsequent browsers to process via cross-site scripting (XSS). Subtle changes introduced into the Web server can radically change the server's behavior (e.g., turning a trusted entity into malicious one), the accuracy of the computation (e.g., changing computational algorithms to yield incorrect results), or the confidentiality of the information (e.g., disclosing collected information).

Controls Over Server Farms

A server farm is a physical security control that uses a network configuration mechanism to monitor and minimize theft of or damage to servers because all servers are kept in a single, secure physical location with a key and lock. If not controlled well, server farms can become a single point of failure and can be a target of internally originated attacks. Only those individuals (e.g., server administrator) who require physical access to the server farm should be given a key to open and close the doors. A two-person control is better.

Examples of logical security controls over a server farm include host and network based IDS, private VLANs, access controls with strong passwords, and good system administration practices (e.g., keeping systems up to date with the latest patches).

Maintaining Server Integrity

To ensure and maintain the integrity of the network servers, it is important to constantly monitor them for signs of malicious activity and other vulnerabilities. Integrity controls include a server farm, a secure demilitarized zone (DMZ), a secure server network with firewalls, or using routers behind the firewall.

Server Load Balancing and Clustering

Server load balancing is fine tuning of a computer system, network, or disk subsystem in order to more evenly distribute the data and/or processing across available resources. The load balancing occurs when network traffic is distributed dynamically across groups of servers running a common application so that no one server is overwhelmed. It increases server availability and application system availability, and could be a viable contingency measure when it is implemented among different websites. In this regard, the application system continues to operate as long as one or more websites remain operational.

Clustering means multiple servers providing the same service. It implies resilience to failure and/or some kind of load balancing between the servers. For example, in clustering, load balancing might distribute the incoming transactions evenly to all servers or it might redirect them to the next available server.

Security Over Web Servers

Security Levels

Recent attacks on websites have shown that computers supporting websites are vulnerable to attacks ranging from minor nuisances to significant service interruptions. Each organization has to decide its sensitivity to risk and how open it wants to be to the external world. When resources are limited, the cost of security incidents should be considered, and the investment in protective measures should be concentrated on areas of highest sensitivity.

There are three levels of Web security techniques that can be applied to Web servers and they include minimum security level 1, penetration resistance level 2, and attack detection and mitigation level 3, and they operate in a cumulative manner meaning that techniques in level 3 are stronger than those in level 1 and level 2.

Security Controls

Several security controls over Web servers include upgrading software and installing patches, using single-purpose servers, removing unnecessary applications, installing external firewalls, administering remote security, restricting server scripts, shielding Web server with packet filtering router, educating and allocating resources, applying separation of privileges principles, installing hardware-based solutions, installing internal firewalls, installing network-based intrusion detection systems, and installing host-based intrusion detection systems.

Limitations of Control Techniques to Secure Web Servers

Today's software is not 100 percent proven secure, and applications of standard Web security techniques cannot guarantee that a Web server will be impenetrable. A Web server should use its stated Web server security techniques in addition to using trustworthy software. Trustworthy means software that can be assessed by studying past vulnerabilities, using software specifically created with security as the principle goal, and using software evaluated by trusted third parties.

Security Testing of Web Servers

Periodic security testing of public Web servers is critical. Without periodic testing, there is no assurance that current protective measures are working or that the security patch applied by the Web server administrator is functioning as advertised. Although a variety of security testing techniques exists, vulnerability scanning is the most common. Vulnerability scanning assists a Web server administrator in identifying vulnerabilities and verifying whether the existing security measures are effective. Penetration testing is also used, but it is used less frequently and usually only as part of an overall penetration test of the organization's network.

DATABASE SYSTEMS

Database Management Systems Software

A database contains facts and figures on various types of information such as sales, costs, and personnel. These files are collectively called the firm's database. A database is a collection of related data about an organization, intended for sharing of this data by multiple users. A database management system (DBMS) is comprised of software, hardware, and procedures. The DBMS acts as a software controller enabling different application systems to access large number of distinct data records stored on direct access storage devices (e.g., disk).

The DBMS should be compatible with the operating system environment and it handles complex data structures. Unauthorized access to data elements is a major concern in a database system due to concentration of data. The DBMS helps in providing user interface with the application system through increased accessibility and flexibility by means of "data views."

Database Considerations

- Design approaches (to use conceptual, logical, or external model)
- Checkpoints (to act as a starting point after a system fails or detects an error)
- Compression techniques (to save storage space and disk I/O operations)
- Reorganization (to reblock and reload records)
- Restructuring (to accommodate logical, physical, and procedural changes)
- Performance monitoring (to identify problems and actions)
- Utility programs (to use routines for various common computing tasks)

Data Dictionary Systems Software

A data dictionary is an alphabetical listing that describes all the data elements (fields) in an application system and tells how and where they are used. It defines each data element's characteristics, properties, and processes, including the size of the data field and record, the volume of records, the data field editing and validation rules with maximum and minimum values, the security levels or ratings, and the frequency of use and of changes of data elements. A data dictionary can be active or passive.

Data Warehouse

The purpose of a data warehouse is information retrieval and data analysis. It stores pre-computed, historical, descriptive, and numerical data. It is the process of extracting and transferring operational data into informational data and loading it into a central data store or "warehouse." Once loaded, users can access the warehouse through query and analysis tools. The data warehouse can be housed on a computer different from production computer.

A data warehouse is a storage facility where data from heterogeneous databases are brought together so that users can make queries against the warehouse instead of against several databases. The warehouse is like a big database. Redundant and inconsistent data are removed from the databases and subsets of data are selected from the databases prior to placing them in a data warehouse. Usually, summary data, correlated data, or otherwise massaged data is contained in the data warehouse.

Database versus Data Warehouse

- A database contains raw data.

- A data warehouse contains massaged (cleaned up) data.

- Users query many points with heterogeneous databases.

- Users query only a single point with a data warehouse.

Data Marts

A data mart is a subset of a data warehouse. It brings the data from transaction processing systems (TPSs) to functional departments (i.e., finance, manufacturing, and human resources) or business units or divisions. Data marts are scaled-down data warehouses, where targeted business information is placed into the hands of more decision makers.

Data Mart versus Data Warehouse

- A data mart provides a detailed data for a specific function of a business.

- A data warehouse provides a summary data for the entire business.

Data Mining

Data mining can be applied to databases as well as to data warehouses. A warehouse structures the data in such a way as to facilitate query processing. Data mining is a set of automated tools that convert the data in the warehouse into some useful information. It selects and reports information deemed significant from a data warehouse or database.

Data mining is the process of posing a series of queries to extract information from the databases. A data warehouse itself does not attempt to extract information from the data contained in the warehouse. One needs a data mining tool to do this.

Data Mining versus Data Auditing

- Data mining is a user tool to select information from a data warehouse.

- Data auditing is an auditing tool to detect fraud, intrusions, and security problems in a data warehouse.

Virtual Databases

A virtual database is created when data from multiple database sources is integrated to provide a total perspective on a specific topic. It is virtual in that such a database does not exist physically, but is created on demand. For example, an auditor comparing performance of a multiplant organization can use virtual database technology to view key operating and financial ratios of each plant side-by-side.

Online Analytical Processing

Online analytical processing (OLAP) programs are available to store and deliver data warehouse information from multidimensional databases. It allows users to explore corporate data from a number of different perspectives, such as product, geography, time, and salesperson.

OLAP servers and desktop tools support high-speed analysis of data involving complex relationships, such as combinations of a company's products, regions, channels of distribution, reporting units, and time periods. Access to data in multidimensional databases can be very quick because they store the data in structures optimized for speed, and they avoid using structured query language (SQL) and index processing techniques. In other words, multidimensional databases have greater retrieval speed and longer update times.

Structured Query Language

The primary components of a structured query language (SQL) database are schemas, tables, and views, parser, optimizer, executor, access rights checker, and access rights grantor or revoker. A schema describes the structure of related tables and views. Tables hold the actual data in the database; they consist of rows and columns. Each row is a set of columns; each column is a single data element. Views are derived tables and may be composed of a subset of a table or the result of table operations (e.g., a join of different tables). A parser is a program that breaks input into smaller chunks so that a program can act upon the information.

SQL is a standard query language for relational DBMSs that is also used to query and update the data managed by the DBMS. The SQL standard, which is used by most commercial DBMSs, includes specific requirements for enforcing discretionary access controls (DACs).

Basically, two types of access control policies are applied to SQL: discretionary access control and mandatory access control.

Discretionary access control is a means by which access to objects is restricted to specific users or groups of users. The access control is discretionary in that the object's owner may pass on access privileges to other users, either directly or indirectly. Privileges are means by which SQL enforces discretionary access control. Privileges are granted with a grant statement and are used to specify an allowable action on a specific object (e.g., to update the rows in a specific table or to a grantee). Grant, revoke, and role statements are available to allocate

Structured Query Language (continued)

individual privileges. The role facility allows a database administrator to create individual roles with corresponding database access requirements. An additional benefit of roles is that a user can have only one role active at a time. For example, this would allow a user to access only payroll related objects when working under the payroll role and only procurement related objects when working under the purchasing role.

Mandatory access control is frequently used with mandatory access control database systems to control inference. Mandatory access controls require support for security labels. These labels are used as the basis for access control decisions. In order to correctly label data, the system must request and receive the security level of data. Encryption and cryptographic checksums are employed to protect the security label from modification.

Aggregation is primarily a mandatory access control problem. The aggregation problem occurs when two pieces of information A and B are classified at level X individually but level Y (Y higher than X) collectively. To limit aggregation, one should limit access as tightly as possible.

Most databases use SQL and many will have Web interfaces that may be vulnerable to typical Web attacks like cross-site scripting (XSS) or SQL injection. The communication link between data and decision layers is the primary attack surface for SQL injection. To understand the scope of a threat surface, all segments of the database system, with an emphasis on entry points, must be examined. The cascading effect of corrupted databases

Structured Query Language (continued)

due to injection into databases content can impact data acquisition servers and data historians. Attackers can use automated malware kits to conduct SQL injection attacks.

Many intrusion prevention systems (IPSs) claim to thwart SQL injection attacks, but their capabilities are weak and are usually based on signatures, which hackers can easily evade. SQL injections in Web applications can be thwarted by binding variables in SQL statements. Unfortunately, many programmers still do not use the bind variables method when developing applications, leaving the database exposed to SQL injection. If not controlled, SQL can lead to slammer worm attack.

Cloud Computing Systems

Cloud computing is a model for enabling ubiquitous, convenient, on-demand network access to a shared pool of configurable computing resources (e.g., networks, servers, storage, applications, and services) that can be rapidly provisioned and released with minimal management effort or service provider interaction. This cloud model promotes availability and is composed of five essential characteristics (i.e., on-demand self-service, broad network access, resource pooling, rapid elasticity, and measured service), three service models (i.e., cloud software as a service, cloud platform as a service, and cloud infrastructure as a service), and four deployment models (i.e., private cloud, community cloud, public cloud, and hybrid cloud). The major issues in cloud computing include security and privacy of data.

Security Downside of Cloud Computing

- System complexity

- Shared multi-tenant environment

- Internet-facing service

- Loss of control

As with any technology, cloud computing services can be turned towards improper or illicit activities such as botnets and cracking mechanisms such as a Wi-Fi protected access (WPA) cracker.

Solutions to the Security Downside of Cloud Computing

- Deploy access control and intrusion detection technologies at the cloud provider, and conduct an independent assessment to verify that they are in place. This partly includes traditional perimeter security measures in combination with the domain security controls. Traditional perimeter security includes restricting physical access to network and devices; protecting individual components from exploitation through security patch deployment; setting as default most secure configurations; disabling all unused ports and services; using role-based access control; monitoring audit trails; minimizing the use of privileges; using antivirus software; and encrypting communications.

- Define trust boundaries between service providers and consumers to ensure that the responsibility for providing security is clear

- Support application and data portability such that the customer can take action to change cloud service providers when needed to satisfy availability, confidentiality, and integrity requirements. This includes the ability to close an account on a particular date and time, and to copy data from one service provider to another.

Security Upside of Cloud Computing (i.e., good news)

The cloud computing paradigm provides opportunities for innovation in provisioning security service that hold the prospect of improving the overall security of some organizations. The biggest beneficiaries are likely to be smaller organizations that have limited numbers of IT administrators and security personnel, and lack the economies of scale available for larger organizations with sizeable data centers. Potential areas of improvement where organizations may derive security benefits from transitioning to a public cloud computing environment include the following:

- Staff specialization
- Platform strength
- Resource availability
- Backup and recovery
- Mobile endpoints
- Data concentration
- Data center–oriented (e.g., redirecting electronic mail records to a cloud to discover widespread spam, phishing, and malware campaigns, and to carry out remedial actions such as quarantining suspect messages and content)
- Cloud-oriented (e.g., reverse proxy products are available that enable unfettered access to a cloud environment, yet maintain the data stored in that environment in encrypted form)

Key Security Considerations in Cloud Computing

- Carefully define security and privacy requirements during the initial planning stage at the start of the system development life cycle

- Determine the extent to which negotiated service agreements are required to satisfy security requirements and the alternatives of suing negotiated service agreements or cloud computing deployment models which offer greater oversight and control over security and privacy

- Assess the extent to which the server and client-side computing environment meets organizational security and privacy requirements

- Continue to maintain security management practices, controls, and accountability over the privacy and security of data and applications

Potential Vulnerabilities in Cloud Computing

- The inherent system complexity of a cloud computing environment and the dependency on the correctness of these components and the interactions among them

- The dependency on the service provider to maintain logical separation in a multi-tenant environment, which is not unique to the cloud computing model

- The need to ensure that the organization retains an appropriate level of controls to obtain situational awareness, weigh alternatives, set priorities, and effect changes in security and privacy that are in the best interests of an organization

Security Requirements of Cloud Computing

- Statutory compliance to laws, regulations, and organization requirements

- Data characteristics to assess which fundamental protections an application's dataset requires

- Privacy and confidentiality to protect against accidental and nefarious access to information

- Integrity to ensure data is authorized, complete, and accurate

- Data controls and access policies to determine where data can be stored and who can access physical locations

- Governance to ensure that cloud computing service providers are sufficiently transparent, have adequate security and management controls, and provide the information necessary for the organization to appropriately and independently assess and monitor the efficacy of those controls

Potential Security Benefits of Using Cloud Computing Services

- The ability to focus resources on areas of high concern as more general security services are assumed by the cloud provider

- Potential platform strength resulting from greater uniformity and homogeneity, and resulting improved information assurance, security response, system management, reliability, and maintainability

- Improved resource availability through scalability, redundancy, and disaster recovery capabilities; improved resilience to unanticipated service demands

- Improved backup and recovery capabilities, policies, procedures, and consistency

- Ability to leverage alternate cloud services to improve the overall security posture, including that of traditional data centers

- Reduced time-to-market metric regarding access provisioning of new applicants

General and Specific Security and Privacy Issues in Cloud Computing

Data processed in a public cloud computing environment and applications running in a public cloud facility can experience different security and privacy exposures than would be the case in an onsite hosted environment. For example, cloud subscribers, who are ultimately responsible for their data processed on provider's systems, will need to require assurances from providers that they are in compliance with the appropriate regulations.

Examples of *general security and privacy issues* in a public cloud environment include (1) not meeting the subscriber's data protection requirements, (2) not providing encryption of data at rest in storage, (3) not knowing the strengths of the encryption algorithm, (4) not knowing the attack surface of a cloud and the likely pool of attackers, and (5) not knowing the expertise level of cloud administrators.

Examples of *specific security and privacy issues* in public cloud computing environment include (1) storing sensitive data without adequate protection due to risk of unintended data disclosure, (2) lack of subscriber awareness over where data is stored and who has or can have access, leading to privacy concerns due to distributed nature of clouds, (3) inability to partition access rights between subscribers, providers, and administrators, thus compromising system integrity, (4) not having both logical separation and physical separation of systems required to protect a subscriber's resources due to multi-tenancy, (5) using a subscriber's browser as a graphical interface, account setup, and resource administration, leading to security flaws, and (6) lack of proper protection of a subscriber's cryptographic keys to ensure a safe use of cryptography from inside a cloud.

Functional Areas of Information Technology Operations

Operating Environment

Activities include data input and output procedures, production program execution procedures, job scheduling practices, and production job turnover procedures.

Computer Operations

Activities such as console operations, system commands and parameters, system backups, system backup alternatives, data file backup methods, tape handling, tape cleaning and degaussing, and preventive maintenance constitute a major work in computer operations. Other activities include system logs and help-desk functions.

Change and Problem Management

Installation of a change/problem management system or service is another end-user service and support tool where problems and changes are logged, tracked, reported, resolved, and implemented. The goals of the computer center operations management should be to

- Stabilize the production environment and limit negative impact (system outages, errors, backouts, and downtime) due to changes or problems.

- Maintain the integrity and security of all program modules, hardware devices, and network components within the production environment.

- Prioritize those changes that are critical to business function versus those changes that can be deferred.

- Coordinate all problems and changes in a controlled and coordinated manner.

- Promote a proactive mode of computer operations instead of a reactive one.

Often, incorrectly implemented changes cause problems. There should be a cross-reference between a change and a problem caused by a change. To some extent, integrity, liability, and availability of computer systems depend on the way the problems and changes are managed, controlled, and secured. Problem management is critical to online processing due to high visibility of problems to end users. Changes can be classified into standard change request, mandatory change requests, and emergency change requests, so that priorities can be established and resources can be allocated accordingly.

Service-Level Management

Service-level management is a better way for the computer center management to improve quality of computing services to system users. The computer center management must define a set of user service levels or service objectives that describe application systems, volume of transactions, processing windows, online system response times, and batch job turnaround times. Without defined service levels to monitor against actual performance determined in the resource utilization function, a computer system's capacity limit is difficult to identify. Without service levels, the computer center management will consider that the capacity of a computer is near its limits when the users begin to complain about computer performance.

By monitoring performance against service levels, the computer center management can identify approaching problems in meeting service objectives. In order to achieve these goals, computer center management needs to develop service level objectives for internal use. Some examples of areas requiring service level objectives are

- System capacity during peak hours in terms of average CPU busy, average demand paging rate, and maximum channel busy
- Number of online users, number of online transactions per minute, and number of batch jobs per hour
- Online system average response time in seconds by application
- Percentage of time the online system is available

Service-Level Management (continued)

- Turnaround time for test and production batch jobs processed under each job class by application

- Number of job reruns and time lost due to job reruns

- Number of abnormal terminations by application program per operating shift

Where applicable, maximum and minimum numbers (range) should be identified for each of these objectives. The rationale behind developing service level objectives internally first is that they provide a basis for negotiating service level agreements with the user community.

After developing service level objectives internally, the computer center management is ready to negotiate with each business user to develop formal service level agreements. Some examples of service level agreements are:

- Average response times for each online application system

- Turnaround times for each batch job by application system

- System availability time (system up-time) by each application system

Service-Level Management (continued)

- Accuracy limits in terms of number of errors by cause for each application system
- Number of job reruns by each application system
- Number of transactions to be processed during peak hours in each application system
- Number of production problems by application system per week
- Computer report delivery times by application system
- A plan for reporting service level problems
- Action priorities if services cannot be delivered
- Scheduled meetings to discuss service levels between end users and computer center management

It is important to remember that these service level agreements are not static. They require adjustments and refinements periodically, such as at least once a year or preferably at the time of renegotiation of the agreement with customers (users).

Separation of Duties in IT Operations and Other IT Functions

The objective is to ensure that no one person has complete control over a transaction throughout its initiation, authorization, recording, processing, and reporting. A similar concept applies equally to any operation performed by IT or user department employees. The rationale is to minimize the incompatible functions, which are not conducive to good internal control structure (i.e., risky) and which can lead to fraud or collusion.

It is important to understand that the degree of separation of duties depends on the job level. This means that there is more separation of duties practiced at the lower levels of the organization than at higher levels. The rationale is that somebody at higher levels needs to be in charge of many functions, activities, and operations.

Incompatible IT functions

- Data entry and production job scheduling

- Computer operations and applications programming

- Computer operations and systems programming

- Application programming and systems programming

- Systems programming and data security administration

- Data security administration and data administration (includes database administration)

- Data administration and quality assurance

- Database administration and applications programming

- Telecommunication network and computer operations

- Quality assurance and applications development/maintenance

- Quality assurance and systems programming

Compatible IT functions

- Quality assurance and data security administration

- Help desk and telecommunication networks

- Job control analysis and job scheduling

- Tape librarian and documentation librarian

- Systems analysis and application programming

Network Management

Scope includes network architecture, network management categories, network changes, and network interoperability.

Attacks on Data Center or Computer Center Operations

- **Maintenance accounts** are one of the most common methods hackers use to break into computer systems, are accounts that still have factory-set or easily guessed passwords.

- **Diagnostic port attacks** allow hackers to access large systems through diagnostic ports meant for third-party maintenance vendors.

- **Keyboard attacks** are data scavenging through resources available to normal system users, which may include advanced software diagnostic tools.

- **Laboratory attacks** are data scavenging through the aid of what could be precise or elaborate equipment.

- **Physical piggybacking** is where an unauthorized person enters a computer center behind an authorized person. Either the door is wide open or the first person lets the second one in.

ENTERPRISE-WIDE RESOURCE PLANNING SYSTEM, CUSTOMER-RELATIONSHIP MANAGEMENT SYSTEM, AND SOFTWARE LICENSING AND PIRACY MANAGEMENT

Enterprise-Wide Resource Planning System

Enterprise-wide resource planning (ERP) system software can help organizations in optimizing their value chain, which requires integrating business processes across organizational boundaries through IT.

Value chain = Business process reengineering + Change management + ERP

ERP systems allow employees to access a full database of information that will allow them to complete their tasks. The information can also be shared with customers and suppliers as needed. The ERP system can track business transactions from their origin (at the customer) to order entry through operations and accounting until the transaction is completed. The objective of ERP systems is to integrate all functions within an organization and to become customer-oriented (customer-centric). Companies are using the ERP system for increased business competitiveness.

Advantages and Disadvantages of ERP Systems

- Advantages of ERP systems include: elimination of costly, inflexible legacy systems, improvement of work processes, increase in access to data for operational decision making, and standardization of IT infrastructure (i.e., hardware, software, operating systems, and databases).

- Disadvantages of ERP systems include: expense and time in implementation, difficulty in implementing change in the organization, risks in using one vendor, and difficulty in integrating with other computer systems.

Customer-Relationship Management System

Marketing departments are acquiring or developing a customer relationship management (CRM) system to survive in the customer-centric environment and to establish a one-to-one business relationship with customers. Some define CRM as a call center solution. Some view it as sales force automation; others as direct mail, marketing automation, or simply a Web page. Many companies see it as a "front-end" application only, interacting at the point-of-contact, point-of- purchase, or customer support. Others believe the secret to CRM success is in the "back-end" activities, such as data mining, data warehousing, data distribution, and data sharing. A properly designed and implemented CRM system encompasses all of these and much more. It is better to view the CRM system as a bridge system, not as a front-end system or back-end system.

Organizations **must do** the following to derive benefits from the CRM system:

- Understand that customers come first, products and services come next

- Understand the customer cycle as "get, keep, grow" or "acquire, support, retain"

- Understand that customers "pull" the company's products or services of their choice

- Understand that marketers "push" company's products or services on to customers

Customer-Relationship Management System (continued)

- Understand that pull and push concepts must be linked together to create interactive, learning relationships between the company and its customers. This linkage, in turn, results in increasing customer satisfaction and loyalty, share of customer, return on sales (ROS), and return on investment (ROI).

- Establish a strong linkage between the CRM system and financial performance such as return on sales (ROS) and return on investment (ROI)

Software Licensing and Piracy Management

Software Licensing

Similar to systems and network devices, operating system software and application software are also a relevant data source or asset for organizations. Software asset and licensing information may be centrally managed by a software asset management tool to track license compliance, monitor usage status, and manage the software asset life cycle. Software license management tools offer a variety of features to automate inventory, utilization monitoring and restrictions, deployment, and patches for software.

A periodic **audit** of software licenses should be conducted to mitigate legal liabilities with software vendors. Ineffective and inefficient management of software license issues can lead to software piracy risks.

Software monitoring is performed for two purposes: illegal acquisition of software and unauthorized use of software. Audit software running on a computer will detect illegal acquisition, which is using unofficially acquired software. This audit can be performed either manually or with automated tools. For example, an organization may audit systems for illegal copies of copyrighted software. This problem is primarily associated with PCs and LANs but can apply to any type of computer system or mobile devices. Another requirement is retention of business records to comply with legal, tax, audit, and regulatory authorities.

Many organizations use a **software-metering program** to ensure that software is properly licensed, as required. System-users are defined to the software metering product, and the product controls and monitors who is using the system and determines whether the user is authorized to use the system. Unauthorized users will be denied access to the system.

Software Licensing (continued)

Risks include (1) telecommuting employees may install illegal software on their home computer which is also used for business purpose and that is not authorized by their employers, (2) regular employees may bring software from home to work that is not authorized by their employers, and (3) disgruntled employees may report illegal copying and using of vendor-developed software to government officers, software vendor representatives, or software alliance or watchdog groups. Developing and monitoring a software inventory management system is an effective control to detect illegal use of copyrighted software.

Piracy Management

The purpose of the U.S. Executive Order on computer **software piracy** (intellectual property) is to prevent and combat computer software piracy by observing the relevant provisions of international agreements in effect in the United States, including applicable provisions of the World Trade Organization (WTO) Agreement on Trade-Related Aspects of Intellectual Property Rights, the Berne Convention for the Protection of Literary and Artistic Works, and relevant provisions of U.S. Federal law, including the Copyright Act.

Software Piracy Policies

The vast majority of the software involved in software piracy legal cases is off-the-shelf, PC software, such as word processing, spreadsheets, graphics, and databases. The issue is illegal use, copying, and distribution of software both inside and outside the organization. Here, illegal means a user has not paid for the software.

Software piracy policies are needed to protect the organization from legal suits by owners. The policy should include:

- Prohibiting illegal copy and use of software.
- Developing a software inventory management system that includes a list of popular application programs. This list can be compared to the organization's purchase orders, the original software, or original documentation manual.
- Checking the hard disks for illegally copied software periodically.
- Making illegal copying of software grounds for employee dismissal.
- Requiring all employees to sign a statement of not using illegal software at their work and not using the illegal software taken from work to home.
- Prohibiting copying of internally-developed software.
- Prohibiting pirated externally-developed software from being brought into the organization.
- Monitoring of all sensitive programs from illegal copying.

Copyright Laws

Copyright laws protect the software. The act of illegally (not paying for) copying, duplicating, or using the software is called software piracy. Internet piracy involves illegally gaining access to and using the Internet. Many companies on the Internet receive customer fees for their research, services, information (e.g., sports and market analysis), and even products), and when unauthorized people use such services illegally, Internet firms lose revenues. Both software piracy and the Internet piracy are growing steadily.

Penalties in Software Contracts

If the customer/client refuses to pay due to nonperformance by vendor/contractor, can the contractor "electronically repossess" the software that he developed/maintained for the customer or supplied to the customer? The question is: Who is right?

Even where it is clear that the client had wrongfully refused to pay for the contractor work, electronic repossession of software is not always justified. The contractor/developer's claim for payments due does not automatically include a right to repossess or disable the software, especially without going to the court. One exception is when the contractor is the owner or has a personal property interest in the software product. Disabling of computer software could interrupt business operations and customer services.

Even where the vendor has an arguable right to "repossess" or disable the software, the manner in which the repossession is executed may itself be wrongful. If a contractor/developer must access the customer/client's computer in order to remove or disable the software, this may constitute a violation of federal and/or state computer crime statutes.

If a contractor disables the client's software, the client can sue the contractor for trespass, intentional interference with contractual relations, and breach of contract.

Automatic disabling mechanisms, such as time/logic bombs, drop-dead devices, Trojan horses, access keys, are the insertion of illegal and unauthorized program code into the computer system, to be activated by the system date on the computer, by turning up a counter, or by occurrence of some specific event or condition. Are these mechanisms legal?

Penalties in Software Contracts (continued)

Software disabling mechanisms by vendor/contractor require advance notice to the client, that is, prior to entering into the software agreement.

Courts do not appreciate the idea that business operations are at the mercy of, or slave to, a computer. The courts would prohibit the vendor from activating the drop-dead device if prior notice is not given to the customer. However, courts would allow a vendor to activate a drop-dead device where notice of the device was included in the contract. In either case, such contractual protection will not protect the vendor/contractor if the vendor itself is in default, that is, nonperformance.

Some of choices the customer can exercise when the software does not work as expected include (1) return the software, (2) cancel the contract, (3) obtain a refund of all or partial sums paid, (4) accept the defective software at a reduced price.

Data and Network Communications and Connections

Computer Data and Communications Networks

Computer networks can be classified according to their scale, bandwidth, and location similar to classifying multiple processors in computers based on their physical size, speed, and memory.

Wired Networks

The lowest scale of wired network is a **personal-area network** (PAN) or home network in a room for an individual's use or to conduct home-based business. For example, a wireless network connecting a computer (e.g., desktop PC, laptop PC, notebook PC, and PDA) with its mouse, keyboard, and printer is a PAN or home network.

The next highest scale of wired network is a **local-area network** (LAN) for use in a single building or campus of buildings connected by personal computers (PCs) and workstations to share peripheral resources (e.g., printers and scanners) and to exchange information. Several topologies are possible for broadcast LANs such as bus, star, tree, ring, and mesh. The combination of a cable and host forms a LAN, and there is no subnet for LANs.

The next highest scale of wired network is a **metropolitan-area network** (MAN) for use in a city for cable television network. MANs are also called as wireless local loop. It interfaces to the network layer and uses packet protocols (e.g., IP, PPP, and Ethernet), which are connectionless, and asynchronous transfer mode (ATM), which is connection oriented. This requires mapping the ATM connection to the other connections.

Wired Networks (continued)

The next highest scale of wired network is **wide-area network** (WAN) for use in a country or continent to run user application systems. A WAN consists of hosts (PCs), which are connected by a communication subnet. The subnet consists of transmission lines and switching elements (routers). Transmission lines move bits between computers using copper wire, optical fiber, or radio links. Routers connect three or more transmission lines. Customers own the hosts whereas telephone companies or Internet service providers (ISPs) own and operate the communication subnet. The combination of a subnet and its hosts forms a WAN.

The highest scale of wired network is the **Internet** for use in all continents (i.e., the entire planet). An internetwork (internet) is established when distinct networks are interconnected (e.g., connecting a LAN and a WAN or connecting two LANs).

Wireless Networks

Wireless PANs are short-range wireless networks (e.g., Bluetooth), using IEEE 802.15 standard, connects computer components without wires and using short-range radio. They use open standards for short-range communications.

Wireless LANs, using IEEE 802.11 standard (Wi-Fi), communicate with other systems through a radio modem and antenna when installing the Ethernet is not feasible in office buildings, airports, hotels, restaurants, and campuses. Wireless LANs serve as an extension to existing wired LANs.

The IEEE 802.11 standard defines how to design interoperable WLAN equipment that provides a variety of capabilities, including a wide range of data rates, quality of service, reliability, range optimization, device link options, network management, and security.

Wireless LANs provide five distribution services (i.e., association, disassociation, re-association, distribution, and integration) and four station services (i.e., authentication, de-authentication, privacy, and data delivery). Distribution services relate to managing cell activities and interacting with stations outside the cell. Station services relate to activity within a single cell (intra-cell), and occur only after the distribution services have taken place.

Wireless MANs, which are fixed broadband networks, are used for high-speed wireless Internet access jobs in a city using IEEE802.16 standard known as worldwide interoperability for microwave access ((WiMAX). It is intended for wireless metropolitan-area networking (MAN) and is an effort to provide seamless mobile access in

Wireless Networks (continued)

much the same as wide-area cellular networks with higher transmission speeds. Security advantages of WiMAX include mutual device/user authentication, improved traffic encryption, and options for securing data within the core network.

Wireless WANS, using IEEE 802.11 standard, are installed for cellular telephone systems using the radio network. A wireless LAN-bridge can connect multiple LANS to form a WAN. Wireless supports varying distances with a direct line-of-sight. Wireless WANS are similar to wireless LANS except that the distances involved are much greater and the bit rates are much slower. Wireless WANS use low bandwidth.

Wireless cellular networks are managed by service providers who provide coverage based on dividing a large geographical service area into smaller areas of coverage called cells. As a mobile phone moves from one cell to another, a cellular arrangement requires active connections to be monitored and effectively passed along between cells to maintain the connection.

In addition to cellular phones, cellular networks support smart phones and cellular data cards. Smart phones offer more functionality than basic cellular phones, including e-mail and Web browsing wirelessly (e.g., Bluetooth and Wi-Fi). Cellular data cards allow laptop users to connect to the Internet anywhere cellular service is available. However, cellular data cards can only access the Internet if the user is within the service provider's network coverage area.

Examples of Wireless Technologies

- Bluetooth technology is used in laptop computers, PDAs, and other mobile devices

- Wireless closed circuit television (CCTV) technology is used in surveillance and monitoring

- Radio frequency (RF) identification technology is used in identification and tracking of items

- 802.11 technology is used in wireless local-area networks (WLANs)

- Mobile radio technology is used in radio transmission

- Wireless mesh network technology is used in transporting data

- Cellular technology is used in cellular modems, routers, and bridges for high-speed wireless data

- WiMAX technology is used in wireless metropolitan-area networks (WMANs)

- Microwave and satellite technology is used in cell phones, PDAs, radio, cable, infrared, and air lasers

Wired Local-Area Networks

A wired local-area network (LAN) is a network that interconnects systems located in a small geographic area, such as an office, all the computers in one building, or all the computers in several buildings in close proximity (i.e., in a campus). LANs can be classified in a number of different ways. Four commonly used classifications include topology, transmission controls, transmission medium, and architectural design.

LAN Architecture

Choosing a LAN software or hardware configuration that will support the desired functional and security features requires an understanding of LAN architectures. Two popular logical architectures that are supported on PC-LAN include client/server architecture and peer-to-peer architecture.

Concepts in Wired LANs

- LAN basic topologies include star, bus, ring, tree, and mesh.

- LAN media access control methods include Ethernet (IEEE 802.3), token bus (IEEE 802.4), IBM token ring (IEEE 802.5), and fiber distributed data interface (FDDI).

- Internet Protocol (IP), which is a packet protocol, is a connectionless protocol so it fits well with the connectionless Ethernet protocol.

- LAN transmission medium includes twisted-pair wire, coaxial cable, and fiber-optic cable.

- LAN transmission methods include unicast, broadcast, and multicast.

- LAN inter-networking devices include routers, bridges, brouters, repeaters, switches, hubs, and gateways.

- Fiber distributed data interface (FDDI) and fiber channel are two ring-based optical LANs, used as backbone networks, and are not successful at the desktop level use.

- FDDI offers an optional bypass switch at each node for addressing failures.

- LANs can link to WANs and other networks using the Internet

Concepts in Wired LANs (continued)

- LANs may use client/server or peer-to-peer architecture
- Transmission media can be guided or unguided.
- Examples of guided transmission media include twisted-pair wire, coaxial cable, and fiber optic cable.
- Examples of unguided transmission media include radio, microwave, infrared, and air lasers.

LAN Security Goals and Features

LAN security goals include (1) maintain the confidentiality of data as it is stored, processed, or transmitted on a LAN, (2) maintain the integrity of data as it is stored, processed, or transmitted on a LAN, (3) maintain the availability of data stored on a LAN, as well as the ability to process and transmit the data in a timely manner, and (4) ensure the identity of the sender and receiver of a message.

LAN Security Concerns and Risks

LAN's major security concerns and risks include distributed file storing (file servers controlling user access to files), remote computing (servers authenticating remote users, system components and applications), topologies and protocols (messages reaching the desired destination), and messaging services (protecting e-mail during transit and in storage). Other security concerns and risks include:

- The possible inherent threats in LANs include both active and passive wiretapping.

- Passive wiretapping includes not only information release but also traffic analysis (using addresses, other header data, message length, and message frequency).

- Active wiretapping includes message stream modifications, including delay, duplication, modification, deletion, or counterfeiting.

- A single-link failure, a repeater failure, or a break in the cable could disable a large part or the entire network.

- When two or more stations transmit at the same time, data frames will collide, leading to unpredictable results and garbled transmission. Neither one gets through. "Who goes next?" is the problem to be resolved. The number of **collisions** will increase as the channel's load increases. When two frames collide, the medium remains unusable for the duration of transmission of both damaged frames. Collision detectors are needed to resolve collision.

LAN Security Concerns and Risks (continued)

- There may not be a backup person for the LAN administrator.

- The backup person, even though designated, may not have been trained adequately to take over the LAN administrator's job duties when needed.

- Changes made to the LAN network may not be transparent to end users.

- LANs can become a single point of failure due to cables and connectivity hardware that could be vulnerable.

- Inadequate LAN management and security policies

- Lack of training for proper LAN usage and security

- Inadequate protection mechanisms in the workstation environment

- Inadequate protection during transmission.

Features Providing High Security in LANs

- Dedicated file server using client/server architecture
- Diskless PCs or workstations remotely booted
- Logical access security control down to lowest level possible (i.e., byte level)
- Encryption of passwords
- Password format control
- Security monitoring, accounting, and reporting
- Network encryption devices
- No disk format command
- Image backup utility programs
- Fault-tolerance design with the use of disk-mirroring, disk-duplicating, or server-mirroring methods
- Reduced system privileges to directories, files, or records
- No remote log-in feature
- Automatic log-out feature after sometime of dormant period
- Printers attached to secured file server

Features Providing Low Security in LANs

- Peer-to-peer architecture
- Allows disk format command
- Shareable printers across the network
- Bootable workstations with local storage facilities
- No directory-, file-, record-, byte-level access controls
- Basic, simple password protection

Client/Server Architecture

Many definitions exist for client/server systems. One broad definition is the coordination of data as application systems are distributed. The application system's processing is divided into two parts (1) client, where users request data services, and (2) server, which furnishes the requested data to the client. In other words, Web pages, documents, and files (e.g., data, video, and audio) are transferred from the server to the client.

Client/server architecture is similar to cooperative processing, which enables the application system to be divided across multiple, different hardware platforms. In other words, the computing process is distributed across multiple, different hardware platforms. This contrasts with distributed processing in that the entire computing process is distributed among several similar platforms. In cooperative processing, a single computing process uses several different connected platforms, while with distributed processing a single computing process runs independently on multiple, similar platforms.

Typical hardware components required in a client/server environment include a personal computer (PC) or workstation capable of storing data, a terminal emulation device, and a physical connection to the host computer system, which are called clients. Servers are powerful computers providing the client computers with a variety of data services. The client and the server are linked via a LAN or other data communications system. The flow of data is mostly one way (i.e., from the server to the client).

Six basic elements of the client/server computing process include (1) data storage, (2) database management system, (3) application system, (4) operating system, (5) display device, and (6) user interface. Elements 1 and 2 are located on the server or host platform, and elements 3 through 6 are located on the client platform.

ClientServer Architecture (continued)

The normal client/server implementation is a two-tiered architecture for simple networks (i.e., one client and one server) and multi-tiered (N-tier) is possible for complex networks. In N-tier architecture, there is one client and several servers (e.g., Web server, application server, database server, and other servers) where client requests are handled by different levels of servers.

Most client/server systems are designed for PCs and LAN-based operating systems. The processing of an application is split between a front-end portion executing on a PC or workstation (**client**) and a back-end portion running on a server.

Four client/server implementation approaches include (1) simple file transfer, (2) application program-ming interface (API), (3) graphical user interface (GUI)-based operating system, and (4) peer-to-peer communications.

Virtual Local-Area Networks

Virtual local-area network (VLAN) technology is an efficient way of grouping users into workgroups to share the same network address space regardless of their physical location on the network. VLAN separates the logical topology of the LANs from their physical topology, and employs the IEEE 802.1Q standard. Users can be organized into separate VLANs according to their department, location, function, application, physical address, logical address, or protocol. Regardless of the organization method used, the goal with any VLAN is to group users into separate communities that share the same resource; thereby, enabling the majority of their traffic to stay within the boundaries of the VLAN.

The logical separation of users and traffic result in a better performance management (i.e., broadcast and bandwidth utilization control). It also facilitates a reduction in configuration management overhead enabling networks to scale at ease. By default, all ports are configured to be members of VLAN1, which is all untagged traffic. As a consequence, VLAN1 may unwisely span the entire network if not appropriately controlled. The risk is even greater if VLAN1 is also used for user VLANs or the management of VLAN. In addition, it is unwise to mix management traffic with user traffic making the management of VLAN an easier target for exploitation.

Trunk links can carry the traffic of multiple VLANs simultaneously. Therein lies a potential security exposure. Trunk links have a native or default VLAN that is used to negotiate trunk status and exchange VLAN configuration information. Trunking also enables a single port to become part of multiple VLANs—another potential security exposure.

Wireless Local-Area Networks

The most widely implemented legacy wireless local-area network (WLAN) technologies are based on the IEEE 802.11 standard and its amendments, which are not capable of using the new IEEE 802.11i standard that is used in robust security networks (RSNs). Wireless LAN transmission protocols include carrier sense multiple access (CSMA), with collision avoidance (CSMA/CA), and with collision detection (CSMA/CD).

Legacy WLANs

Wireless local-area networks (WLANs) are groups of wireless networking nodes within a limited geographic area (e.g., an office building or building campus) that are capable of radio communication. WLANs are usually implemented as extensions to existing wired local-area networks (LAN) to provide enhanced user mobility and network access. Legacy WLANs have limited and weak security-controls, and are particularly susceptible to loss of confidentiality, integrity, and availability. Unauthorized users have access to well-documented security flaws and exploits that can easily compromise an organization's systems and information, corrupt the organization's data, consume network bandwidth, degrade network performance, launch attacks that prevent authorized users from accessing the network, or use the organization's resources to launch attacks on other networks.

Robust Security Networks for WLANs

Based on the IEEE 802.11i standard, robust security networks (RSNs) were found to remedy the security problems of WEP as RSNs provide moderate to high levels of assurance against WLAN security threats through use of a variety of cryptographic techniques. The three types of RSN components are stations (STAs), access points (APs), and authentication servers (ASs).

Campus-Area Networks

A campus-area network (CAN) consists of LANs interconnected within multiple buildings or a short geographic area (e.g., a school campus, office towers, or military base). It can be safely assumed that all the threats, vulnerabilities, and risks applicable to LANs can be equally applicable to CANs due to a common architecture.

Wired Metropolitan-Area Networks

A wired metropolitan-area network (MAN) is configured for a larger geographical area than a LAN, ranging from several blocks of buildings to entire city, for cable television network. MANs can be owned and operated either as public utilities or individual organizations. MANs interconnect two or more LANs. Although MANs depend on moderate-to-high data rates as required for LANs, the error rates and delays would be higher than might be obtained on a LAN. MAN is based on the IEEE 802.6 standard—distributed-queue dual-bus (DQDB) standard. Physically, a MAN consists of a transmission medium and nodes that provide user access to the medium. The DQDB standard is divided into three layers: upper, middle, and lower, as shown in the above.

Wireless Metropolitan-Area Network

Wireless metropolitan-area network (WMAN) employs the worldwide interoperability for microwave access (WiMAX) communication technology using the IEEE 802.16 standard. WiMAX network threats focus on compromising the radio links between WiMAX nodes. These radio links support both line-of-sight (LOS) and non-line-of-sights (NLOS) signal propagation. Links from LOS WiMAX systems are generally harder to attack than those from NLOS systems because an adversary (attacker) would have to physically locate equipment between the transmitting nodes to compromise the confidentiality or integrity of the wireless link. WiMAX NLOS systems provide wireless coverage over large geographic regions (e.g., the size of a city), which expands the potential staging area for both clients and adversaries. Like other wireless networking technologies, all WiMAX systems are susceptible to denial-of-service attacks, eavesdropping, man-in-the-middle (MitM) attacks, message modification, and resource misappropriations.

Wired Wide-Area Networks

A wired wide-area network (WAN) refers to a network that interconnects systems located in a large geographic area, such as a city, a continent, or several continents. A complex network can consist of WANs that span continents or geographic regions within continents and connect smaller, more localized LANs.

WANs connect intelligent terminals, workstations, personal computers, minicomputers, and LANs together. They use public telecommunication facilities to accomplish this connection as well as private. For example, a WAN data link interconnection can be used to connect two or more physical LANs in different geographical locations.

Types of wired WAN Networks include switching networks. Switching is used to share communication channels between many users and can take place in the telephone exchange office, where the user dials into it using a telephone. The exchange can even take place on the user's premises, which enables many users to share a small number of access lines.

The four popular types of switching are message switching, circuit switching, packet switching and hybrid switching. With **message switching**, users can be interconnected on demand without using circuit switches. Messages are forwarded to a final destination (e.g., electronic mail systems). In **circuit switching**, all the lines are connected to telephone exchange or switching offices. Individual users can lease telephone channels and install their own switches. **Packet switching** is another form of message switching used to interconnect all types of users on a general-purpose public data network. In this type, messages are broken up into smaller packets, which are routed independently through the network. X.25 protocol standard is used in packet switching

Wired Wide-Area Networks (continued)

networks. **Hybrid switching** combines circuit switching and packet switching. Computer networks are usually packet switched, occasionally circuit switched, but seldom message switched due to transmission delays and throughput problems.

Fast packet networks, using fiber optic transmission, provide the necessary processing power to keep up with increases in link bandwidth and the necessary flexibility to support different kinds of services and a range of bandwidth requirements. Fast packet networks overcome the main weakness of traditional packet networks by using special control mechanisms to provide the consistent network performance required for video and other real-time services. In traditional packet networks, such as the current Internet, the network may become heavily loaded in a way that degrades these services.

Major Concepts in a Wired Wide-Area Network

- WANs are packet-switched networks, meaning they use routers.

- WAN interconnection devices include bridges, repeaters, routers, switches, multiplexers, modems, and protocol converters.

- WAN networks include (1) private-circuit networks (e.g., ISDN, XDSL, and public and leased lines), (2) circuit-switched networks used in telephone company networks, and (3) packet-switched networks (e.g., X.25, Frame Relay, LAPB, SMDS, ATM, PTM, and VoIP).

- WANs can become a single point of failure due to several ISPs, networks, protocols, and communication lines due to their incompatibility and vulnerability.

The differences between a private (leased) line and public line include:

- A private line provides voice and data transmission services without the public exchange

- A public line provides voice and data transmission services with public exchange

- If a private line fails, its users are cut off from the connection

- If a public line fails, its users are provided with fallback procedures to recover from a disaster or malfunction

---

Major Concepts in a Wired Wide-Area Network (continued)

X.25 standard is an international standard that defines the interface between a computing device and a packet-switched data network (WAN). X.25 implements point-to-point connections between two or more user computers. It is a single point of connection for one user computer and a logical point-to-point (PTP) connection for a number of user computers. This is accomplished through a concept called *virtual circuits* operating in either a permanent mode or a switched mode. The virtual circuits function in the network layer of the ISO/OSI Reference Model. By using X.25, one pays only for the bits sent, unlike circuit-switched or leased lines where one pays for the time regardless of how much was sent. X.25 uses a high-speed shared connection, which is a predecessor to frame relay. Charging is typically by the packet, segment, or character and requires a connection before exchanging data, similar to a telephone call.

Advantages of X.25 virtual circuits include flexibility in providing a range of functions for implementing multiple-protocol enterprise inter-networks when compared with the conventional telecommunication data links. **Disadvantages of X.25** include additional overhead due to handling of multiple protocols and lower throughput due to complex routing decisions.

Broadband Networks

The capacity of a network, measured as the number of bits it can transmit every second, is called bandwidth. Broadband networks are high bandwidth networks due in part to the use of optical fiber and high-speed switches. They carry video, sound, data, and image services. Broadband networks also allow a closer coupling of the computers on a network. Today, any kind of network transmitting at more than 100 million bits per second is considered a broadband network.

Difference Between Narrowband Networks and Broadband Networks

- Examples of narrowband network services include switching networks (WANs) and X.25 standard.

- Examples of broadband networks include frame relay, switched multimegabit data services (SMDS), asynchronous transfer mode (ATM), packet transfer mode (PTM), integrated services digital network (ISDN), digital subscriber line (DSL/ADSL), T lines and carriers, and cable Internet connections.

- Narrowband networks are low bandwidth networks.

- Broadband networks are high bandwidth networks.

- The dividing line between the two networks is not always clear and changes as technology evolves.

Voice over Internet Protocol

VoIP Risks and Opportunities

Voice over Internet protocol (VoIP)—the transmission of voice over packet-switched IP networks—is one of the most important emerging trends in telecommunications. As with many new technologies, VoIP introduces both security risks and opportunities. Lower cost and greater flexibility are among the promises of VoIP for the enterprise, but the technology presents security administrators with significant security challenges. Administrators may mistakenly assume that some digitized voice travels in packets; they can simply plug VoIP components into their already-secure networks and remain secure. Unfortunately, the process is not that simple.

VoIP systems take a wide variety of forms, including traditional telephone handsets, conferencing units, and mobile units. In addition to end-user equipment, VoIP systems include a variety of other components, including call processors/call managers, gateways, routers, firewalls, and protocols.

VoIP General Guidelines

- Separate voice and data on logically different networks. Different subnets with separate RFC 1918 address blocks should be used for voice and data traffic, with separate DHCP servers for each.

- At the voice gateway, which interfaces with the PSTN, disallow H.323, SIP, or MGCP, or Megaco/H.248 connections from the data network. Use strong authentication and access control on the voice gateway system, as with any other critical network management components. Strong authentication of clients towards a gateway is often very difficult. Here, access control mechanisms and policy enforcement may help.

- Use firewalls designed for VoIP traffic, through ALGs or firewall control proxies. Stateful packet filters can track the state of connections, denying packets that are not part of a properly originated call.

- Use IPsec or secure shell (SSH) protocol for all remote management and auditing access. If practical, avoid using remote management at all and do IP PBX access from a physically secure system.

- If performance is a problem, use encryption at the router or other gateway, not the individual end-points, to provide for IPsec tunneling. Since some VoIP endpoints are not computationally powerful enough to perform encryption, placing this burden at a central point ensures that all VoIP traffic emanating from the enterprise network has been encrypted.

VoIP Physical Security Controls

Physical security controls should be installed, including barriers, locks, access control systems, and security guards, which can act as the first line of defense.

VoIP-Ready Firewalls

Because of the inherent vulnerabilities (e.g., susceptibility to packet sniffing) of operating telephony across a packet network, VoIP systems incorporate an array of security features and protocols. Organization security policy should ensure that these features are used. In particular, firewalls designed for VoIP protocols are an essential component of a secure VoIP system.

VoIP Training

Emerging technologies when coupled with network administrators not yet trained on the technology, lax security practices, insufficient controls, and poor understanding of the risks form an especially challenging security environment. Therefore, organizations should carefully consider such issues as administrators' level of knowledge and training in the technology, the maturity and quality of their security practices, controls, policies, and architectures, and their understanding of the associated security risks.

VoIP Quality of Service Issues

- Latency refers to the time it takes for a voice transmission to go from its source to its destination.

- Jitter refers to non-uniform packet delays.

- Packet loss can result from excess latency.

- Bandwidth congestion can cause packet loss and a host of other problems.

- Speed is the key to conquering issues like latency and bandwidth congestion.

Voice Mail Systems

Voice mail (V-mail) or voice messaging systems are computer-based systems with their own input, editing, storage, retrieval, and transmission of information in the form of natural (human) or synthetic speech. V-mail systems can be PC-based or private branch exchange (PBX). A PBX is a telephone branch switch located at an end-user site. The PBX is used to connect two end users or an end user and the telephone company network. Each user is given a voice "mailbox" for his own use. Outgoing and incoming messages can be of any length, or they can be fixed. All messages are date-stamped and time-stamped.

Private Branch Exchange Systems

A private branch exchange (PBX) system is a sophisticated computer-based switch that can be thought of as a small in-house phone company. Failure to secure a PBX can result in exposing the organization to toll fraud (most common), disclosure of proprietary or confidential information due to eavesdropping, unauthorized access to routing and address data, data modification (changing billing information), denial of service by making the equipment inoperable or forced to operate in a degraded state, traffic analysis (observing information about telephone calls and making inferences), lack of external access controls over remote maintenance ports and access to the switch by a potentially large pool of outside parties, and loss of revenue or legal entanglements. The threats to PBX telephone systems are many, depending on the goals of attackers.

Plain Old Telephone Service

Plain old telephone service (POTS) is a basic and conventional voice telephone system with a wired telecommunication connection. It contains a POTS coder/decoder (CODEC) as a digital audio device and a POTS filter (DSL filter). Three major components of POTS include local loops (analog twisted pairs going into houses and businesses), trunks (digital fiber optics connecting the switching offices), and switching offices (where calls are moved from one trunk to another). A potential risk or disadvantage of POTS is eavesdropping due to physical access to tap a telephone line or penetration of a switch. Another disadvantage is phony telephone bills by phone attackers. An advantage of POTS or mobile phone is that they can serve as a backup for PBX and VoIP system during a cable modem outage or DSL line outage.

Virtual Private Networks

A virtual private network (VPN) is a virtual network, built on top of existing physical networks, provides a secure communications tunnel for data/information transmitted between networks. VPN is a protected information system utilizing link tunneling, security controls, and endpoint address translation giving the impression of a dedicated (leased) line. Because a VPN can be used over existing networks such as the Internet, it can facilitate the secure transfer of sensitive data across public networks. VPNs are usually established and managed by VPN gateway devices owned and managed by the organization being protected. Although VPNs can be implemented on top of asynchronous transfer mode or frame relay, or over WAN connections, an increasing popular approach is to build VPNs directly over the Internet. Leased lines (e.g., T1 and T3) are secure but expensive and the Internet is less expensive.

The main components that make VPN secure are encrypted traffic and protected authentication mechanism. The authentication method can be security token, securely distributed certificate, known key, password, or combination of any of these methods. Once the authentication is complete, the VPN should encrypt all traffic between end-points to ensure no data are leaked and to prevent man-in-the-middle attacks. Multifactor identification and authentication is strongly advised to neutralize the effectiveness of brute-force attacks. A common multifactor identification is a combination of a security token, known key, certificate, a password, PIN, or biometrics.

A VPN can allow employees to connect to the Intranet securely, so there are no fears of sensitive information leaving the network unprotected. The Internet alone cannot remove this fear.

Virtual Private Networks (continued)

A VPN is a private network composed of computers owned by a single organization that share information with each other in that organization (e.g., LAN or WAN). On the other hand, a public network is a large collection of organizations or computers who exchange information with each other (e.g., a public telephone system and the Internet).

A VPN blurs the line between a private and public network. With a VPN, a secure, private network can be created over a public network such as the Internet. A VPN can be created using software, hardware, or a combination of the two that provides a secure link between peers over a public network. Control techniques, such as encryption, packet tunneling, and firewalls, are used in a VPN. Tunneling encapsulates a packet within a packet to accommodate incompatible protocols. The packet within the packet could either be of the same protocol or of a completely different one.

The private network is called virtual because it uses temporary connections that have no real physical presence, but consist of packets routed over various computers on the Internet on an ad hoc basis. Secure virtual connections are created between two computers, a computer and a network, or two networks. A VPN does not exist physically.

A VPN is a distributed collection of networks or systems that are interconnected via a public and/or private network but protects their communications using encryption. In effect, a VPN is a private secure distributed network that is transported or tunneled across a public and/or private network. Typically, VPN encryption is implemented at the local network entry points (i.e., the firewall or premise router), thereby freeing the end systems from having to provide the necessary encryption or communication security functions.

Virtual Private Networks (continued)

The placement of the VPN is to maintain the security of the enclave and the requirement that all traffic must pass through the enclave security architecture. This is not to say that encrypted data (e.g., SSL, SSH, and TSL) that entered the VPN tunnel must also be unencrypted prior to leaving the tunnel. However, the data would still have to pass through the respective application proxy. If host-to-host VPN is required, it will be established between trusted hosts.

A VPN solution can be cheaper than conventional networks that run over WAN connections. VPN devices and software provide not only encryption functions but also network access control to secure Internet tunnels between remote sites. A VPN must provide privacy and integrity of data as it traverses the public network. At a minimum, it should provide user authentication, address management, and data encryption security services.

Four types of VPNs exist: secure sockets layer (SSL) VPNs, Internet Protocol security (IPsec) VPNs, ESP in tunnel mode, and firewall-based VPNs. Three primary models for IPsec VPN architectures include gateway-to-gateway, host-to-gateway, and host-to-host. Alternatives to IPsec VPNs include encapsulating security payload tunnel mode and firewall-based VPNs.

Multimedia Collaborative Computing Networks

Multimedia collaborative computing networks include instant messaging (IM) architecture, Internet relay chat (IRC) architecture, remote (virtual) meeting technology, networked whiteboards, cameras, and microphones. Explicit indication of use includes signals to users when collaborative computing devices are activated.

The IM architectures vary in design depending on the services being provided to the end users. There are four possible architectural designs for IM systems: private hosting (i.e., client-to-server), public hosting, client-to-client, and public switched network. The difference between the four architectures is the location of the session data.

The IRC architecture consists of servers and clients. Servers form the backbone of the network, linking components together and using routing capabilities to relay messages to their destinations. All packets are relayed through the server hence the name of the protocol. Clients reside on the machines of users who are chatting on the network. Currently, IRC is mainly designed for group (many-to-many) communication in discussion forums called channels, but also allows one-to-one communications via private message. IRC networks that are in operation need to migrate to newer IM technologies due to the inherent security vulnerabilities with IRC.

Ad Hoc Networks

Networks of nodes that are near each other are called ad hoc networks, where both the routers and the hosts are mobile and running on the same computer (i.e., Nodes = Routers + Hosts). In traditional wired networks, the routers are fixed and the hosts are mobile. In ad-hoc networks, topologies are changing all the time without warning. An ad hoc network is used when a group of users with notebook computers are gathered in one area where the service of IEEE 802.11 standard is not available in that area. A common routing algorithm used in ad hoc networks is ad hoc on-demand distance vector, which determines a route to some destination only when somebody wants to send a packet to that destination (i.e., as needed, meaning ad hoc). Bluetooth has emerged as a very popular ad hoc network standard.

Content Delivery Networks

Content delivery networks (CDNs) are used to deliver the contents of music, movies, sports, or news from content owners' Web sites to end users quickly with the use of tools and techniques such as client caching, server replication, client's request redirection, and a proxy content server to enhance the Web performance in terms of optimizing the disk size and preload time.

Three parties exist in the CDN process to deliver the content to the end users: CDN provider (contractor), Internet service provider (ISP), and the content owner (music or news provider). The CDN contractor delivers the content owner's material to the end users via the ISP for a fee. Server replication is called server mirroring where the content is replicated at multiple, dispersed locations for end users' easy and quick access. The content is redirected without changing the domain name system (DNS). Similar to caching which improves the client's performance, mirroring improves the server's performance.

Value-Added Networks

Value-added carriers lease channels from other common carriers and then provide additional services to customers, using these leased channels. They operate a public data network, where the equipment breaks up the user's data into packets, routes the packets over its network between one location and another, and reassembles them into their original form on the other end. Value-added networks (VANs) take advantage of the economies of scale. Usually, they share a wider bandwidth, which gives faster response time. Some examples of services provided by VANs include bulletin board services, Internet services, electronic data interchange (EDI), and dial-in services.

Wireless Sensor Networks

Wireless sensor networks (WSNs) are networks of interconnected wireless devices that are embedded into the physical environment to provide measurements, for example, of a building security. These devices have built-in processing, storage, and radio frequency (RF) sensors and antennas. These sensors start with low-level sensors and progress toward nodes for high-level data aggregation, analysis, and storage, where data are routed over a network to an automated computer facility. Typical applications of WSNs include monitoring traffic or military activity, protecting physical property, monitoring environmental changes in a building (e.g., humidity, voltage, and temperature), managing machinery and vehicle operation, establishing physical security perimeters for building and facilities, monitoring supply chain management activities, and detecting the presence of chemical, biological, or radiological substances.

Digital Cellular Networks

Today, separate networks are used for voice traffic (the telephone traffic), computer communications (data networks such as the Internet), and video (broadcast or cable television or other specialized networks), which are expensive, time-consuming, and complicated. The day will come soon when a single digital network can potentially be used to transmit all types of data and information (i.e., voice, data, video, and images).

Digital cellular network standards in the world are varied and incompatible with each other. For example, the U.S. uses a code division multiple access (CDMA) standard whereas the rest of the world uses a global system for mobile communications (GSM) standard. Today's cellular network systems are used to transmit both voice and data (e.g., a short message service (SMS) to send and receive text messages). More powerful cellular networks use third-generation (3G) or fourth-generation (4G) networks to send and receive voice, data, video, and images.

Peer-to-Peer Networks

Broadly defined, a peer-to-peer (P2P) network is a distributed computing software architecture that enables individual computers to connect to and communicate directly with other computers. Through this connection, computer users (known as peers) can share communications, processing power, and data files. With respect to file sharing specifically, P2P technology allows decentralized sharing. That is, rather than storing files in a central location to which individual computers must connect to retrieve the files, P2P technology enables individual computers to share directly among themselves files stored on the individual computers. P2P file-sharing programs themselves do not perform the sharing or copying of files; rather, they employ a protocol that facilitates communication between the two peers who wish to share or copy a particular file. Peers can share myriad types of files, including audio, video, software, word processing, and photographs.

By eliminating the need for a central storage point for files, P2P file-sharing technology allows for faster file transfers and conservation of bandwidth (i.e., the capacity to transmit information to and from a computer). In addition, because P2P technology decreases the need for businesses and consumers to store files on their hard drives, it can lower costs by conserving on storage requirements and saving on maintenance and energy costs related to data retrieval, sharing, and processing.

Uses of and risks from P2P technology include the following:

- P2P technology enables users to share communications, processing power, and data files with other users. Use of P2P technology can enhance efficiency by allowing faster file transfers, conserving bandwidth, and reducing or eliminating the need for central storage of files.

Peer-to-Peer Networks (continued)

- P2P technology has a variety of applications, the most common application by far is commercial file-sharing software programs used by consumers to exchange files, such as music, movies, television programs, video games, software, and pornography.

- P2P technology continues to evolve in response to market and legal forces. It appears likely that the uses of P2P technology will expand in the future.

- Consumers face risks when using commercial P2P file-sharing software programs, including risks related to data security, spyware and adware, viruses, copyright infringement, and unwanted pornography.

Converged Networks

A converged network occurs when two different networks are combined, as in the case of data and voice networks. A converged network is subject to vulnerabilities and threats. For example, the same openings that allow voice traffic to pass unimpeded may also either create high-bandwidth covert channels for data infiltration or exfiltration or provide a point of entry for other probes and attacks. Although it may be impossible to examine voice traffic in real time without incurring unacceptable delay, it may be possible to isolate the voice traffic in some way from the rest of the network to minimize the vulnerabilities introduced by opening these entry points. Although firewalls, hardware/software guards, and downgraders serve to separate an enclave from the outside world or the rest of the network, they may not limit latency, jitter, and delay problems in the context of the converged network.

A converged network is a **single point of failure** in a way that totally separate data and voice infrastructures were not because the converged network may not have uninterruptible power supply and fault tolerance mechanisms to facilitate graceful degradation.

Until the technology improves, it might be preferable to isolate the packet-switched digital voice on a separate network from the data network. This isolation is a better approach rather than an ad-hoc box-based mix-and-match solution focused on individual functions.

Optical Networks

Optical networks use fiber-optic cables, which are strands of clear glass fiber. These cables are faster, lighter, secure, durable, expensive, and difficult to install. The optical network can transmit voice, data, and video with greater bandwidth. Existing optical networks can increase their capacity with dense wavelength division multiplexing (DWDM), which enables a single communications channel to carry simultaneously data transmissions from multiple sources without any extra cable. DWDM uses different wavelengths to carry separate streams of data over the same cable at the same time. Prior to DWDM, optical networks could use only a single wavelength per strand.

Synchronous optical network (SONET) is popular in transmitting voice, data, and video over optical networks. Most long-distance telephone systems in the world use SONET to standardize and connect multiple and different long-distance carriers. The goals of SONET are to (1) interwork the multiple carriers with a common signaling standard regarding wavelength, timing, and framing structures, (2) unify the pulse code modulation (PCM) channels, which are incompatible with each other, (3) multiplex different digital channels with different speed in terms of data rates, and (4) provide support for operations, administration, and maintenance systems. SONET is a synchronous system, meaning that the sender and receiver are tied to a common clock, whereas asynchronous transfer mode (ATM) system is not tied to a common clock because it permits irregular cell arrivals. SONET operates at the physical layer of the ISO/OSI model and supports gigabit transmission rates. SONET has a fault tolerance mechanism (i.e., redundancy) in that it has a backup ring to ensure continued transmission if the primary ring fails.

Body Area Networks

Body area network is a new technology that allows communication between ultra-small and ultra-low-power intelligent sensors/devices that are located on the body surface or implanted inside the body. In addition, the wearable/implantable nodes can also communicate to a controller device that is located in the vicinity of the body. These radio-enabled sensors can be used to continuously gather a variety of important health and/ or physiological data (i.e., information critical to providing health care) wirelessly.

Radio-enabled implantable medical devices offer a revolutionary set of possible applications, including smart pills for precision drug delivery, intelligent endoscope capsules, glucose monitors, and eye pressure sensing systems. Similarly, wearable sensors allow for various medical and physiological monitoring (e.g., electrocardiogram, temperature, respiration, heart rate, and blood pressure) and disability assistance.

Radio Frequency Identification Networks

Radio frequency identification (RFID) network systems share information across organizational boundaries, such as *supply chain* applications. RFID systems provide a method for tracking the movement of goods throughout the supply chain. These systems use small tags with embedded microchips containing data about an item and its location to transmit radio signals over a short distance to special RFID readers. These readers then pass the data over a network to a computer for processing the tag's data. These tags, unlike bar codes, do not need line-of-sight contact to be read. RFID systems can be very complex, and implementations vary greatly across industries and organizations.

An RFID system is composed of three components such as a RF subsystem, an enterprise subsystem, and an inter-enterprise subsystem. The four major categories of RFID risk are (1) business process risk (loss of critical and operational records and cloning of tags), (2) business intelligence risk (access to sensitive or proprietary information), (3) privacy risk (profiling individuals using the tagged items), and (4) externality risk (health hazards from electromagnetic radiation).

Network Connections

Network connections consist of connectivity hardware devices and software to share resources and information among the networks. This would enable a network user to establish a communication link with a user from another network, and vice versa. These hardware devices and software move data frames and packets from one cable segment to another. They may use a piggybacking technique of temporarily delaying outgoing acknowledgements of data frames so that they can be attached to the next outgoing data frames.

Network Switches

A computer network has three main components: computers, links, and switches. The web of links and switches carry data between the computers. Links are made of copper (either twisted pair or coaxial cable) or fiber optics. Transmission equipment at each end of the fiber or copper generates the electrical or optical signals. There are also satellite and microwave links that send radio waves through the air. Fiber optics has several advantages over other types of links— most notably its very high bandwidth.

As the information travels through the network, the switches decide which link it will have to traverse next in order to reach its destination. The rules by which the switches and the users' computers coordinate the transmission of information through the network are called protocols.

Bridges and repeaters share the same physical transmission medium to interconnect or extend a local-area network (LAN). Switches and hardware devices are designed for the opposite purpose of bridges and repeaters. Switches, in the form of routers, interconnect when the systems forming one workgroup are physically separated from the systems forming other workgroups. Switches do not extend LANs as bridges and repeaters do. Switches are primarily used to (1) implement multiple, parallel transmission medium segments to which different groups of workstations can be connected, and (2) provide full network bandwidth to multiple groups of systems.

Network switches are devices that provide connectivity between two or more hosts located on the same network segment. They are similar to hubs in that they allow communications between hosts, but, unlike hubs, the switches have more intelligence and send communications to only those hosts to which the communications are addressed. The benefit of this from a security standpoint is that when switches are employed on a network,

Network Switches (continued)

it is much more difficult to eavesdrop on communications between other hosts on the network segment. This is extremely important when a Web server is on a network segment that is used by other hosts. For example, if a hub is used and a host on the demilitarized zone (DMZ) is compromised, an attacker may be able to eavesdrop on the communications of other hosts on the DMZ, possibly leading to the compromise of those hosts or the information they communicate across the network. For example, e-mail servers in their default configurations receive unencrypted passwords; a compromise of the Web server would lead to the exposure of e-mail passwords by sniffing them from the compromised Web server.

Switches can have a negative impact on network-based intrusion detection and prevention systems (IDPSs). Most network switches allow network administrators to configure a specific port on the switch, known as a span port, so that it replicates the entire switch's traffic to the port used by the IDPS. This allows a network-based IDPS to see all traffic on a particular network segment. However, under high loads, the switch might have to stop sending traffic to the span port, causing the IDPS to be unable to monitor network activity. Also, other devices use span ports, and there are typically very few span ports on a switch; therefore, it might not be possible to connect an IDPS to a particular switch because its span ports are all in use.

Bridges

A bridge is a device that connects two or more similar or dissimilar LANs together to form an extended LAN. Bridges are protocol independent devices and are designed to store and then forward frames destined for another LAN. Bridges are transparent to the end-stations connecting through the bridge. Bridges can reduce total traffic on the extended LAN by filtering unnecessary traffic from the overall network. A bridge functions in a MAC/Data Link layer of the ISO/OSI Reference Model. Bridges are similar to switches. Various types of bridges include local bridges, remote bridges, learning bridges, and source routing bridges.

Bridges and routers are lower-level network interconnection devices. Typically network interconnection strategies will involve some combination of bridges and routers. The decision when to use a bridge and when to use a router is a difficult one. Enterprises may use bridging to connect LANs between different buildings on corporate or university campuses. Bridging access point (AP) devices are typically placed on top of buildings to achieve greater antenna reception.

Brouters

Brouters are routers that can also bridge; they route one or more protocols and bridge all other network traffic. Routing bridges are those capable of maintaining the protocol transparency of a standard bridge while also making intelligent path selections, just like a router. Brouters merge the capabilities of bridges and routers into a single, multi-functional device.

Repeaters

Repeaters offer the simplest form of inter-connectivity hardware devices. Multiple cables can be connected by repeaters to make larger networks. They merely generate or repeat data packets or electrical signals between cable segments. Repeaters perform data insertion and reception functions. They receive a message, amplify it, and then retransmit it, regenerating the signal at its original strength in both directions. In their purest form, repeaters physically extend a network. They also provide a level of fault tolerance by isolating networks electrically, so problems on one cable segment do not affect other segments. However, repeaters exert stress on a network's bandwidth due to difficulty in isolating network traffic. Repeaters are independent of protocols and media. A repeater operates in a physical layer of the ISO/OSI Reference Model and performs no data link level functions. Repeaters are similar to hubs.

Summary of Functions of Bridges, Routers, Repeaters, and Switches

- Bridges are generally considered to be faster than routers since the processing they perform is simpler.

- Routers are limited to particular routing protocols, while bridges may be transparent to most routing protocols.

- Bridging protocols are semi-automatic. Routers are automatic and depend on routing tables which typically must be maintained.

- Bridge protocols limit the size of any extended LAN network while routers do not. Routers are used to connect LANs, WANs, and WANs.

- Bridges and repeaters share the same physical transmission medium to interconnect or extend a LAN

- Routers do not propagate broadcast. Bridges do.

- Routers and switches provide the simplest method of local authentication for network infrastructure devices.

- Repeaters and hubs are similar in function.

- Bridges and switches are similar in function.

- Switches do not extend LANS as bridges and repeaters do.

Gateways

A gateway is an interface providing compatibility between networks by converting transmission speeds, protocols, codes, or security measures. In general, a gateway is a device that connects incompatible networks using different communications protocols so that information can be passed from one to the other (i.e., two connection-oriented protocol such as TCP/IP and ATM transport protocol). A gateway transfers information and converts it to a form compatible with the receiving network's protocols (e.g., an e-mail gateway could translate the Internet messages into short messaging system (SMS) messages for mobile phones). Several types of gateway exist, including data gateways, e-mail gateways, application gateways, secure gateways, XML gateways, and VPN gateways.

Which Connectivity Device Operates Where in the Open System Interconnection (OSI) Model Layer?

- A gateway operates in the application layer and transport layer.

- A router operates in the network layer.

- A bridge and switch operates in the data-link layer.

- A repeater and hub operates in the physical layer.

- A network interface card operates at the data-link layer.

- Firewalls operate at lower layers and higher layers. Basic firewalls operate on one or a few lower layers while more advanced firewalls examine all of the layers. Firewalls that examine more layers can perform more granular and thorough examinations. A firewall that only handles lower layers (e.g., data link layer) cannot usually identify specific

Proxies and Reverse Proxies

A **proxy** is a computer with software acting as a barrier between a private network and the Internet by presenting only a single network address to external sites. By acting as a go-between representing all internal computers, the Web proxy protects network identities while still providing access to the Internet. Proxy servers forward application traffic through a firewall. Proxies tend to be specific to the protocol they are designed to forward and may provide increased access control or audit. A proxy server is a firewall component that manages Internet traffic to and from a LAN. The proxy server also provides document caching and access control. A proxy server can improve performance by supplying frequently requested data (e.g., a popular Web page) and can filter and discard requests that the owner does not consider appropriate (e.g., unauthorized access requests).

Reverse proxies are devices that sit between a Web server and the server's clients. The term "reverse proxy" is used because the data flow is the reverse of a traditional (forward) proxy. Reverse proxies can serve as a valuable addition to the security of a Web server.

Reverse proxies should be considered for any high-risk Web server deployment. While they do add risk by requiring the deployment of additional hardware and software, the risk is generally outweighed by the benefits. In addition to the functionality list above, Web proxies are also valuable because they add an additional layer between a Web server and its less trusted users. Due to their highly specialized nature, proxies are easier to secure than Web servers. Proxies also further obfuscate a Web server's configuration, type, location, and other details that are pertinent to attackers. For example, Web servers have banners that frequently reveal the Web

Proxies and Reverse Proxies (continued)

server type and version, and these banners sometimes cannot be changed. With a reverse proxy, this is not an issue because the proxy can rewrite the banner before it is sent to users.

Modems

If computers are connected over long distances, modems are needed. Modem is an acronym for modulator and demodulator. It is a device that modulates and demodulates signals. Modems are primarily used for converting digital signals into quasi-analog signals for transmission over analog communication channels and for reconverting the quasi-analog signals into digital signals. Many additional functions may be added to a modem to provide customer service and control features. Modems can be installed either internally or externally to a computer.

The range of options available on modems is quite large. Simple units do little more than perform the digital-to-analog signal conversion, but more intelligent units can automatically dial phone numbers, store messages for delayed transmission, and perform a number of other functions.

The factors identified in modem selection include (1) the requirements of the communications software and target computer, (2) speed (measured in baud), (3) physical connection (RS-232 and V.35), (4) duplex (full or half), (5) synchronization scheme (asynchronous or synchronous), and (6) dialing (manual or automated).

Major functions of modems include (1) attaching modems to a stand-alone personal computer either internally or externally and (2) attaching modems to network-based personal computers. Two types of modems are cable modems and digital modems.

Port Protection Devices

A port protection device (PPD) is fitted to a communications port of a host computer and authorizes access to the port itself, prior to and independent of the computer's own access control functions. A PPD can be a separate device in the communications stream (typically PPDs are found only in serial communications streams) or it may be incorporated into a communications device (e.g., a modem). PPDs typically require a separate authenticator, such as a password, in order to access the communications port.

One of the most common PPDs is the dial-back modem. In a typical dial-back modem sequence, a user calls the dial-back modem and enters a password. The modem hands up on the user and performs a table look-up for the password provided. If the password is found, the modem places a return call to the user (at a previously specified number) to initiate the session. The return call itself also helps to protect against the use of lost or compromised accounts. This is, however, not always the case. Malicious hackers can use advanced functions such as call forwarding to re-route calls. Another device is a terminal server that acts as a PPD for remote maintenance connection such as router maintenance port.

Multiplexers

A multiplexer is a device for combining two or more channels. A channel is a single path provided from a transmission medium either by physical separation (e.g., cable) or by electrical separation (e.g., frequency- or time-division multiplexing). In optical communications, one encounters wavelength-division multiplexing (WDM), involving the use of several distinct optical sources (e.g., lasers) with each having a distinct center frequency. In general, muitlplexing is the combining of two or more information channels onto a common transmission medium.

Hardware Controllers

A controller is a hardware device that coordinates and manages the operation of one or more input/output devices, such as computer terminals, workstations, disks, and printers. It synchronizes the operations of these devices with the operation of the computer system as a whole. A controller organizes a series of actions from requests received from computer terminals, other controllers, or host computer systems. Many varieties of controllers exist, including communication controller, store controller, cluster controller, and terminal controller.

Protocol Converters

Protocol converters are devices that change one type of coded data to another type of coded data for computer processing. Conversion facilities allow an application system conforming to one network architecture to communicate with an application system conforming to some other network architecture.

Protocol Analyzers

A protocol analyzer is a range of equipment that varies widely in functions and user friendliness. Examples of its functions include password sniffing and packet sniffing performed by sniffers. Protocol analyzers perform password sniffing to capture passwords for unauthorized reuse.

Sniffers are LAN protocol analyzers that capture packets and analyze them for certain attributes. They capture illegally short or long frames typically discarded by standard LAN adapters. Sniffers are programs to capture, interpret, and store packets traversing a network used for later analysis and debugging network problems. Sensitive data such as username (user ID) and password combination, confidential e-mail messages, and file transfers of proprietary data can be sniffed.

The protocol analyzer allows the LAN administrator to see what is happening on the LAN in real time and observe problems as they occur. It is a valuable tool for online testing of service degradation.

Backbone Network

A backbone network is a central network to which other networks connect. Users are not attached directly to the backbone network; they are connected to the access networks, which in turn connect to the backbone. A backbone network provides connection between LANs and WANs. Dumb terminals can be attached directly to the backbone through terminal servers. The backbone network is a high-speed connection within a network that connects shorter, usually slower circuits.

How Do Networks Get Connected?

- Front-end networks connect workstations and servers for file sharing and application processing.

- Back-end networks connect peripherals such as disk drives and high-speed printers.

- A backbone network is a central network to which other networks connect.

Concentrators

The major function of concentrators is to gather together several lines in one central location. Concentrators are the foundation of a fiber distributed data interface (FDDI) network and are attached directly to the FDDI dual ring. Concentrators provide highly fault-tolerant connections to the FDDI rings.

The concentrator allows stations to be inserted and removed with minimal effect on the operation of the ring. One of the functions of the concentrator is to ensure ports (stations) are automatically bypassed in response to a detected fault connection, a high error rate, or when a user powers down the station. This bypass function of the concentrator enhances the reliability of the FDDI ring.

Hubs

A hub can be thought of as a central place from which all connecting lines are made. All the lines coming into a hub must operate at the same speed. Hubs do not amplify the incoming signals, unlike repeaters. Like repeaters, hubs do not examine the IEEE 802 addresses. If two frames arrive at the same time, they will collide, similar to a coaxial cable. Hubs are similar to repeaters.

Definitions of a hub include: (1) it is the link from the remote end users to the central satellite and back to the central satellite dish; (2) it is the link from Ethernet LANs to host computers; and (3) it is another name for the Ethernet concentrator. Although hubs are cheaper than switches, hubs are becoming obsolete due to falling prices of switches and due to better performance of switches over hubs. However, legacy hubs still exist. The backbone network is also used as a hub, but it is not common now.

Connectors

A connector is an electro-mechanical device on the ends of cables that permit them to be connected with, and disconnected from, other cables. The type of cable used determines the type of connector needed (e.g., a thicknet coaxial cable needs Type N connector). For example, connectors join controllers to peripherals (e.g., printers and hard disk drive) and computers.

Network Interface Cards

Network interface cards (NICs) are circuit boards used to transmit and receive commands and messages between a PC and a LAN. NICs are expansion cards and they mediate between the computer and the physical media (e.g., cable) over which transmissions take place. When the network interface card fails, workstations and file servers also fail. *Network adapters*, functioning similarly to NICs, establish a connection to other computers or peripherals, such as a printer in the network. NIC operates at the data-link layer.

Mobile wireless stations need an add-on card called a wireless NIC with a built-in radio and antenna signals to establish connections to the wireless LAN. In a wireless LAN, a station or client can be a laptop/notebook/desktop computer or PDA with a wireless NIC. Usually, the wireless NIC is inserted in the client's PCMCIA slot or USB port.

Front-End Processors

A front-end processor (FEP) is a programmed-logic or stored-program device that interfaces data communication equipment with an input/output bus or the memory of a data processing computer. It reduces the workload of a host computer by performing certain tasks that the host computer would otherwise do. A programmable FEP (PFEP) puts less demand on the host computer by sharing some tasks with the host. The PFEP performs polling, code conversion, and data formatting functions.

Network Nodes

A network node has multiple definitions: (1) it is a physical connection (junction) point where communication lines come to and leave from; (2) in network topology, it is a terminal of any branch of a network or an interconnection common to two or more branches of a network; (3) it is the point at an end of a branch; (4) in a tree structure, it is a point at which subordinate items of data originate; (5) it is the representation of a state or event in terms of a point on a diagram; and (6) in a switched network, it is one of the switches forming the network backbone. Nodes can be distributed to host processors, communication controllers, or terminals. Nodes are labeled as major node, minor node, endpoint node, host node, master node, intermediate node, or terminal node.

Which Network Uses What Topology?

Topology affects security so proper selection and functioning of topology is important to ensure proper security. Several types of topologies exist for several networks, as follows:

- Star topology—All nodes are connected to a single central hub. Traffic is in both directions.

- Bus topology—All nodes are connected to a central cable, called the bus or backbone. Traffic is in both directions.

- Ring topology—All nodes are connected to one another in the shape of a closed loop, so that each node is connected directly to two other nodes, one on either side of it. Traffic is in one direction.

- Mesh topology—Networked components are connected with many redundant interconnections between network nodes. In a true mesh topology, every node has a connection to every other node in the network.

- Hybrid topology—A linear bus backbone connects with the star-configured network.

- **Dial-up telephone services and private branch exchange (PBX) systems** use the star topology.

- **Ethernet** mostly uses the bus topology.

- **Fiber distributed data interface (FDDI)** uses the ring topology.

- **The Internet** uses the mesh topology.

Sockets

Sockets (SOCKS) are end points created in a TCP service by both the sender and the receiver. Each socket has a socket number consisting of the IP address of the host and a port number. For a TCP service to be obtained, a connection must be made between a socket on the sending computer and a socket on the receiving computer. Two or more connections can terminate at the same socket. Connections are identified by the socket number at both ends, and no virtual circuit numbers are used. In TCP/IP, the socket number is the concatenation of the sender's or receiver's IP address and the port number for the service being used. The pair of these sender's and receiver's socket numbers uniquely specifies the connection to the Internet.

Ports

A port has multiple definitions: (1) it is an access point for data entry or exit; (2) it is a connector on a device to which cables for other devices such as terminals and printers are attached; and (3) in a communication network, it is a point at which signals can enter or leave the network en route to or from another network.

A port is identified by a port number assigned either ephemerally or permanently to enable IP packets to be sent to a particular process on a computer connected to the Internet. An ephemeral port number goes out of use when the session ends. All ports should be closed when they are not in use because open and unused ports invite attackers.

Some protocols such as file transfer protocol (FTP) and simple mail transfer protocol (SMTP) use the same permanent port number in all TCP/IP implementations. Note that some connections use TCP protocol for FTP, SMTP, and TELNET services; some use UDP protocol for DNS service; and while others use either TCP or UDP for PING echo service.

TELNET is the TCP/IP standard network virtual terminal protocol that is used for remote terminal connection service and that allows a user at one site to interact with systems at other sites as if that user terminal were directly connected to computers at those sites.

Packet Internet groper (PING) is a TCP/IP diagnostic program that sends one or a series of Internet control message protocol (ICMP) echo packets to a user-specified IP address. The echo packet requests the receiver to reply with an echo reply packet. The PING program measures and displays the round-trip time for replies to

Ports (continued)

return, the number of hosts that are operational, and the number of IP addresses that are valid, and the percentage of returned packets or lost packets. The PING protocol tests the ability of a computer to communicate with a remote computer by sending a query and receiving a confirmation response.

Ports are labeled as serial port, parallel port, terminal port, input/output port, protocol port, disabled port, or communication port. Ports should be closed when not in use because open ports invite attackers.

Subnets

A subnet (also called sub network) has multiple definitions: (1) it is a network that forms part of a larger network; (2) in TCP/IP, it is a part of a network that is identified by a portion of the Internet address; (3) it is a group of nodes with the same network ID; and (4) it is the Ethernet part of a main network.

Portals

A portal is a Web site that acts as a gateway to the Internet. A portal is a collection of links, content, and services designed to guide end users for information search on the Internet (e.g., Yahoo and MSN). A portal is a server that offers access to one or more applications through a single centralized interface. Most portals are Web-based—for them, the portal client is a regular Web browser. The application client software is installed on the portal server, and it communicates with application server software on servers within the organization. The portal server communicates securely with the portal client as needed; the exact nature of this depends on the type of portal solution in use.

Examples of portals include (1) application portals such as SSL portal VPN, which is a Web-based portal providing a user with access to multiple Web-based applications from a single portal website; (2) Ethernet portal, which is connected to the Internet; and (3) mobile (wireless) portals, which provide content and services on users' mobile devices by guiding users to the information they need.

Wireless Devices

The most frequently used handheld wireless devices include personal digital assistants (PDAs), text-messaging devices, smart phones, and Bluetooth.

Wireless Access Points

Wireless access points are devices that act as a conduit to connect wireless communication devices together to allow them to communicate and create a wireless network. For example, employees travelling on business work with wireless-enabled devices can connect to an organization's network via any one of the many public Internet access points or public hot spots.

Domain Controller

A domain controller is a server responsible for managing domain information, such as login identification and passwords.

Programmable Logic Controller

A programmable logic controller (PLC), used in industrial control systems, is a programmable microprocessor-based device designed to control and monitor various inputs and outputs used to automate industrial processes. Since PLC is a first-level decision-making device controlling safety interlocks, it can become a **single point of failure.**

Quality of Service and Quality of Protection

Network congestion occurs when too many network packets are present in the subnet (i.e., too much traffic), thus degrading the network performance in terms of some lost packets or all packets undelivered. The presence of congestion means that the load is temporarily greater than the system resources can handle. Two solutions are available to the congestion problem: either increase the resources or decrease the load.

Quality of service (QoS*)* is a network performance property that specifies a guaranteed throughput level for end-to-end services, which is critical for most composite Web services in delivering enterprise-wide service-oriented distributed systems. Examples of network performance properties include throughput (bandwidth), transit delay (latency), error rates, priority, security, packet loss, and packet jitter.

Quality of protection (QoP) requires that overall performance of a system should be improved by prioritizing traffic and considering rate of failure or average latency at the lower layer protocols.

Denial of quality (DoQ*)* results from lack of quality assurance (QA) methods and quality control (QC) techniques used in delivering messages, packets and services. QA is the planned systematic activities necessary to ensure that a component, module, or system conforms to established technical requirements. QC is the prevention of defective components, modules, and systems. Proper implementation of QA methods and QC techniques can prevent DoQ and DoS and support QoS and QoP.

Denial of service (DoS) is the prevention of authorized access to resources or the delaying of time-critical operations.

---

6   Focus on: **Information Technology and Business Continuity (15–25%)**   **529**

Ways to Improve the QoS and QoP

- Implement service-to-service authentication services, as a part of authentication, authorization, and accountability concepts.
- Implement traffic prioritization rules to improve overall performance of the system.
- Implement WS-Reliability and WS-Reliable Messaging standards for guaranteed message delivery and message ordering. These standards also address rate of failure or average latency at the lower layer protocols. Through WS-Reliable Messaging, Web services can ensure that messages are not lost even if the network is saturated.
- Use queuing networks and simulation techniques for both single service and composite services to assure quality and availability of Web services. For example, enterprise systems with several business partners must complete business processes in a timely manner to meet real-time market conditions. The dynamic and compositional nature of Web services makes end-to-end QoS and QoP management a major challenge for service-oriented distributed systems.
- Ensure that packets corresponding to individual Web service messages are routed accordingly.
- Practice defensive programming techniques and information hiding concept to make the Web service software more robust.
- Implement a service-level agreement (SLA) between an end user organization and a service provider to satisfy specific end user (customer) application system requirements.

BUSINESS CONTINUITY

Business Focused Continuity Management

The entire scope of business continuity management (BCM) should be broader and comprehensive than before and as such its scope should be elevated to the enterprise level, similar to enterprise risk management, enterprise-wide resource planning software, enterprise customer relationship management system, enterprise-wide internal control systems, and enterprise-wide total quality management (TQM) programs. The reason for elevating the earlier and fragmented BCM is to integrate all the relevant pieces now to determine the magnitude of disasters and incidents occurring in the entire enterprise in a timely manner for a better and complete action. The new BCM function should become a business-led initiative, not an IT-led initiative.

In the past, the BCM activities were focused more on information technology (IT) function and less on business functions (e.g., operations, marketing, accounting, human resources, and finance) thus leaving huge gaps and unmitigated risks to the overall enterprise.

The business-led processes should focus on, for example: (1) addressing all business functions, including the IT function; (2) handling IT continuity plans and disaster recovery plans; (3) handling nature-made, man-made, and technology-used disasters; (4) handling kidnapping of key executives and officers; (5) understanding the applicable legal and regulatory requirements; (6) assuring that suppliers/vendors and business partners will continue to provide key raw materials, products, and services, even during disasters or incidents; (7) handling

Business Focused Continuity Management (continued)

cyber-based attacks and terrorism-based attacks targeted at companies by hacking their computer systems and networks and stealing intellectual property (IP) information; (8) implementing a vital records retention program; and (9) obtaining adequate insurance coverage for assets to recover losses.

Implementing a vital records retention program and obtaining adequate insurance coverage is essential to ensuring business continuity management in order to protect assets from accidents, errors, disruptions, attacks, losses, damages, and disasters.

Information Technology Focused Continuity Management

Scope of Contingency Planning

Computer-based application systems and business-related information systems must be available at all times to continue normal business operations and to handle and recover from disasters.

Contingency Plan

Undesirable events occur regardless of a security program's effectiveness. Contingency planning provides a controlled response that minimizes damage and restores operations as quickly as possible. A contingency plan is a document or set of documents that provides a course of action to be followed before, during, and after an undesirable event that disrupts or interrupts IT operations. The document should include procedures for data recovery, hardware recovery, and updating the contingency plan. The planning process should focus on providing a minimum acceptable level of outputs and services, using a combination of top-down and bottom-up approaches. It should also focus on a vital records program considering legal, tax, audit, regulatory, and business requirements.

A contingency plan should detail:

- Individual roles and responsibilities

- Actions to be taken before an undesirable event occurs

- Actions to be taken at the onset of an undesirable event to limit the level of damage, loss, or compromise of assets

- Actions to be taken to restore critical IT functions

- Actions to be taken to re-establish normal IT operations

Contingency Plan (continued)

Contingency plans address both catastrophic events that cause major destruction to IT assets and less-than-catastrophic events that interrupt IT operations but do not cause major destruction. Contingency plans do not concentrate on disaster recovery planning to the detriment of planning for less-than-catastrophic occurrences. As a general rule, the greater the adverse impact of an undesirable event, the lower its probability of occurring. Contingency plans are stored onsite for use in less-than-catastrophic occurrences and offsite so that they will be available when needed.

To handle these undesirable events, organizations should do the following:

- Develop risk profiles
- Establish security priorities
- Identify critical applications

Business Impact Analysis

The business impact analysis (BIA) is a critical step in implementing the contingency plan controls and in the contingency planning process overall. The BIA enables management to characterize the system components, supported business functions, and their interdependencies. The BIA results characterize the consequences of a disruption, which is used to determine contingency planning requirements and priorities.

The BIA should critically (1) examine the business processes and their dependencies,(2) assess costs and benefits, (3) locate single point-of-failures, and (4) identify risks and threats (both physical and environmental). For example, (1) a single point of failure occurs when there is no redundancy in data, equipment, facilities, systems, and programs, and (2) risks in the use of cellular radio and telephone networks during a disaster include security systems and switching offices.

The BIA should be performed during the initiation phase of the system development lifecycle (SDLC) using both quantitative and qualitative tools. Three steps are typically involved in accomplishing the BIA: (1) determining mission or business functions and recovery criticality, (2) identifying resource requirements, and (3) identifying recovery priorities for system resources.

Maximum Tolerable Downtime

Maximum tolerable downtime (MTD) represents the total amount of time the the system owner is willing to accept for a business process outage or disruption and includes all impact considerations. Determining MTD is important because it could leave continuity planners with imprecise direction on (1) selection of an appropriate recovery method, and (2) the depth of detail which will be required when developing recovery procedures, including their scope and content. MTD is also known as maximum allowable outage (MAO), which describes the downtime threshold. MTD and recovery time objective (RTO) replace MAO.

Additional processing time (APT) is required when a system outage may prevent a particular process from being completed, and because it takes time to reprocess the data, that APT must be added to the RTO to stay within the time limit established by the MTD.

Recovery Objectives

Two types of recovery objectives exist: recovery time objective (RTO) and recovery point objective (RPO). The RTO defines the maximum amount of time that a system resource can remain unavailable before there is an unacceptable impact on other system resources, supported business functions, and the MTD.

The RPO represents the point in time, prior to a disruption or system outage, to which business process data can be recovered (given the most recent backup copy of the data) after an outage. Because the RTO must ensure that the MTD is not exceeded, the RTO must normally be shorter than the MTD. For example, a system outage may prevent a particular process from being completed, and because it takes time to reprocess the data, that additional processing time (APT) must be added to the RTO to stay within the time limit established by the MTD. These relationships are shown below.

BIA $\rightarrow$ MTD, RTO, and RPO

RTO < MTD

RTO + APT < MTD

Relationship Between Recovery Point Objective, Recovery Time Objective, and Business Impact Analysis

- A recovery point objective (RPO) is the point in time in which data must be restored in order to resume computer processing.

- A recovery time objective (RTO) is the maximum acceptable length of time that elapses before the unavailability of the system severely affects the organization.

- Maximum tolerable downtime (MTD) is the total amount of time the system owner is willing to accept for a business process outage or disruption and includes all impact considerations.

- Note that the business impact analysis (BIA) must consider the RPO, RTO, and MTD since they are related to and affect each other.

- Note that RPO and RTO are a part of disaster recovery controls and procedures.

- It is important to determine the optimum point to recover the IT system by balancing the cost of system inoperability against the cost of resources required for restoring the system (i.e., recovery cost balancing). The RPO, RTO, MTD, and BIA are part of the recovery cost balancing equation.

Computer Security Incident Management

Security Incident Triad

The security incident triad includes three elements such as detect, respond, and recover. An organization should have the ability to detect an attack, respond to an attack, and recover from an attack by limiting consequences of or impacts from an attack. *Root cause analysis* can be used in the remediation step of the incident response.

Symptoms of Security Incidents

It is always possible that a computer system or network may be compromised by an intentional or unintentional incident. When several symptoms start to appear, a pattern may indicate that a system is under attack and may be worth investigating further. If the adversary is skilled, it may not be very obvious that an attack is underway. The symptoms of an incident could include any of the following:

- Unusually heavy network traffic
- Out of disk space alert or significantly reduced free disk space
- Unusually high CPU usage
- Creation of new user accounts and account in-use when the user is not at work
- Attempted or actual use of administrator-level accounts and locked-out accounts
- Cleared log files and full log files with an unusually large number of events
- Antivirus alerts from a intrusion detection system and disabled antivirus software
- Unexpected patch changes and unexpected changes in configuration settings

Symptoms of Security Incidents *(continued)*

- Computers and communication devices connecting to outside IP addresses

- Requests for information about a system-related data such as user IDs and passwords (i.e., social engineering attempts)

- Unexpected system shutdown or slowdown

Contingency Planning Strategies

A contingency planning strategy normally consists of three parts: emergency response, recovery, and resumption (restoration). **Emergency response** encompasses the initial actions taken to protect lives, limit property damage, and minimize the impact of the emergency. Contingency planning for local-area networks should consider security incident response, backup operations, and recovery plans. **Recovery** refers to the steps taken to continue support for critical functions. A proactive disaster recovery plan includes an uninterruptible power supply, an emergency procedure, and a fire extinguisher. **Resumption** is the return to normal operations. The relationship between recovery and resumption is important. The longer it takes to resume normal operations, the longer the organization will have to operate in the recovery mode.

Disaster Recovery Planning

A disaster recovery plan (DRP) is essential to continued availability of computer systems. The scope of a DRP should include:

- Required response to events or conditions of varying duration and severity that would activate the recovery plan
- Procedures for operating the computer system in manual mode without external electronic connections
- Roles and responsibilities of responders (first and second responders)
- Processes and procedures for the backup and secure storage of information
- Complete and up-to-date logical network diagrams
- Personnel list for authorized physical and cyber access to computer systems
- Communication procedures and list of personnel to contact in the case of an emergency including vendors, network administrators, and support staff (call tree list)
- Current configuration information for all components of systems
- Replacement for hard-to-obtain critical components kept in inventory

Disaster Recovery Planning (continued)

The DRP plan should define a comprehensive backup and restore policy. In formulating this policy, the following should be considered:

- The speed at which data or the system must be restored. This requirement may justify the need for a redundant system, spare offline computer, or valid file-level system backups

- The frequency at which critical data and configurations are changing. This will dictate the frequency and completeness of backups

- The safe onsite and offsite storage of full and incremental backups

- The safe storage of installation media, license keys, and configuration information

- Identification of individuals responsible for performing, testing, storing, and restoring backups

Develop Recovery Site Strategies

Recovery strategies provide a means to restore IT operations quickly and effectively following a service disruption. The strategies should address disruption impacts and maximum allowable outage times identified in the BIA. Several alternatives should be considered when developing the strategy, including cost, allowable outage time, security, and integration with larger, organization-level contingency plans.

The contingency planning coordinator should determine the optimum point to recover the IT system by balancing the cost of system inoperability against the cost of resources required for restoring the system. This is called **recovery cost balancing** where the cost of disruption line and the cost to recover line (on a cost versus time graph) meet will define how long the organization can afford to allow the system to be disrupted or unavailable. Recovery site strategies include selection of offsite storage, rotation of backup tapes between onsite and offsite, and electronic vaulting to store data and programs.

Develop Alternate Recovery Site Strategies

Although major disruptions with long-term effects may be rare, they should be accounted for in the contingency plan. Thus, for all high-impact and moderate-impact systems, the plan should include a strategy to recover and perform system operations at an alternate site/facility for an extended period. Organizations may consider low-impact systems for alternate site processing, but is not required due to their low risk and is dependent on management's decision.

- High-impact systems require mirrored systems with disk replication, high availability systems, and a hot site, a mobile site, a mirrored site, or a combination of these sites

- Medium-impact systems require a warm site

- Low-impact systems require a cold site or a reciprocal agreement

  In general, three types of alternate sites are available:

1. Dedicated site owned or operated by the organization (i.e., company owned or operated, which is very expensive)

2. Reciprocal agreement requiring a memorandum of agreement (MOA) or a memorandum of understanding (MOU) with an internal or external entity. Internal entities may require a MOU while external entities may require a MOA.

3. Commercially leased facility (e.g., cold site, warm site, or hot site)

Develop Alternate Recovery Site Strategies (continued)

Regardless of the type of alternate site chosen, the facility must be able to support system operations as defined in the contingency plan. The three alternate site types commonly categorized in terms of their operational readiness are cold sites, warm sites, or hot sites, progressing from basic to advanced, as follows:

Cold Site → Warm Site → Hot Site

Some organizations use any combination of the above approaches called a hybrid approach. It includes having a hot-site as a backup in case a redundant or reciprocal agreement site is damaged by a separate contingency. Other variations of the three common sites include mobile sites and mirrored sites with similar core features. Exhibit 6.2 shows a comparison of cold sites, warm sites, hot sites, mobile sites, and mirrored sites.

Develop Alternate Recovery Site Strategies (continued)

Alternate Site	Cost	Hardware/ Equipment	Telecommunications	Setup Time	Location
Cold site	Low	None	None	Long	Fixed
Warm site	Medium	Partial	Partial/full	Medium	Fixed
Hot site	Medium/high	Full	Full	Short	Fixed
Mobile site	High	Dependent	Dependent	Dependent	Not Fixed
Mirrored site	High	Full	Full	None	Fixed

Exhibit 6.2 Five alternative sites

Service-Level Agreements for Alternate Recovery Sites

An MOA/MOU or a service-level agreement (SLA) for an alternate site should be developed specific to the organization's needs and the partner organization's capabilities. The legal department and internal audit department of each party must review and approve the agreement. In general, the SLA should address at a minimum, each of the following elements:

- Contract/agreement duration
- Cost/fee structure for disaster declaration and occupancy (daily usage), administration, maintenance, testing, annual cost/fee increases, transportation support cost (receipt and return of offsite data/supplies, as applicable), cost/expense allocation (as applicable), and billing and payment schedules
- Disaster declaration (i.e., circumstances constituting a disaster, notification procedures)
- Site/facility priority access and/or use
- Site availability
- Site guarantee
- Other clients subscribing to same resources and site, and the total number of site subscribers, as applicable

Service-Level Agreements for Alternate Recovery Sites (continued)

- Contract/agreement change or modification process

- Contract/agreement termination conditions

- Process to negotiate extension of service

- Guarantee of compatibility

- Information system requirements (including data and telecommunication requirements) for hardware, software, and any special system needs (hardware and software)

- Change management and notification requirements, including hardware, software, and infrastructure;

- Security requirements, including special security needs

- Staff support provided/not provided

- Facility services provided/not provided (e.g., use of onsite office equipment, and cafeteria)

- Testing, including scheduling, availability, test time duration, and additional testing, if required

Service-Level Agreements for Alternate Recovery Sites (continued)

- Records management (onsite and offsite), including electronic media and hardcopy
- Service-level management (performance measures and management of quality of information system services provided)
- Work space requirements (e.g., chairs, desks, telephones, and personal computers)
- Supplies provided/not provided (e.g., office supplies)
- Additional costs not covered elsewhere
- Other contractual issues, as applicable
- Other technical requirements, as applicable

Implementation, Documentation, Training, and Testing

Once the contingency planning strategies have been selected, it is necessary to make appropriate preparations for implementation, document the strategies, train employees and testing. Many of these tasks are ongoing.

There are several **types of testing**, including reviews, analyses, disaster simulations, end-to-end testing, and full-scale testing.

Reviews

A review can be a simple test to check the accuracy of contingency plan documentation. For instance, a reviewer could check if individuals listed are still in the organization and still have the responsibilities that caused them to be included in the plan. This test can check home and work telephone numbers, organizational codes, and building and room numbers. The review can determine if files can be restored from backup tapes or if employees know emergency procedures. *A checklist is used during reviews to ensure that all items are addressed*.

Analyses

An analysis or *desk checking* may be performed on the entire plan or portions of it, such as emergency response procedures. It is beneficial if the analysis is performed by someone who did not help develop the contingency plan but has a good working knowledge of the critical function and supporting resources. The analyst(s) may mentally follow the strategies in the contingency plan, looking for flaws in the logic or processes used by the plan's developers. The analyst also may interview functional managers, resource managers, and their staff to uncover missing or unworkable pieces of the plan.

Disaster Simulations

Organizations may also arrange disaster simulations. These tests provide valuable information about flaws in the contingency plan and provide practice for a real emergency. While they can be expensive, these tests can also provide critical information that can be used to ensure the continuity of important functions. In general, the more critical the functions and the resources addressed in the contingency plan, the more cost-beneficial it is to perform a disaster simulation.

End-to-End Testing

The purpose of end-to-end testing is to verify that a defined set of interrelated systems, which collectively support an organizational core business area or function, interoperate as intended in an operational environment (either actual or simulated). These interrelated systems include not only those owned and managed by the organization but also the external systems with which they interface.

Generally, end-to-end testing is conducted when one major system in the end-to-end chain is modified or replaced, and attention is rightfully focused on the changed or new system. The boundaries on end-to-end tests are not fixed or predetermined but vary depending on a given business area's system dependencies (internal and external) and criticality to the mission of the organization. Therefore, in planning end-to-end tests, it is critical to analyze the organization's core business functions, the interrelationships among systems supporting these functions, and potential risk exposure due to system failures in the chain of support. It is also important to work early and continuously with the organization's data exchange partners so that end-to-end tests can be effectively planned and executed.

Full-Scale Testing

Full-scale (full-interruption) testing is costly and disruptive while end-to-end testing is least costly and less disruptive. Management of a firm will not allow stopping of normal production operations for the sake of full-interruption testing. Some businesses operate on a 24x7 schedule and losing several hours or days of production time is equal to another disaster, financially or otherwise. Hence, full-scale testing is not advised unless specified by management.

Documentation

The contents of personnel **training program** document should include:

- Purpose of the plan

- Cross-team coordination and communication

- Reporting procedures

- Security requirements

- Team-specific processes (i.e., activation/notification, recovery, and reconstitution phases)

- Individual responsibilities (i.e., activation/notification, recovery, and reconstitution phases)

    The contents of a **testing program** document should include:

- System recovery on an alternate site from backup media

- System performance using alternate equipment

- Coordination among recovery teams (e.g., business continuity planners)

- Restoration of normal operations

Documentation (continued)

- Internal and external connectivity

- Notification procedures

  The contents of an **exercise program** document should include:

- Tabletop exercises (i.e., discussion-based only without the deployment of equipment are useful for low-impact systems)

- Functional exercises (i.e., validation of operational readiness for emergencies are useful for moderate-impact systems with system recovery from backup media)

- Full-scale functional exercises (i.e., a system failover to the alternate site, recovery of a server or database from backup media, and processing from a server at an alternate site are useful for high-impact systems with full system recovery and reconstitution to a known state)

- Personnel exercises (i.e., execution of staff roles and responsibilities)

- Scenario-driven exercises (i.e., simulation of operational emergency environment such as a power failure or a fire in a data center). Functional, full-scale functional, and personnel exercises are examples of scenario-driven exercises.

Contingency Plan Maintenance

The IT contingency plan must always be maintained in a ready state for use immediately upon notification.

Periodic reviews of the plan must be conducted for currency of key personnel and vendor information, system components and dependencies, the recovery strategy, vital records, and operational requirements. While some changes may be obvious (e.g., personnel turnover or vendor changes), others will require analysis. The BIA should be reviewed periodically and updated with new information to identify new contingency requirements and priorities. Changes made to the plan are noted in a record of changes, dated, and signed or initialed by the person making the change. The revised plan (or plan sections) is circulated to those with plan responsibilities. Because of the impact that plan changes may have on interdependent business processes or information systems, the changes must be clearly communicated and properly annotated in the beginning of the maintenance document.

Fault-Tolerance Mechanisms

Modern fault-tolerance mechanisms can play an important role in maintaining data and system integrity as they increase system resilience. Resilience is the ability of a computer system to continue to perform its tasks after the occurrence of faults and operate correctly even though one or more of its component parts are malfunctioning. Traditional system fault-tolerance mechanisms, such as logs and locks, cannot handle serious malicious code attacks or cyberattacks. The ultimate goal is to ensure that computer systems are reliable and available for system users to provide continuity of business operations.

Examples of Fault-Tolerance Mechanisms

- Develop error detection, error correction, and redundant processing policies and procedures to maintain integrity of data and systems.

- Install mechanisms such as fail-stop processors and redundancy mechanisms with built-in fault detection, error recovery, and failure recovery abilities combined with system reliability measurement metrics (e.g., mean-time-to-failure (MTTF), mean-time-to- repair (MTTR), and mean-time-between-failures (MTBF).

- Install fault-tolerant hardware methods as they increase system resilience.

- Install a robust operating system so it can handle unexpected system failures.

Fault-Tolerant Hardware Methods

Hardware methods such as disk arrays (i.e., RAIDs), disk striping, disk mirroring, server mirroring, disk duplexing, block mirroring, disk replication, disk imaging, disk farming, or checkpointing should be used in combination to improve the performance of data storage media regardless of the type of computer used. A gap between a computer's CPU performance and its data storage subsystem performance causes imbalance which, in turn, degrades online system response time and batch job turnaround time.

Robust Operating Systems

An operating system must be robust enough to withstand system failures. Operating systems' response to failures can be classified into three general categories: (1) system reboot, (2) emergency system restart, and (3) system cold start.

Relationship of Business Continuity Management to ISO Standards

The International Organization for Standardization (ISO) standard 22301 focuses on business continuity management systems and requirements in order to prepare for, to protect against, and to reduce the likelihood of occurrence of disasters or disruptive incidents (i.e., man-made, nature-made, or technology-used). The goal is to respond to and recover from disasters and incidents and to improve business continuity capabilities.

Other ISO standards related to business continuity management include the 15489 standard which provides general guidance to records management and the 13606 standard which provides guidance to electronic health records communication.

FINANCIAL ACCOUNTING AND FINANCE: BASIC CONCEPTS OF FINANCIAL ACCOUNTING

Financial accounting is the language of business. All business transactions will eventually end up in financial statements. Accounting principles are used to classify, record, post, summarize, and report the business transactions between various parties involved. Accountants apply their professional standards to analyze business transactions, prepare estimations, and report business events. The business transactions data accumulated in the chart of accounts are used to prepare the financial statements of an organization.

Accounting Principles and Qualities of Accounting Information

Accounting Principles

If the management of a company could record and report financial data as it saw fit, comparisons among companies would be difficult, if not impossible. Thus, financial accountants follow generally accepted accounting principles (GAAP) in preparing reports. These reports allow investors and other stakeholders to compare one company to another.

Business Entity Concept

The individual business unit is the business entity for which economic data are needed. This entity could be an automobile dealer, a department store, or a grocery store. The business entity must be identified, so that the accountant can determine which economic data should be analyzed, recorded, and summarized in reports.

Cost Concept

The historical cost concept is the basis for entering the *exchange price or cost of an asset* into the accounting records. Using the cost concept involves two other important accounting concepts: (1) objectivity and (2) the unit of measure. The objectivity concept requires that the accounting records and reports be based upon objective evidence (i.e., final agreed upon amount). The unit of measure concept requires that economic data be recorded in dollars.

Matching Concept

The matching concept, which is based on accrual accounting, refers to the matching of expenses and revenues (hence net income) for an accounting period. Under the accrual basis, revenues are reported in the income statement in which they are earned. Similarly, expenses are reported in the same period as the revenues to which they relate. Under the cash basis of accounting, revenues and expenses are reported in the income statement in the period in which cash is received or paid.

Other Accounting Concepts

The materiality concept implies that errors, which could occur during journalizing and posting transactions, should be significant enough to affect the decision-making process. The accounting period concept breaks the economic life of a business into time periods, and requires that accounting reports be prepared at periodic intervals. The revenue recognition concept, which is based on accrual accounting, refers to the recognition of revenues in the period in which they are earned.

Qualities of Accounting Information

The accounting function collects the raw data from business transactions and converts them into information useful to the decision maker. In this regard, the accounting information should contain two qualitative characteristics: (1) primary and (2) secondary qualities.

Accounting Cycle

Financial accounting provides accounting information for use by those outside and inside the organization. This information is used by current investors and potential investors to determine the future benefits they will receive if they hold or acquire ownership in a business. Creditors and lenders use this information to assess the creditworthiness of an organization. Other users of this information include employees, unions, customers, the general public, and governmental units.

The basic accounting equation is: Assets = Liabilities + Equity

Cash-Basis versus Accrual-Basis

The two approaches of accounting are **cash-basis** accounting and **accrual-basis** accounting. With the **cash-basis of accounting**, revenues are recognized when cash is received, and expenses are recognized when cash is paid out. The primary advantages of cash-basis accounting are the increased reliability due to the fact that transactions are not recorded until complete and the simplicity due to the fact that fewer estimates and judgments are required.

Steps in the Accounting Cycle

The accounting cycle records the effect of economic transactions upon the assets, liabilities and owners' equity of an organization. The accounting cycle involves eight steps: (1) analysis of transactions, (2) journalizing of transactions, (3) posting to the ledger, (4) trial balance and working papers, (5) adjusting journal entries, (6) closing journal entries, (7) preparing financial statements, and (8) reversing journal entries.

Different Formats of Financial Statements

- **A statement of financial position** provides information about an entity's assets, liabilities, and equity and their relationships to each other at a moment in time. The statement delineates the entity's resources structure—major classes and amounts of assets—and its financial structure—major classes and amounts of liabilities and equity.
- **Statements of earnings and of comprehensive income** together reflect the extent to which and the ways in which the equity of an entity increased or decreased from all sources other than transactions with owners during a period.
- **A statement of cash flows** (SCFs) directly or indirectly reflects an entity's cash receipts classified by major sources and its cash payments classified by major uses during a period, including cash flow information about its operating, financing, and investing activities.
- **A statement of investments by and distributions to owners** reflects an entity's capital transactions during a period—the extent to which and in what ways the equity of the entity increased or decreased from transactions with investors as owners.

Account Analysis

Account analysis helps the internal auditor to be able to reconstruct balance sheet accounts from account balances and journal entries and understand the account classifications and posting error correction process through journal entries.

INTERMEDIATE CONCEPTS OF FINANCIAL ACCOUNTING

Bonds

Bonds result from a single agreement. However, a bond is intended to be broken up into various subunits. Notes and bonds have similar characteristics. These include a written agreement stating the amount of the principal to be paid, the interest rate, when the interest and principal are to be paid, and the restrictive covenants.

The stated interest rate on a note or bond often differs from the market interest rate at the time of issuance. When this occurs, the present value of the interest and principal payments will differ from the maturity, or face value. **Outstanding debt may be reacquired or retired before its scheduled maturity. Usually, this is caused by changes in interest rates or in cash flows**.

Leases

A lease agreement involves at least two parties (lessor, lessee) and an asset. The lessor, who owns the asset, agrees to allow the lessee to use it for a specified period of time for rent payments. *The key point in leases is the transfer of risk of ownership*. If the transaction effectively transfers ownership to the lessee, then it should be treated as a sale even though the transaction takes the form of a lease. Here, the substance, not the form, dictates the accounting treatment. Two types of leases exist: capital and operating lease.

Accounting by Lessees

Statement of Financial Accounting Standards (SFAS) 13, *Accounting for Leases*, requires lessees to classify every lease as either an operating lease or capital lease. A capital lease, not operating lease, is an installment purchase of the property.

A lease meeting any one of the following four criteria (criteria 1) should be accounted for as a capital lease by the lessee:

1. The lease transfers ownership of the property to the lessee by the end of the lease term. If the title is transferred, the lease is assumed to be a purchase and the assets should be capitalized.

2. The lease contains a bargain purchase option.

3. The lease term is equal to 75% or more of the estimated economic life of the leased property. However, if the beginning of the lease term falls within the last 25% of the total estimated economic life of the leased property, including earlier years of use, this criterion shall not be used for purposes of classifying the lease.

4. The present value at the beginning of the lease term of the minimum lease payments, excluding that portion of the payments representing executory costs such as insurance, maintenance, and taxes to be paid by the lessor, including any profit thereon, equals or exceeds 90% of the excess of the fair value of the leased property.

Accounting by Lessor

From the standpoint of the lessor, if at inception a lease meets any one of the preceding four criteria (criteria 1) and in addition meets **both** of the following criteria (criteria 2), it shall be classified as a sales-type lease or a direct financing lease. Otherwise, it shall be classified as an operating lease.

- Collectibility of the minimum lease payments is reasonably predictable. Estimation of uncollectibility based on experience with groups of similar receivables is not a reason for applying this criteria.

- No important uncertainties surround the amount of un-reimbursable costs yet to be incurred by the lessor under the lease. The necessity of estimating executory costs such as insurance, maintenance, and taxes to be paid by the lessor shall not by itself constitute an important uncertainty.

A lessor has four types of choices in classifying a lease: (1) sales-type leases; (2) direct financing leases; (3) operating leases; and (4) participation by third parties.

Lease Involving Real Estate

Lease involving real estate can be divided into four categories: (1) leases involving land only, (2) leases involving land and buildings, (3) leases involving equipment as well as real estate, and (4) leases involving only part of a building.

Sale-Leaseback Transaction

Sale-leaseback transactions involve the sale of property by the owner and a lease of the property back to the seller. If the lease meets one of the criteria (criteria 1) for treatment as a capital lease, the seller-lessee shall account for the lease as a capital lease; otherwise, as an operating lease.

Accounting and Reporting for Leveraged Leases

From the standpoint of the lessee, leveraged leases shall be classified and accounted for in the same manner as nonleveraged leases.

Pensions

The principal focus of SFAS 87, *Employers' Accounting for Pensions* is the present value of the pension obligation, the fair value of plan assets, and the disclosure of net pension costs and of the projected benefit obligation. The critical accounting issues are the amount to be expensed on the income statement and the amount to be accrued on the balance sheet.

Intangible Assets

Typically intangibles lack physical existence and have a high degree of uncertainty regarding their future benefits. These assets have value because of the business advantages of exclusive rights and privileges they provide.

Intangible assets are initially recorded at **cost**. Therefore, the costs of intangible assets, except for goodwill, are relatively easy to determine. These assets must be amortized over their expected useful life but not to exceed forty years. An organization must use straight-line amortization, unless it can prove that another method is more appropriate. The amortization of intangible assets over their useful lives is justified by the going concern assumption.

Copyrights, trademarks, and patents that have a separate identity apart from the enterprise as a whole are identifiable as intangible assets.

Research and Development

Research and Development Costs

SFAS 2, *Accounting for Research and Development (R&D) Costs*, requires R&D costs to be expensed as incurred except for intangible or fixed assets purchased from others having alternative future uses. Thus, the cost of patents and R&D equipment purchased from third parties may be deferred, capitalized, and amortized over the assets' useful life. However, internally developed R&D may not be deferred and therefore should be expensed. R&D done under contract for others is not required to be expensed per SFAS 2. The costs incurred would be matched with revenue using the completed-contract or percentage-of-completion method. The key accounting concept is expense as incurred and disclose and disclose total R&D expenses per period on face of income statement or notes.

Software Developed for Sale or Lease

The costs that are incurred internally to create the software should be expensed as R&D costs until technological feasibility is established. Thereafter, all costs should be capitalized and reported at the lower of unamortized cost or net realizable value. Capitalization should cease when the software is available for general release to customers.

Software Developed for Internal Use

Software must meet two criteria to be accounted for as internally developed software: (1) the software's specifications must be designed or modified to meet the reporting entity's internal needs, including costs to customize purchased software and (2) during the period in which the software is being developed, there can be no plan or intent to market the software externally, although development of the software can be jointly funded by several entities that each plan to use the software internally.

ADVANCED CONCEPTS OF FINANCIAL ACCOUNTING

Business Combinations

According to the Financial Standards Accounting Board (FASB), a business combination occurs when an entity acquires net assets that constitute a business or acquires equity interests of one or more other entities and obtains control over that entity or entities. Business combinations may be friendly or hostile takeovers. Purchase accounting is the only acceptable accounting method for all business combinations; the pooling-of-interest method is not.

Computation and Allocation of Cost of a Combinee

The cost of a combinee is the total of the amount of consideration paid by the combinor, the combinor's direct "out-of-pocket" costs of the combination, and any contingent consideration that is determinable on the date of the business combination.

The FASB requires that the cost of a combinee must be allocated to assets (other than goodwill) acquired and liabilities assumed based on their estimated fair values on the date of the combination. Any excess of total costs over the amounts thus allocated is assigned to goodwill. Methods for determining fair values include: present values for receivables and most liabilities, net realizable value less a reasonable profit for work in process and finished goods inventories, appraised values for land, natural resources, and nonmarketable securities, and individual fair values for patents, copyrights, franchises, customer lists, and unpatented technology.

Consolidation of Financial Statements

The purpose of consolidated financial statements is to present for a single accounting entity the combined resources, obligations, and operating results of a group of related corporations such as parent and subsidiaries. Only subsidiaries not actually controlled should be exempted from consolidation. Usually, an investor's direct or indirect ownership of more than 50% of an investee's outstanding common stock has been required to evidence the controlling interest underlying a parent-subsidiary relationship. Actual control is more important than the controlling interest in situations such as liquidation or reorganization (bankruptcy) of a subsidiary or control of a foreign subsidiary by a foreign government. GAAP requires the use of the cost method of accounting for investments in unconsolidated subsidiaries because the subsidiaries generally are neither controlled nor significantly influenced by the parent company.

Partnerships

A partnership is an association of two or more people to carry on as co-owners of a business for profit. Competent parties agree to place their money, property, or labor in a business and to divide the profits and losses. Each person is personally liable for the debts of the partnership. Express partnership agreements may be oral or written.

Duties, Rights, and Powers of Partners

The duties, rights, and powers of partners are both expressed (in the agreement) and implied (created by law).

The statutory law in most states is the Uniform Partnership Act.

Ordinary matters are decided by a majority of the partners. If the partnership consists of two persons who are unable to agree and the partnership agreement makes no provision for arbitration, then dissolution is the only remedy.

The following matters require the unanimous consent of the partners:

- Change the essential nature of the business by altering the original agreement or reducing or increasing the partners' capital.
- Embark on a new business or admit new members.
- Modify a limited partnership agreement.
- Assign partnership property to a trustee for the benefit of creditors.
- Confess a judgment.
- Dispose of the partnership's goodwill.
- Submit a partnership agreement to arbitration.

Duties, Rights, and Powers of Partners (continued)

- Perform an act that would make impossible the conduct of the partnership business.

    Partners have the following powers:

- Power to contract

- Power to impose tort liability

- Power over property

- Financial transactions

Liabilities and Authorities of a General Partner

General partners are liable for:

- Fraudulent acts of other partners
- Debts attributable to limited partner notes to the partnership
- Debts related to the purchase of real property without each partner's consent

General partners have no authority to:

- Do any act in violation of the certificate.
- Do any act that would make it impossible to carry on the ordinary business of the partnership.
- Confess a judgment against the partnership.
- Possess or assign partnership property for other than partnership purposes.
- Admit a person as a general partner.
- Admit a person as a limited partner unless the right to do so is given in the certificate.
- Continue the business with partnership property on the death, retirement, or incapacity of a general partner unless the right to do so is given in the certificate.

Partnership Accounting

A partner's share of the partnership assets or profits may be determined in a suit for an accounting. These suits are equitable in nature and must be filed in a court of equity. A partner is entitled to a formal accounting in the following situations:

- The partnership has been dissolved.

- An agreement calls for an accounting at a definite date.

- A partner has withheld profits arising from secret transactions.

- An execution has been levied against the interest of one of the partners.

- One partner does not have access to the books.

- The partnership is approaching insolvency, and all parties are not available.

Actions Against Other Partners

Typically a partner cannot maintain an action at law against the other partners, because the indebtedness among the partners is undetermined until there is an accounting and all partnership affairs are settled. *The few exceptions to this rule are if:*

- The partnership is formed to carry out a single venture or transaction,
- The action involves a segregated or single unadjusted item or account, or
- The action involves a personal covenant or transaction entirely independent of the partnership affairs.

Admitting a New Partner

If a partnership admits a new partner, the new partner is liable to the extent of his capital contribution for all obligations incurred before his admission. The new partner is not personally liable for such obligations.

Asset Distribution of Partnership

If a firm is insolvent and a court of equity is responsible for the distribution of the partnership assets, the assets are distributed in accordance with a rule known as **marshalling of assets**. The firm's creditors may seek payment out of the firm's assets and then the individual partner assets. The firm's creditors must exhaust the firm's assets before recourse to the partners' individual assets.

Foreign Currency Transactions

The buying and selling of foreign currencies result in variations in the exchange rate between the currencies of two countries. The selling spot rate is charged by the bank for current sales of the foreign currency. The bank's buying spot rate for the currency is less than the selling spot rate; the spread between the selling and buying spot rates represents gross profit to a trader in foreign currency. Factors influencing fluctuations in exchange rates include a nation's balance of payments surplus or deficit, differing global rates of inflation, money-market variations such as interest rates, capital investment levels, and monetary policies and actions of central banks.

A multinational corporation (MNC) headquartered in the United States engages in sales, purchases, and loans with foreign companies as well as with its own branches, divisions, investees, and subsidiaries in other countries. If the transactions with foreign companies are denominated in terms of the U.S. dollar, no accounting problems arise for the U.S.-based MNC. If the transactions are negotiated and settled in terms of the foreign companies' local currency unit, then the U.S. company must account for the transaction denominated in foreign currency in terms of U.S. dollars. This foreign currency translation is accomplished by applying the appropriate exchange rate between the foreign currency and the U.S. dollar.

Translation of Foreign Currency Financial Statements

When a U.S.-based MNC prepares consolidated or combined financial statements that include the operating results, financial position (balance sheet), and cash flows of foreign subsidiaries or branches, the U.S. company must translate the amounts in the final statements of the foreign entities from the entities' functional currency to U.S. dollar. Similar treatment must be given to investments in other foreign investees for which the U.S. company uses the equity method of accounting.

Current/Noncurrent Method for Foreign Exchange Rates

Current assets and current liabilities are translated at the exchange rate in effect on the balance sheet date of the foreign entity (that is, the current rate). All other assets and liabilities, and the components of owners' equity, are translated at the historical rates in effect at the time the assets, liabilities, and equities first were recognized in the foreign entity's accounting records. In the income statement, depreciation expense and amortization expense are translated at historical rates applicable to the related assets, while all other revenue and expenses are translated at an average exchange rate for the accounting period.

Monetary/Nonmonetary Method for Foreign Exchange Rates

Monetary assets and liabilities, which are expressed in a fixed amount, are translated at the current exchange rate. All other assets, liabilities, and owners' equity amounts are translated at appropriate historical rates. In the income statement, average exchange rates are applied to all revenue and expenses except depreciation expense, amortization expense, and cost of goods sold, which are translated at appropriate historical rates.

Current Rate Method for Foreign Exchange Rates

All balance sheet accounts other than owners' equity are translated at the current exchange rate. Owners' equity amounts are translated at historical rates. To emphasize the functional currency aspects of the foreign entity's operations, all revenue and expenses may be translated at the current rate on the respective transaction dates, if practical. Otherwise, an average exchange rate is used for all revenue and expenses.

Foreign Currency Transaction Gains and Losses Excluded from Net Income

- Foreign currency transactions that are designated as, and are effective as, economic hedge of a net investment in a foreign entity, commencing as of the designation date.

- Intercompany foreign currency transactions that are of a long-term investment nature, when the entities to the transaction are consolidated, combined, or accounted for by the equity method.

Foreign Currency in Highly Inflationary Economies

The functional currency of a foreign entity in a highly inflationary economy can be identified as the reporting currency (e.g., the U.S. dollar for a U.S.-based MNC). A highly inflationary economy is defined as the one having cumulative inflation of 100% or more over a three-year period. The financial statements of a foreign entity in a country experiencing severe inflation are remeasured in U.S. dollars.

Income Taxes Related to Foreign Currency Translation

The following are the procedures for the interperiod and intraperiod tax allocation to determine the effects of foreign currency translation:

- Interperiod tax allocation for temporary differences associated with transaction gains and losses that are reported in different accounting periods for financial accounting and income taxes.

- Interperiod tax allocation for temporary differences associated with translation adjustments that do not meet the criteria for nonrecognition of deferred tax liabilities for undistributed earnings of foreign subsidiaries.

- Intraperiod tax allocation for translation adjustments are included in the stockholders' equity section of the balance sheet.

Disclosure of Foreign Currency Translation

Aggregate transaction gains or losses of an accounting period should be disclosed in the income statement or in a note to the financial statements. Changes in cumulative translation adjustments during an accounting period should be disclosed in a separate financial statement, in a note to financial statements, or in a statement of stockholders' equity.

FINANCIAL STATEMENT ANALYSIS

Financial statement analysis requires a comparison of the firm's performance with that of other firms in the same industry, comparison with its own previous performance, and/or both. Primary users of financial statements include managers, investors, and creditors and lenders. *The real value of financial statements is in their predictive power about the firm's future earnings potential and dividends payment strength.*

A company's **annual report** presents four basic financial statements, including: a statement of income (income statement), a statement of financial position (balance sheet), a statement of retained earnings, and a statement of cash flows. Income statement summarizes the firm's revenues and expenses over an accounting period.

An **income statement** presents the results of operations for a given time period. Net sales are shown at the top; after which various costs, including income taxes, are subtracted to obtain the net income available to common stockholders. A report on earnings and dividends per share is given at the bottom of the statement.

A **balance sheet** is a statement of the firm's financial position at a specific point in time. The firm's assets are shown on the left-hand side of the balance sheet while the claims against these assets (the claims against these) are shown on the right-hand side. *The assets are listed in the order of their liquidity or the length of time it takes to convert assets into cash. The liabilities are listed in the order in which they must be paid.*

A **statement of retained earnings** shows how much of the firm's earnings were not paid out in dividends. Retained earnings represent a claim against assets, not assets per se. Retained earnings do not represent cash and are not "available" for the payment of dividends or anything else. A positive retained earnings means that the firm has earned an income, but its dividends have been less than its reported income. Due to differences between accrual and cash accounting practices, a firm may earn money, which shows an increase in the retained earnings, but still could be short of cash.

A **statement of cash flows** reports the impact of a firm's operating, investing, and financing activities on cash flows over an accounting period. This statement shows how the firm's operations have affected its cash flows and presents the relationships among cash flows from operating, investing, and financing activities of the firm.

Types of Financial Statement Analysis

Common size analysis expresses items in percentages, which can be compared with similar items of other firms or with those of the same firm over time. For example, common size balance sheet line items (both assets and liabilities) are expressed as a percentage of total assets (e.g., receivables as X percent of total assets). Similarly, common size income statement line items are expressed as a percentage of total sales (e.g., cost of goods sold as X percent of total sales).

Variations of common size analysis include: vertical analysis and horizontal analysis. **Vertical analysis**, which expresses all items on a financial statement as a percentage of some base figure, such as total assets or total sales. Comparing these relationships between competing organizations helps to isolate strengths and areas of concern.

In **horizontal analysis**, the financial statements for two years are shown together with additional columns showing dollar differences and percentage changes. Thus, the direction, absolute amount, and relative amount of change in account balances can be calculated. Trends that are difficult to isolate through examining the financial statements of individual years or comparing with competitors can be identified.

Trend analysis shows trends in ratios, which gives insight whether the financial situation of a firm is improving, declining, or stable. It shows a graph of ratios over time, which can be compared with a firm's own performance as well as that of its industry.

Comparative ratios show key financial ratios, such as current ratio and net sales to inventory, by industry, such as beverages and bakery products. These ratios represent average financial ratios for all firms within an

Types of Financial Statement Analysis (continued)

industry category. Many ratio data-supplying organizations are available and each one designs ratios for its own purpose, such as small firms or large firms. Also, the focus of these ratios is different, too, such as creditor's viewpoint or investor's viewpoint. Another characteristic of the ratio data-supplying organization is that each has its own definitions of the ratios and their components. A caution is required when interpreting these ratios due to these differences.

Single ratios or simple ratios. Certain accounts or items in an organization's financial statements have logical relationships with each other. If the dollar amounts of these related accounts or items are expressed in fraction form, then they are called ratios. These ratios are grouped into five categories: liquidity ratios, asset management ratios, debt management ratios, profitability ratios, and market value ratios.

Limitations of Financial Statement Ratios

- The use of ratio analysis could be limiting for large, multidivisional firms due to their size and complexity—two conditions that mask the results. However, they might be useful to small firms.

- Typically, financial statements are not adjusted for price-level changes. Inflation or deflation can have a large effect on the financial data.

- Since transactions are accounted for on a cost basis, unrealized gains and losses on different asset balances are not reflected in the financial statements.

- Income ratios tend to lose credibility in cases where a significant number of estimated items exist, such as amortization and depreciation.

- Seasonal factors affect and distort ratio analysis, which can be minimized by using average figures in calculations.

- Be aware of "window dressing" and "earnings management" techniques used by firms to make them look financially better than what they really are. Management manipulates the financial statements to impress the credit analysts and the stock market investors (i.e., management fraud).

Limitations of Financial Statement Ratios (continued)

- Certain off-balance-sheet items do not show up on the financial statements. For example, leased assets do not appear on the balance sheet, and the lease liability may not be shown as a debt. Therefore, leasing can improve both the asset turnover and the debt ratios.

- Attaining comparability among organizations in a given industry is an extremely difficult problem, since different organizations apply different accounting procedures. These different accounting procedures require identification of the basic differences in accounting from organization to organization and adjustment of the balances to achieve comparability.

- Do not take the ratios on their face value since a "good" ratio does not mean that the company is a strong one or that a "bad" ratio means that the company is a weak one. This implies that ratios should be evaluated and interpreted with judgment and experience and considering the firm's characteristics and the industry's uniqueness.

TYPES OF DEBT AND EQUITY

Types of Debt

Debt is of two types: (1) long-term debt and (2) short-term debt. Debt maturities affect both risk and expected returns.

- Short-term debt is riskier than long-term debt.
- Short-term debt is less expensive than long-term debt.
- Short-term debt can be obtained faster than long-term debt.
- Short-term debt is more flexible than long-term debt.

Sources of Short-Term Debt

By definition, short-term debt (credit) is any liability originally scheduled for payment within one year. The four major sources of short-term credit are: (1) accruals, (2) accounts payable, (3) bank loans, and (4) commercial paper.

Use of Security Collateral in Short-Term Financing

The security agreement of the Uniform Commercial Code (UCC) provides guidelines for establishing loan security. Secured loans are expensive due to recordkeeping costs. Financially weak companies are required to put up some type of collateral to protect the lender, while financially strong companies generally are not even though they are encouraged to do so.

Long-Term Debt

Long-term debt is often called funded debt, a term used to define the replacement of short-term debt with securities of longer maturity (e.g., stocks, bonds). Many types of long-term debt instruments are available including term loans, bonds, secured notes, unsecured notes, marketable debt, and nonmarketable debt.

Factors Influencing Long-Term Financing Decisions

Long-term financing decisions require a great deal of planning since a firm commits itself for many years to come. The long-term nature combined with uncertainty makes long-term financing risky, requiring careful consideration of all factors involved.

Types of Equity

When management decides to acquire new assets, it has the option of financing these assets either with equity, debt, or a combination. The definition of common equity is the sum of the firm's common stock, additional paid-in capital, preferred stock, and retained earnings. The common equity is the common stockholders' total investment in the firm. Sources of long-term capital include common stocks, preferred stocks, debt (loans, bonds, and notes), leases, and option securities.

Common Stocks

The common stockholders are the owners of a corporation. Common stock is the amount of stock management has actually issued (sold) at par value. Par value is the nominal or face value of a stock and is the minimum amount for which new shares can be issued. The component "additional paid-in capital" represents the difference between the stock's par value and what new stockholders paid when they bought newly issued shares. Retained earnings are the money that belongs to the stockholders and that they could have received in the form of dividends. Retained earnings are also the money that was plowed back into the firm for reinvestment.

Book value of the firm = Common stock + Paid-in capital + Retained earnings = Common equity

Book value per share = Book value of the firm divided by common shares outstanding

It should be interesting to note that par value, book value, and market value will never be equal due to conflicting relationships.

Legal Rights of Common Stockholders

Since the common stockholders are the owners of a firm, they have the following rights: the right to elect the firm's directors, and the right to remove the management of the firm if they decide a management team is not effective. Common stock holders have preemptive rights to purchase any additional shares sold by the firm.

Put and Call Option

A put option is the right to sell stock at a given price within a certain period. A call option is the right to purchase stock at a given price within a certain period.

Preferred Stock

Preferred stock is issued to raise long-term capital for many reasons: When neither common stock nor long-term debt can be issued on reasonable terms, during adverse business conditions, a firm can issue preferred stock with warrants when the common stock is depressed, to bolster the equity component of a firm's capital structure, a firm can issue convertible preferred stock in connection with mergers and acquisitions, and to issue a floating rate preferred stock to stabilize the market price.

Major Provisions of Preferred Stocks

Major provisions include priority to assets and earnings, par value, cumulative dividends, convertibility into common stock, voting rights, participation in sharing the firm's earnings, sinking fund requirements, maturity date, and call provisions.

Pros and Cons of Preferred Stock from Issuer and Investor Viewpoints

From an issuer's viewpoint, the **advantages** of financing with preferred stock are: fixed financial cost, and no danger of bankruptcy if earnings are too low to meet fixed charges, and avoidance of sharing control of the firm with new investors.

From an issuer's viewpoint, the **disadvantage** of financing with preferred stock is a higher after-tax cost of capital than debt due to nondeductibility of preferred dividends. The lower a company's tax bracket, the more likely it is to issue preferred stock.

From an investor's viewpoint, the **advantages** of financing with preferred stock are: steadier and more assured income than common stock, preference over common stock in the case of liquidation, and tax exemption for preferred dividends received.

From an investor's viewpoint, the **disadvantages** of financing with preferred stock are: no legally enforceable right to dividends, even if a company earns a profit, and for individual investors, after-tax bond yields could be higher than those on preferred stock, even though the preferred stock is riskier.

FINANCIAL INSTRUMENTS

Currency Derivatives

- **Forward contracts**. In the forward exchange market, one buys a forward contract for the exchange of one currency for another at a specific future date and at a specific exchange ratio.

- **Futures contracts**. A futures contract is a standardized agreement that calls for delivery of a currency at some specified future date.

- **Options and Warrants**. An **option** is a contract that gives its holder the right to buy or sell an asset at some pre-determined price within a specified period of time. Pure options (financial options) are created by outsiders (investment banking firms) rather than by the firm itself; they are bought and sold by investors or speculators. **Warrants** are options issued by a company that give the holder the right to buy to a stated number of shares of the company's stock at a specified price. Warrants are distributed along with debt, and they are used to induce investors (a sweetener) to buy a firm's long-term debt at a lower interest rate than otherwise would be required.

Real options are used for investment in real assets and their value is determined as follows:

Project discounted cash flow value = (Cash flows) ÷ (1 + Risk-free cash flow)

Swaps

A swap exchanges a floating-rate obligation for a fixed-rate one, or vice versa. There are two types of swaps: currency swaps and interest-rate swaps. With currency swaps, two parties exchange interest obligations on debt denominated in different currencies. At maturity the principal amounts are exchanged, usually at a rate of exchange agreed upon in advance. With an interest-rate swap, interest-payment obligations are exchanged between two parties, but they are denominated in the same currency. There is not an actual exchange of principal. If one party defaults, there is no loss of principal per se.

Credit Derivatives

Total Return Swaps

Credit derivatives unbundle default risk from the other features of a loan. The original lender no longer needs to bear the risk; it can be transferred to others for a price. The party who wishes to transfer is known as the protection buyer. The protection seller assumes the credit risk and receives a premium for providing this insurance. The premium is based on the probability and likely severity of default.

Credit Swaps

A credit swap, also known as a default swap, is similar in concept to the total-return swap, but different in the detail. The protection buyer pays a specific premium to the protection seller, insurance against a risky debt instrument deteriorating in quality. The annuity premium is paid each period until the earlier of the maturity of the credit swap agreement or a specific credit event occurring, usually default.

Other Credit Derivatives

Spread-adjusted notes involve resets based on the spread of a particular grade of security over Treasury securities. An index is specified, and quarterly and semiannual resets occur, where one counterparty must pay the other depending on whether the quality yield spread widens or narrows. Usually the spread is collared with a floor and cap.

Credit options involve puts and calls based on a basket of corporate fixed-income securities. The strike price often is a specified amount over Treasury securities. With **credit-sensitive notes**, the coupon rate changes with the credit rating of the company involved. If the company is downgraded, the investor receives more interest income; if upgraded, less interest income.

Hidden Financial Reporting Risk

Off-balance-sheet accounting practices include: hiding debt with the equity method, hiding debt with lease accounting, hiding debt with pension accounting, and hiding debt with special-purpose entities. In all these cases, debt is underreported, which creates a financial reporting risk. Investors and creditors charge a premium for the financial reporting risk. Consequently, the cost of capital goes up and stock prices and bond prices go down.

CASH MANAGEMENT

Cash Controls

To be presented as cash on the balance sheet, it must be available to meet current obligations. Cash includes such items as coins, currency, checks, bank drafts, checks from customers, and money orders. Cash in savings accounts and cash in certificates of deposit maturing within one year can be included as current assets preferably under the caption of short-term investments, but not as cash. Petty cash and other imprest cash accounts can be included in other cash accounts.

Current assets are those assets expected to be converted into cash, sold, or consumed within one year or within the operating cycle, whichever is longer. Current assets are properly presented in the balance sheet in the order of their liquidity. Some of the more common current assets are cash, marketable securities, accounts receivable, inventories, and prepaid items.

Cash Items Excluded

Certain cash items are not presented in the general cash section of the balance sheet. They include compensating balances, other restricted cash, and exclusions from cash.

Compensating Balances

Borrowing arrangements are made with a lending institution to ensure the availability of a line of credit. The classification of compensating balances on the balance sheet depends on whether the compensation relates to short-term or long-term borrowing. If held for short-term borrowing, it should be presented separately in current assets. If held for long-term borrowing, it should be classified as a noncurrent asset under Investments or Other Assets.

Other Restricted Cash

Cash balances can be restricted for special purposes such as dividend payments, acquisition of fixed assets, retirement of debt, plant expansion, or deposits made in connection with contracts or bids. Since these cash balances are not immediately available for just any use, they should be presented separately in the balance sheet. Classification as current or noncurrent is dependent upon the date of availability or disbursement.

Exclusions from Cash

Items that should not be presented as cash are postage stamps, postdated checks, travel advances, IOUs, securities, investments in federal funds, and checks deposited and returned because of insufficient funds. Certificates of deposit should be reflected in the temporary investment account, since they are not available for use until the maturity date.

Bank Reconciliation

Every organization should prepare a bank reconciliation schedule periodically (e.g., monthly) to reconcile the organization's cash record with the bank's record of the organization's cash.

Cash requires a good system of internal control, since it is so liquid and easy to conceal and transport. Segregation of duties is an important part of the system of internal control for cash. No one person should both record a transaction and have custody of the asset. Without proper segregation, it is easier for an employee to engage in lapping and kiting.

Float

Float is an amount of money represented by items (both check and noncheck) outstanding and in the process of collection. The amount of float incurred is determined by two factors: the dollar volume of checks cleared, and the speed with which the checks are cleared. The relationship between float and these two factors can be expressed as

Float = Dollar volume × Collection speed

The cost of float pertains to the potential for earning income from nonearning assets, as represented by items in the process of collection. This cost of float is an opportunity cost—the firm could have fully invested and earned income had the funds been available for investment and not incurred float.

Hedging

In a financial futures **hedging** transaction, a firm takes a futures position that is opposite to its existing economic, or more commonly called, "cash" position. By taking the opposite position in the financial futures market, the firm can protect itself against adverse interest rate fluctuations by locking in a given yield or interest rate.

Controls Over Cash

Cash is required to pay employee wages and salaries, buy raw materials and parts to produce finished goods, pay off debt, and pay dividends, among other things. Cash is received from customers for the sale of goods and the rendering of services. Customer payments come into the organization in various forms such as checks, bank drafts, wire transfers, money orders, charge cards, and lockboxes.

Cash Account Balances

- Take an inventory of cash accounts open. Since each account maintains cash balances, the potential exists to improve control over cash.

- Perform account reconciliations periodically and ensure that the person doing the reconciliation has no cash management duties.

- Review the account of compensating balances held at the banks. Focus on eliminating or reducing the amount of compensating balances.

- Review cash account balances to see if they are kept too high for fear of being overdrawn. Try to bring these balances down to the bare minimum without being overdrawn. This will improve the idle cash situation.

- Review the fees charged by the bank for the number of accounts open and understand the reasons for charging the service fees.

Payables

- Establish policies concerning the average payment period. The payment period is calculated by dividing the accounts payable balance by the average daily credit purchases.

- Use remote disbursement banks preferably with zero balance.

- Perform aging of the accounts payable periodically.

Receivables

- Review billing and collection policies and procedures.

- Minimize the elapsed time between sale and release of invoice to the customer.

- Reduce the long time between invoice preparation and entry of the invoice into the receivables system.

- Identify receivable backlogs and determine their impact on cash position.

- Minimize the time that is required to record the payment and to remove it from the receivable subledger. If the time lag is too long, collection resources will be wasted pursuing accounts that have already paid.

- Perform aging of receivables.

- Establish procedures related to the types of collection efforts including customer statements, dunning letters, phone calls by trained in-house staff, referral to a collection agency, and so forth.

- Establish policies toward selling the receivables or clarify the policies toward using the receivables as collateral for financing purposes.

Electronic Techniques to Control Cash

Electronic Funds Transfer

Electronic funds transfer (EFT) systems allow organizations to pay their bills without actually writing checks. EFT eliminates bank float as "good" funds move quickly from customer accounts to vendor accounts at their respective banks. EFT accelerates cash inflow for the company receiving payment.

The automated clearing house (ACH) clears debits and credits created by electronic funds transactions. The ACH clears all transactions each day by properly debiting and crediting to the correct accounts. The ACH then routes these cleared transactions to the proper member banks.

Electronic Data Interchange

The electronic data interchange (EDI) system is another major step toward a payment acceleration scheme. EDI is not only used to place purchase orders with vendors for raw materials and finished goods, but also is used to send invoices and receive payments. The invoice is automatically created by the EDI system, which is then sent to the customer. After receiving the goods, the customer authorizes an electronic payment with virtually no float. EDI involves a third party as a middleperson to transmit and receive electronic messages between vendors and customers.

Management of Current Assets

Effective cash management requires a working capital policy, which refers to the firm's policies regarding the desired level for each category of current assets and how current assets will be financed.

Current assets fluctuate with sales and represent a large portion (usually greater than 40%) of total assets. Working capital management is important for both large and small firms alike.

Cash Conversion Cycle Model

The cash conversion model defines the length of time from the payment for the purchase of raw materials to the collection of accounts receivable generated by the sale of the final product. It is an important model since it focuses on the conversion of materials and labor to cash.

The cash conversion cycle begins the day a bill for labor and/or supplies is paid and runs to the day receivables are collected. The cycle measures the length of time the firm has funds tied up in working capital. The shorter the cash conversion cycle, the smaller the need for external financing and thus the lower the cost of such financing. This would result in increase in profits.

Approaches to Shorten the Cash Conversion Cycle

- Reduce the inventory conversion period by processing and selling goods more quickly.
- Reduce the receivables conversion period or days sales outstanding by speeding up collections.
- Lengthen the payables deferral period by slowing down payments.

Working Capital Asset Investment Policies

Appropriate working capital policies are needed to support various levels of sales. Three such policies include:

1. Relaxed (liberal) working capital policy. Sales are stimulated by the use of a credit policy that provides liberal financing to customers which results in a high level of accounts receivable. This is a policy which maximizes the current assets. Accounts receivable will increase as the credit sales increase for a relaxed policy and the opposite is true for the restricted policy.

2. Moderate working capital policy. This is a policy which falls between liberal and tight working capital policy.

3. Restricted (tight) working capital policy. A policy that minimizes current assets. A tight policy lowers the receivables for any given level of sales, or even the risk of a decline in sales. This policy provides the highest expected return of investment and entails the greatest risk. The firm would hold minimal levels of safety stocks for cash and inventories.

Working Capital Financing Policies

A good working capital financing policy is needed to handle seasonal or cyclical business fluctuations and a strong or weak economy. When the economy is strong, the working capital is built up and inventories and receivables go up. When the economy is weak, the working capital goes down along with inventories and receivables. Current assets are divided into permanent and temporary, and the manner in which these assets are financed constitutes the firm's working capital financing policy.

A firm's working capital asset investment policy, including the cash conversion cycle, is always established in conjunction with the firm's working capital financing policy. Three financing policies are available to manage working capital, including maturity matching, aggressive, and conservative approach.

Advantages and Disadvantages of Short-Term Credit

Short-term credit is generally riskier and cheaper than using long-term credit. There is a trade-off between risk and profits in using short-term credit. The three financing policies (i.e., maturity matching, aggressive, and conservative) differ in the relative amount of short-term debt financing each uses in that aggressive policy uses the greatest amount, conservative policy uses the least amount, and maturity-matching policy uses the right amount.

Management of Cash

On one hand, adequate cash serves as protection against a weak economy and can be used to pay off debts and to acquire companies. On the other hand, too much cash makes a firm vulnerable to corporate raiding or takeovers.

Cash = Currency + Bank demand deposits + Near-cash marketable securities

Near-cash marketable securities = US Treasury bills + Bank certificates of deposit (CDs)

Effective cash management is important to all organizations, whether profit-oriented or not. The scope of cash management encompasses cash gathering (collection) and disbursement techniques and investment of cash. Since cash is a "nonearning" asset until it is put to use, the goal of cash management is to reduce cash holdings to the minimum necessary to conduct normal business.

Advantages of Holding Adequate Cash and Near-Cash Assets

- Taking trade discounts. Suppliers offer customers trade discounts—a discount for prompt payment of bills. Cash is needed to take advantage of trade discounts. Cost of not taking trade discounts could be high.

- Keeping current ratios and acid-test ratios in line with those of other firms in the industry requires adequate holdings of cash. Higher ratios give a strong credit rating. A strong credit rating enables the firm both to purchase goods and services from suppliers and provide favorable terms and to maintain an ample line of credit with the bank. A weak credit rating does the opposite.

- Holding ample supply of cash could help to acquire another firm, to handle contingencies such as labor strike, to attack competitors' marketing campaigns, and to take advantages of special offers by suppliers.

Cash Management Efficiency Techniques

A cash budget, showing cash inflows and outflows and cash status, is the starting point in the cash management system. The techniques used to increase the efficiency of management include: cash flow synchronization, use of float, speeding collections, slowing disbursements, and transfer mechanisms.

Management of Marketable Securities

Reasons for Holding Marketable Securities

Two basic reasons for holding marketable securities (e.g., U.S. Treasury bills, commercial paper, and certificates of deposits) are: (1) they are used as a temporary investment, and (2) they serve as a substitute for cash balances. Temporary investment occurs when the firm must finance seasonal or cyclical operations, when the firm must meet some known financial requirements such as new plant construction program, a bond about to mature, quarterly tax payments, and when the proceeds from stocks and bonds are used to pay for operating assets.

Criteria for Selecting Marketable Securities

The selection criteria for a marketable security portfolio include default risk, taxability, and relative yields. Several choices are available for the financial manager in selecting a marketable securities portfolio and they all differ in risk and return. Most financial managers are averse to risk and unwilling to sacrifice safety for higher rates of return. The higher a security's risk, the higher its expected and required return, and vice versa. A trade-off exists between risk and return.

Risks in Marketable Securities

Default risk, interest rate risk, purchasing power risk, and liquidity risk face the financial manager in managing the portfolio of marketable securities.

Risks in Inventory

Inventories are least liquid assets (greatest risk) because they take a long time to convert into cash. They can be damaged, spoiled, or stolen.

VALUATION MODELS

Inventory Valuation

The three types of manufacturing inventory are raw materials, work in process (WIP), and finished goods, and is the largest current asset.

Inventory Cost Flow Methods

- **Specific identification method**, where the cost of the specific items sold are included in the cost of goods sold, while the costs of the specific items on hand are included in the inventory. This method is used for valuing jewelry, fur coats, automobiles, and high-priced furniture.

- **Average cost method**, where the items in the inventory are priced on the basis of the average cost of all similar goods available during the period. Weighted-average method or moving-average technique is used for calculating the ending inventory and the cost of goods sold.

- **First-in, first-out (FIFO) method**, where goods are used in the order in which they are purchased; the first goods purchased are the first used. The inventory remaining must represent the most recent purchase. Cost flow matches the physical flow of the goods, similar to the specific identification method.

- **Last-in, first-out (LIFO) method**, where it matches the cost of the last goods purchased against revenue. The ending inventory would be priced at oldest unit cost. LIFO is the most commonly used method.

- **Next-in, first-out (NIFO) method**, which is not currently acceptable for purposes of inventory valuation. NIFO uses replacement cost. When measuring current cost income, the cost of goods sold should consist not of the most recently incurred costs but rather the cost that will be incurred to replace the goods that have been sold.

Inventory Valuation Methods

Generally, **historical cost** is used to value inventories and cost of goods sold. In certain circumstances, though, departure from cost is justified. Some other methods of costing inventory include:

- Net realizable value

- Lower of cost or market

However, **market cost** is limited by a floor and ceiling cost. Market cannot exceed net realizable value, which is the estimated selling price minus the cost of completion and disposal (ceiling). Market cannot be less than net realizable value minus a normal profit margin (floor). Lower of cost or market can be applied to each inventory item, each inventory class, or total inventory.

Inventory Estimation Methods

An organization may estimate its inventory to compare with physical inventories to determine whether shortages exist, to determine the amount of inventory destroyed in a fire or stolen, or to obtain an inventory cost figure to use in monthly or quarterly (interim) financial statements. Two methods of estimating the cost of ending inventory are (1) the gross margin method and (2) the retail inventory method.

The **gross margin method** is based on the assumption that the relationship between gross margin and sales has been fairly stable. Gross margin rates from prior periods are used to calculate estimated gross margin. The estimated gross margin is deducted from sales to determine estimated cost of goods sold. Estimated cost of goods sold is then deducted from cost of goods available for sale to determine estimated inventory cost.

The **retail inventory method** is used by organizations that mark their inventory with selling prices. These prices are converted to cost using a cost/price (cost-to-retail) ratio. The cost/price ratio is simply what proportion cost is to each sales dollar. This cost/price ratio is applied to ending inventory stated at retail prices to estimate the cost of ending inventory.

Financial Asset Valuation

Policy decisions that are most likely to affect the value of the firm include: investment in a project with large net present value, sale of a risky operating division that will now increase the credit rating of the entire company, and use of more highly leveraged capital structure that results in a lower cost of capital.

Establishing or predicting the value of a firm is an important task of the financial manager since maximizing the value of his firm is a major goal. Here the focus is on maximizing shareholders' wealth. Similar to capital budgeting decisions, the financial manager can use "discounted cash flow" (DCF) techniques to establish the worth of any assets (e.g., stocks, bonds, real estate, and equipment) whose value is derived from future cash flows. *The key concept of DCF is that it takes time value of money into account. The value of a firm is a combination of bond valuation, common stock valuation, and preferred stock valuation.*

Bond Valuation

A bond valuation model shows the mathematical relationships between a bond's market price and the set of variables that determine the price. For example, bond prices and interest rates are inversely related. Corporate bonds are traded in the over-the-counter market.

A bond represents an annuity (i.e., interest payments) plus a lump sum (i.e., repayment of the par value), and its value is found as the present value of this payment stream. The equation to find a bond's value is

Value of bond = I(Present value of annuity) + M(Present value of lump sum)

Where I is dollars of interest paid each year (i.e., Coupon interest rate $\times$ Par value = Coupon interest payment), and M is par (maturity) value.

Common Stock Valuation

Investors buy common stock for two main reasons: (1) to receive dividends, and (2) to enjoy capital gain. Dividends are paid to stockholders at management's discretion since there is no legal obligation to pay dividends. Usually stockholders have an expectation to receive dividends even though in reality they may not. If the stock is sold at a price above its purchase price, the investor will receive a capital gain. Similarly, if the stock is sold at a price below its purchase price, the investor will suffer capital losses.

The value of a common stock is calculated at the present value of the expected future cash flow stream (i.e., expected dividends, original investment, and capital gain or loss). Different aspects of these cash flow streams is the determination of the amount of cash flow and the riskiness of the amounts, and knowing what alternative actions affect stock prices.

Preferred Stock Valuation

Preferred stock is a hybrid stock—has elements of both bonds and common stock. Most preferred stocks entitle their owners to regular fixed dividend payments. The value of the preferred stock can be found as follows:

$$VPS = DPS \times KPS$$

Where VPS is the value of the preferred stock

DPS is the preferred dividend

KPS is the required rate of return on preferred stock

Business Valuation

Business valuation is valuing the worth of a business entity, whether in whole or part. The value of a business is derived from its ability to generate cash flows consistently period after period over the long term. Business valuation can be performed at various milestones such as new product introduction; mergers, acquisitions, divestitures, recapitalization, and stock repurchases; capital expenditures and improvements; joint venture agreements; and ongoing review of performance of business unit operations.

There are 12 models to help management in making sound decisions during valuation of a business opportunity. These models, in the order of importance and usefulness, include: (1) book value model, (2) accounting profit model, (3) liquidation value model, (4) replacement cost model, (5) discounted abnormal earnings model, (6) price multiples model, (7) financial analysis model, (8) economic-value-added model, (9) market-value-added model, (10) economic profit model, (11) net present value model, and (12) discounted cash flow model.

CAPITAL BUDGETING

Capital budgeting decisions deal with the long-term future of a firm's course of action. Capital budgeting is the process of analyzing investment projects and deciding whether they should be included in the capital budget which, in turn, outlines the planned expenditures on fixed assets such as buildings, plant, machinery, equipment, warehouses, and offices.

Methods to Rank Investment Projects

Payback Method

Payback is the expected number of years required to recover the original investment in a capital budgeting project. The procedure calls for accumulating the project's net cash flows until the cumulative total becomes positive. The shorter the payback period for a project, the greater the acceptance of the project, and the greater the liquidity for that project. Risk can be minimized by selecting the investment alternative with the shortest payback period. Initial investment money can be recouped quickly. Two payback methods include regular payback and discounted payback where the latter is better than the former.

$$\text{Payback period} = \text{Investment} \div \text{After-tax cash flows}$$

Net Present Value Method

A simple method to accommodate the uncertainty inherent in estimating future cash flows is to adjust the minimum desired rate of return. Discounted cash flow (DCF) techniques, which consider the time value of money, were developed to compensate for the weakness of the payback method. *Two examples of DCF techniques include (1) the net present value (NPV) method and (2) the internal rate of return (IRR) method.*

NPV is equal to the present value of future net cash flows, discounted at the marginal cost of capital. The approach calls for finding the present value of cash inflows and cash outflows, discounted at the project's cost of capital, and adding these discounted cash flows to give the project's NPV. The rationale for the NPV method is that the value of a firm is the sum of the values of its parts.

NPV = (After-tax cash flows) × (Present value of annuity) − (Initial investment)

The NPV index or profitability index is the present value of after-tax cash flows divided by initial investment. Accounting rate of return is annual after-tax net income divided by initial or average investment. When the profitability index or cost-benefit ratio is one, the NPV is zero.

Regular Internal Rate of Return

In the regular internal rate of return (IRR) method, the discount rate that equates the present value of future cash inflows to the investment's cost is found. In other words, the IRR method is defined as the discount rate at which a project's NPV equals zero.

Modified Internal Rate of Return

Academics prefer the NPV method, while business executives favor the IRR method. The reason business executives prefer the IRR method is that they find IRR "more natural" to analyze investments in terms of percentage rates of return rather than dollars of NPV.

The regular IRR method can be modified to make it a better indicator of relative profitability and hence better for use in capital budgeting. The new measure is called the modified IRR (MIRR) and it is the discount rate at which the present value of a project's cost is equal to the present value of its terminal value. The terminal value is the sum of the future values of the cash inflows, compounded at the firm's cost of capital. In other words, the MIRR is the discount rate that forces the present value of the costs to equal the present value of the terminal value.

Postaudit of Capital Projects

A postaudit is a comparison of the actual and expected results (both costs and savings) for a given capital project and explanation of variances, if any. A postaudit is a good learning exercise and is practiced by most successful organizations. The lessons learned from the postaudit can be used to fine-tune the forecasts of costs and benefits and to improve business operations.

Project Cash Flows and Risk Assessment

Project Cash Flows

It is important to note that capital budgeting decisions must be based on annual cash flows, not accounting income, and that only incremental cash flows are relevant to the accept or reject decision. Cash flows and accounting income can be different due to depreciation expense, which is a noncash expense. Since we are interested in net cash flows, it is obtained by adding depreciation expense to the net income after taxes.

Incremental cash flows represent the changes in the firm's total cash flows that occur as a direct result of accepting or rejecting the project. It is the net cash flow that can be traceable to an investment project. Sunk costs, opportunity costs, externalities, and shipping/installation costs are examples of special problems that can occur in determining incremental cash flows.

Project Risk Assessment

Risk analysis is important to capital budgeting decisions. Three separate and distinct types of project risk include (1) the project's own stand-alone risk, (2) corporate risk (within-firm risk), and (3) market risk (beta risk).

A **project's own stand-alone risk** is measured by the variability of the project's expected returns. A project's **corporate risk** is measured by the project's impact on the firm's earnings variability. It does not consider the effects of stockholders' diversification.

A project's **market (beta) risk** is measured by the project's effect on the firm's beta coefficient. Market risk can-not be eliminated by diversification. If the project has highly uncertain returns, and if those are highly correlated with those of the firm's other assets and also with most other assets in the economy, the project will have a high degree of all types of risk. A company whose beta value has decreased due to a change in its marketing strategy would apply lower discount rate to expected cash flows of potential projects.

Market risk is important because of its direct effect on a firm's stock prices. It has been found that both market risk and capital risk affect stock prices. Corporate risk for weak firms increases significantly compared to strong firms. This is because weak firms would have difficulty in borrowing money at reasonable interest rates, which, in turn, would decrease profits. The decrease in profits would be reflected in the price of the stock.

Risk to a company is affected by both project variability and how project returns correlate with those of the company's prevailing business. Overall company risk will be lowest when a project's returns exhibit low variability and negative correlation.

Techniques for Measuring Stand-Alone Risk

With this technique, one is interested in determining the uncertainty inherent in the project's cash flows. Three techniques are available for assessing a project's stand-alone risk: sensitivity analysis, scenario analysis, and Monte Carlo simulation.

Techniques for Measuring Market or Beta Risk

Beta risk is that part of a project's risk that cannot be eliminated by diversification. It is measured by the project's beta coefficient. Two methods are available to estimate the betas of individual projects: (1) the pure play method and (2) the accounting beta method.

In the **pure play method**, the company tries to find several single-product firms in the same line of business as the project being evaluated, and it then applies these betas to determine the cost of capital for its own project.

The **accounting beta method** fills the gap of the pure play method in finding single-product, publicly traded firms by applying against a large sample of firms. The project's beta is determined by regressing the returns of a particular company's stock against returns on a stock market index. Betas determined by using accounting data rather than stock market data are called accounting betas.

Project Risks and Capital Budgeting

Capital budgeting can affect a firm's market risk, its corporate risk, or both. It is difficult to develop a good measure of project risk due to difficulty in quantifying either risk.

Two methods for incorporating project risk into the capital budgeting decision process include (1) certainty equivalent approach and (2) risk-adjusted discount rate approach.

Capital Rationing

The amount of funds available to a firm is limited even though acceptable capital budget projects are many. A firm will approve an independent project if its NPV is positive. It selects the project with the highest NPV when faced with mutually exclusive projects. Management cannot or would not want to raise whatever funds are required to finance all of the acceptable projects. When capital budget must be limited, this situation is called capital rationing.

Capital rationing is a constraint placed on the total size of the firm's capital investment. A drawback of capital rationing is that it is not maximizing a firm's stock value since it deliberately forgoes profitable projects. Because of this negative effect, only a few firms ration their capital.

International Capital Budgeting

The techniques for domestic capital budgeting are equally applicable to the international capital budgeting process. However, three types of risks exist in the international area: (1) cash flow risk, that is, cash flow estimation is much more difficult, (2) exchange rate risk, that is, exchange rate fluctuations add to the riskiness of the foreign investment, and (3) sovereignty risk, that is, the possibility of deliberate foreign government acts that reduce or eliminate cash flows.

COST OF CAPITAL EVALUATION

The rate of return on a security to an investor is the same as the cost of capital to a firm, which is a required return on its investments. Any increase in total assets of a firm's balance sheet must be financed by an increase in one or more of capital components (i.e., debt, preferred stock, retained earnings, common stock). Like any other resources, capital has a cost. The cost of capital must reflect the average cost of the various sources of long-term funds used, that is, one or more of capital components used.

Cost of Debt

The cost of debt is calculated as $Kd (1 - T)$ where Kd is the interest rate on debt and T is the firm's marginal tax rate. The government pays part of the cost of debt (equal to tax rate) because interest is deductible for tax purposes. The value of the firm's stock depends on after-tax cash flows. Here we are interested in acquiring a new debt (marginal cost of debt) to finance a new asset, and past financing is a sunk cost and is irrelevant for cost of capital calculation purposes.

The key point is to compare the rate of return with after-tax flows. After-tax cost of debt is less than before-tax cost due to tax savings resulting from an interest expense deduction that reduces the net cost of debt.

Cost of Preferred Stock

The cost of preferred stock (Kp) is the preferred dividend (Dp) divided by the net issuing price (Pn) or the price the firm receives after deducting flotation costs. This is $Kp = Dp/Pn$. Since preferred dividends are not tax deductible, there are no tax savings unlike interest expense on debt.

Cost of Retained Earnings

If management decides to retain earnings there is an opportunity cost involved, that is, stockholders could have received the earnings as dividends and invested this money somewhere else. Because of this opportunity cost, the firm should earn on its retained earnings at least as much as the stockholders themselves could earn in alternative investments of comparable risk such as the cost of common stock equity.

Cost of Common Stock

The cost of common stock (Ke) is higher than the cost of retained earnings (Ks) due to flotation costs involved in selling new common stock. The equation is:

$$Ke = \frac{D1}{p_0(1-F)} + g$$

Where D1 is the dividends, Po is the stock price, F is the percentage flotation cost incurred in selling the new stock, Po (1 − F) is the net price per share received by the firm.

When a stock is in equilibrium, its required rate of return (Ks) should be equal to its expected rate of return (Kes)

$$Ks = Krf = Rp \text{ or } Kes = (D1/Po) + g$$

where Krf is the risk-free rate

Rp = Risk premium

D1/Po is the stock's dividend yield

g is the stock's expected growth rate.

Cost of Common Stock (continued)

Three methods are commonly used to calculate the cost of common stock: (1) the capital asset pricing model (CAPM) approach, (2) the bond-yield-plus-risk-premium approach, and (3) the discounted cash flow (DCF) approach. The DCF approach does not consider the risk explicitly while the other two approaches do consider the risk explicitly.

CAPM Approach

The CAPM model is used to determine the required rate of return on an asset, which is based on the idea that any asset's return should be equal to the risk-free rate plus a risk premium rate that reflects the asset's non-diversifiable risk. Note that the non-diversifiable risk cannot be eliminated through diversification because it is a part of systematic risk.

$Ks = Krf + (Km - Krf) bi$

Where Krf is the risk-free rate (e.g., U.S. Treasury bond or bill rate)

$(Km - Krf)$ is equal to the risk premium

Km is the expected rate of return on the market or on "average" stock

bi is the stock's beta coefficient (an index of the stock's risk).

Drawbacks of the CAPM approach include: a stockholder may be concerned with total risk rather than with market risk only. Beta coefficient may not measure the firm's true investment risk. This approach will understate the correct value of the required rate of return on the stock, Ks, and it is difficult to obtain correct estimates of the inputs to the model to make it operational.

Examples of the CAPM approach include: deciding whether to use long-term or short-term Treasury bonds for risk-free rate, difficulty in estimating the beta coefficient that investors expect the firm to have in the future, and difficulty in estimating the market risk premium.

Bond-Yield-Plus-Risk-Premium Approach

The bond-yield approach provides a "ballpark" estimate of the cost of equity, not a precise number, since it uses ad hoc, subjective, and judgmental estimate.

Ks = Bond rate + Risk premium

A firm's cost on common equity is found by adding a risk premium (say 2 to 4%) based on judgment to the interest rate on the firm's own long-term debt.

Discounted Cash Flow Approach

The discounted cash flow (DCF) approach is also called the dividend-yield-plus-growth rate approach, and calculated as

$Ks = Kes = D1/Po$ + Expected growth (g)

Investors expected to receive a dividend yield ($D1/Po$) plus a capital gain (g) for a total expected return of Kes. At *equilibrium*, this expected return would be equal to the required return (Ks). $Ks = Kes$.

Weighted-Average and Marginal Cost of Capital Concepts

An optimal (target) capital structure is a mix of debt, preferred stock, and common stock that maximizes a firm's stock price. The goal of the finance manager should be then to raise new capital in a manner that will keep the actual capital structure on target over time. The firm's weighted-average cost of capital (WACC) is calculated based on the target proportions of capital and the cost of the capital components, all based on after-tax costs. The WACC could be used as a "hurdle rate" for capital investment projects, and is computed as:

$$WACC = W_dk_d(1 - T) + W_pk_p + W_sk_s$$

where W_d, W_p, and W_s are the weights used for debt, preferred stock, and common stock, respectively. The weights could be based either on book values or market values and the latter is preferred over the former. If a firm's book value weights are close to its market value weight, book weights can be used.

As the firm tries to raise more money, the cost of each dollar will at some point rise. The marginal cost concept can be applied here: The marginal cost of any item is the cost of another unit of that item, whether the item is labor or production. The marginal cost of capital (MCC) is the cost of the last dollar of new capital that the firm raises, and the MCC rises as more and more capital is raised during a given period. The MCC schedule shows how the weighted-average cost of capital changes as more and more new capital is raised during a given year.

The break point is the dollar value of new capital that can be raised before an increase in the firm's weighted-average cost of capital occurs. The break point is total amount of lower-cost of capital of a given type divided by fraction of this type of capital in the capital structure.

Issues in Cost of Capital

Capital budgeting and cost of capital estimates deal with *ex ante* (estimated) data rather than *ex post* (historical) data. Because of this, we can be wrong about the location of the investment opportunity schedule (IOS) and the marginal cost of capital (MCC). Consequently, a project that formerly looked good could turn out to be a bad one. By solving these issues, refinements can be made. Other issues include

- Depreciation-generated funds

- Privately owned and small business firms

- Measurement problems

TAXATION SCHEMES

Tax Shelters

Some U.S. corporations take advantage of loopholes in the U.S. tax code and open corporate offices, manufacturing plants, and service firms in foreign countries to avoid or shelter from various types of taxes imposed in the U.S. These tax shelters or tax havens are legal but unethical until the tax loopholes are closed by the U.S. Congress. In a way, U.S. corporations want to benefit from the tax differentials that exist between the U.S. and foreign countries and pay little or no taxes in the U.S.

Examples of Taxation Schemes

- Sales tax
- Use tax
- Value-added tax (VAT)
- Income tax
- Property tax
- Ad valorem tax
- Accumulated earnings tax
- Capital stock tax
- Unrelated business income tax
- Gift tax
- Estate tax
- Excise tax
- Unified transfer tax

Differences between Tax Reporting and Financial Reporting

The net income computed for financial accounting purposes will be different from taxable income reported on the corporation's income tax return, and therefore, reconciliation between these two types of income is essential to ensure accuracy. The starting point for the reconciliation is net income per books, which is the financial accounting net income. Additions and subtractions are entered for items that affect net income per books and taxable income differently.

MERGERS, ACQUISITIONS, AND DIVESTITURES

A merger is defined as the combination of two firms to form a single firm. A merger can be a friendly merger or a hostile merger. In a friendly merger, the terms and conditions of a merger are approved by the management of both companies, while in a hostile merger, the target firm's management resists acquisition.

Types of Mergers

- Horizontal. Same line of business

- Vertical. With supplier or customer

- Congeneric. In the same general industry

- Conglomerate. With unrelated business

- Beachhead. To enter a new industry

Merger Analysis

Whatever type of merger is used, the underlying theory of merger analysis is capital budgeting techniques. The objective is to determine whether the present value of the cash flows expected to result from the merger exceeds the price that must be paid for the target company. The acquiring firm performs the capital budgeting analysis.

The merger analysis can focus on four areas such as a strategic merger, an operating merger, a financial merger, or a strategic alliance arrangement. In a **strategic merger**, economies of scale concept is at the focus, which means increasing market share for products and services; eliminating duplicate functions, departments, divisions, manufacturing plants, warehouses, or offices; reducing the raw material suppliers' source base; decreasing the number of marketing distribution channels, and increasing the overall efficiency of the entire company. What the senior management is expecting to see from the strategic merger is that the performance of the post-merged firm is significantly better than that of the pre-merged firm. A strategic merger appears to be best type of merger due to its long-term survivability or sustainability than the other types of mergers.

An **operating merger** is a merger in which operations of the firms involved are integrated in the hope of achieving synergistic benefits. In most cases, the operating merger is similar to the strategic merger in terms of their common goals and objectives to achieve.

A **financial merger** is one in which the merged companies will be operated independently and from which no significant operating economies of scale are expected. The post-merger cash flows are simply the sum of the

Merger Analysis (continued)

expected cash flows of the two companies if they continued to operate independently. It also means restructuring the acquired company to improve the cash flows and unlock its hidden value.

A **strategic alliance arrangement**, although not a merger in its true meaning, occurs when a large and highly established company with proven products, markets, and distribution channels wishes to invest its money in a small and emerging company in the areas of new research and development activities that could help the large company in its growth.

After completing the merger analysis, value of the target firm should be assessed in order to determine an educated price. Both cash flows and a discount rate are essential in valuing the target firm. Cash flows can be developed using a set of pro forma income statements for a number of years (say five years). These net cash flows are discounted at the overall cost of capital, if both debt and equity are used to finance the merger. If only equity is used then the cost of equity should be used. The price paid to acquire the target firm is a summation of the discount net cash flows at the appropriate cost of capital.

Types of Divestitures

At least, three types of divestitures can exist: spinoffs, selloffs, and closeoffs.

- **Spinoffs** occur where a large company establishes a new corporation based on the assets from one of its operating divisions. The stock of the new corporation was titled to the stockholders of the parent firm. The operating division or a business unit becomes an independent company through the issuance of shares in it, on a pro-rata basis, to the parent company's shareholders. It also occurs when a company sells one of its operating divisions to its existing shareholders, and the shareholders receives new stock representing separate ownership rights in the division.

- **Selloffs** include selling the entire business unit or its assets, whether as a whole or in parts. The total value of a firm is greater than the sum of the values of its individual operating units if each unit were sold separately. This means some units are good with hidden value while other units are bad with little or no value.

- **Closeoffs** include discontinuing an unprofitable product line and closing a losing department, facility, business unit, or division.

Leveraged Buyouts

Often, a leveraged buyout (LBO) is an alternative to a merger. There is a controversy whether LBOs are a good or a bad idea for a company or the economy as a whole. Some argue that LBOs might destabilize the economy because of the disruptive forces involved in the deal. Others argue that LBOs can stimulate lethargic or complacent management.

Holding Companies

A holding company is a company that owns stock in another company and exercises control. The holding company is called the parent company and the controlled companies are called subsidiaries or operating companies. A holding company is taxed on profits, cannot issue tax-free bonds, and is subject to normal government regulations.

Role of Investment Bankers in Mergers and Acquisitions

An investment banker and a lawyer are usually involved with a merger by helping to arrange mergers, advising target companies in developing and implementing defensive tactics, and helping to value target companies. For these services, a fee and commissions are paid to the investment banker.

Role of Regulators in Mergers and Acquisitions

Business mergers can be friendly or hostile. Of particular importance is developing defensive tactics to block hostile mergers. Some commonly used tactics include: changing the bylaws to require a supermajority of directors instead of a simple majority to approve a merger; educating the target firm's stockholders that the price being offered is too low; raising antitrust issues in the hope that the U.S. Justice Department will intervene; persuading a white knight more acceptable to the target firm's management that it should compete with the potential acquirer; and taking a "poison pill," which includes management committing a kind of suicide to avoid a takeover, borrowing on terms that require immediate repayment of all loans if the firm is acquired, selling off the assets at bargain prices to make the firm less attractive to the potential acquirer, granting lucrative golden parachutes to the firm's executives to drain off some cash, taking on a huge debt, and leaving behind assets of questionable value. The U.S. Federal Trade Commission (FTC) also plays an active role in mergers and acquisitions to balance the competitive situation.

MANAGERIAL ACCOUNTING: GENERAL CONCEPTS

One can think of managerial accounting (MA) and financial accounting (FA) topics as the two sides of a coin because one side provides information to the other side, and each side shares some common information with each other. For example, internal managers and executives share and use some financial accounting reports such as balance sheets, income statements, statements of cash flows, and other customized financial reports. Some activities are similar between MA and FA (e.g., recordkeeping) while most of the activities (e.g., decision making) are different.

MA concepts and decisions are non-sequential, unstructured, non-programmed, and non-routine in nature and are mostly handled by high-level management. The reverse is not true with FA concepts and decisions as they are structured, rule bound, programmed, and routine in nature.

COSTING SYSTEMS

Target Costing

Target costing is a better way of controlling a product's cost. A target cost is the allowable amount of cost that can be incurred on a given product to develop, produce, and deliver it, and still earn the required profit margin. It is a market-driven cost in which cost targets are set by considering customer requirements and competitive environment. Cost targets are achieved by focusing and improving both process design and product design. Market research indicates that the target price is what customers are willing to pay for a product or service. Both the target cost and target price concepts, which are related to each other, are equally applicable to products and services.

Target cost = Target price − Profit margin

Target price = Target cost + Profit margin

Traditional Costing

Traditional costing systems use a cost plus approach, where production costs are first estimated, then a profit margin is added to it to obtain a product price that the market is going to pay for it. If the price is too high, cost reductions are initiated. It is a cost-driven approach where customer requirements and competitive environment are not considered.

Traditional cost = Traditional price − Profit margin

The cost to manufacture a product is necessary for external reporting (e.g., inventory valuation and cost of goods sold determination) and internal management decisions (e.g., price determination, product mix decisions, and sensitivity analysis). One of the goals of cost accounting is to provide information for management planning and control and determination of product or service costs. This is achieved through the accumulation of costs by department and/or by product. Although the terminology differs between manufacturing and service industries, the principles of cost accounting are the same.

Activity-Based Costing

Activity-based costing (ABC) is a management system that focuses on activities as the fundamental cost objects and uses the costs of these activities as building blocks for compiling the costs of other cost objects. ABC helps management in controlling costs through its focus on cost drivers. ABC can provide more accurate product cost data by using multiple cost drivers that more accurately reflect the causes of costs. Inaccurate product cost information can lead to cross-subsidization of products. This results in systematic under-costing of products due to lower overhead rate. These cost drivers can be both non-volume-based as well as volume-based drivers.

Benefits of Activity-Based Costing System

- Better cost control
- Accurate product cost information
- Lower information processing costs
- Individual costs allocated to products via several cost drivers
- Better make-or-buy decisions
- Focus on activities where costs are incurred and accumulated instead of products

Just-in-Time Costing

Just-in-time (JIT) costing system starts with completed production units (outputs) and then assigns manufacturing costs to units sold (sales) and units not sold (inventories). This is called **backflush costing** because it works backwards by recording the costs of production when outputs are completed. It does not cost products as they move from raw materials stage to work-in-process stage and then to finished goods stage. JIT costing is in contrast with the standard costing where the latter builds the costs of products as they move from raw materials stage to work-in-process stage and then to finished goods stage.

Standard Costing

Standard costs are predetermined costs or estimated costs requiring a startup investment to develop them. Ongoing costs for maintenance of standards can be lower than for an actual-cost system. Standard costs should be attainable and are expressed on a per-unit basis. Without standard costs, there is no flexible budgeting system since the latter is developed at different volumes of production using standard costs per unit. In a way, a standard cost is a budget for a single unit of production or sales. Various types of variances can occur when using the standard costing system.

Types of Standards

- Perfection (ideal or theoretical) standards

- Currently attainable standards

Types of Variances

In general, **price variance** is the difference between actual unit prices and budgeted unit prices multiplied by the actual quantity of goods sold, used, or purchased.

Price variance = (Actual unit price − Standard unit price) × Actual inputs purchased

In general, **efficiency variance** is of two types: material efficiency and labor efficiency. Possible reasons for material efficiency variances include (1) quality of materials (2) workmanship, (3) choice of materials, (4) mix of materials, and (5) incorrect standards.

Efficiency variance is the difference between the quantity of actual inputs used and the quantity of inputs that should have been used multiplied by the budgeted price.

Efficiency variance = (Inputs actually used − Inputs that should have been used)
× Standard unit price of inputs

Specifically, **direct materials variance** is of two types: (1) price and (2) quantity. The price variance is actual price paid per unit of input (AP) minus standard price established per unit of input (SP) multiplied by actual quantity of input used in production (AQ).

Direct materials price variance = (AP − SP) × AQ

The materials price variance is unfavorable if AP is greater than SP and favorable if AP is less than SP.

Types of Variances (continued)

The *quantity variance* is actual quantity of input used in production (AQ) minus standard quantity of input that should have been used in production (SQ) multiplied by standard price established per unit of input (SP).

Direct materials quantity variance = $(AQ - SQ) \times SP$

The materials quantity variance is unfavorable if AQ is greater than SQ and favorable if AQ is less than SQ.

Specifically, **direct labor variance** is of two types: (1) rate and (2) efficiency. The rate variance is actual price paid per unit of input (AP) minus standard price established per unit of input (SP) multiplied by actual quantity of input used in production (AQ).

Direct labor rate variance = $(AP - SP) \times AQ$

The labor rate variance is unfavorable if AP is greater than SP and favorable if AP is less than SP.

The efficiency variance is actual quantity of input used in production (AQ) minus standard quantity of input that should have been used in production (SQ) multiplied by standard price established per unit of input (SP).

Direct labor efficiency variance = $(AQ - SQ) \times SP$

The labor efficiency variance is unfavorable if AQ is greater than SQ and favorable if AQ is less than SQ.

Types of Variances (continued)

Specifically, **overhead variance** is of four types: (1) spending variance, (2) efficiency variance, (3) budget variance, and (4) volume variance. Variances (1) and (2) are part of variable overhead variances while variances (3) and (4) are part of fixed overhead variances.

Spending variance = Actual variable overhead − (Actual hours × Budget rate)

Efficiency variance = Budget rate × (Actual hours − Standard hours)

The budget variance is sometimes called the fixed overhead spending variance. It is calculated as the difference between actual fixed costs and budget fixed costs.

The volume variance is sometimes called the idle capacity variance. This is computed as Budget fixed costs−Standard hours allowed for actual output at standard rate.

Although labor rates are known from the union contract, unfavorable labor price variance can occur due to:

- The use of a "single average standard labor rate" for a given activity that requires different labor rates (the averaging effect)
- The assignment of a high-skilled worker earning more money to an activity that should have been assigned to a less-skilled worker earning less money

Effects of Variance Prorations

Generally accepted accounting principles (GAAP) and income tax laws require that financial statements show actual costs of inventories and cost of goods sold. Consequently, variance prorations (difference between actual costs and standard costs) are required if they result in a material change in inventories or operating income. A good benefit of proration is that it prevents managers from setting standards aimed at manipulating income. By setting loose standards, managers can take the resulting favorable variance into current income. If managers do not have to prorate variances, they can more easily affect a year's operating income by how they set standards.

Reporting of Variances

Interim reporting of variance differs in that some firms write off all variances monthly or quarterly to cost of goods sold while others prorate the variances among inventories and cost of goods sold. Most firms will follow the same reporting practices for both interim and annual financial statements.

COST CONCEPTS

Absorption and Variable Costing Methods

The cost of goods sold, which is larger than all of the other expenses combined in a product cost, can be determined under either the absorption costing or variable costing method.

Under **absorption costing**, all manufacturing costs are included in finished goods and remain there as an inventory asset until the goods are sold. Management could misinterpret increases or decreases in income from operations, due to mere changes in inventory levels, to be the result of business events, such as changes in sales volume, prices, or costs. Absorption costing is necessary in determining historical costs for financial reporting to external users and for tax reporting.

Variable costing may be more useful to management in making decisions. In variable costing (direct costing), the cost of goods manufactured is composed only of variable manufacturing costs—costs that increase or decrease as the volume of production rises or falls. These costs are the direct materials, direct labor, and only those factory overhead costs that vary with the rate of production. The remaining factory overhead costs, which are fixed or nonvariable costs, are generally related to the productive capacity of the manufacturing plant and are not affected by changes in the quantity of product manufactured. Thus the fixed factory overhead does not become a part of the cost of goods manufactured but is treated as an expense of the period (period cost) in which it is incurred.

Management's Use of Absorption and Variable Costing Methods

Controlling Costs

All costs are controllable in the long run by someone within a business, but they are not all controllable at the same level of management. For example, plant supervisors, as members of operating management, are responsible for controlling the use of direct materials in their departments. They have no control, however, of insurance costs related to the buildings housing their departments. For a specific level of management, **controllable costs** are costs that can be influenced by management at that level, and **non-controllable costs** are costs that another level of management controls. This distinction is useful in fixing the responsibility for incurring costs and for reporting costs to those responsible for their control.

Pricing Products

Many factors enter into determining the selling price of a product. In the **short run**, a business is committed to its existing manufacturing facilities. The pricing decision should be based on making the best use of such capacity. The fixed costs cannot be avoided, but the variable costs can be eliminated if the company does not manufacture the product. The selling price of a product, therefore, should at least be equal to the variable costs of making and selling it. Any price above this minimum selling price contributes an amount toward covering fixed costs and providing income.

In the **long run**, plant capacity can be increased or decreased. If a business is to continue operating, the selling prices of its products must cover all costs and provide a reasonable income. Hence, in establishing pricing policies for the long run, information provided by absorption costing procedures is needed.

Planning Production

Planning production also has both short-run and long-run implications. In the **short run**, production is limited to existing capacity. Operating decisions must be made quickly before opportunities are lost. For example, a company manufacturing products with a seasonal demand may have an opportunity to obtain an off-season order that will not interfere with its production schedule nor reduce the sales of its other products. The relevant factors for such a short-run decision are the additional revenues and the additional variable costs associated with the off-season order. If the revenues from the special order will provide a contribution margin, the order should be accepted because it will increase the company's income from operations. For **long-run** planning, management must also consider the fixed costs.

Analyzing Market Segments

Market analysis is performed by the sales and marketing function in order to determine the profit contributed by market segments. A **market segment** is a portion of business that can be assigned to a manager for profit responsibility.

Analyzing Contribution Margins

Another use of the contribution margin concept to assist management in planning and controlling operations focuses on differences between planned and actual contribution margins. However, mere knowledge of the differences is insufficient. Management needs information about the causes of the differences. The systematic examination of the differences between planned and actual contribution margins is termed **contribution margin analysis**.

Since contribution margin is the excess of sales over variable costs, a difference between the planned and actual contribution margin can be caused by (1) an increase or decrease in the amount of sales or (2) an increase or decrease in the amount of variable costs. An increase or decrease in either element may in turn be due to (1) an increase or decrease in the number of units sold (quantity factor) or (2) an increase or decrease in the unit sales price or unit cost (unit price or unit cost factor).

Technical Aspects of Absorption and Variable Costing Methods

An understanding of the inventory costing method is important for several reasons such as: (1) in measuring product costs and inventories, (2) determining income, (3) deciding between making or buying a product, (4) setting prices, and (5) planning product mix to produce or sell.

Two major methods of inventory costing are absorption costing and variable costing, and they differ in whether fixed manufacturing overhead is an "inventoriable" cost (i.e., whether such overhead is included in the inventory or not). Other names used for fixed manufacturing overhead are fixed factory overhead or indirect manufacturing cost.

Other Cost Concepts

- Actual costs

- Average costs

- Budgeted costs

- Common costs

- Conversion costs

- Current costs

- Direct costs

- Expired costs

- Fixed costs

- Full costs

- Historical costs

- Indirect costs

Other Cost Concepts (continued)

- Joint costs
- Long-run costs
- Marginal costs
- Mixed costs
- Period costs
- Prime costs
- Product costs
- Short-run costs
- Standard costs
- Step costs
- Sunk costs

Other Cost Concepts (continued)

- Unexpired costs

- Variable costs

- Avoidable costs

- Unavoidable costs

- Controllable costs

- Noncontrollable costs

- Out-of-pocket costs

- Embodied costs

- Displaced costs

- Discretionary costs

- Opportunity costs

- Incremental costs

Other Cost Concepts (continued)

- Differential costs
- Replacement costs
- Implicit costs
- Imputed costs
- Committed costs
- Uncommitted costs
- Rework costs
- Engineered costs

Cost Behavior

Costs have a behavior pattern. For example, costs vary with volumes of production, sales, or service levels, with the application of the amount of resources, and with the timeframe used. Knowing the cost-behavior information helps in developing budgets, interpreting variances from standards, and making critical decisions.

Assumptions Underlying Cost Classifications

1. The cost object must be specified since costs are variable or fixed with respect to a chosen cost object. Cost objects can be product-based or activity-based.

2. The time span must be specified. Costs are affected by the time span. The longer the time span, the higher the proportion of total costs that are variable and the lower the fixed costs. Costs that are fixed in the short run may be variable in the long run. There should be a cause-and-effect relationship between the cost driver and the resulting costs. The cost driver may be either an input (e.g., direct labor hour or machine hour) or an output (finished goods). For example, fixed manufacturing costs decline as a proportion of total manufacturing costs as the time span is lengthened from the short run to the medium-run to the long run.

3. The relevant range for changes in the cost driver must be specified. Each of the cost-behavior patterns such as variable cost, fixed cost, or mixed cost has a relevant range within which the specified cost relationship will be valid. Constraints such as labor agreements and plant capacity levels set the relevant range. If volume exceeds the relevant range, total fixed costs would increase if a new plant is built, and unit variable costs would increase if overtime must be paid.

Cost Estimation Approaches

Four approaches are available to estimate costs including: (1) industrial engineering method, (2) conference method, (3) account analysis method, and (4) quantitative analysis method of current or past cost relationships. The first three methods require less historical data than do most quantitative analyses. Therefore, cost estimations for a new product will begin with one or more of the first three methods.

RELEVANT COSTS

Differential Analysis

Managers must consider the effects of alternative decisions on their businesses. Differential analysis reports the effects of alternative decisions on total revenues and costs. Planning for future operations involves decision making. For some decisions, revenue and cost data from the accounting records may be useful. However, the revenue and cost data for use in evaluating courses of future operations or choosing among competing alternatives are often not available in the accounting records and must be estimated. These estimates include relevant revenues and costs. The relevant revenues and costs focus on the differences between each alternative. Costs that have been incurred in the past are not relevant to the decision. These costs are called **sunk costs.**

Differential revenue is the amount of increase or decrease in revenue expected from a course of action as compared with an alternative. **Differential cost** is the amount of increase or decrease in cost that is expected from a course of action as compared with an alternative.

Differential income or loss is the difference between the differential revenue and the differential costs. Differential income indicates that a particular decision is expected to be profitable, while a differential loss indicates the opposite.

Differential analysis focuses on the effect of alternative courses of action on the relevant revenues and costs.

Application of Relevant Cost Concept

When deciding whether to accept a special order from a customer, the best thing to do is to compare the total revenue to be derived from this order with the total relevant costs incurred for this order. The key terms are incremental relevant costs and incremental relevant revenues. The relevant costs are those that vary with the decision.

COST-VOLUME-PROFIT ANALYSIS

Cost-volume-profit (CVP) analysis helps managers who are making decisions about short-term duration and for specific cases where revenue and cost behaviors are linear and where volume is assumed to be the only cost and revenue driver. CVP is an approximation tool and low-cost tool.

CVP analysis is a straightforward, simple-to-apply, widely used management tool. CVP analysis answers questions such as, how will costs and revenues be affected if sales units are up or down by x percent? If price is decreased or increased by x percent? A decision model can be built using CVP relationships for choosing among courses of action. *CVP analysis tells management what will happen to financial results if a specific level of production or sales volume fluctuates or if costs change.*

Methods for Calculating Break-Even Point (BEP)

Equation Method

The equation method is more general and thus is easier to apply with multiple products, with multiple costs and revenue drivers, and with changes in the cost structure. At BEP, the operating income is zero. The formula is:

(Unit sales price $\times$ number of units) $-$ (Unit variable cost $\times$ number of units) $-$ Fixed costs $=$ Operating income

or

Sales $-$ Variable costs $-$ Fixed costs $=$ Operating income

Contribution-Margin Method

Contribution-margin (CM) is equal to sales minus all variable costs. BEP is calculated as follows:

BEP $=$ Fixed costs/Unit contribution margin

Graphic Method

A CVP chart results when units are plotted on the x-axis and dollars on the y-axis. The BEP is where the total-sales line and total-cost line intersect. The total sales line begins at the origin because if volume is zero, sales revenue will be zero, too.

CVP Assumptions and Their Limitations

Assumptions of CVP Analysis

- The behavior of total revenues and total costs is linear over the relevant range of volume.

- Selling prices, total fixed costs, efficiency, and productivity are constant.

- All costs can be divided neatly into fixed and variable components. Variable cost per unit remains constant.

- A greater sales mix will be maintained as total volume changes.

- Volume is the only driver of costs.

- The production volume equals sales volume, or changes in beginning and ending inventory levels are zero.

Limitations of CVP Analysis

- Volume

- Unit prices of inputs

- Efficiency

- Changes in production technology

- Civil wars

- Employee strikes

- Laws and regulations

- *Profits are affected by changes in factors besides volume.* A CVP chart must be analyzed together with considering all assumptions and their limitations.

Ways to Lower the BEP

- Reducing the overall fixed costs

- Increasing the CM per unit of product through increase in sales prices

- Increasing the CM per unit of product through decreases in unit variable costs

- Increasing the CM per unit through increase in sales prices and decreasing unit variable costs together

- Selecting a hiring freeze for new employees

- Limiting merit increase for senior executives

- Cutting the annual percentage salary rate increase for all salaried employees

- Reducing overtime pay for all employees to reduce labor costs

- Reducing the number of employees on payroll

- Improving employee productivity levels

- Increasing machine utilization rates

Sensitivity Analysis in CVP Model

A CVP model developed in a dynamic environment determined that the estimated parameters used may vary between limits. Subsequent testing of the model with respect to all possible values of the estimated parameters is termed a sensitivity analysis.

Sensitivity analysis is a management tool that will answer questions such as: What will operating income be if volume changes from the original prediction? What will operating income be if variable costs per unit decrease or increase by x percent? If sales drop, how far can they fall below budget before the BEP is reached? The last question can be answered by the margin of safety tool. The margin of safety is a tool of sensitivity analysis and is the excess of budgeted sales over the break-even volume.

Changes in Variable and Fixed Costs on CVP Analysis

Organizations often face a trade-off between fixed and variable costs. Fixed costs can be substituted for variable costs and vice versa. This is because variable costs and fixed costs are subject to various degrees of control at different volumes—boom or slack.

Contribution Margin versus Gross Margin

Contribution margin (CM) is the excess of sales over all variable costs, including variable manufacturing, marketing, and administrative categories. **Gross margin** (GM), also called gross profit, is the excess of sales over the cost of the goods sold. Both CM and GM would be different for a manufacturing company. They will be equal only when fixed manufacturing costs included in cost of goods sold are the same as the variable nonmanufacturing costs, which is a highly unlikely event.

Profit-Volume Chart versus CVP Chart

The profit-volume chart is preferable to the CVP chart because it is simpler to understand. This chart shows a quick, condensed comparison of how alternatives on pricing, variable costs, or fixed costs affect operating income as volume changes. The operating income is drawn on the y-axis and the x-axis represents volume (units or dollars).

Effect of Sales Mix and Income Taxes on CVP

Sales mix is the relative combination of quantities of products that constitute total sales. A change in sales mix will cause actual profits to differ from budgeted profits. It is the combination of low-margin or high-margin products that causes the shift in profits, despite achievement of targeted sales volume.

There will be a different BEP for each different sales mix. A higher proportion of sales in high contribution margin products will reduce the BEP. A lower proportion of sales in small contribution margin products will increase the BEP. Shifting marketing efforts to high contribution margin products can increase the operating income and profits.

TRANSFER PRICING

Transfer pricing involves inter- or intracompany transfers, whether domestic or international. A transfer price is the price one unit of a corporation charges for a product or service supplied to another unit of the same corporation. The units involved could be either domestic or international, and the products involved could be intermediate products or semifinished goods.

Transfer Pricing Methods

- Market-based

- Cost-based

- Negotiated

Transfer Pricing Management

Goal congruence exists when individual goals, group goals, and senior management goals coincide. Under these conditions, each unit manager acts in his own best interest, and the resulting decision is in the long-term best interest of the company as a whole. A transfer price method should lead to goal congruence.

A sustained high level of **managerial effort** can lead to achievement of goals. A transfer price method promotes management effort if sellers are motivated to hold down costs and buyers are motivated to use the purchased inputs efficiently.

Senior management should allow a high level of **unit autonomy** in decision making in a decentralized organization. This means that a transfer price method should preserve autonomy if unit managers are free to make their own decisions and are not forced to buy or sell products at a price that is unacceptable to them.

Dual Pricing in Transfer Pricing

Dual pricing uses two separate transfer-pricing methods to price each inter-unit transaction. This is because seldom does a single transfer price meet the criteria of goal congruence, managerial effort, and unit autonomy. An example of dual pricing is when the selling unit receives a full-cost plus markup-based price and the buying unit pays the market price for the internally transferred products.

International Transfer Pricing

The multinational corporation (MNC) must deal with transfer pricing and international taxation, and therefore, a knowledge of international laws related to these areas is important. A transfer is a substitute for a market price and is recorded by the seller as revenue and by the buyer as cost of goods sold. The transfer pricing system should motivate unit managers not to make undesirable decisions at the expense of the corporation as a whole.

Transfer Pricing Choices

- Market-based pricing

- Cost-based pricing

Taxes and Transfer Pricing

Intercompany transactions from an MNC point of view are subject to Section 482 of the Internal Revenue Code of the United States. Section 482 gives the Internal Revenue Service (IRS) the authority to reallocate income and deductions among subsidiaries if it determines that this is necessary to prevent tax evasion, the illegal reduction of taxes. The key test is whether intercompany sales of goods or services appear to be priced at arm's-length market values. Among items the IRS will scrutinize include trademarks, patents, research and development cost, and management services.

RESPONSIBILITY ACCOUNTING

Accountability of Managers

Managers are responsible and accountable for their decisions and actions in planning and controlling the resources of the organization. Resources include physical, human, and financial resources. Resources are used to achieve the organization's goals and objectives. Budgets help to quantify the resources required to achieve goals. Each manager should receive a periodic actual performance reports compared to performance targets and a periodic actual production reports with variances compared to production plans related to her own department or function that she is responsible for.

Responsibility Centers

Each manager is in charge of a responsibility center and is accountable for a specified set of activities and operations within a segment of the organization. The degree of responsibility varies directly with the level of the manager. Responsibility accounting is a system that measures the plans and actions of each responsibility center. Four types of responsibility centers are common:

1. Cost center (accountable for costs only)

2. Revenue center (accountable for revenue only)

3. Profit center (accountable for revenues and costs)

4. Investment center (accountable for investments only)

OPERATING BUDGETS

Operating Budget Systems

A budgeting system includes both expected results and historical or actual results. A budgeting system builds on historical, or actual, results and expands to include consideration of future, or expected, results. A budgeting system guides the manager into the future.

Budget System $\longrightarrow$ Forward Looking

Historical Cost System $\longrightarrow$ Backward Looking

A budget is a quantitative expression of a plan of action. It will aid in the coordination of various activities or functions throughout the organization. The master budget by definition summarizes the objectives of all subunits of an organization.

Benefits of Operating Budgets

- Budgets are planning "tools." Budgets force managers to look into the future and make them prepare to meet uncertainties and changing business conditions.

- Budgets provide a starting point for discussing business strategies. In turn, these strategies direct long-term and short-term planning. Therefore, strategic plans and budgets are interrelated and affect one another.

- Budgeted performance is better than historical data for judging or evaluating employee performance. This is because employees know what is expected of their performance. A major drawback of using historical data is that inefficiencies and bad decisions may be buried in past actions.

- Budgets can be a valuable vehicle for communication with interested parties. Budgets help coordinate activities of various functions within the organization to achieve overall goals and objectives.

- Budgets are control systems. Budgets help to control waste of resources and to search out weaknesses in the organizational structure.

- A budget should be implemented so as to gain acceptance by employees. This requires a "buy-in" by employees, senior management support, and lower-level management involvement.

Benefits of Operating Budgets (continued)

- A budget should be set tight, but attainable and flexible. A budget should be thought of as a means to an end, not the end in itself.

- A budget should not prevent a manager from taking prudent action. Nonetheless, he should not disregard the budget entirely.

Different Dimensions in Operating Budgets

The time period for budgets varies from one year to five or more years. The common budget period is one year and broken down by quarters and months. Four types of budgets emerge from the time coverage and update point of view: short-term, long-term, static, and continuous budgets:

1. Short-term budgets (operating budgets) have a time frame of one to two years.

2. Long-term budgets (strategic budgets) have a time frame of three to five or more years.

3. Static budgets are the original budgeted numbers, which are not changed. The time frame does not change.

4. Continuous budgets are also called rolling budgets, where a twelve-month forecast is always available by adding a month in the future as the month just ended is dropped. The timeframe keeps changing in continuous budgets.

How Operating Budgets Are Prepared

The **master budget** (static budget) is developed after the goals, strategies, and long-range plans of the organization have been determined. It summarizes the goals of the subunits or segments of an organization. This information summarizes, in a financial form, expectations regarding future income, cash flows, financial position, and supporting plans. The functions of budgets include planning, coordinating activities, communicating, evaluating performance, implementing plans, motivating, and authorizing actions. It contains the operating budget.

A detailed budget is prepared for the coming fiscal year along with some less-detailed amounts for the following years. Budgets may be developed from the **top-down** or the **bottom-up approach**. With the top-down approach, upper management determines what it expects from subordinate managers. Subordinate managers may then negotiate with upper management concerning the items they feel are unreasonable. With the bottom-up approach, lower-level managers propose what they expect to accomplish and the required resources. Upper management then makes suggestions and revisions. Budgets may be used for long-range planning, but the typical planning-and-control budget period is one year. This annual budget may be broken down into months or quarters and continuously updated.

Operating Budgeting Techniques

- Incremental budgeting
- Flexible budgeting
- Zero-base budgeting
- Program planning budgeting
- Performance budgeting

Advantages of Operating Budgets

- Compel planning
- Provide performance criteria
- Promote communication and coordination

Limitations of Operating Budgets

- Be aware that budgeted items are a mixture of fixed and variable cost components. Accordingly, mixed costs cannot be used for linear projection.

- Be aware that budgeted items include some direct costs and some allocated costs. Direct costs are more useful for decision making than allocated costs. Responsibility accounting favors direct and controllable costs, not allocated and uncontrollable costs.

- The nature of volume levels needs to be understood. Most budgets are based on a single level of volume (point estimates) while multiple volume levels (range estimates) would be better for decision making.

- The kind of assumptions made during the budget development process need to be known. Understand the budget preparer's state of mind: optimistic, most likely, or pessimistic outcomes. Each of these outcomes would bring a different type of realism to the budget numbers.

- The variances from budgets need to be analyzed very carefully. Performance reports show the variations between the actual and the budgets—an element of control. Corrective action requires determination of underlying causes of variation. Variation could be favorable or unfavorable.

ECONOMIC/FINANCIAL ENVIRONMENTS

International Organization Structures

The organization structure of the Multinational Corporation (MNC) evolves over time due to changes in economic policies, tax laws, government regulations, and political structures. The organizational structure of the MNC varies, in which each manager's level has a varied degree of authority and responsibility.

MNCs are firms with significant foreign direct investment assets. They are characterized by their ability to derive and transfer capital resources worldwide and to operate facilities of production and penetrate markets in more than one country, usually on a global scale. **Multinational enterprise (MNE)** has been a popular term because it reflects the fact that many global firms are not, technically speaking, "corporations." The terms **transnational corporation** and **supranational corporation** are often used within the United Nations system, in which many internationalists argue that the operations and interests of the modern corporation "transcend" national boundaries.

Information Flows and Organization Structures of MNCs

- With the international division or department, information flows from subsidiaries to the vice president of the international division.

- In MNCs organized by product line, information flows from subsidiaries to the vice president of the product line.

- In an MNC organized by function, information flows from subsidiary to headquarters according to specific business function, that is, marketing, manufacturing, or accounting.

- When MNCs are geographically organized, the subsidiary information is collected within a geographic area and then sent to headquarters.

- With the matrix form, information flows in two directions: from the subsidiary to the geographic location headquarters and by product line to MNC headquarters.

Models of Multinational Business

Another dimension to the organization of MNCs is the attitude of headquarters management toward multinational business. These attitudes can be classified into three models: (1) ethnocentric (home-country oriented), (2) polycentric (host-country oriented), and (3) geocentric (world-oriented). *The host country refers to that nation in which an MNC establishes a subsidiary in a local country. The home country (parent country) refers to that nation in which an MNC establishes a subsidiary in a foreign country.*

The attitudes of headquarters management also affect the location of decision making. Basically, three types of decision making may result: (1) centralized, (2) decentralized, and (3) semi-centralized or semidecentralized.

Types of International Strategies

International firms typically develop their core strategy for the home country first. Subsequently, they internationalize their core strategy through international expansion of activities and through adaptation. Eventually, they globalize their strategy by integrating operations across nations.

Ethnocentric Strategy

Following World War II, U.S. enterprises operated mainly from an **ethnocentric** perspective. These companies produced unique goods and services, which they offered primarily to the domestic market. The lack of international competition offset their need to be sensitive to cultural differences. When these firms exported goods, they did not alter them for foreign consumption—the costs of alterations for cultural differences were assumed by the foreign buyers. In effect, this type of company had one strategy for all markets.

Multidomestic Strategy

The multidomestic firm has a different strategy for each of its foreign markets. In this type of strategy, "a company's management tries to operate effectively across a series of worldwide positions with diverse product requirements, growth rates, competitive environments, and political risks. The company prefers that local managers do what is necessary to succeed in R&D, production, marketing, and distribution, but holds them responsible for results." In essence, this type of corporation competes with local competitors on a market-by-market basis.

Global Strategy

The global corporation uses all of its resources against its competition in a very integrated fashion. All of its foreign subsidiaries and divisions are highly interdependent in both operations and strategy. Therefore, whereas in a multidomestic strategy the managers in each country react to competition without considering what is taking place in other countries, in a global strategy, competitive moves are integrated across nations. The same kind of move is made in different countries at the same time or in a systematic fashion.

Transnational Strategy

The transnational strategy provides for global coordination (like the global strategy) and at the same time it allows local autonomy (like the multidomestic strategy). The challenges managers of transnational corporations face are to identify and exploit cross-border synergies and to balance local demands with the global vision for the corporation. Building an effective transnational organization requires a corporate culture that values global dissimilarities across cultures and markets.

International Strategic and Tactical Objectives

Organizations generally establish two kinds of measurable objectives:

1. **Strategic objectives**, which are guided by the enterprise's mission or purpose and deal with long-term issues, associate the enterprise to its external environment and provide management with a basis for comparing performance with that of its competitors and in relation to environmental demands. Examples of strategic objectives include: to increase sales, to increase market share, to increase profits, and to lower prices by becoming an international firm.

2. **Tactical objectives**, which are guided by the enterprise's strategic objectives and deal with shorter term issues, identify the key result areas in which specific performance is essential for the success of the enterprise and aim to attain internal efficiency. For example, they identify specifically how to lower costs, to lower prices, to increase output, to capture a larger portion of the market, and to penetrate an international market.

Technology and Global Strategy

Technology has been at the root of the most dramatic changes occurring in commerce today. It now enables organizations to integrate their systems, where changes in one part ripple throughout the system, causing shifts in the other parts. Therefore, no strategy has been left untouched. Electronic networks and the Internet have enabled organizations to decentralize business activities and to outsource activities to other organizations.

Forms of International Business and Marketing Strategies

One can classify international business into three categories: (1) trade, (2) intellectual property rights (trademarks, patents, and copyrights) and international licensing agreements, and (3) foreign direct investment. To the marketer, these broad categories describe three important methods for entering a foreign market. To the lawyer, they also represent the form of doing business in a foreign country and the legal relationship between parties to a business transaction. Each method brings a different set of problems to the firm because the level of foreign penetration and entanglement in various countries is different. Trade usually represents the least entanglement, and thus, the least political, economic, and legal risk, especially if the exporting firm is not soliciting business overseas or maintaining sales agents or inventories there. An investment in a plant and operations overseas usually represents the greatest market penetration and thus, the greatest risk to the firm.

Trade

Trade consists of the import and export of goods and services. **Exporting** is the term generally used to refer to the process of sending goods out of a country, and **importing** is used to denote when goods are brought into a country. However, a more accurate definition is that *exporting is the shipment of goods or the rendering of services to a foreign buyer located in a foreign country. Importing* is then defined as *the process of buying goods from a foreign supplier and entering them into the customs territory of a different country.* Every export entails an import, and vice versa.

Exporting

Trade is often a firm's first step into international business. Compared to the other forms of international business (licensing and investment), trade is relatively uncomplicated. It provides the inexperienced or smaller firm with an opportunity to penetrate a new market, or at least to explore foreign market potential, without significant capital investment and the risks of becoming a full-fledged player (that is, citizen) in the foreign country. For many larger firms, including multinational corporations, exporting may be an important portion of their business operations.

Firms that have not done business overseas before should first prepare an export plan, which may mean assembling an export team, composed possibly of management and outside advisors and trade specialists. Their plan should include the assessment of the firm's readiness for exporting, the export potential of its products or services, the firm's willingness to allocate resources (including financial, production output, and human resources), and the selection of its channels of distribution. The firm may need to modify products, design new packaging and foreign language labeling, and meet foreign standards for product performance or quality assurance. The firm must also gauge the extent to which it can perform export functions in-house or whether these functions should best be handled indirectly through an independent export company. Export functions include foreign marketing, sales and distribution, shipping, and handling international transfers of money.

Importing and global sourcing

Here, importing is presented from the perspective of the global firm for which importing is a regular and necessary part of their business. **Global sourcing** is the term commonly used to describe the process by which a firm attempts to locate and purchase goods or services on a worldwide basis. These goods may include, for example, raw materials for manufacturing, component parts for assembly operations, commodities such as agricultural products or minerals, or merchandise for resale.

Government Controls over Trade

Tariffs and Nontariff Barriers

Both importing and exporting are governed by the laws and regulations of the countries through which goods or services pass. Nations regulate trade in many ways. The most common methods are **tariffs** and **nontariff barriers**. Tariffs are import duties or taxes imposed on goods entering the customs territory of a nation. Tariffs are imposed for many reasons, including the collection of revenue, the protection of domestic industries from foreign competition, and political control (e.g., to provide incentives to import products from politically friendly countries and to discourage importing products from unfriendly countries).

Nontariff barriers are *all barriers to importing or exporting other than tariffs*. Nontariff barriers are generally a greater barrier to trade than are tariffs because they are more insidious. Unlike tariffs, which are published and easily understood, nontariff barriers are often disguised in the form of government rules or industry regulations and are often not understood by foreign companies. Countries impose nontariff barriers to protect their national economic, social, and political interests. Imports might be banned for health and safety reasons. Imported goods usually have to be marked with the country of origin and labeled in the local language so that consumers know what they are buying. One form of nontariff barrier is the **technical barrier to trade**, or **product standard** (e.g., safety standards, electrical standards, and environmental standards). A **quota** is a restriction imposed by law on the numbers or quantities of goods, or of a particular type of good, allowed to be imported. Unlike tariffs,

Tariffs and Nontariff Barriers (continued)

quotas are not internationally accepted as a lawful means of regulating trade except in some special cases. An **embargo** is a total or near total ban on trade with a particular country, sometimes enforced by military action and usually imposed for political purposes. A **boycott** is a refusal to trade or do business with certain firms, usually from a particular country, on political or other grounds.

Trade Liberalization and the World Trade Organization

Trade liberalization refers to the efforts of governments to reduce tariffs and nontariff barriers to trade. In 1995, the Geneva-based **World Trade Organization (WTO)**, was created to administer the rules and to assist in settling trade disputes between its member nations. WTO was the successor to the **General Agreement on Tariffs and Trade (GATT)**.

All WTO nations are entitled to **normal trade relations** with one another. This is referred to as **Most Favored Nation (MFN)** trading status. This means that a member country must charge the same tariff on imported goods, and not a higher one, as that charged on the same goods coming from other WTO member countries. Trade liberalization has led to increased economic development and an improved quality of life around the world.

Intellectual Property Rights and International Licensing Agreements

Intellectual property rights are a grant from a government to an individual or firm of the exclusive legal right to use a copyright, patent, or trademark for a specified time. Copyrights are legal rights to artistic or written works, including books, software, films, music, or to such works as the layout design of a computer chip. Trademarks include the legal right to use a name or symbol that identifies a firm or its product. Patents are governmental grants to inventors assuring them of the exclusive legal right to produce and sell their inventions for a period of years. Copyrights, trademarks, and patents compose substantial assets of many domestic and international firms. As valuable assets, intellectual property can be sold or licensed for use to others through a licensing agreement.

International licensing agreements are contracts by which the holder of intellectual property will grant certain rights in that property to a foreign firm under specified conditions and for a specified time. Licensing agreements represent an important foreign market entry method for firms with marketable intellectual property. For example, a firm might license the right to manufacture and distribute a certain type of computer chip or the right to use a trademark on apparel such as blue jeans or designer clothing. It might license the right to distribute Hollywood movies or to reproduce and market word-processing software in a foreign market, or it might license its patent rights to produce and sell a high-tech product or pharmaceutical. United States firms have extensively licensed their property around the world, and in recent years have purchased the technology rights of Japanese and other foreign firms.

Technology Transfer

The exchange of technology and manufacturing know-how between firms in different countries through arrangements such as licensing agreements is known as technology transfer.

International Franchising

Franchising, a form of licensing, is the most common form of franchising known as a business operations franchise, usually used in retailing. Under a typical franchising agreement, the franchisee is allowed to use a trade name or trademark in offering goods or services to the public in return for a royalty based on a percentage of sales or other fee structure. The franchisee will usually obtain the franchiser's know-how in operating and managing a profitable business and its other "secrets of success" (ranging from a "secret recipe" to store design to accounting methods).

Some Legal Aspects of franchising

Franchising is a good vehicle for entering a foreign market because the local franchisee provides capital investment, entrepreneurial commitment, and on-site management to deal with local customs and labor problems. However, many legal requirements affect franchising.

Foreign Direct Investment

The term **foreign investment**, or **foreign direct investment**, refers to the ownership and active control of ongoing business concerns, including investment in manufacturing, mining, farming, assembly operations, and other facilities of production. A distinction is made between the home and host countries of the firms involved. The **home country** refers to that country under whose laws the investing corporation was created or is head-quartered. For example, the United States is home to multinational corporations such as **Ford, Exxon**, and **IBM**, to name a few, but they operate in **host countries** throughout every region of the world.

Of the three forms of international business mentioned earlier, foreign investment provides the firm with the most involvement, and perhaps the greatest risk, abroad. Investment in a foreign plant is often a result of having had successful experiences in exporting or licensing, and of the search for ways to overcome the disadvantages of those other entry methods. For example, by producing its product in a foreign country instead of exporting, a firm can avoid quotas and tariffs on imported goods, avoid currency fluctuations on the traded goods, provide better product service and spare parts, and more quickly adapt products to local tastes and market trends. Manufacturing overseas for foreign markets can mean taking advantage of local natural resources, labor, and manufacturing economies of scale. Foreign investment in the United States is often called reverse investment. Most of the foreign investment in the United States has come from the United Kingdom and recently from China.

Multinational corporations wishing to enter a foreign market through direct investment can structure their business arrangements in many different ways. Their options and eventual course of action may depend on many factors, including industry and market conditions, capitalization of the firm and financing, and legal considerations.

Foreign Direct Investment (continued)

Some of these options include the start-up of a new foreign subsidiary company, the formation of a joint venture with an existing foreign company, or the acquisition of an existing foreign company by stock purchase. Stock ownership gives the investing corporation tremendous flexibility when investing abroad.

The **wholly owned foreign subsidiary** is a "foreign" corporation organized under the laws of a foreign host country, but owned and controlled by the parent corporation in the home country. Because the parent company controls all of the stock in the subsidiary, it can control management and financial decision making.

The **joint venture** is a cooperative business arrangement between two or more companies for profit. A joint venture may take the form of a partnership or corporation. Typically, one party will contribute expertise and another the capital, each bringing its own special resources to the venture. Joint ventures exist in all regions of the world and in all types of industries. Where the laws of a host country require local ownership or that invest-ing foreign firms have a local partner, the joint venture is an appropriate investment vehicle. **Local participation** refers to the requirement that a share of the business be owned by nationals of the host country.

Another method of investing abroad is for two companies to **merge** or for one company to acquire another ongoing firm. This option has appeal because it requires less know-how than does a new start-up and can be concluded without disruption of business activity.

CULTURAL/POLITICAL ENVIRONMENTS

Different Local/Regional Cultures

Culture is the collective meaning a people put into their unique life-space. It is the pattern of attitudes, beliefs, customs, and traditions that generally expresses the way the average person in that place thinks and behaves. Culture gives people a sense of who they are, of belonging, of how they should behave, and of what they should be doing. Culture is a distinctly human capacity for adapting to circumstances and transmitting this coping skill and knowledge to subsequent generations. Culture itself is an attempt, consciously or unconsciously, by a people to transmit to future generations their acquired wisdom and insight relative to their knowledge, beliefs, customs, traditions, morals, law, art, communication, and habits.

Corporate culture affects how an organization copes with competition and change, whether in terms of technology, economics, or people. The work culture stimulates or constricts the energies of personnel, whether through slogans and myths or taboos. Now management is more cognizant of its customs and traditions, rules and regulations, policies and procedures—such components of culture are being used to make work more enjoyable, to increase productivity, and to meet customer needs and competitive challenges.

Effects of Cultures

Persons of dissimilar backgrounds usually require more time than those of the same culture to become familiar with each other, to be willing to speak openly, to share sufficiently in common ideas, and to understand one another. Therefore, education and training of global leaders must include formal learning in the various cultural dimensions. With globalization of business, managers and leaders need to become more transnational and transcultural in their thinking, planning, and involvement with people.

Global Manager's Dilemma

Global managers operating transnationally are commonly faced with the following situation: In one country something is a lawful or accepted practice, and elsewhere it is illegal. Bribes, for example, may be a common way of doing business to ensure service in the host-country culture, but quite illegal in the home country culture.

Global planning not only requires an effective international management information system, but input from a variety of locals at different levels of sophistication. Even when there are apparent similarities of peoples in geographic regions, cultural differences may require alteration of strategic market planning. For example, North American companies and unions discovered this in Canada when they tried to treat their operations in Canada as mere U.S. extensions. Europeans realized this in Bolivia and Argentina where a common cultural heritage is altered by political and social conditions.

Regional Cultures

Even in the United States, there are cultural differences between the south and the north and between the east and the west regions. Food habits, language, accent, pace of life, work attitudes, and values are different. Culture also affects decision-making capacity.

Global Communication Insights

All behavior is communication because all behavior contains a message, whether intended or not. Communication is not static and passive, but rather it is a continuous and active process without beginning or end. A communicator is not simply a sender or a receiver of messages but can be both at the same time. Culture poses communication problems because there are so many variables unknown to the communicators. *As the cultural variables and differences increase, the number of communication misunderstandings increases.*

High- and Low-Context Communications

Anthropologist Edward Hall makes a vital distinction between high-context and low-context cultures, and how this matter of context impacts communications. A high-context culture uses high-context communications—that is, information is either in the physical context or internalized in the person. Japan, Saudi Arabia, and Africa are examples of cultures engaged in high-context communications, as are the Chinese and Spanish languages. However, a low-context culture employs low-context communications—most information is contained in explicit codes, such as words. North American cultures engage in low-context communications, whether in Canada or the United States, and English is a low-context language.

General Characteristics of the Emerging Work Culture

- Enhanced quality of work life

- Autonomy and control over their work space

- Organizational communication and information orientation

- Participation and involvement in the enterprise

- Creative organizational norms or standards

- High performance and improved productivity

- Emphasis on new technology utilization

- Emphasis on research and development

- Emphasis on entrepreneurialism

- Informal and synergistic relationships

Cultural Awareness Learning Program

The aim of the Canadian International Development Agency's training program is to instill seven skills that could be offered as the objectives of all cultural awareness learning. These seven skills can be applied to understand people, whether they are local, regional, or international. These skills are:

- **Communicate respect** to transmit (both verbally and nonverbally) positive regard, encouragement, and sincere interest.

- **Be nonjudgmental** to avoid moralistic, value-laden, evaluative statements, and to listen in such a way that the other can fully share and explain itself.

- **Personalize knowledge and perceptions** to recognize the influence of one's own values, perceptions, opinions, and knowledge on human interaction, and to regard such as relative, rather than absolute, for more tentative communications.

- **Display empathy** to try and understand others from "their" point of view, to attempt to put oneself into the other's life space, and to feel as they do about the matter under consideration.

- **Practice role flexibility** to be able to get a task accomplished in a manner and time frame appropriate to the learner or other national, and to be flexible in the process for getting jobs done, particularly with reference to participation and group maintenance or morale.

Cultural Awareness Learning Program (continued)

- **Demonstrate reciprocal concern** to truly open up a dialogue, take turns talking, share the interaction responsibility, between groups, and promote circular communication.

- **Tolerate ambiguity** to be able to cope with cultural differences, try to accept a degree of frustration, and deal with changed circumstances and people.

Cross-Cultural Negotiations

Negotiating across cultures is far more complex than negotiating within a culture because foreign negotiators have to deal with differing negotiating styles and cultural variables simultaneously. In other words, the negotiating styles that work at home generally do not work in other cultures. As a result, cross-cultural business negotiators have one of the most complicated business roles to play in organizations. They are often thrust into a foreign society consisting of what appears to be "hostile" strangers. They are put in the position of negotiating profitable business relationships with these people or suffering the negative consequences of failure. And quite often they find themselves at a loss as to why their best efforts and intentions have failed them.

How to Avoid Failure in International Negotiations?

Negotiators in a foreign country often fail because the local counterparts have taken more time to learn how to overcome the obstacles normally associated with international/cross-cultural negotiations. Failure may occur because of time and/or cost constraints. Effective cross-cultural negotiators understand the cultural differences existing among all parties involved, and they know that failure to understand the differences serves only to destroy potential business success.

How Much Must One Know about the Foreign Culture in Negotiations?

Realistically, it is nearly impossible to learn everything about another culture, although it may be possible if one lives in the culture for several years. The reason for this is that each culture has developed, over time, multifaceted structures that are much too complex for any foreigner to understand totally. Therefore, foreign negotiators need not have total awareness of the foreign culture; they do not need to know as much about the foreign culture as the locals, whose frames of reference were shaped by that culture. However, they will need to know enough about the culture and about the locals' negotiating styles to avoid being uncomfortable during (and after) negotiations. Besides knowing enough not to fail, they also need to know enough to win.

Strategic Planning for International Negotiations

Strategic planning for international negotiations involves several stages: (1) preparation for face-to-face negotiations, (2) determining settlement range, (3) determining where the negotiations should take place, (4) deciding whether to use an individual or a group of individuals in the negotiations, and (5) learning about the country's views on agreements/contracts. Tactical planning for international negotiations involves determining how to obtain leverage, use delay tactics, and deal with emotions.

Ethical Constraints in Foreign Negotiations

Business ethics and corporate social responsibility place constraints on negotiators. For example, a negotiator's ethical concerns for honesty and fair dealings, regardless of the power status of negotiating parties, will affect the outcome. There is no global standard or view of what is ethical or unethical behavior in business transactions—what is viewed as unethical behavior in one culture may be viewed as ethical in another culture, and vice versa. For instance, if a negotiator on one side "pays off" an influential decision maker on the other side to obtain a favorable decision, it would be an unethical business practice in some cultures (and illegal in the United States), but it would be quite acceptable in other cultures.

International Management Theories

Theory Z refers to a Japanese style of management that is characterized by long-term employment, slow promotions, considerable job rotation, consensus-style decision making, and concern for the employee as a whole. **Theory T and Theory T+** are complementary theories based on Southeast Asian assumptions that at work is a necessity but not a goal itself; people should find their rightful place in peace and harmony with their environment; absolute objectives exist only with God; in the world, persons in authority positions represent God, so their objectives should be followed; and people behave as members of a family and/or group, and those who do not are rejected by society.

Global Mindsets

Cultural forces represent another important concern affecting international Human Resources (HR) management. In addition to organizational culture, national cultures also exist. **Culture** is composed of the societal forces affecting the values, beliefs, and actions of a distinct group of people. Cultural differences certainly exist between nations, but significant cultural differences exist within countries also. One only has to look at the conflicts caused by religion or ethnicity in Central Europe and other parts of the world to see the importance of culture in international organizations. Convincing individuals from different ethnic or tribal backgrounds to work together may be difficult in some parts of the world.

Geert Hofstede defined five dimensions of culture: power distance, individualism, masculinity/femininity, uncertainty avoidance, and long-term orientation.

LEGAL AND ECONOMIC CONCEPTS

Definition of Contracts

Contracts are governed by state common law. A contract is a binding agreement that the courts will enforce. It is a promise or a set of promises for the breach of which the law gives a remedy, or the performance of which the law in some way recognizes a duty. A promise manifests or demonstrates the intention to act or to refrain from acting in a specified manner.

Requirements of Contracts

- Mutual assent
- Consideration
- Legality of object and subject matter
- Capacity (competent parties)

Classification of Contracts

Contracts can be classified according to various characteristics, such as method of formation, content, and legal effect. The standard classifications are express or implied contracts; bilateral or unilateral contracts; valid, void, voidable, or unenforceable contracts; and executed or executory contracts. These classifications are not mutually exclusive. For example, a contract may be express, valid, bilateral, executory, and informal.

Other Types of Contracts

- Doctrine of promissory estoppel
- Quasi contracts

Nature of Key Economic Indicators

Business conditions relate to business cycles. Decisions such as ordering inventory, borrowing money, increasing staff, and spending capital are dependent on the current and predicted business cycle. For example, decision making in preparation for a recession, such as cost reduction and cost containment is especially different and difficult. Also, during a recession, defaults on loans can increase due to bankruptcies and unemployment.

Specific Types of Key Economic Indicators

- Leading indicators (change in advance of other variables; e.g., capital goods purchases)

- Coincident indicators (change at the time as other variables change; e.g., inflation, unemployment)

- Lagging indicators (change after the other variables change; e.g., unemployment)

Other Types of Key Economic Indicators

- Gross national product (GNP)
- Gross domestic product (GDP)
- Net national product (NNP)
- Consumer price index (CPI)
- Producer price index (PPI)

Methods of Measuring Economic Performance

Unemployment

The key point is that the level of output depends directly upon total or aggregate expenditures. A high level of total spending means: It will be profitable for the various industries to produce large outputs, and it will be profitable for various resource suppliers to be employed at high levels. Hence,

Total spending = Private sector spending + Public sector spending

Inflation

If aggregate spending exceeds the full-employment output, the excess spending will have the effect of increasing the price level. Therefore, excessive aggregate spending is inflationary. Government intervenes to eliminate the excess spending by cutting its own expenditures and by raising taxes so as to curtail private spending. The inverse relationship between unemployment and inflation is embodied in the Phillips curve.

Those who suffer from inflation include fixed money income groups, creditors, and savers, while those who benefit from inflation include flexible money income groups, debtors, and speculators.

Deflation

Deflation is a decrease in prices. Deflation can be induced through contractionary monetary and fiscal policies. If deflation occurs in the United States, it becomes cheaper for other countries to buy U.S. goods. Deflation can arise automatically due to an excess of imports over exports.

IMPACT OF GOVERNMENT LEGISLATION AND REGULATION ON BUSINESS

Government impacts business in many ways. This impact is felt through regulations to control environment, labor practices, safety at workplace, product liability, import and export laws, banking practices, and other areas. Government also impacts business through depreciation laws and tax credits to control investment levels in the economy by the private sector. Using fiscal and monetary policies, government controls employment, production, inflation, interest rates, government spending, and money supply in the economy.

Governmental Legislation and Regulation

U.S. governmental legislation and regulation includes both state and federal government. The scope of state regulation includes pricing by public utility companies while the scope of federal regulation covers price fixing, deceptive pricing, price discrimination, and promotional pricing.

U.S. Sherman Act

The U.S. Sherman Act of 1880 is the primary, first tool of antitrust enforcement. The Act declared any combination, contract, or conspiracy in restraint of trade made among the states or with foreign countries illegal. The Act also made it illegal to monopolize, attempt to monopolize, or conspire to monopolize any portion of interstate commerce or any portion of trade with foreign nations. However, the Sherman Act did not state exactly what types of action were prohibited.

U.S. Clayton Act

The U.S. Clayton Act of 1914 was designed to strengthen and clarify the provisions of the Sherman Act. It defines specifically what constitutes monopolistic or restrictive practices, whereas the Sherman Act does not. The goal of the Clayton Act is to curb anticompetitive practices in their incipiency. Under the Clayton Act, by simply showing a probable, rather than actual, anticompetitive effect would be enough cause for a violation of the act. This means the Clayton Act is more sensitive to anticompetitive practices than the Sherman Act.

U.S. Federal Trade Commission Act

Like the Clayton Act, the U.S. Federal Trade Commission (FTC) Act was designed to prevent abuses and to sustain competition. The FTC Act declared "unfair methods of competition" in commerce" as unlawful and authorizes the FTC to issue "cease and desist" orders prohibiting "unfair methods of competition" and "unfair or deceptive acts or practices." These orders provide injunctive relief by preventing or restraining unlawful conduct. *One of the goals of the FTC is to enforce antitrust laws and to protect consumers.*

U.S. Robinson-Patman Act

The U.S. Congress passed the Robinson-Patman Act in 1936 to protect small competitors by amending the Clayton Act. It is often called the "chain store act." The Robinson-Patman Act amended the price discrimination section of the Clayton Act. It was aimed at protecting independent retailers and wholesalers from "unfair discriminations" by large chain stores and mass distributors, which were supposedly obtaining large and unjustified price discounts because of their purchasing power and bargaining position.

U.S. Wheeler-Lea Act

In 1938, the U.S. Wheeler-Lea Act was passed as an amendment to the FTC Act. The Wheeler-Lea Act makes "unfair or deceptive acts or practices" in interstate commerce illegal; thus, it is designed to protect consumers rather than competitors. Now, the FTC has the authority to prohibit false and misleading advertising and product misrepresentation.

U.S. Celler Antimerger Act

The U.S. Celler Antimerger Act of 1950 also amended the Clayton Act by making it illegal for a corporation to acquire the assets, as well as the stock, of a competing corporation if the effect is to greatly reduce competition or to tend to create a monopoly.

Government's Monitoring of Environmental Issues

The U.S. Environmental Protection Agency (EPA) protects and enhances the environment today and for future generations to the fullest extent possible under the laws enacted by Congress. The agency's mission is to control and abate pollution in the areas of air, water, solid waste, pesticides, radiation, and toxic substances. Its mandate is to mount an integrated, coordinated attack on environmental pollution in cooperation with state and local governments.

EPA: Air and Radiation

The air activities of the EPA Agency include: development of national programs, technical policies, regulations for air pollution control, enforcement of standards, development of national standards for air quality, emission standards for new stationary and mobile sources, and emission standards for hazardous pollutants, technical direction, support, and evaluation of regional air activities, and provision of training in the field of air pollution control.

EPA: Water

The EPA Agency's water quality activities represent a coordinated effort to restore the nation's waters. The functions of this program include: development of national programs, technical policies, and regulations for water pollution control and water supply, ground water protection, marine and estuarine protection, enforcement of standards, water quality standards and effluent guidelines development, technical direction, support, and evaluation of regional water activities, development of programs for technical assistance and technology transfer, and provision of training in the field of water quality.

EPA: Solid Waste and Emergency Response

The U.S. Office of Solid Waste and Emergency Response provides policy, guidance, and direction for the EPA agency's hazardous waste and emergency response programs. The functions of these programs include: development of policies, standards, and regulations for hazardous waste treatment, storage, and disposal, national management of the Superfund toxic waste cleanup program, development of guidelines for the emergency preparedness and "community right to know" programs, development of guidelines and standards for underground storage tanks, enforcement of applicable laws and regulations, analysis of technologies and methods for the recovery of useful energy from solid waste, and provision of technical assistance in the development, management, and operation of waste management activities.

EPA: Pesticides and Toxic Substances

The U.S. Office of Pesticides and Toxic Substances is responsible for: developing national strategies for the control of toxic substances, directing the pesticides and toxic substances enforcement activities, developing criteria for assessing chemical substances, standards for test protocols for chemicals, rules, and procedures for industry reporting and regulations for the control of substances deemed to be hazardous to man or the environment, and evaluating and assessing the impact of existing chemicals, new chemicals, and chemicals with new uses to determine the hazard and, if needed, develop appropriate restrictions.

Specific Trade Legislation and Regulations

U.S. Tied Aid Practices

U.S. tied aid refers to foreign assistance that is linked to the purchase of exports from the country extending the assistance. Tied aid can consist of foreign aid grants alone, grants mixed with commercial financing or official export credits (mixed credits), or concessional (low-interest-rate) loans.

U.S. Export-Import Bank

Exports play a vital role in any economy by creating jobs and generating economic growth. Most industrialized nations have programs to help companies export, that is, sell their products abroad. These programs, collectively referred to as "export promotion," include offering business counseling and training and giving representational assistance, as well as providing market research information, trade fair opportunities, and export financing assistance. These programs can play an important role in increasing the exports of a country's goods and services in sectors of the economy in which it is competitive. Although the U.S. Export-Import Bank (Eximbank) was created to facilitate the financing of both US exports and imports, it has been used almost exclusively to finance US exports.

Methods, Restrictions, and Barriers of International Trade

A country has a trade deficit when it consumes more than it produces and imports the difference from other countries. A country will become a debtor nation when there is a huge trade deficit and when it borrows to finance the domestic budget deficit.

A country should strike a balance between the national savings rate and the budget deficit, specifically by reducing the deficit without endangering long-term economic growth. An imbalance is created when the savings rate is declining and the budget deficit is increasing. The national savings rate should be sufficient to meet the needs of both private sector investments and government borrowing. A country should focus on long-term investment as a way to enhance its competitiveness in the global marketplace.

Methods of Restricting the Trade via Tariffs

A tariff is a tax imposed on imported goods, usually as a percentage of the product's value. Import duties, or tariffs, have been a source of government revenue far longer than income and value-added taxes. Goods entering a country are taxed at an *ad valorem* (percent of value) basis. Many foreign countries prefer to use tariffs since it is relatively easy to check and control as goods come through designated ports.

Methods of Restricting the Trade via Import Quotas

A quota is simply a quantitative restriction applied to imports. Under GATT/WTO, import quotas are supposed to be banned, but there are so many exceptions that the ban is not that useful. In fact, as tariffs have been reduced as an instrument of protection, the tendency has been to replace them with quotas.

Methods of Restricting the Trade via Domestic Content Laws

Another way many countries have attempted to assure the participation of domestic producers has been through domestic content laws. These laws stipulate that when a product is sold in the marketplace, it must incorporate a specified percentage of locally made components. These laws must meet "local content requirements."

Methods of International Trade: Export Promotion Programs

As each country's economic advancement is dependent on its success in trading with other countries, the way that country promotes its exports will be of great importance. Therefore, it is important to ensure that the funds allocated are being channeled into areas with the greatest potential returns. A budget for export promotion programs would be a good start. For a government to promote these programs requires good internal controls, program evaluation criteria, proper program accountability, enhanced planning, and decision making. *Export promotion programs, export loans, credit guarantees, and insurance are some examples of promoting international trade.*

Methods of International Trade: Trade Agreements

The aim of U.S. trade negotiations is to remove foreign barriers to imports and unfair governmental incentives to exports, thus encouraging the free flow of international trade. The principal multinational trade regime has been the World Trade Organization, which requires the negotiations of concerned countries in liberalizing the trade and removing tariffs and other barriers—which is not an easy thing to accomplish.

Methods of International Trade: Technology Policies

Technology policies, the financial market structures, and the business/government relationships of other nations will receive greater significance in the more closely integrated global marketplace.

Theory of Comparative Advantage

Increased total world output is a good argument for free trade between countries. Incentives exist for trade to develop along the lines of comparative advantage. Countries achieve comparative advantage in certain goods due to international differences in demand or supply.

The law of comparative advantage explains how mutually beneficial trade can occur when one country is less efficient than another country in the production of all commodities. The less efficient country should specialize in and export the commodity in which its absolute disadvantage is smallest, and should import the other commodity.

The **HO theorem** states that a country will have a comparative advantage in, and therefore will export that good whose production is relatively intensive in the factor with which that country is relatively well endowed. For example, a country that is relatively capital-abundant compared with another country will have a comparative advantage in the good that requires more capital per worker to produce.

International Laws: World Trade Organization

The World Trade Organization's (WTO's) coverage includes improved procedures over unfair trade practices; trade in services, intellectual property rights, and trade-related investments, and to provide increased coverage to the areas of agriculture, textiles and clothing, government procurements, trade, and the environment.

International Laws: North American Free Trade Agreement

The North American Free Trade Agreement (NAFTA) was intended to facilitate trade and investment throughout North America (United States, Canada, and Mexico). It incorporates features such as the elimination of tariff and nontariff barriers. NAFTA also supports the objective of locking in Mexico's self-initiated, market-oriented reforms.

Impacts and Implementation of NAFTA

NAFTA's system for avoiding and settling disputes among the member countries is a critical element of the agreement. The agreement includes mechanisms such as the establishment of committees and working groups and an early consultation process to help the parties avoid disputes. These mechanisms have helped the governments resolve important trade issues and have kept the number of formal dispute settlement cases relatively low.

International Laws: European Union

The European Union (EU), often called the Common Market, is a supranational legal regime with its own legislative, administrative, treaty-making, and judicial procedures. To create this regime, several European nations have surrendered substantial sovereignty to the EU. European Union law has replaced national law in many areas and the EU legal system operates as an umbrella over the legal systems of the member states. The EU law is vast and intricate.

The EU's Council, the Commission, the Parliament, and the Court of Justice

- **The Council** consists of representatives of the ruling governments of the member states. The European Community Treaty requires the Council to act by a qualified majority on some matters and with unanimity on others.

- **The Commission** is independent of the member states. Its twenty commissioners are selected by council appointment. They do not represent member states or take orders from member state governments. The Commission is charged with the duty by acting only in the best interests of the Union, and serves as the guardian of the Treaties. The Commission largely maintains EU relations with GATT and WTO. The Commission proposes and drafts EU legislation and submits to the Council for adoption.

- **The Parliament** historically played an advisory role. The European Parliament has the power to put questions to the Commission and the Council concerning Union affairs. It also has the power, so far unused, to censure the Commission, in which event all the Commissioners are required to resign as a body. As a minimum, the Parliament has a right to be consulted and to give an "opinion" as part of the EU legislative process. The opinion is not binding upon the Commission or Council.

- **The Court of Justice** is to ensure that in the interpretation and application of Treaty "the law" is observed. There are fifteen Justices (one from each state) that make up the European Court of Justice. If a conflict arises between Union law and the domestic law of a member state, the Court of Justice has held that the former prevails. When there is no conflict, both Union law and domestic law can coexist.

International Laws: Other Regional Groups

- Several groups have been formed in Africa including UDEA, CEAO, and ECOWAS. The purpose is to establish a common customs and tariff approach toward the rest of the world and to formulate a common foreign investment trade.

- Regional groups have been established in Latin America and the Caribbean (CARICOM, CACM, LAFTA/LAIA). The Latin American Free Trade Association (LAFTA) had small success in reducing tariffs and developing the region through cooperative industrial sector programs. These programs allocated industrial production among the participating states. In 1994 some 37 nations signed the Association of Caribbean States agreement with long-term economic integration goals.

- The Gulf Cooperations Council (GCC) was formed between Bahrain, Kuwait, Oman, Qatar, Saudi Arabia, and United Arab Emirates with objectives to establish freedom of movement, a regional armaments industry, common banking and financial systems, a unified currency policy, a customs union, a common foreign aid program, and a joint, international investment company, the Gulf Investment Corporation.

- The Andean Common Market (ANCOM) was founded by Bolivia, Chile, Colombia, Ecuador, and Peru in 1969 primarily to counter the economic power of Argentina, Brazil, and Mexico and to reduce dependency upon foreign capital. Later, Venezuela joined and Chile left the group. ANCOM Commission has not been

International Laws: Other Regional Groups (continued)

an activist on behalf of regional integration like the EU Commission. It mostly reacts to proposals put forth by the Junta, the administrative arm of ANCOM.

- The Association of Southeast Asian Nations (ASEAN) was formed in 1967 by Indonesia, Malaysia, the Philippines, Singapore, and Thailand. Brunei joined in 1984, Vietnam in 1995. The Bangkok Declaration establishing ASEAN as a cooperative association is a broadly worded document, but with little supranational legal machinery, to implement its stated goals.

- East Asian Integration, ranging from Japan in the north to Indonesia in the south, has formed the Asia-Pacific Economic Cooperation (APEC) consisting of 18 Asian-Pacific nations and other countries including the United States. East Asia, unlike Europe, has not developed a formal Common Market with uniform trade, licensing, and investment rules. Late in 1994, the APEC nations targeted free trade and investment for developed countries by the year 2010 and developing countries by the year 2020.

Appendix: Sarbanes-Oxley Act of 2002

The U.S. Sarbanes-Oxley Act of 2002 (SOX Act) contains provisions affecting the corporate governance, auditing, and financial reporting of public companies, including provisions intended to deter and punish corporate accounting fraud and corruption. The SOX Act generally applies to those public companies required to file reports with Securities and Exchange Commission (SEC) under the Securities Exchange Act of 1933 and the Securities Exchange Act of 1934 and registered accounting firms. This appendix contains only the SOX Act titles and sections that are of interest to internal auditors. Visit www.pcaobus.org or www.aicpa.org for SOX.

Title II of the Act addresses auditor independence. It prohibits the registered external auditor of a public company from providing certain non-audit services to that public company audit client. Title II also specifies communication that is required between auditors and the public company's audit committee (or board of directors) and requires periodic rotation of the audit partners managing a public company's audits.

Titles III and IV of the Act focus on corporate responsibility and enhanced financial disclosures. Title III addresses listed company audit committees, including responsibilities and independence, and corporate responsibilities for financial reports, including certifications by corporate officers in annual and quarterly reports, among other provisions. Title IV addresses disclosures in financial reporting and transactions involving management and principal stockholders, and other provisions such as internal control over financial reporting.

More specifically, Section 404 of the Act establishes requirements for companies to publicly report on management's responsibility for establishing and maintaining an adequate internal control structure, including controls over financial reporting and the results of management's assessment of the effectiveness of internal control over financial reporting. Section 404 also requires the firms that serve as external auditors for public companies to attest to the assessment made by the companies' management, and report on the results of their attestation and whether they agree with management's assessment of the company's internal control over financial reporting.

TITLE II—AUDITOR INDEPENDENCE

Section 201: Services Outside the Scope of Practice of Auditors

Registered accounting firms cannot provide certain non-audit services to a public company if the firm also serves as the auditor of the financial statements for the public company. Examples of prohibited non-audit services include bookkeeping, appraisal or valuation services, internal audit outsourcing services, and management functions.

TITLE III—CORPORATE RESPONSIBILITY

Section 301: Public Company Audit Committees

Listed company audit committees are responsible for the appointment, compensation, and oversight of the registered accounting firm, including the resolution of disagreement between the registered accounting firm and company management regarding financial reporting. Audit committee members must be independent.

Section 302: Corporate Responsibility for Financial Reports

For each annual and quarterly report filed with SEC, the CEO and CFO must certify that they have reviewed the report and, based on their knowledge, the report does not contain untrue statements or omissions of material facts resulting in a misleading report and that, based on their knowledge, the financial information in the report is fairly presented.

Section 304: Forfeiture of Certain Bonuses and Profits

The CEO and CFO of the issuer have to reimburse the issuer for any bonus or profits from sale of securities during the 12 month period following the filing of a financial document that required an issuer to prepare an accounting restatement due to misconduct.

Section 308: Fair Funds for Investors

The civil penalties can be added to the disgorgement fund for the benefit of the victims of a security law violation. A disgorgement sanction requires the return of illegal profits.

TITLE IV—ENHANCED FINANCIAL DISCLOSURES

Section 404: Management Assessment of Internal Controls

This section consists of two parts. First, in each annual report filed with SEC, company management must state its responsibility for establishing and maintaining an internal control structure and procedures for financial reporting; it must also assess the effectiveness of its internal control structure and procedures for financial reporting. Second, the registered accounting firm must attest to, and report on, management's assessment of the effectiveness of its internal control over financial reporting.

Section 406 (c): Code of Ethics

This section must provide for an enforcement mechanism and protection for persons reporting questionable behavior (i.e., whistleblowing). The board of directors must approve any waivers of the code for directors, executives, or officers of the organization.

Section 407: Disclosure of Audit Committee Financial Expert

Public companies must disclose in periodic reports to SEC whether the audit committee includes at least one member who is a financial expert and, if not, the reasons why.

About the Author

S. RAO VALLABHANENI is an educator, author, publisher, consultant, and practitioner in business with more than 30 years of management and teaching experience in auditing, accounting, manufacturing, and IT consulting in both the public and private sectors. He is the author of more than 60 trade books, study guides, review guides, monographs, audit guides, and articles in auditing and IT. He holds 24 professional certifications in business management in the Accounting, Auditing, Finance, IT, Manufacturing, Quality, and Human Resource fields.

Index

A

ABC inventory control system, 89

Absorption and variable costing methods, 656–660

management's use of, 657–659

contribution margins, analyzing, 659

controlling costs, 657

market segments, analyzing, 659

planning production, 658

pricing products, 658

technical aspects of, 660

Activity analysis, 213

Activity-based costing (ABC), 650

Activity network diagrams, 187

Ad-hoc networks, 496

Affinity diagram, 186

Alternative market channels, 53

Amoral management, 25

Andean Common Market (ANCOM), 732

Application development, 366–411

end-user computing, 405–407

audit challenges of, 406

audit and control risks over, 406

scope of, 405

suggested controls over, 407

information system development models in, 373–374

tools for, 375

knowledge-based systems, 407–411

artificial intelligence technology, 407

expert systems, 410–411

neural network systems, 409

parsers, 408

malware inserted during software development and maintenance work, categories of, 397–398

program change management and control, 398

software acquisition methodology, 370–372, 379–384

alternative approaches to, 379–382

due care and due diligence reviews in, 383–384

guidelines, 371

modification alternatives, 372

software assurance, safety, security, and quality, 385

software reviews, inspections, traceability analysis, and walkthroughs, 395–396

software testing objectives, approaches, methods, and controls, 389

traditional approaches, 366–370

version control and version management, difference between, 399–405

Application development (continued)
access controls over changes, 402
application software maintenance controls, 404
change control board, 405
check-in and check-out procedures, 403
configuration control, 401
configuration management, 400
system stages, 404
Artificial intelligence technology, 407
Asia-Pacific Economic Cooperation (APEC), 733
Association of Southeast Asian Nations (ASEAN), 733
Attribute listing, 200
Audit committee, roles and responsibilities of, 17–18
types of audits in governance, 18
Automated clearing house, 606

B
Backbone network, 519
Backflush costing, 651
Backflush Inventory Deduction, 96
Balanced scorecard system, 76–78
indicators, 77
measures, 77
perspectives, 78
Baldrige, Malcolm, National Quality Award, 190
Benchmarking, 68
Best Alternative to a Negotiating Agreement (BATNA), 256
Blasting, creating, and refining, 200
Board of directors
basic ethical and legal principles for, 4–10
duties, 3
independence, need for, 11
member liabilities, 12

Body area networks, 504
Bonds, 565
Bonus incentives policy, 230
Boston Consulting Group (BCG)
matrix model, 170
Bottleneck management, 66
Broadband networks, 485
Business continuity, 531–558
alternative recovery site strategies, 545–547
service-level agreements for, 548–550
contingency plan maintenance, 556
fault-tolerance mechanisms, 556
fault-tolerant hardware methods, 557
robust operating systems, 558
contingency planning strategies, 541
disaster recovery planning, 542–543

implementation, documentation, training, and testing, 550
  analyses, 551
  disaster simulations, 552
  documentation, 554–555
  end-to-end testing, 552
  full-scale testing, 553
  reviews, 551
management, 531–541
  business focused, 531–532
  computer security incident, 539–541
  information technology focused, 532–538
recovery site strategies, 544–547
relationship to ISO standards, 558
Business cycles, schemes in, 51–64
  sales pricing objectives and policies, 51

marketing product life cycles, 55–64
  pricing objectives, 51
  procurement and supply chain management, 52–55
Business development life cycles, 112–114
  causes behind, 113
  consumer durable goods, 114
  consumer nondurable goods, 114
  growth concepts in, 114
Business ethics, 18–28
  audit, 28
  codes of conduct, 20
  financial disclosures, 21
  gatekeepers, roles and responsibilities of, 26–27
  interactions between law, ethics, and economics, 19
  key principles, 22

  management
    models of, 25
    scope of, 19
  normative approach vs. descriptive approach, 24
  types of, 23
Business impact analysis (BIA), 535, 538
Business process analysis, 65–67
  bottleneck management, 66
  focusing steps, 67
  theory of constraints, 66
  workflow analysis, 66
Business process reengineering and business process improvement, 67

C
Capital budgeting, 621–629
  capital projects, postaudit of, 624

Index

Capital budgeting (*continued*)
  capital rationing, 628
  investment projects, methods to
    rank, 622
    net present value, 623
    payback, 622
  internal rate of return, 623–624
    modified, 624
    regular, 623
  international capital budgeting,
    629
  project cash flows, 625
  risk assessment, 626
    and capital budgeting, 628
    market or beta, 627
    stand-alone, 627
Carrying or holding costs, 82, 83
Cash management, 599–613
  account balances, 603
  bank reconciliation, 601

cash conversion cycle model,
  607–608
  approaches to shorten, 608
  controls, 599, 603
  current assets, management
    of, 607
  efficiency techniques, 611
  electronic techniques, 606
    electronic data interchange
      (EDI), 606
    electronic funds transfer
      (EFT), 606
  float, 602
  hedging, 602
  items excluded, 600–601
    compensating balances, 600
    exclusions from cash, 601
    other restricted cash, 600
  marketable securities, management
    of, 612–613

criteria for selecting, 612
  inventory, risks in, 613
  reasons for holding, 612
  risks in, 613
  payables, 604
  receivables, 605
  scope of, 610
  working capital
    asset investment policies, 608
    financing policies, 609
Cause-and-effect (C&E) diagram,
  186, 200
Celler Antimerger Act (U.S.), 721
Cellular networks, wireless, 466
Centralization, 43
Change management techniques,
  271–274
  agents of change, 271
  organizational development as
    change program, 274

process, factors in, 273
resistance to change, 272
types of, 272
Check sheets, 185
Chief executive officer, roles of, 13
CIA Exam
content specifications, xxi–xxix
exam-taking tips and techniques,
xix–xx
study preparation resources, xv–xvii
CIA triad, 275
Clayton Act (U.S.), 719
Closeoffs, 644
Cloud computing systems, 435–438
key security considerations in, 439
potential security benefits of, 442
potential vulnerabilities in, 440
security downside of, 436–437
security and privacy issues in, 443
security requirements of, 441

security upside of, 438
Cluster organizations, 48
Codes of conduct, 20
Committees, types of, 250
Communication skills, 132–139
barriers to, 138
decoding, 134
encoding, 133
feedback, 135
formal and informal, 137–138
medium, 134
organizational dynamics in, 139
process, factors in, 136
receiver, 135
sender, 133
Competitive analysis, portfolio
techniques of, 169–171
Boston Consulting Group (BCG)
matrix model, 170
General Electric (GE) model, 171

Competitive industries, competitive
strategies related to, 165
Concentrators, 520
Conflict management, 251–262
collaborative problem solving, 261
alternatives to, 261
interpersonal differences, solution
for, 262
negotiation, 251–257
added-value (AVN), 257
Best Alternative to a Negotiating
Agreement (BATNA), 256
compromise vs. collaboration
in, 255
definition of, 252
elements of, 253
modes of, 254
opposition to, 253
process of, 252
skills, 251

Index

Conflict management (*continued*)
  prevention and control methods, 259
    group or organizational, 259
    personal, 259
  resolution choices and techniques,
    260
  triggers, 259
Connectors, 521
Consumer durable goods, 114
Consumer nondurable goods, 114
Consumer Credit Protection Act
  (U.S.), 231
Content delivery networks, 497
Contingency design alternatives,
  41–44
  centralized and decentralized, 43
  line and staff organizations, 44
  span of control, 42
    narrow and wide, 42
    tall and flat, 42

Contingency planning, 532–534, 541
  strategies, 541
Contracts, 713–714
  classification of, 714
  definition of, 713
  requirements of, 714
  types of, 714
Control chart, 186
Control environment, 233
Converged networks, 502
Corporate governance, 1–16
  basic ethical and legal principles for
    managers, executives, officers,
    and board of directors, 4–10
    summary of, 10
  board of directors' duties, 3
  board independence, need for, 11
  board member liabilities, 12
  chief executive officer, roles of, 13
  definition, 1

  global practices in, 14–15
  improving, 13
  insider trading scandals, 12
  issues, 2
  principles, 1
  process, role of internal audit
    in, 16
Corporate risk management,
  34–37
  best practices in, 37
  methodology, 34
  tools, 36
  types of risk, 35
Corporate social responsibility,
  29–33
  definition, 29
  economic, 30
  ethical, 31
  legal, 30
  philanthropic, 31

pyramid layers of, 33
social audit, 32
Cost behavior, 665
Cost-benefit analysis, 212
Cost of capital evaluation, 629–637
common stock, 632–635
bond-yield-plus-risk-premium,
635
CAPM approach, 634
discounted cash flow approach,
635
debt, 630
issues in, 637
preferred stock, 630
retained earnings, 631
weighted-average and marginal
cost of capital concepts, 636
Cost classifications, assumptions
underlying, 666
Cost concepts, 661–664

Cost estimation approaches, 667
Cost-volume-profit (CVP) analysis,
669–676
assumptions and their limitations,
671–672
BEP, ways to lower, 673
break-even point (BEP), methods
for calculating, 670
contribution-margin, 670
equation, 670
contribution margin vs. gross
margin, 675
effect of sales mix and income
taxes on, 676
graphic method, 671
profit-volume chart vs. CVP chart,
675
sensitivity analysis, 674
variable and fixed costs, changes
in, 674

Costing systems, 648–655
activity-based (ABC), 650
backflush costing, 651
Just-in-time costing, 651
standard, 651
types of, 651
variance prorations, 655
variances, types of, 652–654
target, 648
traditional, 649
Costs, relevant, 668–669
application of concept, 669
differential analysis, 668
Credit derivatives, 597–598
credit options, 598
credit-sensitive notes, 598
credit swaps, 598
spread-adjusted notes, 598
total return swaps, 597
Crosby quality model, 190

Cultural/political environments, 703–713
  emerging work culture, general characteristics of, 707–709
    cultural awareness learning program, 708–709
    global communication insights, 705–706
      high- and low-context, 706
  global manager's dilemma, 704
  global mindsets, 713
  international management theories, 712
  local/regional cultures, 703–704
    effects of, 704
  negotiations, 710–712
    avoiding failure in, 710
    ethical constraints in, 712
    foreign culture, knowledge of, 711
    cross-cultural, 710
    strategic planning for, 711
    regional cultures, 705
Currency derivatives, 596
Customer-relationship management system, 455–456

D

Data systems, electronic. *See* Electronic data systems
Database systems, 427–452
  cloud computing systems, 435–438
    key security considerations in, 439
    potential security benefits of, 442
    potential vulnerabilities in, 440
    security downside of, 436–437
    security and privacy issues in, 443
    security requirements of, 441
    security upside of, 438
    considerations, 428
  data dictionary systems software, 428
  data marts, 430
  data mining, 431
    vs. data auditing, 431
  data warehouse, 429, 430
  information technology operations, functional areas of, 444–448
    change and problem management, 445
    computer operations, 444
    operating environment, 444
    service-level management, 446–448
    separation of duties in, 449–452
  online analytical processing, 432
  software, 427
  structured query language (SQL), 433–435
  virtual databases, 432

Debt and equity, types of, 590–595
  common stock, 593–594
    legal rights of stockholders, 593
    put and call option, 594
  long-term debt, 591
  long-term financing decisions,
      factors influencing, 591
  preferred stock, 594
    major provisions of, 594
    pros and cons of, 595
  short-term debt, sources of, 590
  short-term financing, use of security
      collateral in, 591
Decentralization, 43
Decision analysis, 195–203
  problem solving, 195–203
    and creativity, 197
    differences in methods of, 197
    impediments to, 196
    process, 195

  prospective and retrospective
      methods in, 198
  tools and techniques for, 199
  traits and behaviors, 203
Decision making, 204–214
  facets of, 206
  models, 207
  vs. problem solving, 214
  pure strategy and mixed strategy
      in, 210
  tools and techniques for, 211–213
  types of data used in, 208
  types of decisions, 209
Decision table, 211
Decision trees, 211
Deflation, measuring, 717
Delphi technique, 201
Demilitarized zones (DMZs), 311–312
  architecture, 312
  purpose, 311

Deming quality model, 189
Departmentalization, types of, 45
Devil's advocate techniques, 212
Differential analysis, 211
Digital cellular networks, 499
Digital watermarking, 362
Disaster recovery planning,
    542–543
Discriminant analysis, 211
Distribution requirements planning
    (DRP), 101
Domain controller, 528

E
Economic/financial environments,
    687–702
  foreign direct investment, 701–702
  intellectual property rights and
      international licensing
      agreements, 699–700

Index

Economic/financial environments
(continued)
international organization
structures, 687
international strategies, 689–692,
693
business and marketing, 693
ethnocentric, 690
global, 691
multidomestic, 690
objectives, 692
transnational, 691
multinational business models
of, 689
multinational corporations
(MNCs), information flows and
organization structures of, 688
technology and global strategy, 693
international franchising, 700
technology transfer, 700

trade, 694–
exporting, 695
importing and global sourcing,
696
liberalization and the World Trade
Organization (WTO), 698
tariffs and nontariff barriers,
697–698
Edisonian method, 200
Electronic data interchange (EDI), 606
Electronic data systems, 104–112
electronic commerce, 104–107
electronic data interchange (EDI)
security issues, 105, 109
e-mail security, 105
financial transactions security
issues, 106
information transactions security
issues, 106
infrastructure, 107

security issues, 104–105
software, 107
electronic data interchange (EDI),
109–112
benefits of, 112
system, 110–111
mobile commerce, 108
cyber threats, 108
risks, 109
scope of, 108
Electronic funds transfer (EFT), 606
Emerging industries, competitive
strategies related to, 164
Employee empowerment, 235
Employee selection policy, 227
Encoding, 133
Encryption, 347–365
alternatives to, 351–352
cryptographic key systems, basic
types of, 352–353

cryptographic mechanisms
  to protect data-at-rest, 357–359
  to protect data-in-transit, 360
cryptography
  alternatives to 361–363
  basic uses of, 354–356
  digital signatures, 354
    certificates, 356
    digitized, 355
    electronic, 355
  foundational concepts, 347–348
  methods of, 349
    summary of, 364–365
  modes of, 350
  types of, 349
Enterprise risk management, 37–39
  alternative risk-transfer tools, 38
  approaches and dimensions to, 38
  definition, 37
  implementation of, 39

internal auditing role in, 39
Enterprise-wide resource planning
    (ERP) system, 453–454
  advantages and disadvantages of,
    454
Environmental Protection Agency
    (EPA), 721–723
  air and radiation, 722
  pesticides and toxic substances,
    723
  solid waste and emergency
    response, 723
  water, 722
Equal employment opportunity policy,
    228
Ethics. See Business ethics
European Quality Award, 191
European Union international trade
    laws, 730–731
Expectancy theory, 217

F
Federal Trade Commission Act (U.S.),
    720
Financial accounting and finance,
    559–564
  accounting cycle, 562–563
    cash-basis vs. accrual-basis, 562
    steps in, 563
  accounting principles, 559
  advanced concepts of, 571–583
    business combinations,
      571–572
    financial statements,
      consolidation of, 573
    foreign currency transactions,
      579
    partnerships, 573–578
  basic concepts of, 559
  business entity concept, 560
  cost concept, 560

Index

Financial accounting and finance
(*continued*)
   financial statements, different
      formats of, 564
      account analysis, 564
   intermediate concepts of, 565–571
      bonds, 565
      intangible assets, 569
      leases, 565–568
      pensions, 568
      research and development,
        570–571
      matching concept, 560
      qualities of accounting information,
        561
Financial disclosures, 21
Financial instruments, 596–599
   credit derivatives, 597–598
      credit options, 598
      credit-sensitive notes, 598

      credit swaps, 598
      spread-adjusted notes, 598
      total return swaps, 597
   currency derivatives, 596
   hidden financial reporting risks, 599
   swaps, 597
Financial statement analysis,
    584–589
   ratios, limitations of, 588–589
   types of, 586–587
Financial transactions security issues,
    106
Firewalls, 293–303
   advantages of, 302
   disadvantages of, 303
   limitations of, 300
   management of, 301
   purpose, 293–294
   technology, 294
      application firewalls, 296

      application-proxy gateways, 297
      dedicated proxy servers, 298
      packet filtering, 295
      personal firewalls or firewall
        appliances, 299
      stateful inspection, 296
Float, 602
Flowcharting, 185–186, 211
   in decision making, 211
Focus group, 249
Forecasting, 172–175
   regression analysis, 173
   sensitivity analysis, 174
   simulation models, 175
   time-series analysis, 172
Foreign currency transactions,
    579–583
   financial statements, translation of,
    580
   foreign exchange rates

current/noncurrent method for, 580
current rate method for, 581
monetary/nonmonetary for, 581
gains and losses excluded from net
 income, 581
translation
 disclosure of, 583
 income taxes related to, 582
Foreign direct investment, 701–702
Forward contracts, 596
Fragmented industries, competitive
 strategies related to, 163
Franchising, international, 700
Front-end processors, 522
Functional departments, 45
Futures contracts, 596

G
Gatekeepers, roles and
 responsibilities of, 26–27

General Electric (GE) model, 171
General pricing decision model, 51
Global analytical techniques,
 155–158
 buyers, bargaining power of, 158
 existing firms, rivalry among, 157
 new entrants, threat of, 156
 substitute products or services,
  pressure from, 157
 suppliers, bargaining power of, 158
Global competition, sources and
 impediments, 166
Global markets, evolution of, 166–167
 strategic alternatives to compete,
  167
Goal congruence principle, 22
Goal-setting theory, 217
Golden Rule, 22
Governance. *See* Corporate
 governance

Governmental legislation and
 regulation, 718–733
 Celler Antimerger Act (U.S.), 721
 Clayton Act (U.S.), 719
 Environmental Protection Agency
  (EPA), 721–723
  air and radiation, 722
  pesticides and toxic substances,
   723
  solid waste and emergency
   response, 723
  water, 722
 European Union international trade
  laws, 730–731
 Federal Trade Commission Act
  (U.S.), 720
 international trade, methods,
  restrictions, and barriers of,
  725–728
  domestic content laws, 726

Index

Governmental legislation and
    regulation (*continued*)
    export promotion programs, 727
    import quotas, 726
    technology policies, 728
    theory of comparative advantage,
      728
    trade agreements, 727
  North American Free Trade
    Agreement (NAFTA), 729
  Robinson-Patman Act (U.S.), 720
  Sherman Act (U.S.), 719
  tied aid practices (U.S.), 724
  U.S. Export-Import Bank, 724
  Wheeler-Lea Act (U.S.), 721
  World Trade Organization (WTO),
    729
Group dynamics, 221–225
  behaviors, 221
  decision making, 221–222
  factors affecting, 222
  development, 223–224
  effectiveness, criteria and
    determinants of, 225
  organizational politics (OP), 224
Gulf Cooperations Council (GCC),
  732

H
Hardware controllers, 517
Hardware and software guards,
  308–310
  attacks on, 310
  implementations, 310
  purpose, 308
  technology, 309
Hatch Act (U.S.), 231
Hedging, 602
Herzberg's two-factor theory, 216
Histogram, 185

Holding companies, 645
Hourglass organizations, 47
Hubs, 520
Human resources management, 226
  bonus incentives policy, 230
  employee selection policy, 227
  equal employment opportunity
    policy, 228
  pay administration policy, 229
  policies, purpose of, 226
  recruiting policy, 227
  records retention policy, 232
  safety policy, 232
  transfers and promotions policy,
    228
  wage garnishments policy, 231

I
Identification and authentication (I&A),
  333–346

application authentication techniques
for devices, 339
for system users, 338
authorization mechanisms, 336–337
basic mechanisms, 334
identity management, 340–342
integrating methods, 344–346
four-factor, 346
one-factor, 344
three-factor, 346
two-factor, 345–346
principal forms of, 335
privilege management, 343
weak and strong, 335
Illegal and improper acts, incentives and temptations for engaging in, 234
Imagineering, 199

Immoral management, 25
Industry environments, 163–166
competitive industries, competitive strategies related to, 165
emerging industries, competitive strategies related to, 164
fragmented industries, competitive strategies related to, 163
global competition, sources and impediments, 166
Inflation, measuring, 717
Information protection, 313–332
methods, 317
privacy
impact assessments, 332
laws, compliance with, 332
management, 330–331
risks, 331
risks, 313–314
threats and vulnerabilities, 315–316

Information security, 275–282
controls, 277
impact analysis, 279
key concepts in, 280–282
objectives, 275
accountability, 276
assurance, 277
policies, 278
Information technology operations, functional areas of, 444–448
change and problem management, 445
computer operations, 444
operating environment, 444
service-level management, 446–448
separation of duties in, 449–452
attacks on data center or computer center operations, 452

Index 757

Information technology operations,
functional areas of (*continued*)
compatible functions, 451
incompatible functions, 450
network management, 451
Information transactions security
issues, 106
Information system development
models in, 373–374
tools for, 375
prototyping, 375–376
software engineering,
377–378
cleanroom, 377
computer-aided, 378
Insider trading scandals, 12
Internal audit
role of in corporate governance
process, 16
role in ERM implementation, 39

International Organization for
Standardization (ISO)
framework, 115–122, 415
certification process, 115
ISO 9000 standards
benefits of, 116
in quality management,
117–118
standards
most popular, 122
other, 119–121
International organization structures,
687
International trade, methods,
restrictions, and barriers of,
725–728
domestic content laws, 726
export promotion programs, 727
import quotas, 726
technology policies, 728

theory of comparative advantage,
728
trade agreements, 727
Interrelationship digraph, 187
Inventory distrubution methods, 102
Inventory levels and profit levels, 80
Inventory management techniques
and concepts, 78–103
ABC inventory control system, 89
alternative shipping carriers, costs
of, 103
calculating when to order, 88
carrying costs vs. ordering costs vs.
stock-out costs, 83
dependent demand systems, 79
distribution requirements planning
(DRP), 101
distribution systems, 100
double order point system, 100
single order point system, 100

independent demand systems, 79
inventory distrubution methods, 102
inventory levels and profit levels, 80
investment in inventory, 81
   carrying or holding costs, 82
   ordering costs, 82
   stock-out costs, 83
just-in-time (JIT) strategy, 90
   inventory, 93
   layout, 95
   lean operations, 95
   partnerships, 94
   production, 91
   production processing, 93
   purchasing, 92
   quality, 94
   scheduling, 94
   transportation, 93
Kanban production and inventory
   systems, 97–99

logistics, forward vs. reverse, 103
management decisions, 86
   calculating how much to order
     using EOQ, 86
   EOQ assumptions, 87
   sensitivity analysis and EOQ, 88
materials requirements planning
   (MRP), 96
optimal order quantity, 84
periodic review system, 101
quick response (QR) retail
   systems, 99
reorder point, 85
safety stock vs. stock-outs, 89
sales replacement system, 101
warehouse inventory control, 102
warehouse shipments, 102

J
Juran quality model, 189

Just-in-time (JIT) costing, 651
Just-in-time (JIT) strategy, 90
   inventory, 93
   layout, 95
   lean operations, 95
   partnerships, 94
   production, 91
     processing, 93
   purchasing, 92
   quality, 94
   scheduling, 94
   transportation, 93

K
Kanban production and inventory
   systems, 97–99
Key economic indicators, 715–716
   nature of, 715
   types of, 715–716
Kiertsu, 15

Index 759

Knowledge-based systems, 407–411
  artificial intelligence technology,
    407
  expert systems, 410–411
    and conventional systems,
      difference between, 411
    safety and security risks in, 411
  neural network systems, 409
  parsers, 408

L

Latin American Free Trade
     Association (LAFTA), 732
Lean operations, 95
Leapfrogging, 199
Leases, 565–568
  accounting
    by lessees, 566
    by lessor, 567
  involving real estate, 567

leveraged, accounting and reporting
    for, 568
  sale-leaseback transaction, 568
Leveraged buyouts (LBOs), 645
Line and staff organizations, 44
Local-area network (LAN)
  campus-area network (CAN), 479
  virtual (VLAN), 477
  wired, 463, 468–476
    architecture, 468
    client/server architecture,
      475–476
    concepts in, 469–470
    features providing high security
      in, 473
    features providing low security
      in, 474
    security concerns and risks,
      471–472
    security goals and features, 470

  wireless, 465, 478–479
    legacy, 479
    robust security networks for, 479
Logistics, forward vs. reverse, 103

M

Malware, 397–398
Management science, 211
Management skills, 235–241
  defined, 235
  employee development, role of
    leaders in, 239–241
  functions, 235
  information-processing styles, 237
  leadership categories, 238
  leadership theories, 237
  personality factors for leaders,
    238
  roles, 236
  types, 236

Management, strategic. *See* Strategic management

Management structures and organization systems, 49

Managerial accounting, 647

Marketing distribution, channels of, 54

Marketing intermediaries, 53, 54
selecting, 54

Maslow's needs hierarchy theory, 216

Materials requirements planning (MRP), 96

Matrix diagram, 187

Matrix organizations, 44

Maximum tolerable downtime (MTD), 536, 538

Means-end cycle, 22

Mentoring, 239–240

Mergers, acquisitions, and divestitures, 640–646

Closeoffs, 644
holding companies, 645
investment bankers, role of, 645
leveraged buyouts (LBOs), 645
mergers
analysis, 642–643
types of, 641
regulators, role of, 646
selloffs, 644
spinoff vs. divestiture, 644

Metropolitan-area network (MAN)
wired, 463, 480
wireless, 465–466, 480

Might-equals-right principle, 22

Mobile commerce, 108
device threats, 108
risks, 108
scope of, 108

Modems, 515

Moral management, 25

Multimedia collaborative computing networks, 495

Multinational corporations (MNCs), information flows and organization structures of, 688

Multiplexers, 517

N

Negotiation, 251–257
added-value (AVN), 257
Best Alternative to a Negotiating Agreement (BATNA), 256
compromise vs. collaboration in, 255
definition of, 252
elements of, 253
modes of, 254
opposition to, 253
process of, 252
skills, 251

Index

Network connections, 506–513
  bridges, 509, 511, 513
  brouters, 509, 511
  gateways, 512, 513
  repeaters, 510, 511, 513
  routers, 513
  switches, 507–508, 511, 513
Network interface cards, 521
Network nodes, 522
Network organizations, 48
Network topologies, 523
Networks
  ad-hoc, 496
  backbone, 519
  body area, 504
  broadband, 485
  campus-area (CAN), 479
  content delivery, 497
  converged, 502
  digital cellular, 499
  multimedia collaborative computing, 495
  optical, 503
  peer-to-peer (P2P), 500–501
  quality of service and quality of protection, 529–530
  radio frequency identification (RFID), 505
  subnets, 526
  value-added, 497
  wired, 463–464, 468–476, 481–484
    local-area networks, 463, 468–476
    metropolitan-area networks, 480
    wide-area networks, 481–484
  wireless, 465–467, 478–479
    metropolitan-area networks, 480
    technologies, examples of, 467
    legacy WLANs, 478–479
  wireless sensor (WSN), 498

Neural network systems, 409
North American Free Trade Agreement (NAFTA), 729

O
Occupational Safety and Health Administration (OSHA), 232
Online analytical processing, 432
Operating budgets, 681–686
  advantages of, 685
  benefits of, 682–683
  different dimensions in, 683
  limitations of, 686
  preparation of, 684
  systems, 681
  techniques, 685
Operating systems, 416–417
Operations research, 202
Optical networks, 503
Ordering costs, 82, 83

Organizational behavior, 215–220
    motivation
        defined, 216
        strategies, 218–220
        theories, 216–217
    theory, 215
Organizational effectiveness,
        criteria and determinants
        of, 50
Organizational politics (OP), 224
Organizational structures, 40–50
    risk/control implications of, 40–41
        classifying organizations, 40
        organization defined, 40
        theories of organization, 40
        theories of organizing, 41
    types of, 41–50
        cluster organizations, 48
        contingency design alternatives,
            41–44

organizational effectiveness,
        criteria and determinants of, 50
    customer classification of
        departments, 46
    departmentalization, types of, 45
    functional departments, 45
    geographic location of
        departments, 46
    hourglass organizations, 47
    management structures and
        organization systems, 49
    network organizations, 48
    new configurations, 47
    product-service departments, 46
Outsourcing business processes,
        123–131
    benefits of, 128–129
    examples of, 124
    reasons for, 125
    risks in, 126–127

    scope of, 123
    vendor governance, 130
    vendors, service-level agreements
        for, 131

P
Pareto diagram, 185, 200
Parsers, 408
Partnerships, 573–578
    accounting, 577
    actions against other partners,
        578
    admitting a new partner, 578
    asset distribution of, 578
    duties, rights, and powers of
        partners, 574–575
    liabilities and authorities of general
        partner, 576
Pay administration policy, 229
Payoff table, 212

innovation, traditional vs.
reverse, 59
new products
development steps, 59
failure, causes of, 60
policy, 61–62
packaging and branding, 57
product classification, 56
product definition, 55
product mix and product lines, 56
service marketing, overcoming
obstacles in, 64
service quality, problems in, 64
services, characteristics of, 63
strategy, 55
Product-service departments, 46
Production process flows, 69
Productivity, 72–75
effectiveness, efficiency, and
economy, 75

industry evolution, 162
market signals, 161
Ports, 525–526
Pricing objectives, 51
Prioritization matrices, 187
Private branch exchange (PBX)
systems, 490
Process decision program chart, 187
Procurement and supply chain
management, 52–55
alternative market channels, 53
marketing distribution, channels
of, 54
marketing intermediaries, 53, 54
selecting, 54
reverse purchasing vs. reverse
marketing, 52
Product life cycles, marketing, 55–64
audit, 58
concept, 57

Peer-to-peer (P2P) networks,
500–501
Pensions, 568
Performance, 71
Performance measurement systems,
70
Periodic review system, 101
Personal-area network (PAN)
wired, 463
wireless, 465
Plain old telephone service (POTS),
491
Plan-do-check-act (PDCA) cycle, 188
Planning process, strategic. See
Strategic planning process
Port protection device (PPD), 516
Portals, 527
Porter's competitive strategies,
159–162
competitive analysis, 161

improvement, 73–74
   criteria for, 73
   measurement
      components of, 73
      guidelines for, 74
Professional principle, 22
Programmable logic controller
   (PLC), 528
Project management, 263–270
   audit, 270
   basic guidelines, 263
   controls, 264
   governance mechanisms, 269
   organization, 264
   PERT approach, 266–268
      time dimensions, 268
   problems in, 264
   scheduling techniques, 265
   techniques, 263
Protocol analyzers, 518

Protocol converters, 518
Prototyping, 375–376
Proxies and reverse proxies,
   514–515
Prudent person concept, 22

Q
Quality management. *See* Total
   Quality Management (TQM)
Quick response (QR) retail
   systems, 99

R
Radio frequency identification (RFID)
   networks, 505
Reality check, in decision making, 213
Records retention policy, 232
Recovery objectives, 537, 538
Recruiting policy, 227
Regression analysis, 173

Related-party transactions, examples
   of, 148
Responsibility accounting,
   679–680
   managers, accountability of, 679
   responsibility centers, 680
Reverse proxies, 514–515
Reverse purchasing vs. reverse
   marketing, 52
Reversible data hiding, 363
Risk analysis, 213
Risk management. *See* Corporate
   risk management; Enterprise
   risk management
Robinson-Patman Act (U.S.), 720
Routers, 304–306
   accounts and passwords, 305
   configuration management, 306
   purpose, 304
   table integrity, 306

Index

S

Saddle point, 210

Safety policy, 232

Safety stock, 81, 89

Sales pricing objectives and policies, 51

Sales replacement system, 101

Sarbanes-Oxley Act of 2002, 735–740

    Title II—Auditor Independence, 736

        Section 201: Services Outside the Scope of Practice of Auditors, 736

    Title III—Corporate Responsibility, 737–738

        Section 301: Public Company Audit Committees, 737

        Section 302: Corporate Responsibility for Financial Reports, 737

Section 304: Forfeiture of Certain Bonuses and Profits, 738

Section 308: Fair Funds for Investors, 738

Title IV—Enhanced Financial Disclosures, 739–740

    Section 404: Management Assessment of Internal Controls, 739

    Section 406(c): Code of Ethics, 739

    Section 407: Disclosure of Audit Committee Financial Expert, 740

Scatter diagram, 185

Security. *See* Information security; System security

Selloffs, 644

Sensitivity analysis, 174

Sensors, 307

Servers, 419–426

    farms, controls over, 423

    integrity, maintaining, 423

    load balancing and clustering, 424

    server-based threats, 422

    types, 421–422

    web

        control techniques to secure, limitations of, 426

        security over, 425–426

        security testing of, 426

Sherman Act (U.S.), 719

Shipping carriers, alternative, 103

Simulation models, 175

Six-sigma quality program, 191–194

    players, 193–194

    tools, 192

Social audit, 32

Social responsibility. *See* Corporate social responsibility

Sockets, 524

Software engineering, 377–378
    cleanroom, 377
    computer-aided, 378
Software. *See also* Application
    development
    contracts, penalties in, 461–462
    licensing, 457–458
    piracy management, 458–460
        copyright laws, 460
        policies, 459
Software guards. *See* Hardware and
    software guards
Spinoffs, 644
Stakeholder relationships, 140–149
    initiatives, shareholders and
        corporations, 141
    business mergers, acquisitions,
        and divestitures, handling, 149
    marketing and salespeople, dealing
        with, 147

purchasing agents, buyers, and
    commodity/service experts,
    dealing with, 145–146
related parties and third parties,
    handling, 147
related-party transactions,
    examples of, 148
scope of, 140
shareholder lawsuits, 142
whistleblowing actions, protecting
    employees from, 143–144
Steganography, 361
Stock-outs, 89
    costs, 83
Storyboarding, 202
Strategic alliance arrangement, 643
Strategic business units (SBUs), 16
Strategic decisions, 167–168
    analysis of, 167
    capacity expansion, 168

new businesses, entry into, 168
Strategic management, 150–153
    control, 153
    formulation, 151
    grand strategy, 150
    implementation, 152
    process, 150
Strategic planning process, 153–155
    mission, 154
    objectives, 154
    portfolio plan, 155
    strategies, 155
Stratification, 203
Structured query language (SQL),
    433–435
Subnets, 526
Success-failure analysis, 212
Supply chain management. *See*
    Procurement and supply chain
    management

Index   **767**

Swaps, 597

System infrastructure, 412–426
  information technology control
    frameworks, 412–415
  mainframe computers, terminals,
    and workstations, 417–418
  operating systems, 416–417
  servers, 419–426
    farms, controls over, 423
    integrity, maintaining, 423
    load balancing and clustering,
      424
    server-based threats, 422
    types, 421–422
    web, security over, 425–426

System security, 282–292
  access control, 283–285
    policies, 286–292
    principles, 285
  access rights and permission, 285

T

T-analysis, 202

Target cost, 648

Target price, 648

Taxation schemes, 638–640
  examples of, 639
  tax reporting and financial reporting,
    differences between, 640
  tax shelters, 638
    tax havens, 638

Team building, 242–250
  committees, types of, 250
  group context, individuals in, 243
  group structures, 243
  methods used in, 244
  role of worker as individual or team
    member, 242
  team performance, assessing,
    245–246
  types, 247–249

Theory of comparatie advantage, 728

Theory of constraints, 66

Theory T, 712

Theory T+, 712

Theory Z, 712

Tied aid practices (U.S.), 724

Time-series analysis, 172

Total factor productivity, 72

Total Quality Management (TQM),
  176–194
  concurrent engineering, 182
  cost of quality (COQ), 183–184
    appraisal costs, 184
    failure costs, 184
    prevention costs, 183
  elements of, 176
  plan-do-check-act (PDCA)
    cycle, 188
  quality
    areas of agreement on, 177

areas needing improvement in, 178
assurance, 181
audit, 181
circles, 181
control, 181
council, 181
definitions and criteria of, 179
drivers, examples of, 180
metrics, 184
models and awards, 188–191
tools, 185–187
six-sigma quality program, 191–194
players, 193–194
tools, 192
Transfer pricing, 676–679
choices, 678
dual pricing in, 678
international, 678

management, 677
methods, 677
taxes and, 679
Transfers and promotions policy, 228
Tree diagram, 186
TRIZ theory, 203

U
Unemployment, measuring, 716
U.S. Export-Import Bank, 724

V
Value-added networks, 497
Valuation models, 613–621
business, 621
inventory, 613–616
cost flow methods, 614
inventory estimation methods, 616

inventory valuation methods, 615
financial asset, 617–620
bond valuation, 618
common stock valuation, 619
preferred stock valuation, 620
Value analysis, 199
Various types of risks, 35
Virtual databases, 432
Virtual local-area network (VLAN), 477
Virtual private networks (VPNs), 492–494
Voice over Internet protocol (VoIP), 486–490
firewalls, 488
general guidelines, 487
physical security controls, 488
quality of service issues, 489
risks and opportunities, 486
training, 489
voice mail systems, 490

Index

W

Wage garnishments policy, 231
Wald criterion, 210
Warehouse inventory control, 102
Warehouse shipments, 102
Wheeler-Lea Act (U.S.), 721
Whistleblowing actions, protecting
  employees from, 143–144
Wide-area network (WAN), 463,
  481–484
  wired, 481–484
  major concepts in, 483–484
Wireless access points, 528
Wireless devices, 527
Wireless sensor networks (WSNs),
  498
Workflow analysis, 66
Working stock, 81
World Trade Organization (WTO),
  698, 729
  trade liberalization and, 698

X

X.25 standard, 484